**Literature and violence in North Arabia**

Cambridge Studies in Cultural Systems

Clifford Geertz, editor

1 The anthropological romance of Bali 1597–1972: Dynamic perspectives in marriage and caste, politics and religion
James A. Boon

2 Sherpas through their rituals
Sherry B. Ortner

3 Literature and violence in North Arabia
Michael E. Meeker

# Literature and violence in North Arabia

MICHAEL E. MEEKER

*University of California, San Diego*

CAMBRIDGE UNIVERSITY PRESS

*Cambridge*
*London New York Melbourne*

Published by the Syndics of the Cambridge University Press
The Pitt Building, Trumpington Street, Cambridge CB2 1RP
Bentley House, 200 Euston Road, London NW1 2DB
32 East 57th Street, New York, NY 10022, USA
296 Beaconsfield Parade, Middle Park, Melbourne 3206, Australia


First published 1979

Printed in the United States of America
Typeset by Lehigh Rocappi, Pennsauken, New Jersey
Printed and bound by The Murray Printing Company, Westford, Massachusetts

*Library of Congress Cataloging in Publication Data*

Meeker, Michael E.

Literature and violence in North Arabia.

(Cambridge studies in cultural systems)

Bibliography: p.

1. Bedouins in Arabia.
2. Nomads - Near East.
3. Nomads - Africa, North.
4. Arabic poetry - Arabia - History and criticism.
5. Near East - Civilization.
6. Africa, North - History.
7. Muslim Saints - Africa, North.

I. Title. II. Series.
DS219.B4M36 953 76-47194
ISBN 0 521 22074 2

The cover illustration is from a drawing of an Aramaic inscription that appeared in Charles Huber's *Journal d'un Voyage* (1889). Huber observed the inscription in Teyma, southwest of the Nefûd desert. It is probably part of a funerary monument dating from around the fifth century B.C. The drawing evokes some of the themes of the present book which suggest a relationship between the importance of "literary" metaphors in Bedouin oral traditions and the character of Arabian political history since ancient times. Although the principal features of the human face, eyes, brows, and nose, are represented, a phonetic inscription appears in the place of the mouth.

*To*
Gesine

When no one has made the Hajj (the pilgrimage) for seven years, one shall arise one morning and see that the Kaaba (the sacred house in Mecca) has disappeared so that no one can find a trace of it. Then one shall find that the Koran has disappeared from its copies leaving the paper glistening white, without a letter on them. Then the Koran shall be blotted out of men's hearts so that no one shall remember a word of it, and men shall again amuse themselves with the old poems, songs, and tales of the Time of Ignorance (pre-Islamic Arabia).

al-Ghazâlî's description of the prelude to the coming of the Antichrist, quoted in writings of Snouck Hurgronje.

# Contents

# Figures



# Maps

# Preface

The arid zone which stretches across North Africa, through the central Near East, and into Central Asia includes the sites of the earliest civilizations. Since ancient times, an urban way of life based upon elaborate forms of commerce and industry has flourished in this part of the world. But beyond the great cities, the hinterlands have been the setting of a very different kind of society. In the deserts and steppes of the arid zone, the way of life of the nomadic herding peoples did not involve the complex political and economic institutions which were characteristic of urban centers. For a long while, the states and empires, which were centered upon the cities of the Near East, were not fundamentally affected by their relationship with the peoples of the hinterlands, but about fifteen hundred years ago this began to change. Formerly peripheral peoples, whose traditions had first taken shape under the conditions of their pastoral experiences, began to play an important role in Near Eastern history. Eventually some of these peoples, such as the Arabs and the Turks, came to dominate many of the ancient urban centers of the arid zone, and Near Eastern civilization was reconstructed around their ideals and values. This period reached a high point more than a few centuries ago. In recent years, the towns, villages, and tribes of the hinterlands have come to play a less important role in the course of Near Eastern history. In particular, nomadic herders are no longer a crucial dimension of social life in the hinterlands, as they were only a few decades ago. Even more decisively, their tribes and chiefs are no longer a political factor fundamental to the design of the state and the extent of its powers, as they were in much of the Near East before World War I. Nevertheless, those periods when such peoples occupied much of the terrain beyond the urban centers have left a deep imprint upon the present shape of culture and society in this part of the world.

For an account of the pastoralists' impact upon Near Eastern civilization, one must go back to the fourteenth-century writings of Ibn Khaldûn. In his philosophy of history, *The Muqaddimah,* he viewed a nomadic herding way of life as one in which men were unusually constrained by natural conditions. This situation, he believed, fostered the human qualities of physical endurance and moral fortitude, making the peoples of the deserts and steppes a reservoir of energetic capacities and a driving force, sometimes for good and sometimes for bad, in the cyclical fortunes of the Near Eastern polity.

In this book, I have re-examined this relationship of human character and natural conditions among the pastoralists. To do so, I have drawn upon the work of those Western ethnographers who observed the North Arabian Bedouins around the turn of this century. At the time, these Bedouins were still independent of the direct control of any government, still only superficially involved with the doctrines and rituals of Islam, and while their way of life was not exactly what it was many centuries ago, the distinctive dimensions of that life were virtually the same as they had been for almost two millennia.

One of the ethnographers of the North Arabian Bedouins, Alois Musil, devoted himself to a painstaking collection of their oral compositions. These materials are especially revealing of the kind of men the Bedouins once were and the kind of world in which they once lived. In particular, the oral compositions which Musil collected testify to a remarkably developed form of literary consciousness among these peoples and suggest that such a consciousness was a direct product of a trenchant political dilemma inherent in their pastoral way of life. Once this relationship between a form of artistic expression and a pattern of historical circumstances is understood, it can be studied as evidence of an epoch of popular experience in the Near East.

The very conception of this book was an intimate part of my association with Lloyd A. Fallers and James T. Siegel in the early seventies. Our conversations about anthropology were in many ways the place where this book began. Besides these two individuals, I would not have been able to carry out this study without the support of a number of other friends and colleagues. Raymond Scheindlin, who taught me classical Arabic, guided me in my initial approaches to the Rwala dialect. My former teachers at the University of Chicago, Clifford Geertz, David M. Schneider, and Nur Yalman, supported me on a number of crucial occasions over the years. My wife, Gesine Meeker, edited the final draft of the manuscript and eliminated many obscurities. I would like to thank my students for their interest in the problems of this book, many of which were developed in class lectures.

I would also like to express appreciation to various organizations which provided me with support and assistance. Most of all, I am grateful to the Society for the Humanities, Ithaca, New York, for sponsoring the initial research which led to this book. The Department of Anthropology at the University of California, San Diego, both its faculty and staff, helped in various ways when the manuscript was being prepared for publication. During my initial months as a Fellow for the National Endowment for the Humanities, the final manuscript was completed.

Dale F. Eickelman provided me with a number of valuable criticisms of earlier versions of the book. In addition, he has generously allowed me to use the story in section 3 of Chapter 12 which he and Bouzekri Draioui have translated in their article, "Islamic myths from western Morocco," *Hespéris-Tamuda* 14 (1973), pp. 195–225. I am also grateful for permission to use the following materials: The story in section 4 of Chapter 12 was taken from *Islam Observed* by Clifford Geertz (New Haven: Yale University Press, 1968), pp. 32–5. Figure 8 was adapted from a diagram which appeared in "The proliferation of segments in the lineage of the Bedouin of Cyrenaica" by Emrys Peters, *Journal of the Royal Anthropological Institute* 90 (1960), pp. 29–51. Figure 9 was adapted from a diagram which appeared in "Some structural aspects of the feud among the camel-herding Bedouin of Cyrenaica" by Emrys Peters, *Africa* 37 (1967), pp. 261–82. Figure 10 was adapted from a diagram in "The socio-political organization of a Berber 'taraf' tribe: pre-protectorate Morocco" by Amal Rassam (Vinogradov). This article appeared in *Arabs and Berbers: From Tribe to Nation in North Africa,* edited by Ernest Gellner and Charles Micaud (London: Duckworth, 1973), pp. 67–83. Map 2 was adapted from a map entitled "Pastoral zones" in *The Sanusi of Cyrenaica* by E.E. Evans-Pritchard (Oxford: Clarendon Press, 1949). Map 3 was reproduced from a map entitled "The Divisions of the Hasa Tribe" in *The Sanusi of Cyrenaica.*

M.M.

# Note on transliteration and translation

Musil devised a system of recording the Rwala dialect which he hoped would accurately indicate its sound values in a Western script. There is a debate about the degree to which he was successful. He has been criticized quite sharply by Cantineau (1937). Since few readers of this book will be familiar with the Rwala dialect, I have changed and simplified Musil's script so that the reader with some knowledge of Arabic might easily recognize Rwala cognates. The system of transliteration which I have adopted is widely used in English. I have also taken the liberty of transliterating Musil's *ẓ* as a *ḍ* in accordance with Cantineau's criticisms.

Musil's vowelizations of the Rwala dialect have been preserved since he is virtually the sole authority on this matter. Occasionally the combination of a standard English transliteration and Musil's vowelizations leads to words or phrases which are not easily read. There seems to be no perfect solution to the problem of presenting Musil's texts. I have attempted a reasonable compromise that might not prove too onerous for readers. My presumption is that anyone interested in the details of the Rwala texts will consult Musil's original work.

In the course of preparing such a large corpus of spoken Arabic for publication, Musil and his editors inevitably made a number of mistakes. In general, I have corrected only a very few typographical errors. To go further than this would demand a thorough editing of Musil's texts. This was a task which lay outside both the field of my interests as well as my competency. Except for the change in transliteration systems, Musil's texts are presented just as they were presented in his ethnography.

For the sake of consistency, Musil's vowelizations of names of persons, groups, and places in Arabia have been adopted throughout the text. In a number of instances, however, standard English equivalents of Arabic terms have been used, as in the case of Koran, Grand Sherif, Mecca, etc. Quotes from authors other than Musil have often retained their methods of transliterating Arabic. In Chapter 12, where two Moroccan stories of a saint are discussed, I have adopted the same system of transliteration as was used by the translators of the materials in question.

The following system has been used for transliterating the Arabic of the Rwala texts:

| Arabic Radical | Musil's translit-eration | The present translit-eration | Arabic Radical | Musil's translit-eration | The present translit-eration |
|---|---|---|---|---|---|
| ء | ’ | ’ | ط | ṭ | ṭ |
| ب | b | b | ظ | none* | ẓ |
| ت | t | t | ع | ʻ | ʻ |
| ث | t̲ | th | غ | ṛ | gh |
| ج | ğ | j | ف | f | f |
| ح | ḥ | ḥ | ق | { ḳ / ž } | q |
| خ | ḫ | kh | ك | { k / č } | k |
| د | d | d | ل | l | l |
| ذ | d̲ | dh | م | m | m |
| ر | r | r | ن | n | n |
| ز | z | z | ه | h | h |
| س | s | s | و | w | w |
| ش | š | sh | ى | j | y |
| ص | ṣ | ṣ | | | |
| ض | ẓ | ḍ | | | |

* merged with the letter ض in Musil's system

The following explanations for the pronunciation of classical Arabic are intended to guide the reader who is not familiar with the Arabic language. These explanations are not always consistent with the pronunciation of the Rwala dialect.

| | |
|---|---|
| ’ | a glottal stop, like the *tt* in bottle, Brooklynese style. |
| ṣ, ḍ, ṭ, ẓ | emphatic consonants. |
| th | like the *th* in thimble. |
| dh | like the *th* in the. |
| ḥ | an aspirated *h*, midway between *h* and *kh*. |
| kh | like the *ch* in Bach. |
| sh | like the *sh* in shake. |
| ʻ | a fricative which is pronounced in the throat. |
| gh | like a guttural French *r*. |
| q | like *k*, but pronounced further back in the mouth. |
| â, î, û | long vowels. |

The remaining letters are pronounced more or less the same as in English.

Musil's translations of the Rwala materials vary in quality. His English versions of the narratives of raiding and warfare are probably especially reliable. However, it is clear that he sometimes translates quite freely. One tale begins: "In 1902 the head chief . . . was invited by the Turkish

Government . . ." Another bears the mark of explanatory interpolation: "A camel thus abandoned is called . . ." Unfortunately, his failure to include a transcription of the Arabic means that the authenticity of the narratives can never be precisely evaluated. The possibility of discovering, however, a consistent design in the composition of a particular tale is good evidence that Musil was reasonably faithful to the original version.

Musil dealt with the poems of raiding and warfare in a different way. He provides a transcription of the Arabic together with an annotated English translation. Since the terms of the poetry are often highly technical, his translations sometimes tend to be ethnographic explanations. This is also generally true of all his glosses of Bedouin terms. They are more commentaries than literal definitions. In some places, however, Musil seriously distorts the poetry. This often happens when he reacts to the curious starkness and sobriety of Rwala poetry by lending it dramatic coloring that is more in accord with Western conceptions of heroic poetry. Despite their faults, Musil's English versions of the poetry must be the starting place for any analysis, since there is no dictionary of this Bedouin dialect.

# Part I

# The epoch of Near Eastern pastoral nomadism in Arabia

There is, however, among the Bedouins themselves, a great variety of dialects . . . but they all agree in pronouncing each letter with much precision, expressing its exact force or power, which . . . is never the case among the inhabitants of towns. The Bedouins also agree universally in using, as common, many select words, which in the towns would be called "literal terms" . . . and in speaking with grammatical accuracy.

Burckhardt, *Notes on the Bedouins and the Wahabys* (1831), pp. 372–3.

# 1. The ethnography of Near Eastern tribal societies

## 1

The Rwala are one of the tribes of the 'Aneze group of Bedouins found in North Arabia (the desert areas now divided between Saudi Arabia, Jordan, Syria, and Iraq). At the turn of the century they were camel-herding nomads. As one of the most vigorous and militant Bedouin tribes, they were an important factor in the politics of North Arabia and, to a lesser extent, in the politics of the Arabian peninsula. Their chief, Prince an-Nûri, was perhaps the most noted Bedouin chief of the northern deserts and steppes. On some occasions, he was recognized as the leader of a confederation of many tribes in this part of Arabia. He was also able to dominate various settled peoples. One of his sons, for example, was for a time the lord of the oasis of al-Jowf. During World War I, the Rwala, led by the prince, were among the tribes who fought against Ottoman military contingents. Following the war, they and their chiefs were also important elements in the political disputes and conflicts among the Grand Sherif of Mecca, the House of Eben Rashîd, and the House of Eben Sa'ûd.

During these troubled times, Alois Musil, a Czech Orientalist, traveled in North Arabia and became a close friend of the prince. While there he devoted himself to a study of Bedouin ethnography and Arabian topography.[1] The result was a painstaking documentation of Bedouin life during the last years in which these peoples would play their traditional role in Arabian affairs. The Arabian Bedouins of today are much milder men than their nineteenth-century forebears. They serve in a national army, receive the benefits of state schools and subsidies, and concern themselves with the profits and losses of animal herding.[2] The times in which Bedouin tribes dominated large sections of Arabia as free and independent political agents are past, and Musil's books present as detailed a glimpse of those times as we shall ever have.

One of Musil's most important works, *The Manners and Customs of the Rwala Bedouins,* borrows its title from Lane's book describing the Egyp-

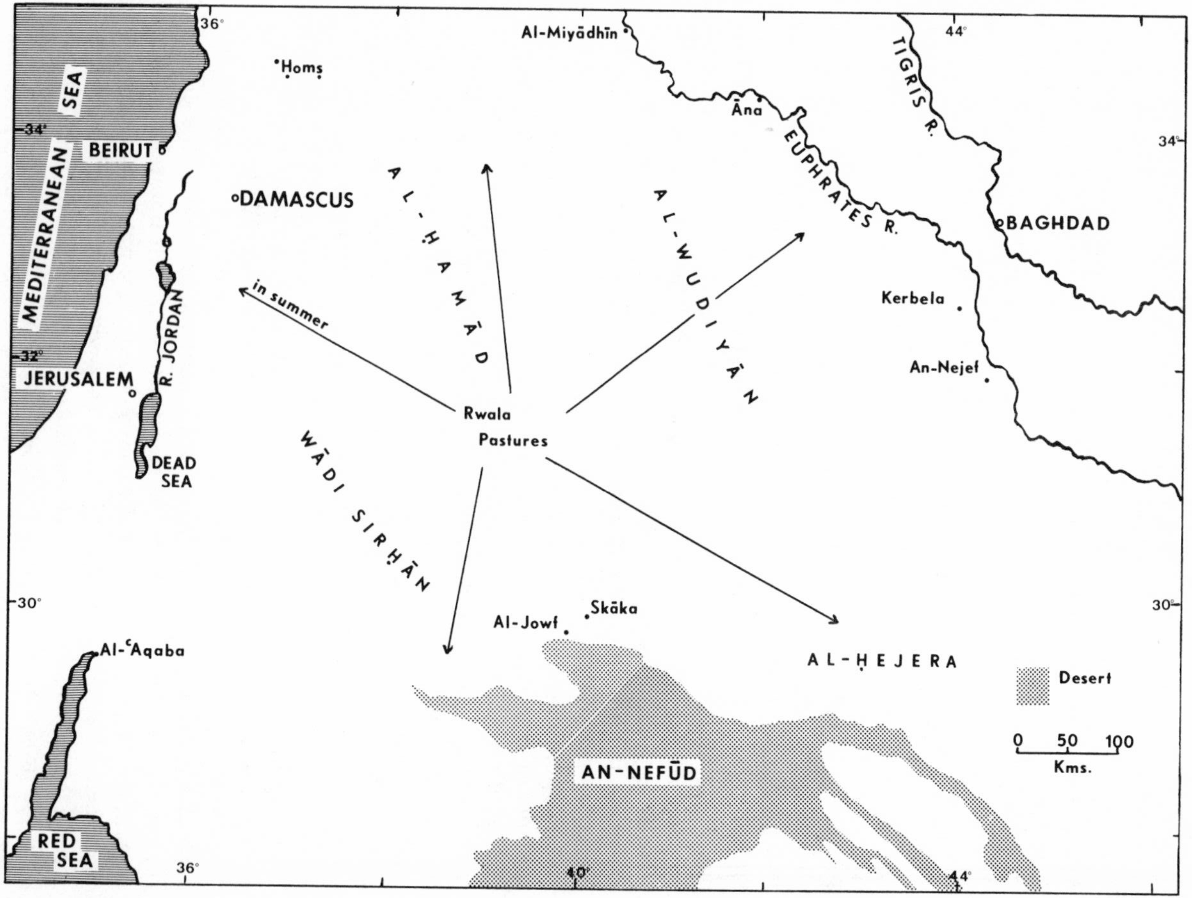


Map 1. North Arabia

tians in the first half of the nineteenth century.[3] Musil may have thought of this ethnography as a Bedouin counterpart to Lane's remarkable portrayal of Cairene society. If so, it is an impressive fulfillment of this ambition and may be ranked among the best ethnographies. The unique aspect of this work is its inclusion of Rwala poems, songs, ditties, narratives, and expressions along with an extensive number of notes regarding these materials. The poetry in particular could be termed the flesh of the ethnography. Again and again Musil ends his discussion of chiefs, camping grounds, food, marriage, children, camels, horses, hospitality, vengeance, and war with poems that deal directly or indirectly with the ethnographic category. Unlike other Western ethnographies of the Bedouins, this record of Rwala oral traditions provides us with a window from which to view Bedouin thoughts and Bedouin passions. It is the only opportunity we have to examine at firsthand just what kind of men the Bedouins were.

The portion of Musil's book that is of interest here, Chapter XXI, entitled "War and Peace," deals with Rwala political traditions. This is the longest chapter in the book, and the largest part of it is devoted to narratives, stories, anecdotes, songs, poems, and ditties having a direct relation to raiding or warfare. One section of the chapter presents several narratives of warfare accompanied by poems that refer more or less directly to the warfare recounted by the narrative. Unfortunately, the narratives, unlike the poems, are not given in Arabic, although they are frequently interspersed with Arabic phrases when a technical or figurative expression is used. This omission presents certain difficulties, and others arise with regard to deficiencies in Musil's transcriptions of Rwala poetry. Nevertheless, Musil's materials are the best Arabian Bedouin source materials that we have. They are far better than the materials with which anthropologists must often work, and they can be checked against the North Arabian texts collected by Carlo Landberg (on the fringes of the tribal area) and by Robert Montagne (after the political independence of the tribes had been compromised).[4]

Musil's study can in addition be supplemented with the work of others. Landberg, who also traveled and lived in Arabia around the turn of the century, has provided us with a small glossary wholly devoted to the Bedouin dialects of North Arabia and another extensive glossary of three volumes on the dialect of Dathînah, which includes numerous comments on North Arabic.[5] Cantineau has written two long articles on the phonetics and grammar of the Bedouin dialects of North Arabia.[6] And finally, Doughty and Montagne are important ethnographic sources for the Bedouin neighbors of the Rwala.[7] There are significant gaps in this body of material; nevertheless, it represents an unusual and impressive amount of ethnographic, lexicological, and grammatical documentation. Certainly very few tribal peoples have had so much attention devoted to their traditions before their independent political status was compromised. And it is possible that Musil's account of a nomadic people's way of life accompanied by an extensive collection of their oral traditions might well be unique. Seventy years after the completion of his Rwala expeditions, a close examination of his Rwala materials seems well overdue. This is especially the case since the Bedouin world he described has not persisted into our time, and there is no possibility of an addition to the ethnography of the free Bedouin tribes of Arabia.

## 2

Musil's Rwala materials exemplify the best efforts of Western ethnographers over the past century, but are also important for other reasons. They are drawn from a kind of peoples, the pastoral nomads, who had a great impact upon Near Eastern history. Until very recently such peoples were found throughout the arid zone that stretches from western North Africa, through the central Near East, and into eastern Central Asia. The way of life of these peoples was so intimately bound to the peculiar environment of this area that they were found almost everywhere within it and very few places outside of it.

It is tempting to consider that the influence of these peoples might even explain, more efficiently than any other single feature of Near Eastern history, why the arid zone today is one of the world's distinctive ethnographic regions. Perhaps the values of the pastoral nomads have somehow left their mark upon the traditions of all the peoples of this region. In this way, an unusual environment that led to an unusual way of life would be the basis for understanding why the peoples of such a far-flung area share so much in common.

Strong arguments can be advanced against such a perspective. Pastoral nomadism, as a way of life, is only vaguely associated with any particular cultural pattern. It is true that pastoral nomads everywhere usually have a reputation for aggressiveness. It is also true that they typically have an impressive concern with the political alliances of tribal groups and subgroups. Such a concern is not surprising given their aggressiveness. But besides these very general features, pastoral nomadism as a way of life cannot be associated with any particular cultural pattern.[8]

In addition to this, the similarity of popular traditions all over the arid zone is very likely a product of the history of our own era. If we had at our disposal an ethnography of the ancient world around 1500 B.C., it is questionable whether we would perceive the arid zone as a distinctive ethnographic region. About two millennia later, however, a large part of this vast region was swept by Islamic politico-religious movements, and by 1500 A.D., the townsmen, peasants, and tribesmen of this part of the

world shared a moral tradition in common. Pa
other hand, dates from much earlier times. The
and sheep, a process which is surely coordinate
pastoral nomadism, is thought to have taken plac
nium B.C. at the very latest.[9] The early appearance o
therefore, precludes it from explaining a cultural un
come about only in recent times.

We should not, however, dismiss too hastily such a pe
as a crucial feature of Near Eastern history. In the Nea
find a remarkable similarity among the traditions of ... s
throughout a large region. The explanation for such a ... omenon among peoples who have never been politically united in an important way and who have never been part of a tightly integrated economic order indicates that a force was at work all over the arid zone and only in that zone. Islamization, the spread of a religious faith, is usually offered as an explanation for this uniformity. But could Islam by itself have become so deeply rooted among the diverse peoples of such a vast area, unless it was somehow a response to a life experience which all these peoples shared in common? Let us consider pastoral nomadism once again, but not as a way of life that was everywhere and at all times the same way of life. Let us consider what might have made pastoral nomadism in the arid zone proper quite different from such a way of life on the various peripheries of this region.

The crucial feature which all forms of pastoral nomadism share in common is the problem of vulnerable domestic wealth. It is hard to protect wealth in herds. It is easy to plunder wealth in herds. This is why almost all, if not all, pastoral peoples are aggressive and concerned with their political organization. Historically, they are in contest over the possession of vulnerable domestic wealth. However, in the arid zone proper, this vulnerability is coupled with a certain form of pastoral nomadism. Here extreme arid conditions resulted in independent little herding groups across the desert and steppe. The domestic wealth of such groups was that much more vulnerable because the strategy of organizing scattered and independent little groups in protective political alliances was less effective. This situation is reflected by the atomistic form which political alliances tended to take among the pastoral nomads in the arid zone proper. They had to be constructed upon the relationship of individual political actors rather than be based upon the systematic relationships of clans and tribes.[10]

More crucial than this, the pastoral nomads of the arid zone proper were in contact with the centers of civilization from very early times. This contact, I suggest, is the key to a historical process. These pastoral nomads had ready access to the technological advances which were continually taking place in the centers of civilization. They tended to acquire not

ology itself, but those items which seemed to be of use in a strug- th other men over vulnerable domestic wealth. In particular they nded to acquire personal instruments of aggression. Their herds gave them the wealth to purchase outright such instruments. And their problem of vulnerable domestic wealth inspired in them the desire for such instruments. This volatile combination of motivations and circumstances will be termed "Near Eastern pastoral nomadism." Such a distinctive form of pastoral nomadism was simultaneously a way of life and a historical process. It was a way of life with anarchical tendencies, which tended to become increasingly anarchical as a result of a steady popular investment in increasingly efficient personal instruments of aggression.

The forces which led to Near Eastern pastoral nomadism may well have been at work at a very early date in certain parts of the arid zone. It is even possible that the evolution of the state in the Near East is intertwined with the relationship of settled and nomadic life. In any case, Kupper's study of the nomads in Mesopotamia during the time of the kings of Mari indicates that, by about 2000 B.C., nomadic sheep-herders, some of whom were more turbulent and some of whom were less so, were exerting considerable pressure upon sedentary peoples there.[11] And Bulliet's recent study of the place of the camel in the ancient world suggests that by about 1000 B.C. the forces of Near Eastern pastoral nomadism were beginning to play a significant role. Tribes of camel-herding nomads appeared in North Arabia, and the effort to convert the camel into a mount of war was under way.[12]

In his book, *The Camel and the Wheel,* Bulliet is concerned with the gradual replacement of carts and wagons by camels as beasts of burden, particularly in ancient long-distance trade. He has argued that this replacement came about primarily because the use of camels as pack animals was more efficient than the use of wheeled devices and draft animals. In developing this view, he has suggested that the gradual increase in the economic importance of camels in ancient times may have been closely related to the spread of camel-herding nomadism during the same period. His views also imply that a good deal of the technology necessary for using camels, not only as pack animals but also as riding mounts, may have been developed in connection with long-distance trade. Whatever the case, the camel-herders who appear on the scene in North Arabia around 1000 B.C. were, or soon became, riders of camels, unlike other early camel-herders. And in the course of the first millennium B.C., these camel-riders gradually converted their beasts into formidable mounts of war. Bulliet believes that the decisive turning point in this conversion was the development of the North Arabian camel saddle, sometime between 500 and 100 B.C.[13] Such an advance enabled the North Arabian Bedouins to enter our own era with a popular military capacity that was truly awesome in its setting in the desert and steppe. The camel was a personal instrument of aggression, which far and away transcended any defensive capacity that nomadic or sedentary peoples outside the centers of civilization were able to employ against it. To seek protection from camel-herding tribes, the peoples of the desert and steppe were themselves obliged to become riders of beasts or to become the subjects of such riders.[14]

During the first millennium A.D., various kinds of peoples, who were either themselves mounted pastoralists, associated with mounted pastoralists, or associated with the political conditions of mounted pastoralism, began to have a considerable impact upon the entire arid zone including the centers of civilization. The most dramatic example of this impact is the brief political domination of a large part of the arid zone by Arabian peoples during the seventh and eighth century A.D. and the eventual Islamization of so many Near Eastern peoples as a result of this domination. The early Muslims, of course, were not simply a group of pastoral nomadic peoples, although such peoples were an important element among them. But they were very much representatives of a society which was marked by a background of mounted pastoral nomadism. Indeed, this background was the crucial fact of Arabian society which did much to determine the very character of both urban and rural life in this part of the world until very recent times.[15]

The move of the Arabians into areas beyond their homeland was followed by more or less similar moves on the part of other peoples whose societies were marked by a background of mounted pastoral nomadism. However, it would be difficult to argue that the cultural uniformity of the peoples in the arid zone could be explained even as a result of the combined influence of the Arabian, Turkish, and Mongolian domination of various parts of this zone. Rather these movements of peoples, like the process of Islamization, represent only the most visible results of forces at work within popular political experience all over the Near East. There was constant pressure among the pastoral nomads all over the arid zone to invest in personal instruments of aggression. With time, this investment embroiled men increasingly in political strategies and struggles. This problem inevitably touched the sedentary peoples who were in contact with the pastoral nomads - that meant the vast majority of sedentary peoples in the arid zone proper. Indeed, since there was never any clear boundary between nomadic and sedentary life, the threat of popular political turmoil was very much a problem of sedentary life, even though it originated in the conditions of nomadic life. And so in the course of time, a cultural uniformity crystallized as a result of a sweeping process which was imperceptibly at work on the level of popular motivations and circumstances and quite visibly at work in connection with dramatic histori-

The cultural uniformity which we now find in the arid zone, however, does not reflect the traditions of a people bent upon violence. On the contrary, it does reflect by and large a moral reaction to the *threat* of popular political turmoil. The process of Islamization itself can be viewed in part as a moral response to the problem which arose from the circumstances of Near Eastern pastoral nomadism. All over the arid zone, different social elements and diverse peoples found a solace in a religion which announced the possibility of a community of peace based upon the sober and decent behavior of the individual. There was such a response because men everywhere shared the problems of a life experience that was touched by the threat of popular political anarchy.

Islam was forged in an area that was troubled by one of the most anarchical forms of Near Eastern pastoral nomadism. The spread of Islam is even closely linked with the spread of the Arabian mounted pastoral nomads themselves. In a sense, the Arabians afflicted the Near East with one of the most vigorous forms of Near Eastern pastoral nomadism at the same time as they were the carriers of an effective moral response to the problems created by Near Eastern pastoral nomadism.[16]

The peculiar character of the cultural patterns which peoples all over the arid zone share suggests the important historical role which the forces of Near Eastern pastoral nomadism played. All over the arid zone proper, popular traditions can be described in terms of three cultural themes. First, we find, more or less everywhere, an agonistic rhetoric of political association. The public world is conceived of as the scene of an uncertain struggle among men. The very concept of an individual or an association cannot be entirely separated from a political interest or concern.[17] Second, we find, more or less everywhere, humanistic religious values. These values are sometimes exemplified by a religious personality such as a saint. They are sometimes invoked as a moral standard of proper personal acts and proper personal beliefs. In both respects, they tend to turn upon conceptions of exemplary personal behavior. Third, we find, more or less everywhere, social norms of personal integrity and familial propriety. The norms of personal integrity often take the form of concepts of honor whereby an individual or group is under the constant scrutiny of others. The norms of familial propriety are usually most impressively elaborated in connection with the seclusion of women.

Only one of these three cultural themes - the political - is obviously related to Near Eastern pastoral nomadism. However, the other two themes, which are more characteristic of traditional Near Eastern urban and peasant societies, can be plausibly related to the political theme.[18] Where relationships in general are considered uncertain, would not religious values crystallize around the sanctity of the person? Would not men find the promise of peace, the promise of respite from the uncertainty of relationships, in examples and definitions of a common, simple humanity? And where relationships in general are considered uncertain, would not social norms proliferate around the proper forms by which men recognize and cope with this fact of life? Is not the Near Eastern man of honor a man who faces other men more or less aggressively with mutual self-respect? Is not the Near Eastern proper family a family which is designed as a peaceful interior that is protected and concealed from a disorderly exterior?

Quite plausibly, the characteristic cultural themes of Near Eastern traditions indicate a history of popular political turmoil. And quite plausibly, the Near Eastern pastoral nomads, a people afflicted by political disorder, but also a people who thrived upon political disorder, were an important source of this turmoil. An understanding of the traditions of these peoples therefore promises some insight as to why the Near East today is a distinctive ethnographic region by and large different from any other ethnographic region of the world.

## 3

Fully aware of the historical importance of Near Eastern tribal peoples, some Orientalists, such as Musil and Landberg, worked to lay the ethnographic and philological foundations for a study of their traditions. They failed, however, to advance any important interpretative view of these traditions. More recently, Near Eastern anthropologists have developed various interpretations of Near Eastern tribal societies, but they have pursued an excessively narrow approach. An inordinate amount of attention has been devoted to the implications of tribal genealogies whereas many other features of tribal traditions have been neglected. And in general there has been very little concern with the importance of tribal materials for an understanding of Near Eastern history.

Yet it is appropriate to begin with what the anthropology of Near Eastern tribal society has accomplished in recent years. This consists of a body of discussion which anthropologists term "segmentary theory." This theory not only provides the lens with which more or less all anthropologists today perceive Near Eastern tribal societies, it also raises, despite its narrow conception, a central issue about the character of these societies.

The first important elaboration of segmentary theory appears in E. E. Evans-Pritchard's book on the Nuer, a group of cattle-herders and agriculturalists living in the southern Sudan.[19] In this study, Evans-Pritchard advanced a thesis about the political functions of Nuer genealogies. He next applied a similar thesis to the Cyrenaican Bedouins; others later developed his ideas in connection with other peoples.[20] With time, the opinion emerged that segmentary theory provided some understanding of the politics of many so-called primitive peoples as well as an especially good understanding of the politics of Near Eastern tribal peoples.

The key examples of what became known as segmentary politics were indeed certain Near Eastern peoples: the Cyrenaican Bedouins, the Somali nomads of the Horn of Africa, and the Berbers of the Atlas.[21] Among these groups of Near Eastern tribal peoples, but not among many others and as we shall see not among the Rwala Bedouins, anthropologists were able to document extensive tribal genealogies in a patrilineal idiom. In some few instances, a single complete tribal genealogy, sometimes including hundreds of thousands of men, purported to map the patrilineal kinship relationships of all male members of the tribal society, both living and dead. That is to say, the tribal genealogy traced the relationships of all living men through their dead male ancestors to a single tribal ancestor. A diagram of the form of such a map, which illustrates the tendency for the map to split into pairs of descendants at its upper levels, is presented in Figure 1.

According to segmentary theory, this genealogical map is inspired by the problem of the political relationships among separate little herding groups. The principal function of the map is to provide a paradigm of political alliances in the idiom of patrilineal descent. Let us suppose then that the map in Figure 1 terminates with names of the patrilineal ancestor of each little herding group. These names are represented by the letters A, B, C, D, E, F, G, and H. While the men of each little group also conceive of their relationships in a patrilineal idiom, these conceptions are not im-

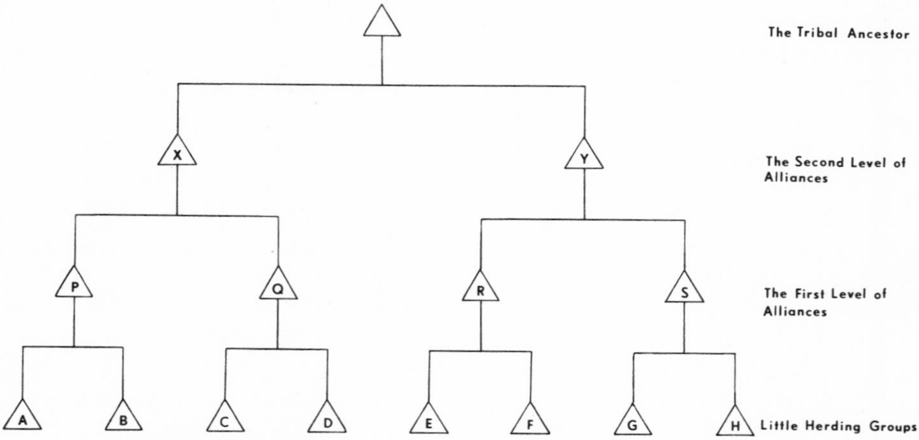


Figure 1. The form of a politically segmenting genealogy

portant for the political relationships between little groups. They are therefore omitted from further consideration.

The Near Eastern tribal peoples devoted to such genealogical maps do indeed contend that they represent political alliances of a sort. They sometimes note, for example, that the descendants of P are obliged to unite against the descendants of Q in a conflict of interests between the two groups: an occasion of cattle-theft, a dispute over water rights, a purposeful or accidental homicide, etc. Likewise, the descendants of P and Q are said to unite, whatever their internal discords, under the name of X in any similar conflict with the descendants of Y. In this way, the genealogical map does seem to be a paradigm of political alliances in the idiom of patrilineal descent.

The existence of such a tribal genealogical map and its political function is then explained by anthropologists as a product of the character of pastoral nomadic societies. They have no elaborate governmental institutions which might serve to regulate the relationships of little herding groups. The little herding groups are relatively independent, but potentially in competition for resources. The result is a minimal "governmental" institution for moderating this competition: the tribal genealogy. The genealogy provides a framework for dealing with disputes. As a conceptual structure, it depends only upon simple, one might even say primitive ideas: the idea of the person and the idea of elementary familial relationships - father and sons, brother and brother. Elementary familial relationships among males in this way become the basic elements for conceiving of a tribal political structure. The tendency for the "fathers" in the upper level of the genealogy to have only two "sons," for example, suggests that the structure of the genealogy consistently pits two groups of equal size against one another. A stalemate is thereby created; political conflict is moderated and controlled. Evans-Pritchard characterized this form of political structure as "ordered anarchy."

In recent years, segmentary theory has been severely criticized. The theory can be attacked, for example, on purely formal grounds. While it implies that the nomads are practical men who think in terms of self-interest, it fails to explain the highly formal way by which they conceive of their self-interest. Besides being practical, the nomads would seem as well to be dogmatic. Their imagination fails to conceive of relationships other than in terms of a model of paternal authority and filial unity. They apply this model indiscriminately and mechanistically to both near relations and distant relations. The murder of a man of group A by a man of group B might, for example, precipitate a feud between these two neighboring groups, a conflict involving a few score of people. Is it also possible that similar events, the murder of a man of group A by a man of group E, might precipitate tribal war among tens of thousands of peoples?

Such an improbable consequence, while implicit in the notion of a segmentary political structure, was explained away by various modifications of segmentary theory. It was argued that the genealogy was not a literal definition of political alliances, but only a guideline by which political problems and situations were approached in a preliminary way. While there is much to be said for such a view of the genealogies, it too can be criticized on formal grounds. Is it correct, for example, to identify the genealogy with a desire to moderate or to control disputes? Some indigenous commentaries on genealogical relationships do not insist on how groups unite with others for protection, nor do they insist on how the genealogy provides a means of conflict resolution. On the contrary, they suggest that the genealogy reveals how tribal society is pervaded by political conflict. The genealogy, from the perspective of some Near Eastern indigenous commentaries, does not reveal how tribal peoples are interested in peace, but how they are interested in war.[22] The Near Eastern tribal genealogy can be plausibly viewed as the product of men who define themselves as a society of men struggling with one another, a society in which men do not come together to live in peace, but come apart to live by war.

There are now many Near Eastern anthropologists who believe that the entire question of political segmentation and tribal genealogies should be set aside as an exhausted area of research. So long as segmentary theory is conceived as a problem of describing political alliances, they are no doubt correct. Yet the segmentary theorists in general, and Evans-Pritchard in particular, have touched upon a distinctive feature of Near Eastern tribal societies. They have focused attention on a curious cultural artifact of these societies, and they have associated this artifact with the pastoral way of life. The growing disillusionment with segmentary theory is accompanied then by the abandonment of a still unresolved formal problem. The question is not whether Near Eastern tribal peoples actually adhere to genealogical principles in their political behavior, but why they should have conceived of such a bizarrely formal paradigm of political relationships with such disturbing implications. Let us consider the formal features of such a paradigm and thereby raise the problem of a distinctive Near Eastern tribal rhetoric.

The principles of the politically segmenting genealogy suggest a kind of political language. A political group arises simultaneously with the breakage of a political group. The existence of relationships is associated with the violence of relationships. This political language is somewhat reminiscent of metaphorical language. A metaphor turns upon the problematic forging of a connection between two things which are not necessarily connected. A metaphor is thereby explicitly fictional in character. It reveals an association where there is no necessary association. Its form reveals, in other words, a distinctive mind playfully at work precisely in that what is associated is uncertainly associated. The fusion and fission of groups described by the tribal genealogy constitute, one might suggest, a purely "political metaphor." Meaning is associated with relationships in that the genealogy does nothing more than tabulate relationships. The meaning of the relationships so tabulated, however, is uncertain. The value of every cooperative relationship turns upon the problem of an equivalent hostile relationship. Indeed, every cooperative relationship is also conceivably a hostile relationship. Relationships are meaningful, they intrigue and fascinate, they have fictional value, precisely because they are uncertain in just these ways. The metaphor at the heart of the politically segmenting genealogy suggests a play of relationships. The disturbing aspect of such a play is its close association with violence.

## 4

When the politically segmenting genealogy is considered as a form of political language, we find that it raises a question about the meaning which anthropologists have attempted to attribute to genealogical traditions. The genealogy suggests a play of relationships around a problem of political violence. In so far as this is the case, it cannot be precisely described as a device for the control of political conflicts. And while the genealogy does at least define the boundaries of political conflict, ethnographers have long since observed that the actual fusion and fission of tribal groups in the course of political events never strictly respected these boundaries.[23]

This view of genealogical traditions as a form of political language therefore raises the broader issue of how a peculiar historical experience led to a peculiar political rhetoric among the tribal peoples of the Near East. Eventually we must consider why some tribal peoples were more concerned with genealogical representations than others, but for now the politically segmenting genealogy can be set aside as simply one artifact among others of a distinctive political language. Once this is done, the North Arabian Bedouins can be recognized as a crucial example of a tribal people in the Near East, even though they were not expecially interested in genealogies. For among these Bedouins, the connection between a pervasive problem of political violence and the circumstances of pastoral nomadism is especially clear.

Around the turn of the century, a struggle with weapons dominated the traditions of the North Arabian Bedouins to a degree that was probably unparalleled anywhere else in the arid zone.[24] At the same time, these Bedouins also practiced an unusually pure form of mounted pastoral nomadism. They did not engage in either agriculture or hunting in any important way, and for the most part, they did not herd any animals that could not be ridden, such as goats, sheep, or cattle. In the next chapter, we shall consider how these two extreme features of the way of life of these people, political violence and mounted pastoralism, were closely interconnected.

# 2. The personal voice and the uncertainty of relationships

## 1

An examination of the circumstances of camel-herding nomadism enables us to determine the peculiar freedoms and constraints which characterize such a way of life. In this way we can understand how the traditions of the North Arabian Bedouins were the result of certain avenues which were either opened up or closed off as they became involved in a mounted pastoral way of life. In North Arabia, the Bedouins lived as little groups wandering with their herds in search of pasture. Setting aside the question of who might have made up each group and just how stable group membership in each might have been, the groups themselves, viewed as herding groups, were more or less self-sufficient and independent from a material point of view. They had herds from which they satisfied their material needs. They had the steppe on which the herds grazed. There was only a question of moving with the herds in search of pasture.

This necessity to move with the herds had implications for the quality of each group's relationships with other groups. As a mobile group, the herders were not tied to any specific territory. They did not and they could not conceive of their relationship with the land in the same terms as settled peoples did. It was their possession of herds on which they depended, not their possession of land. And by the same token, this group mobility undercut the possibility of (as well as the necessity for) routinized and systematic relationships with other groups, as groups. As among all nomadic peoples, there were certain restrictions placed upon the possibility of developing either ceremonial or practical relationships among groups. Such relationships were perhaps not out of the question, but they were necessarily limited by the group's mobility.

The uniqueness of camel-herding nomadism as one type of nomadism, however, becomes evident when one considers the character of the principal resource on which such a life depended. The Bedouins lived a life of camel-herding. The needs of their camels determined the character of their nomadic life. Note two peculiar aspects of this Bedouin means of existence. The camel, as a possession necessary for survival, is uniquely vulnerable. The camel can be removed from its owner. It can be run off at a trot. And yet the camel must be ranged and therefore cannot be surely protected. Unlike land, camels are not very easy to defend. Unlike land, they can be seized in an inadvertent moment. Unlike wealth in land, wealth in camels can vanish almost instantaneously. This feature of the camel as a principal resource allows us to understand why notions of property and possession were in question among the Bedouins.

Now let us consider a second, still more disturbing aspect of the camel. The camel, a vulnerable domestic necessity, is also an aggressive political instrument. The camel, as a mount, makes the camel, as a possession, even more tenuous. As a domestic necessity, the camel provides meat and milk. Its hair, woven into tent cloth, provides shelter, its dung, fuel, and its urine, bath water. But as a mount, the camel can also be used against other men. One can ride to distant unknown groups, steal their camels, and ride home again, sometimes without even revealing one's identity. The character of this central possession, therefore, throws into question the concept of possession. It is easier to steal camels than to defend them. Possession, in other words, is inseparable from a capacity for theft.

From these relatively simple features of mounted camel-herding nomadism, simple but not exactly duplicated by any other form of pastoral nomadism, we can begin to understand the distinctive features of Bedouin political and social forms. The simultaneous vulnerability of camels together with the aggressive potential of camels gave rise to a Bedouin political concern of us versus them. That is to say, North Arabian Bedouin culture was a highly political culture. The vulnerability of domestic possessions (camels) precipitated by the aggressive potential of a political resource (camels) carried men away from a materially productive domestic life toward an uncertain, agonistic, political adventurism. The identity of men did not turn so much upon their wise management of resources or their mastery of intricate and delicate skills. It turned instead upon their political abilities, the capacity to deal with other men and the capacity to struggle with other men. The two highest qualities of a man were closely connected with the formation of policy (political speech) and the achievement of political ends (political action).

The character of the camel as a domestic necessity *and* a political instrument provides us with an understanding of why Bedouin culture is appropriately discussed as a political culture. It is, however, difficult for anyone not familiar with the North Arabian Bedouins to appreciate the degree to which they invested themselves in political activities. There was an awesome political instrument at hand which determined the character of this investment. There was no means of controlling the availability of this instrument. Everyone more or less could partake in camel-raiding since anyone could steal a camel. No group could monopolize the means (camels) of camel-raiding. The more camels a group possessed, the harder it was to protect these numerous herds. The more camels a group possessed, the more enemies they had acquired in amassing these herds, and therefore the more they were surrounded by enemies who lacked and desired camels.

As a consequence, we find that North Arabian Bedouin culture turned in large part upon the notion that violence lay at the center of political life. Men tended to think of themselves, their possessions, and their relationships in terms of this violence. They saw themselves as men on mounts who contested other men on mounts. They were camel-riders who stole from and fought with other men. They saw their possessions as signs of their heroic capacities. They saw their chiefs as men who led them either offensively or defensively against other men. They saw their relationships with other men, their political associations, as resources which could be used against other similar associations. Strategies, skills, techniques, leadership, and relationships crystallized around the problem of mounted political violence. To a remarkable degree Bedouin culture was polarized around the exercise of political violence, an exercise conceived sometimes as an absorbing and joyful play of life and sometimes as a serious struggle against death.

## 2

Turning to Charles M. Doughty's *Travels in Arabia Deserta,* we find these features of Bedouin life more or less implicit in the insights of a keen observer. Doughty describes the Central Arabian Bedouins sometime around 1876. These tribes were more subject to the hegemony of dynasties situated in the Arabian towns than the North Arabian Bedouins, more dependent upon sheep and goats, more closely tied to specific territories, and more Islamized. Nevertheless, their political conventions bore the stamp of the North Arabian camel-herders who often moved south and raided among them.

Reading through Doughty's account, we find that the Central Arabian Bedouins were sometimes driven to steal camels through desperation. Lacking the means of survival and lacking the proper avenues for acquiring such a means, men were forced to take extreme measures. Or was there possibly more to the matter than this? Was it that men only knew how to survive by means of camels, or rather by means of stealing camels? Camel-theft occurred among these Bedouins, not occasionally as a practical necessity, but persistently as a way of life. Such a distinction is made by Doughty himself in a passage which describes certain Bedouins with a "wolfish" self-identity:

> The habalîs, "desert fiends," are dreaded by the nomad tribesmen, as the Beduw themselves among settled country and oasis folk. Commonly the habalîs are some young miscreants that, having hardly any head of cattle at home, will desperately cast themselves upon every cruel hazard: yet others are strenuous solitary men, whose unquiet mettle moves them from slothing in the tent's shadow to prowl as the wolf in the wilderness.[1]

The acquisition of camels by theft holds some fascination for the Bedouins. Men come alive as they plot and strive to steal a camel. Doughty, who was called Khalîl by the Bedouins, puts the question to a Bedouin friend:

> "But why wear out thy life thus? Is Mohammed a Beduwy to go cattle lifting?" At this word he looked up, and "*Tóma,* Khalîl, said he with a weary breath, *tóma*! it is the desire of having, and more having, thus the world is made; I live with the Beduw, and I do as the Beduw, also I may win a camel."[2]

A desire not only of having, but also of winning, manifests itself in the exercise of camel-theft. It is, one might say, the desire to make a certain kind of life for oneself. As such a desire, it disrupts and unsettles the desert scene. In one place, Doughty depicts this scene as a turbulent sea of raids and counterraids:

> Their ghrazzus and counter-ghrazzus are the destruction of the Aarab. Reaving and bereaved they may never thrive; in the end of every tide it is but an ill exchange of cattle. So in the eyes of nomads, the camel troops of the Fukara were all "mingled" cattle and uneven, that is, not home-born-like, but showing to be robbed beasts out of several dîras. Motlog's son said to me, he who should be great sheykh after him, "Ay, wellah! All our camels are harrâm (of prey taken in the forays), and not our lawful own."[3]

There is, in the words of Doughty, an ill exchange of cattle among the Bedouins. The raids and counterraids are conceived as a diseased form of commerce or communication. The camel herd itself is unlawfully possessed and consists of mingled animals stolen from diverse groups. As a form of property it is improper and uneven, a forbidden object.

Just as a life at home is a life built upon uneven, mingled, and forbidden possessions, so life abroad, in the form of organized raiding parties, is decked out as a ritualized occasion. Life abroad assumes a certain formal grandeur. Doughty observes:

> It happened strangely that whilst Bishr was out against them a main ghrazzu of the Wélad Aly had mounted to go and set upon Bishr. These hostile squadrons by a new adventure met with each other in the wilderness. An hundred thelûl riders cover the ground of a regiment. It is a brave sight, as they come on with a song, bowing in the tall saddles, upon the necks of their gaunt stalking beasts, with a martial shining of arms. The foemen in sight, the sheukh descend with the long lances upon their led horses; and every sheykh's back-rider, *radîf,* who is also his gun-bearer, now rides in the thelûl saddle.[4]

The contrast of a great political life abroad with a tawdry, colorless domestic life does not accurately characterize, of course, the whole of Bedouin existence. It only constitutes one of its possible themes or rhythms. Elsewhere in Doughty's account we begin to perceive an intricate field of intimate social relationships, a field which nonetheless is not altogether unrelated with the problem of political adventurism abroad. Consider, for example, an incident in which camel-theft is invoked as an innocent youthful activity while an attempt to defend possessions at all costs is condemned as vicious behavior:

"Ah-ha! and eigh me!" sighed the unhappy father of a valiant son, that this day lay rotting in his shallow burial before the time; "we ride only a cattle-lifting, but ye slay men:" so he ended with a great drawn sob; Tollog sighed after him, as he was a father, and they sat on in silence.[5]

In this incident, the aggrieved father has come to demand blood money from the victims of his son's raiding party who in trying to protect their herds shot and killed the son. We discover in this same passage that the father claims a relationship with the victims of the raid so that he may ask for the higher blood price that prevails among close kin. When Doughty enquires of the defendant why they consent to pay the blood money, he is told that they fear the hostility (of their close relations who plunder them!) that might follow upon a refusal. Strategies of threat and extortion are intertwined with expressions of a mild sociability, a generous hospitality, and a warm, human sympathy.

The Bedouins seem to come alive in the context of raiding and that raiding is conceivable as a way of life. The occasions for raiding and warfare lend the movement and design of groups a certain ceremonial aspect. They are ornamented with songs and organized with a certain grandeur. At the same time, an intricate field of social relationships turns explicitly upon warm and frank expressions of inner feelings and implicitly upon extortions and threats. These features of Bedouin life are all the more striking when one considers another people of the Arabian deserts and steppes who do not herd animals and who do not have a tribal life. These are the "despised" Ṣleyb (or Solubba), a class of people who have no herds, wander in tiny groups, and generally live by their industry. The Ṣleyb are interesting because their way of life is very nearly the obverse of the Bedouin way of life. Let us examine again Doughty's comments on this matter:

I admired the full-faced shining flesh-beauty of their ragged children . . . These alien and outcast kindreds are of fairer looks than the hunger-bitten Beduw. [The Solubba] have food enough in the desert . . . of their hunting and gipsy labour: for they are tinkers of kettles and menders of arms, in the Beduin menzils. They batter out upon the anvil hatchets . . . and grass-hooks for cutting forage, and steels for striking fire with the flint, and the like. They are besides woodworkers, in the desert acacia timber, of rude saddle-trees for the burden-camels, and of the thelûl saddle-frames, of pulley reels . . . for drawing at any deeper wells of the desert, also of rude milk vessels, and other such husbandry: besides, they are cattle surgeons, and in all their trade (only ruder of skill) like the smiths' caste or Sunna.[6]

The Ṣleyb are a people of many accomplishments. They know how to perform intricate and delicate tasks. They make things. They labor patiently. They look closely at how things work. They, not the Bedouins, are the camel surgeons, even though they do not herd camels.

The Bedouins are dependent upon the Ṣleyb. The Ṣleyb by their skills and crafts supply all those products which the Bedouins need for their camel-herding way of life. The relationship between the Ṣleyb and the Bedouins is an important relationship in practical, utilitarian terms. The important point, however, is this: The Bedouins do not recognize their dependence upon the Ṣleyb nor do they appreciate their abilities. Instead, they pretentiously view the Ṣleyb as politically dependent upon them. The Bedouins look down upon the Sleyb as politically weak, as men without honor. They are the "despised" Ṣleyb.

And yet, the way of life of the Ṣleyb is relatively unvexed by the tribulations which afflict the Bedouins. Doughty observes:

The Solubby household go then to settle themselves remotely, upon some good well of water, in an unfrequented wilderness, where there is game. They only (of all men) are free of the Arabian deserts to travel whithersoever they would; paying to all men a petty tribute, they are molested by none of them. Home-born, yet have they no citizenship in the Peninsula. No Beduwy, they say, will rob a Solubby, although he met him alone, in the deep of the wilderness, and with the skin of an ostrich in his hand, that is worth a thelûl.[7]

Just as the Ṣleyb cannot plunder, so they are not plundered. There is no significance in robbing the defenseless. Similarly just as the Ṣleyb cannot plunder, so they do not own herds, the principal means and ends of plunder. And lacking the means to plunder, lacking the ends of plunder, they are viewed as men without "citizenship," without either home groups or homelands. In the Bedouins' eyes, the Ṣleyb are men who are dispossessed, men who live in desolation. In the Bedouins' eyes, Ṣleyb life is an empty one: "The Solubba or *Slèyb,* besides this proper name of their nation, have some other which are epithets. West of Hâyil they are more often called *el-Khlûa* or *Kheluîy,* "the desolate," because they dwell apart from the Kabâil, having no cattle nor fellowship."[8] Still another Bedouin opinion views the Ṣleyb as former Bedouins who were deprived of their herds and so fell to their lowly position. And let us recall that the Ṣleyb in general are better off, they eat better, and are healthier than the Bedouins. The Bedouins cannot appreciate the industry of the Ṣleyb. They cannot appreciate the security of their domestic way of life and its more decent material rewards. The Bedouins instead are captivated by some promise which they find in a life of fellowship and herds.

At this point, we should spell out just how such a way of life challenges some familiar anthropological presuppositions. As the Bedouins put their relationships and their beasts into the play of a political life, their possession of herds became more uncertain. They did not ride, that is to say, in order to secure a tranquil domestic life. As the Bedouins put their relationships and beasts into play, they did not more certainly possess herds, but then they did not altogether lose them. Rather, between the taking of a camel and the losing of a camel, there opened a fascinating life of political adventure. Similarly, as the Bedouins joined and cooperated with other men in order to struggle with still other men, they did not attempt to discover and to realize the inherent value of social life. It was not exactly fellowship which they valued above all else, just as it was not the possession of herds which they valued above all else. Rather, between their joining with some men on the occasion of breaking with still other men, there opened a fascinating political life.

In this sense, a Bedouin involvement in a life of violent contests and extreme risks was a product of the power of the human imagination, not a result of biological or psychological drives which push men relentlessly toward aggressions against one another. The marshaling of riders against other riders was a captivating alternative for the Bedouins, for by such an alternative their life became far more charged with promises, even as it became far more charged with threats. A desire for "possibilities" seized upon the camel, and men were lured into a life of manifold hopes and fears. Let us now attempt to understand more precisely the forms of these peculiar hopes and fears.

## 3

Even though they were on the very threshold of the Holy Cities of Arabia, the North Arabian Bedouins around the turn of the century were not impressed by Islam. Unlike many of the Bedouin tribes of Central Arabia who somewhat haphazardly performed a number of Islamic rituals, the Rwala considered "Islam weak, as it cannot free the settlers from their miseries."[9] Nor were they attracted to the more parochial myths and rituals current among the settlers of Arabia at the time. Instead, Musil observes that they unequivocally rejected the cult of saints:

> The Bedouins know of no communion with the saints. In the whole inner desert there is not a single holy grave or shrine erected in honor of a saint. In fact they have no saints whatever. When they make their short sojourns in the settled territory, where by every village the dome of a shrine rises above the real or imaginary grave of some man or woman whom public opinion considers to be a saint, they never pay attention to these domes. In their opinion the

latter commemorate the saints of the settlers and breeders of goats and sheep . . .

Worship of the saints has never been known among the Rwala and presumably never will be. The hereafter does not trouble the Bedouins much, and their idea of it is only hazy; nor have they any permanent burying places . . . but bury their dead wherever death overtakes them.[10]

As an example of a tribal and archaic world, the North Arabian Bedouin world seems sober and drab. There was among these Arabian Bedouins no great ceremonial life, which brought together the little herding groups. There were no artistic productions or ritual exchanges, such as we find in the South Seas or in the Pacific Northwest. There were no celebrations of kingship such as we find in Africa. There was no conception of a sacred order of the pure and the impure within which groups were hierarchically related, such as we find in South Asia. There was no conception of political authority as a feature of a heavenly order, such as we find in East Asia. In the midst of the little herding groups there was almost no form, almost nothing for the ethnographer to describe.

This exceptional aspect of the Arabian Bedouin world is the basis for a common Western perception of the Arabian desert and steppe as an environment hostile to man. As the Western eye detects the absence of society and industry, it views nature rather than man as the cause of this poverty of public form. Let us examine this Western perception as it appears in Doughty's work:

Now longwhile our black booths had been built upon the sandy stretches, lying before the swelling white Nefûd side: the lofty coast of Irnàn in front, whose cragged breaches, where is any footing for small herbs nourished of this barren atmosphere, are the harbour of wild goats, which never drink. The summer's night at end, the sun stands up as a crown of hostile flames from that huge covert of inhospitable sandstone bergs; the desert day dawns not little and little, but it is noontide in an hour. The sun, entering as a tyrant upon the waste landscape, darts upon us a torment of fiery beams, not to be remitted till the far-off evening. – No matins here of birds; not a rock partridge-cock, calling with blithesome chuckle over the extreme waterless desolation. Grave is that giddy heat upon the crown of the head; the ears tingle with a flickering shrillness, a subtle crepitation it seems, in the glassiness of this sun-stricken nature: the hot sand-blink is in the eyes, and there is little refreshment to find in the tents' shelter; the worsted booths leak to this fiery rain of sunny light. Mountains looming like dry bones through the thin air, stand far around about us: the savage flank of Ybba Moghrair, the high spire and ruinous stacks of el-Jebâl, Chebàd, the coast of Helwàn! Herds of weak nomad camels waver dispersedly, seeking pasture in the midst of this hollow fainting country, where but lately the swarming locusts have fretted every green thing. This silent air burning about us, we endure breathless till the assr: when the dazing Arabs in the tents revive after their heavy hours. The lingering day draws down to the sun-setting; the herdsmen, weary of the sun, come again with the cattle, to taste in their menzils the first sweetness of mirth and repose. – The day is done, and there rises the nightly freshness of this purest mountain air: and then to the cheerful song and the cup at the common fire. The moon rises ruddy from that solemn obscurity of jebel like a mighty beacon: – and the morrow will be as this day, days deadly drowned in the sun of the summer wilderness.[11]

As he surveys the Bedouin world, Doughty finds no great public scene. He perceives in its place a threatening natural environment, a scene of wastes and ruins. In the midst of these wastes and ruins, he perceives as well "weak," "wavering," "fainting," "breathless," "dazed," "weary" men and animals. Only in the narrow confines of the camp, the *menzil,* does he find "mirth and repose." Only around the little "common fire" does he discover "the cheerful song and the cup."

These last remarks direct our attention to the interior life of the little herding group. Perhaps here we may find the existence of cultural forms that we have failed to find among the little herding groups. What form then does the internal life of these groups take? Are there perhaps domestic activities to draw the interests and concerns of the Bedouins away from the promises and threats of political adventurism abroad? If so, the fascination with the camel as a political instrument would be weakened, and with its weakening the problem of uncertain political relationships would likewise subside. Let us first examine quite briefly the implications of herding camels as a practical domestic activity.

Camel-herding obliged the Bedouins to move constantly in order to find pasture and water. It was an arduous occupation which determined many routine day-to-day activities. We must not, however, let our "sedentary" perspective on life mislead us in our estimation of this situation. Paradoxically, Arabian Bedouin camel-herding was not a labor-intensive activity. Nor was it an activity which required an elaborate coordination of groups and individuals or the mastery of precise and diverse skills. Outside the necessity for movement, there was little to be done with the herds from day to day. They needed only to be ranged by a few youths. Camel-herding, that is to say, required neither a precise organization of labor nor elaborate practical skills. There were few opportunities for the cooperative and few opportunities for the industrious.

Two decisive indications of the practical poverty of Bedouin life can now be cited. Even where there was a necessity for cooperation or industry, such tasks were shifted upon women for whom they constituted more of a burden than a pleasure. And from Doughty's account, we learn that the day-to-day life of the Bedouin camp was typified by indolence and verbal strife. If one scans over the entries under "Bedouins" in Doughty's index, these two qualities of the herding life are fully evident: "their minds distempered by idleness and malice," "their mouths full of cursing and lies and prayers," "their deceitful hearts," "they are melancholy despisers of their own things," "they toil not," "their slumbering indolence," "their hypocrisy and iniquity," "factious spirits and infirm heads," "their meditations always of treachery," "their half-feminine raging of the tongue," "have no experience of public burdens," "they clamour in their causes." These are not Doughty's simple prejudices, they are marvelously displayed in his various accounts of the Bedouins.

The important conclusion which we reach is this. The domestic life of the little herding group in so far as it was based upon practical, utilitarian activities did not provide the framework for an elaborate organization of the little group itself. To perform the function of raising camels, the herders needed only to move together. Within this single requirement, a great deal of practical indolence and verbal conflict could be tolerated. The *external problem,* a political life, was the central most important problem which demanded organization. And also the *external problem,* unlike the practical care of camels, was a fascinating problem. The political life, while dangerous, was also interesting. It was a life that was far more replete with intriguing, strategical variations than the common-sense life of animal breeding. When there was political promise (herds to be plundered), men came alive and came together. When there was a political threat (enemy raiders on the horizon), men came alive and came together. When there was neither political promise nor a political threat, men relapsed into lassitude and bickering.

At this point, however, we must take a second glance to discover that these conclusions and impressions, while substantially correct, are far from an accurate portrayal of every moment of Arabian Bedouin life. They overlook an important area of personal life, where an intricate and delicate cultural form might be developed and elaborated in the interludes between political activities. We catch a glimpse of this form and its connection with political promises and threats in the following quote from Doughty, which differs crucially from the last quote we considered:

> The nomad's mind is ever in the ghrazzu; the knave would win, and by whose loss he recks not, neither with what improbity: men in that squalid ignorance and extreme living, become wild men. The Aarab are not all thus; but, after their strait possibility, there are virtuous and higher human spirits, amongst them; especially of the well-faring and sheykhs, men enfranchised from the pining daily carefulness of their livelihood, bred liberally and polished in the mejlis, and entertainers of the public guests. Human life, where the poor hardly find passage by foul and craggy ways, full of cruel gins, is spread out more evenly before them. These are the noblemen of the desert, men of ripe moderation, peacemakers of a certain erudite and subtle judgment.[12]

Unlike the preceding quote from Doughty, he does not here perceive men and animals as "weak," "fainting," and "breathless" in the hostile desert environment. He perceives instead a vigorous kind of "extreme" and "wild" life, a life of contests and risks. And over and against this life he places again the scene of the Bedouin camp, here in the form of the *mejlis,* the sitting of the men in the chief's tent. Note that the *mejlis* and the men who dominate it are now described in opposition to, but also in connection with, the life of political struggle. It is a scene of conciliation and its central figure, the chief, is a man of "ripe moderation," a peacemaker "of a certain erudite and subtle judgment." Here indeed Doughty perceives a peaceful, domestic life which takes on a harmonious form, but one whose character as a scene of conciliation is directly tied to the life of political struggle. The "mirth and repose" of the camp is that of political men in a political association. Still looking under "Bedouins" in Doughty's index we find another series of references which seem at first to contradict blatantly those listed above: "their cheerfulness and hilarity," "mildness and forbearance at home," "fathers of hospitality," "their countenance grave with levity," "the cheerful musing Bedouin talk," "their eloquent utterance," "they are smiling speakers," "they are full of great words," "Arabians are very tender of other men's opinions," "herdsmen they are naturally of the contemplative life," "their good humour," and "are easily cast down by derision."

Where the central interest and concern of life is a struggle among men, the central responses of men must take the form of political skills. When social life is disrupted by political conflict, men must be able to deal with other men in deeds, but then again they must also be able to deal with other men in words. One cannot say that a world of uncertain relationships is a completely formless, chaotic world, one can only say that such a world takes a peculiar form. It takes the form of men who are dealing with other men in the form of "personal deeds and words." The person, as a political actor and speaker, emerges as a central conception.

The form of the deed is the crucial element at the center of a Bedouin political struggle; the form of the word is the crucial element when there is no conflict. In the space and time between one move of the camp to the next, between one raid and the next, between one tribal conflict and the next, there was a world of Bedouin leisure. And there was, as well, nothing with which to fill this world of leisure other than talk. It was a talk of voices that grew out of and reflected the lack of practical or artistic activities, the lack of a complex day-to-day practical cooperation among men, as well as the absorbing concerns and interests of a political life in which relationships were in question. Bedouin talk was therefore at the very center of a Bedouin formal life. Bedouin words, far more than Bedouin actions, were the center of an effort to work out the various possibilities and impossibilities of uncertain political relationships. These words reveal systematic strategies for putting together a kind of political order in spite of uncertain political relationships. From the forms of a Bedouin voice, one can begin to understand with some precision the shape of Bedouin experience.

The prominence of the voice in the desert and steppe did not escape Doughty's attention. His books include a remarkable amount of recorded Arabian speech and of commentary on the character of this speech. In the following passage, for example, we see a direct connection between a manner of speaking and sentiments of political association:

> Asiatics, the Aarab are smiling speakers. All Beduin talk is one manner of Arabic, but every tribe has a use, *loghra,* and neighbours are ever chiders of their neighbours' tongue. "The speech of them, they will say, is somewhat 'awry,' *awaj.*" In the mouth of the Fukara sheykhs, was a lisping of the terminal consonants. The Moahîb talk was open and manly. In that dry serenity of the air, and largely exercised utterance of the many difficult articulations of their language, the human voice, *hess,* is here mostly clear and well-sounding; unless it be in some husk choking throat of heart-sore misery.[13]

The form of the voice becomes the fragile means of defining a political world. The voice itself appears in the desert as a striking human artifact commanding attention. It is an impressive form, "largely exercised" and "mostly clear and well-sounding," but it is also constructed uncertainly of "many difficult articulations."

When we examine Musil's Rwala materials we discover an impressive tradition of oral recitations which touch upon extraordinary political events. As men sit around the campfire or sit in the tent of a chief, they devote their attention from time to time to formal political recitations: narratives and poems of raiding and warfare. These recitations are "literary" constructions which ponder the implications of uncertain relationships. They are explicitly conceived as uncovering the significance of what men have experienced in their political lives (narratives of raiding and warfare) or what they are able to make of the significance of their political lives (poems of raiding and warfare). In a society where men's relationships with one another are in question, the literary voice crystallizes as a center of a formal life. Let us now turn to examine the shape of this voice.

## 4

Where property and commerce are in question, productive activities cannot easily become the center of political or social life. The Arabian Bedouins, as a result, were not industrious. Their practical arts were not impressive and their esthetic arts were almost nonexistent. Where the relationships of groups are uncertain, political and social life cannot be extensively conventionalized. The Arabian Bedouins, as a result, did not have elaborate political ceremonies or rituals of any kind. They even lacked political institutions which would tend to fix and to formalize group relationships in any elaborate way.

If we look for a domain of Arabian Bedouin life where groups were coordinated and activities were formalized, if we look for a domain where relationships and skills were structured in a complex way, we find only the domain of intertribal raiding and warfare. Such occasions were indeed to some extent ceremonialized and ritualized. The raiders or warriors assembled in a traditional manner. They were the masters of certain traditional strategic skills, such as riding, handling a lance, and (in the nineteenth century) firing a rifle. They sang songs, paid homage to a chief or leader, and displayed their hostile intentions in certain traditional ways. They attacked their enemies with the intent of achieving certain traditional ends. All these "forms" by which men came together and acted together were, however, generated around a violent struggle which erupted at the very center of political and social life. Raiding and warfare were ceremonies and rituals which were structured around the uncertainty of relationships, the central feature of Arabian Bedouin experience.

Arabian Bedouin political and social forms were thus more strategic than ceremonial in their design. Without an occasion of political conflict, the actual relationships of groups were not only routinely unobservable as processes, they were also indeterminable. We must therefore forego any attempt to describe the structure of relationships among the Bedouins and focus our attention on that domain where form did indeed proliferate and ramify. This, we have seen, is the domain of the person speaking in the context of uncertain relationships. At the center of this domain, we find the personal voice with a certain structure that is generated around a certain problem. As we analyze the most thoughtful productions of this voice - the Rwala oral traditions collected by Musil - we shall discover metaphors of leaders and followers and of strategies and policies which raise the problem of composing the voice in the midst of uncertain relationships. At the root of political and social forms, that is to say, we shall discover a problem of constructing the voice.

One cannot understand the life of men without an understanding of what they could wish to make of their lives. The study of a society must be to some extent the study of its unique forms of life. The study of its history must be likewise the study of the thriving and perishing of these forms. Having located among the Arabian Bedouins a distinctive cultural form, some concepts especially suitable for an understanding of such a form may be introduced.

The crucial problem of the personal voice among the North Arabian Bedouins was its problematic constitution in the context of uncertain relationships. Such a problem has its counterpart in Western literary criticism, where the constitution of a distinctive literary voice becomes the central concern of a textual analysis.[14] In particular, the recent Western discussion of the concepts of semeiology might be of some use for an understanding of certain features of North Arabian Bedouin materials. For semeiology, as a child of structural linguistics, touches directly upon the question of the construction of the voice. In semeiology, as in structural linguistics, the voice is seen as a structure. It is a thing that is made by certain rules. If one understands these rules, one can "deconstruct" the productions of a voice.[15] One can potentially take them apart by textual analysis and in doing so, understand how and why they were put together.

The key structural metaphor in semeiological studies of the voice is phonetic writing.[16] Phonetic writing is like a portrait of the voice. Once we have this portrait before our eyes, we may discuss the form which it takes and the problems inherent in this form. The speaking voice, when phonetically written, for example, is seen to consist of a chain of signifiers. The signifiers are the limited number of sound elements (phonemes) by which a particular language is vocalized. Any more or less phonetic representation illustrates this character of the voice. Take, for example, the letters on this page. Even though English is not written phonetically in the strictest sense, it is written so that letters and various combinations of letters have a sound value. English writing, as a visual image, depicts sound values rather than ideal values as does the ideogram. This written page then depicts a voice as consisting of a chain of letters. The letters represent a limited number of vocalizations, which follow one another in various combinations. The temporal chain of the speaking voice becomes on the written page a spatial chain of written letters.

During the past two centuries or so, semeiological concepts have pervaded Western philosophical, literary, and historical interpretations. This trend is closely related to the critical examination of traditional institutions. As all values and ideals are brought into question, the discussion of human affairs reverts increasingly to universal levels of human experience. Words are no longer considered to refer to transcendental ideals or existent realities. Instead, language is more nearly conceived as a problematic construction. A concern with the composition of the personal voice in response to the uncertainties of experience replaces an unquestioned commitment to traditional institutions. Values and ideals are interpreted in terms of their function in a particular form of discourse rather than as timeless truths which stand beyond a speaker or writer.

This modern trend is prefigured by developments in the Near East several millennia before our time. Phonetic writing first appeared in the eastern Mediterranean among peoples of Semitic origins sometime after 2000 B.C.[17] In this same general area of the arid zone, there was eventually a general fascination with the idea of religious scriptures which promised a resolution of personal afflictions and social problems. Even the illiterate peoples of the hinterlands who had never experienced life in a town or city were able to conceive of phonetic writing as religious icons.

The epoch of Near Eastern pastoral nomadism is closely correlated with these developments. It therefore seems possible that this unique period, during which the personal voice was composed in a setting of uncertain relationships, may lie behind some of the most distinctive features of Near Eastern civilization. In so far as this might be the case, a study of the North Arabian Bedouins, perhaps the most extreme representatives of Near Eastern pastoral nomadism, promises to provide an understanding of the archaic foundations of the religious and political traditions of the arid zone.

As we examine the personal vocalizations of the Rwala Bedouins, we shall find political metaphors reminiscent of the formal structure of the voice as a chain of distinct signs which differ from one another and require interpretations. The North Arabian Bedouins, it sometimes seems, would hope to build a substantial political world upon a metaphor of the voice. The North Arabian Bedouins, it also sometimes seems, are able to discover no substantial feature of their experience other than the uncertain value of such a metaphor of the voice.

Throughout this book, I shall refer to the various Rwala images that are derived from the formal structure of the voice as metaphors of signification. Where political experience becomes problematic in the course of armed conflicts, we find some such metaphors of signification in the Rwala materials. Political violence is imaged as a series of problematic differences. There are substitutions and replacements (as the basis of a political strategy), rearrangements and articulations (of men in battle), and repetitive flashes and explosions (of swords or of rifles). By means of these images, political violence would seem to hold the promise of a meaning as it provides an occasion for the composition of thoughts and actions. It is therefore intriguing and fascinating. But by means of these same images, political violence would also seem to raise the threat of an uncertain meaning which carries the threat of death. It is therefore dreadful and terrifying. In the Rwala materials, as we shall see, the violence of the desert and steppe appears as a dream of the personal voice written large. It is a dream that sometimes degenerates into a nightmare.

# 3. The composition of the voice and the popular investment in political adventures

## 1

In this chapter we shall examine several personal accounts of raiding expeditions. These accounts, which seem at first glance to be no more than literal reports of a series of events, are in fact thoughtful compositions. As compositions, we shall find, they reveal just how deeply a Bedouin self-identity was implicated in the pursuit of strategic opportunities which involved aggression against other men. In this way we can understand through a literary document the dimensions of the threat of popular political adventurism among the North Arabian Bedouins.

In his chapter on "War and Peace," Musil includes about a dozen personal accounts of raiding expeditions that he recorded in North Arabia. Most of these stories, and all those we shall consider, were told to him by Bleyhân eben Ḍeri. This man was a member of the Sba‘a tribe, Bedouin neighbors of the Rwala. Each story is a more or less factual account of an actual occasion when a group of men set out to plunder the herds of other men. Most of Bleyhân's stories relate his own personal experiences whereas a few are secondhand versions of the experiences of other men.

We shall be concerned with two aspects of each story. First, a story concerns a time and a place different from that in which it is told. It relates the incidents of a raiding expedition, an occasion when men look for some opportunity for plunder. In the midst of such an occasion, companionship, mounts and riding skills, weapons and fighting skills, and indeed the body and the mind, have a significance which they do not have in the ordinary tedium of everyday life. On a raid, the Bedouins have taken up the most potent resources available to them and invested them in an adventure which holds the promise of great reward.

Second, the story itself is an expressive occasion apart from the raiding expedition which it describes. Something about a man's relationship with these adventures leads him to construct an account of the experience. This second aspect of the story indicates how men's interest in raiding is an intimate, personal investment in a certain way of life. During the course of a raiding expedition, men pursue definite strategies and definite ends, but the outcome of these strategies and ends is very much in question. When a raid fails, or, worse still, when a raid leads to disaster, a question is raised about this project where so much is at stake. After the raid is over, this question persists and surfaces in the form of a story. In these stories then we find that a vocal response to experience becomes a metaphor of a more active investment in political experience. The problem of composing the voice as a response to experience becomes a key metaphor behind the design of the narration of a strategic effort to secure a personal advantage. An investment in the risks of a life of raiding is revealed in a preoccupation with images of the uncertain composition of a personal voice.

The first example to be considered demonstrates in a striking way the two sides of a life of raiding. It is a story of a raid which fails. Bleyhân overtly suggests that the failure can be explained by some deficiency in resources or by some mere chance of circumstances. On the other hand, as he composes his story, he also raises a figurative question about what might be made of the raid in purely expressive terms. The inability to succeed in raiding raises a question about a personal identity, and this question is imaged as a problem of composing a voice. Here is the tale which Bleyhân told to Musil:

Kâseb eben 'Omeym once invited us to join him on a plundering expedition, *'ayyarna.* There were twelve of us on ten she-camels, *mrâdîf.* Having mounted our camels in our camp between at-Tinf and al-Ghurâb, we first drank from al-Mshâsh and headed for Qelîb Hdeyb and Ṣwêr, passing the settlement of Skâka. Stopping for a chat with the inhabitants of this settlement, *naqarna 'ala-hl hâk al-bleydât,* we learned that there were some Rwala camping between Ambaṭ and the Nefûd. On our way to them we attacked some haymakers, but returned everything to them, *addeynâhom,* when we found them to be inhabitants of al-Jowf. Soon afterwards we found tracks, evidently made by the 'Abdelle. Water we found in the shallow hollows, *ḥwâya,* of the rocky eminence at al-Jeba'. To the east of these we concealed ourselves in a small deep gully, where fires could be lit without being seen from the outside, *sha'eyyeb alli nâreh mâ tnâwer.* But the notorious Khalaf abu Ḥathlên of the Ṣqûr, who with his band of robbers had a hiding place near by, soon discovered our presence and, creeping to the very bank of our gully, observed us from above and called his men. Suddenly we found ourselves surrounded on all sides. The menacing band cried as with one voice:

"Where are ye from, ye crowd down there?"

We were just then preparing for supper. Jumping away from the fire, we lay down on our bellies - for we feared they might shoot - and began to crawl out of the gully. A few of us answered: "We are the sons of 'Obeyd and ye - whence are ye? We entreat you by Him who strengthens, who speaks the truth and punishes with cowardice him that lies."

"He need not punish us with cowardice. We are the Ṣqûr. Your language told us that ye are really 'Obeyd's sons. And which ones?"

"Of the Eben Meṣreb kin."

So they brought their camels and sat down with us to supper. There were twelve of them in all. Next morning we rode out together against the ‘Abdelle, whose herds we soon sighted south of Kasr Ambaṭ. Then we concealed ourselves. As soon as it grew dark, we fettered our camels near the place and crept towards the camp. At midnight we were close to the tents, *nestaqeṭ ‘aleyhom.* But they were not arranged in rows; some stood in the full light on the level land, others were hidden in the darkness of the dale. This fact prevented us from coming in between them without being noticed by some of the watchmen, *w-lâ ṣâr lena medla’ ‘aleyhom.* On Khalaf's advice four camel riders were to make a feint attack, *ḥaḍḍâyât,* in order to draw attention to themselves; and so it was done, but the ‘Abdelle would not be deceived. Only a few offered resistance, while the others, posting themselves in smaller groups at various points, counter-attacked with such vehemence that we could only run back quickly to our fettered she-camels. But the ‘Abdelle pursued us even there, and one of them, Ḥbeyrân by name, shot two of our good animals. Then we fled with the Nefûd on our left after our leader Khalaf, the ‘Abdelle keeping close at our heels and sending their stones [bullets] after us rapidly. To save ourselves we fettered the left foreleg of our best camel and left it with both the saddle and ribbons to the pursuers. A camel thus abandoned is called *qa‘ayyed redde,* signifying that the pursued will not harm the pursuer any more. However, the ‘Abdelle did not stop. O Allâh, what toil we had to escape with our bare lives! Behind us there was uninterrupted lightning, and the stones [bullets] fell among us like so much hail. A terrible fright took hold of us, *yaṭeqna-l-mṣâṣ,* and we were about to disperse, when at the last moment Eben Sa‘îd with his troop came up with us before sunrise, threw himself upon the ‘Abdelle, and thus rescued us from their hands. So we returned to our people camping in Wâdi al-Miyâh not far from the aṣ-Ṣaqri wells, without having achieved anything.

The story illustrates how these tales are not exactly contrived as fictional diversions. The tale is factual and realistic in its tone; it documents a series of past events. Some other stories are almost tedious in their details of who took part in a raid, along what route they rode, and where they stopped for water or encamped. The story, in other words, is about an actual experience that is over. The problems it raises are the actual problems of raiding. The fears which it recounts are the real fears of confronting other hostile men. There is presumably no problem and no fear present in the expressive occasion itself, but only the memory of a past, but not quite forgotten experience, which for some reason sticks in the mind and takes the peculiar form of this particular story.

Let us examine the story more closely. Bleyhân may recite only facts. But what facts does he cite, and what is the form of those facts? There are in this regard two types of metaphor with which we shall be particularly concerned in this story. First, there is the suggestion that as men go out looking for victims, a voice takes on a life. This is the initial metaphor with which the tale begins. However, after only a few lines, a second more poetic metaphor appears with the prospect of the failure of the raid. It raises the question of the value of a voice which arises out of raiding. The prospect of meeting another hostile group and being unable to come to grips with that group is conceived by an illiterate man as an uncertain reading of experience. Let us see how fruitful these concepts might be as a basis for analyzing Bleyhân's account of his adventures abroad.

Bleyhân, the author of this story, begins by first invoking the author of a raid: "Kâseb . . . once invited us . . ." He begins by displacing what will follow from himself, the present time, and the present place on to another man, another time, and another place. Bleyhân seems to insist with this beginning that what follows concerns the problems of men engaged in a political action, but the way in which he does so suggests some resemblance between these problems and men engaged in an expressive action. Raids have authors, just as stories have authors.

In the next line, Bleyhân cites the resources available for this raid, the means by which a political action, not an expressive action, will unfold. There were twelve men on ten she-camels. In this citation of a fact, we may note the first of several suggestions of a lack or a deficiency. The raiders are short of resources: they lack two camels. If things do not go well, it is perhaps for lack of camels. Bleyhân prepares himself in advance for encountering some problem which cannot be overcome and which must somehow be explained away. But what is the nature of this problem? Is it a practical problem of inadequate political resources or improper political procedures? This overtly seems to be the case. Or is it a problem of making sense of this political occasion of raiding during which resources prove lacking and procedures deficient? Covertly we shall find this seems to be the case.

Bleyhân next recounts when and where the raiding party drank from a spring. It is a simple, even banal event which marks every Bedouin trip abroad in the desert. But then we might note that on this occasion, the party finds along the way another resource other than camels to sustain their progress. And then we might further observe that this resource, which will enable them to proceed, is also something to wet the tongue, the device by which this tale is articulated. The raiders move along on camels; their progress is articulated by the tongue. A voice arises out of the adventure of a raid. Bleyhân has shifted from the citation of one kind of practical resource (camels) to another kind of practical resource (water). Both items sustain the progression of a political action, but the second item is suspiciously associated with the progression of an expressive action: a vocalization. The raid begins as a practical matter and now ever so slightly touches upon an expressive matter.

Next the raiders stop to chat with the inhabitants of the settlement of Skâka. They have temporized by taking a trip on camels, a practical step they are required to take in order to search out a victim to plunder. Now they temporize by talking, something which they are not required to do but merely happen to do. Notice that they seem to achieve their purpose by talking when they did not achieve it by searching on camels. As they chat with the people of Skâka, they learn of the presence of a possible victim. They come upon an opportunity to struggle with other men by means of words (a chat) rather than deeds (a ride abroad). We shall find that this is the first suggestion that an essential problem is more apparent in the words which deal with struggle than in the struggle itself. In these lines, that is to say, we find the implication that some problem of political experience not only touches, but only becomes fully apparent in, some feature of expression. These implications appear not so much as an explicit insight as a dark suggestion concealed in the tale.

In the lines which follow, however, there is first a return, or so it seems, to a concern with purely practical matters. On their way to discover the whereabouts of the Rwala, they first encounter the haymakers, whom they mistakenly assault and plunder. The initial suggestion of insufficient resources (they are two camels short) is here supplemented with an instance of improper procedures (they misidentify their allies as enemies). But Bleyhân is not simply insisting that success and failure in a life of raiding is only a practical matter of sufficient resources and proper procedures. The assault upon the haymakers links the problem of procedures with a problem of identification. The question of what men do is touched by the question of who men are. A little later, another problem of identification will be linked with the qualities of men's voices. There the question of who men are will be resolved by a recognition of the way in which they speak.

The tale recounts the progress of a raiding expedition, but it also involves a progression of another kind. We are moving from a problem of resources to a problem of procedures, from a problem of procedures to a problem of who men are, and from a problem of who men are to a problem of how men speak. As the events of a raiding expedition unfold, there is a deepening concern about a personal identity and a personal voice. This deepening concern, we shall see, foreshadows a critical occasion when Bleyhân was unable to respond to political experience and his death at the hands of other men seemed near.

After restitution of the haymakers' losses, the raiders discover the tracks of the 'Abdelle (a group associated with the Rwala) whose presence was communicated to them by the inhabitants of Skâka. These tracks are a string of impressions in the desert. This is the first of several metaphors of signification to appear in the tale. The tracks indicate the presence of a dangerous victim who will eventually be encountered. But the tracks also raise the problem of a reading. They are a form of signification. They must be interpreted. At this crucial point, Bleyhân again turns to cite a place where the raiders find water. Overtly, they drink to sustain themselves in their efforts to locate and to plunder other men. Covertly, the tongue is moistened at just that moment when the problem of composing a response to the presence of other men becomes imminent. But before Bleyhân tells us of their meeting with the 'Abdelle, he first develops further the question of who men are and how they speak.

The day, the time of activity, comes to an end. The night, the time of passivity, begins. The raiders make camp in "a small deep gully" and light their fires. The camp is the place where men pause in their political activities. Here they seek some repose. Here they nourish themselves. But now this camp is described in terms of its relationship with a hostile world. The camp, a place of refuge, is restricted to the space of "a small deep gully." As Bleyhân fixes upon this occasion, there is a suggestion that men are hemmed in by a situation of hostility. The camp, a place of peace, is confined to a narrow cleavage in the landscape. A question, we shall see, is about to be raised about whether men might find a place for themselves in the midst of political uncertainty.

Suddenly the raiders in the camp find themselves surrounded on all sides by an unseen enemy. They jump away from the light of the fire. They lie down on their bellies. They attempt to crawl out of the gully. As a situation of political hostility presses in upon them, the camp in the gully becomes a trap, and the men of the camp resort to wild and desperate gestures. They resemble snakes which twist and crawl as their nest is disturbed. Here is an overt image of the problem which has until now remained covert. This episode suggests not only anxiety about a situation of political hostility relentlessly pressing in upon the raiders, but also an anxiety about whether the raiders might be able to respond to this threat in any coherent or effective way.

This problem of a coherent and effective response to political hostility anticipates the critical occasion which arises in the final episode. Here, however, Bleyhân's central concern is the connection of this problem with the issues of who men are and how they speak. When the raiding party is discovered and surrounded by the robbers, it is only a confrontation of voices which takes place, not a confrontation of men with mounts and weapons. Bleyhân insists upon this feature of the events: "Khalaf . . . observed us from above *and called his men.* Suddenly we found ourselves surrounded on all sides. The menacing band cried *as with one voice:* 'Where are ye from, ye crowd down there?' " [my italics]. A vocal summons leads to a vocal threat which takes the form of a demand for *identification.* At this point, the raiders jump away from the fire and then answer the robbers by identifying themselves and demanding in return an identification: "We are the sons of 'Obeyd and ye – whence are ye?" A vocal confrontation between two groups has raised the problem of identification. A question of who men are is raised as they come across one another and call out to one another in the darkness of night. And indeed, is not this the very problem of the tale? Is not Bleyhân working over the problem of his identity as he thinks about a life he leads by struggling with other men? Is he not trying to vocalize the problem of who he is as he recalls this occasion when he went out to contest other men?

The robbers do not attack Bleyhân and his companions, let us note, because they have recognized their accent: "We are the Ṣqûr," they call out. "Your language told us that ye are really 'Obeyd's sons." An identity, who one is, emerges as the central concern of this episode and who one is is explicitly linked to how one speaks. But the most important line appears just after the raiders identify themselves and demand the identity of the robbers in return. It takes the form of a moral about speaking the truth: "We entreat you by Him who strengthens him who speaks the truth and punishes with cowardice him that lies."[1] Here we learn that God lends a power to him who speaks the truth and takes power away from him who speaks lies. Recognizing the truth about the facts of an actual struggle, one might say, is the very basis of constituting an identity and a voice. Only in this way might one hope to survive. A failure to recognize the truth of an actual struggle reduces one to fear and trembling before the unknown. The episode suggests that who one is and what one says really matter in an important way. For in this confrontation between the robbers and the raiding party, everything turns upon a question of identities and voices.

But does Bleyhân's insistence on the importance of identities and voices necessarily imply that who men are and how they speak are the sure bases for resolving the problem of a coherent and effective response to the problem of political hostility? Another incident, a more disturbing incident than the robbers' ambush of the raiding party, is about to follow. As they come across the 'Abdelle for whom they have been searching, Bleyhân and his companions will be reduced to a state of paralyzed terror. As they find what they have been looking for, they will fall into the state of powerlessness which should be reserved for him who lies. They will be both unable to act and unable to speak. The issue of identities and voices has been raised because the viability of an identity and a voice will be in question when the raiders are faced with a situation to which they cannot respond.

The raiders locate the 'Abdelle on the next day. They wait till midnight. They creep toward the enemy camp. But there is a problem. There is a difficulty in forming a strategy for overcoming the 'Abdelle. This is an elaboration upon the previous metaphor of the camel tracks. A difficulty of forming a military strategy is described as a difficulty of reading the enemy camp: *"But they were not arranged in rows; some stood in the full light* on the level land, *others were hidden in the darkness* of the dale. This fact prevented us from coming in between them without being noticed by some of the watchmen" [my italics]. The 'Abdelle camp does not have the aspect of an orderly text. Its tents, the signifiers of this text, are not arranged in rows. As a text, moreover, the 'Abdelle camp cannot be clearly interpreted. Some of its signifiers can be plainly seen, but others are obscure. The problem of formulating a military strategy is figured as the problem of reading a text. The problem of penetrating the enemy camp and dispersing the enemy party is figured as a problem of a difficult reading. There has been a shift from a scene of men communicating their identities uncertainly with their voices to a scene where men attempt an uncertain reading of an enemy camp. This shift occurs with the anticipation of the serious and even desperate struggle to follow.

The metaphor of a reading which anticipates a struggle raises in an explicit way the question of what is to be made of life. The text of the enemy as a group of signs which cannot be surely interpreted reflects the problem of a voice which cannot piece together an experience in a sure way. And this problem of how to come to grips with the 'Abdelle, how to understand the strategic design of their camp and respond to it, is rooted in the actual danger, the very real threat which the 'Abdelle represent for the raiders. We are nearing the moment of truth. Now the adequacy of resources and procedures is to be tested in a serious confrontation.

The strategy which the raiders adopt attempts to convert their problem into an advantage. They hope to capitalize upon the very readiness of the 'Abdelle to respond to an attack. A small party of the raiders will attempt to lure the enemy off their guard by means of a feint attack. If the 'Abdelle respond precipitously, they will fall an easy prey to the main body of the raiders. This strategy, however, proves deficient. With the failure of the feint attack, the situation is reversed. Bleyhân and his companions become the prey and the 'Abdelle become the predators. It is the memory of this situation which Bleyhân has been dreading since his tale began, but just what is it that is dreadful about this situation? Is it the actual threat of death? No doubt, at the very moment of the experience itself, Bleyhân feared death. But now we are examining Bleyhân's recollection of this moment. Why has this particular moment in which death was near received the concern of an elaborate recollection? And what is the form which this recollection takes? Let us examine what significance Bleyhân attributes to this threat of death.

With the counterattack, the raiders become the prey instead of the predator. Here, instead of searching out hostility, they begin to retreat from it: "We could only run back quickly to our fettered she-camels." And as they attempt to retreat, hostility closes in upon them relentlessly: "But the 'Abdelle pursued us even there." And here is the first sign of desperation in the form of a depletion of resources: "One of them . . . shot two of our good animals." Setting out on camels to plunder the herds of other men, they are now in a situation of losing the very resources that were the basis of their aggressive intentions. They resort to full flight, but still the 'Abdelle follow them. And here is the second sign of desperation in the form of a hopeless procedure: they attempt to buy off their pursuers with their best camel fully saddled and decorated with ribbons. Setting out on camels to plunder the herds of other men, they are now willing to sacrifice their best camel in order to escape the aggressive intentions of other men. The 'Abdelle, however, will not stop. The 'Abdelle are interested in more than camels, they are bent upon killing men. The depletion of resources and a hopeless procedure are now followed by a state of paralyzed terror: "O Allâh, what toil we had to escape with our bare lives! Behind us there was uninterrupted lightning, and the stones [bullets] fell among us like so much hail. A terrible fright took hold of us." The raiders toil unsuccessfully to escape the hostile presence of other men. They then perceive this hostile presence as a looming metaphor of signification. They perceive *repetitive flashes of light* (the lightning of the rifle shots) and *repetitive thuds of sound* (the hail of the bullets). The hostile presence of other men takes the form of a structure of differences, but there is now no strategy by which Bleyhân and his companions can wrest something from this structure. It represents neither a sign from which a meaning can be deciphered nor a situation from which a prize might be won. This is a structure of differences which cannot, however, be differentiated, "there was *uninterrupted* lightning," and which threatens death, "the bullets fell among us like so much hail." Unable to respond in any way, Bleyhân and his companions are seized with fright. They are no longer the masters of a hostile situation in the desert and steppe, they are instead its victims.

This is the memory that Bleyhân has been dreading from the very beginning of his tale. He has been dreading a circumstance in which all his political resources are depleted and all his political procedures are ineffective. He has been dreading this circumstance in which there seems to be nothing which he can do because the death of an identity and a voice is near. This circumstance represents a moment when nothing can be made of life, and for a North Arabian Bedouin like Bleyhân this is a moment of depletion, ineffectiveness, and paralysis in the face of the hostile presence of other men.

In the last lines, however, we find a resolution of this dreadful circumstance. By happenstance, Bleyhân is able to end his tale of a harrowing experience with the fact of his narrow escape: "Eben Sa'îd . . . thus rescued us from their hands." But then the tale is not quite ended, and its resolution is not quite complete. He adds a final line which indicates some deficiency which nevertheless persists: "So we returned to our people . . .

without having achieved anything." The problem of lending life a value, this problem which touches every human deed and word that becomes the object of a reflection, persists and remains, even though the immediate threat of death has been evaded. But the problem is not so great as it was at the moment of paralysis, for Bleyhân and his companions are not only free to try again, but free to think over what it all might have meant.

## 2

In the preceding tale, the sense of a life of raiding is thrown into question as men are reduced to a state of paralysis. In the next tale, we find a contrary suggestion. Here Bleyhân demonstrates that no matter what impediment is encountered in the course of a plundering expedition, there is always an alternative of some sort, even if it is no more than an ironic expression of a lack of alternatives. Where action is no longer possible the play of a vocal expression continues. The central metaphor of signification in this story is one of constant "articulations" in the midst of a life of plundering which sometimes succeed and sometimes fail, but nevertheless continue. This account concerns the experience of other men, not the experiences of the storyteller. It is still a factual account, which carefully includes names and places, but is now quite plainly told as an amusing diversion. Bleyhân speaks again:

Four members of the Hweyshân kin went on a raid on foot, *ḥanshalow*. Ḥeyrân eben Mesleṭ was their leader. They crossed aṣ-Ṣwâb, heading for Mesopotamia against the Shammar then encamped at ad-Demîm and as-Saba‘, east of al-Miyâdhîn. As soon as the herds were sighted they separated, two stealing at night up to the place where the herds were resting, *al-marḥ*. One called *qa‘îda* stayed with their clothing, the other crawled half-naked to the camels, intending to unfetter a few and drive them towards his comrade. Succeeding in unfettering them, he hurried the animals toward the spot where they had agreed to meet when a certain star had reached a certain height. He was pursued, however, but when the *qa‘îda* man guarding the clothing began to shoot at the pursuers, they halted. After waiting a long time for the other two comrades they finally rode away with their booty, *menser*. The other two had no success owing to the vigilance of the dogs, who, on scenting the man approaching the herd, began to bark, causing both of them, the *qa‘îda* as well as the plunderer, to flee. Then they hid in a gully and the following night went out to plunder again. Allâh having granted them booty, they hastened with it towards the Euphrates. Yet the Shammar pursued and overtook them by the ford. There the robbers abandoned their booty and fled. But they now tried a third time to take booty, *‘âwadow thâleth nôba*. This time they got two camels and, after breaking her iron fetters, a mare. One man galloped away with the she-camels, the other rode the mare. But this animal balked, and he was left far behind his comrade. When he urged her by blows to run faster, she began to neigh and would not stir. Finally, he had to abandon the mare and try to overtake his comrade on foot. Thirsty and hungry he at last sat down below a slope, fearing that he would perish miserably. In this distress he said with a sign: "O Allâh, if thou desirest my welfare, then either feed me or take my soul to thyself!" And it happened by Allâh's will that the unfortunate man's comrade was hiding a little higher up on the same slope and sighted him from there. Descending to him, he heard his words and rolled down a stone which fell almost at his side. Alarmed by this the exhausted man cried out: "O Allâh, thou dost not hasten to send food, but my soul thou wouldst have at once!" At this his comrade began to laugh and gave him enough to eat and drink from the supplies carried by the camels. They luckily reached the Euphrates, crossed it, and remained all day on its right bank hidden in the thicket resting. While there they saw a large troop of the Shammar, who were out on a raid against the ʿAneze, approaching the Euphrates. One half of them forded the river the same day, while the other remained on the left bank. Our *ḥenshel* [raiders on foot] drew near the Shammar, whose mares had been left to graze among the bushes, stole two docile ones, and, mounting them, drove the camels before them into the desert, finally reaching their kin without further mishap.

The story is about humble men of action who have limited means. They are not raiders, but thieves. They are not on camels or horses; instead they proceed on foot. They have only simple devices at their disposal. They utilize these devices in the course of simple strategies. In the course of the tale they sometimes succeed, and they sometimes fail. The repeated failures do not, however, raise the dreadful concerns which appeared in the previous story. On the contrary, as Bleyhân relates how men keep trying despite repeated failures, he suggests that they always have some alternative at their disposal.

At one point one of the men is stripped of all his devices and reduced to desperation. This situation is decisive. What does a man do when there is nothing he can do? Here the message of his story becomes clear. Where men of action can no longer articulate deeds by means of devices, where men of action can no longer undertake any kind of action, they still have the possibility of vocally articulating the very irony of their predicament.

This story, like the last story, is about the relationship of deeds and words, but the relationship here takes a different form. Words do not reveal more clearly than deeds the problem of making something of life. Words, in the form of an active expression of the irony of wanting to make something of life but being unable to do so, become the last resort of a humble man caught in a desperate situation. Let us examine how this might be so.

The tale begins with four men who split into two pairs in order to attempt a camel- or horse-theft. The first pair adopts a strategy of articulations. A passive member of the pair *(qaʿîda),* who is armed with a device which makes a sound (the gun), stays behind. An active member (the plunderer), who has only his own body (he is half-naked) and therefore lacks devices, approaches the enemy camp to effect a theft. There he unfetters a few camels and hurries away with them to meet at the agreed-upon place and time. The passive member then employs his gun at a crucial moment to prevent the owners of the camels from pursuing the plunderer.

An active man without devices silently articulates a deed of theft (he unfetters the camels). A passive man with a device which makes a sound paralyzes at a crucial moment the owners of the camels (they "halted" for fear of being shot). The first episode suggests that in order to articulate a life of plundering, a device which makes a sound must be added to a strategy of silent deeds. Ever so slightly, Bleyhân's concern with a gun as the instrument that finally effected the theft suggests a concern with another device which makes a sound. The first episode seems to touch upon a question: What is the role of the voice within a life of plundering?

Let us, however, look more closely at the conclusion of the first episode and the series of episodes which follow it. When the man without devices unfetters the camels, he hurries to the spot where all four thieves were to meet "when a certain star had reached a certain height." The star suggests that there is support from a precise understanding of how the world works. Its role reminds us of the maxim which appeared in the previous tale: God strengthens him who speaks the truth. Recognizing the nature of reality is the condition for getting by in this world. But note that the prearranged meeting by means of the *silent* star does not mark the successful completion of the theft. The thief is followed by the owners of the camels, and the employment of the gun becomes necessary to effect the theft. A device which makes a sound, this incident suggests, must somehow be added to a clear understanding of how the world works. Let us now read a little further.

The second pair of thieves fails to arrive at the prearranged meeting place, and the tale continues. We next learn of the first attempt of the second pair of thieves to plunder animals. They are prevented from approaching a camp because of the dogs' barks. Again a device which makes a sound (the dogs) is crucial with respect to an attempt to plunder animals. Now, however, the device prevents the attempt rather than effects its completion. In their second attempt the two thieves make more substantial progress. They succeed in approaching a camp and seizing camels, but they fail to escape with their booty when they are caught attempting to ford the river. Now in the absence of a device which makes a sound (there is only the river, a silent feature of nature like the star), a strategy of theft again fails. Let us note here that the river and its association with a life of plunder will be raised again in the concluding lines of the tale. In their third attempt, the two thieves succeed again in approaching a camp. They take two camels and a horse. One man successfully articulates a theft as he rides away on one of the camels with the other in tow. The second man manages to unfetter the horse (articulation) and mount her, but he fails to make the horse carry him (inarticulation). When he resorts to beating the horse, the beast neighs (articulates a sound) but does not move (inarticulation of an action).

Now we can at last see that Bleyhân is being mischievous. The gun is an effective device which makes a sound, but the sound of the gun has only a tangential role in effecting the theft. It is the gun's bullets which the enemy fears, not the gun's sounds. In contrast, it is the dogs' barks which effectively prevent the first theft of the second pair. So it is the actual sound of the dogs which proves crucial in contrast to the secondary and incidental aspect of the gun's sounds. And where the sound of a device proves absolutely crucial, a theft is aborted. The river, a silent feature of nature which does not make a sound, now marks the scene of the abortion of the third attempt. Again we see that a device which makes a sound must be added to a strategy of theft even though, when such a device proved absolutely crucial, the second attempt at theft failed. Finally, we have another device, the horse, and a fourth attempt to plunder animals. By all rights, the horse, a device for locomotion, should transport the thief away from the enemy camp to safety. The horse, however, will not go. Instead the beast does no more than utter a sound. Bleyhân's ironic intent here surfaces for all to see. It here becomes clear that in each case the sound of a device has an ironic relationship with the thieves' attempt to accomplish a theft. We can see that Bleyhân is suggesting that a device which makes a sound has an ironic relationship with a life of plunder. A sound is an inessential aspect of success (the shots). A sound is an essential aspect of failure (the barks). Nevertheless, without a sound there is a failure (first the star and then the river), while at the same time a sound indicates a failure where success was imminently anticipated (the neigh). Let us read a little further to confirm this interpretation.

Abandoning the horse and fleeing on foot, the second member of the second pair eventually falls into desperate straits. He has no horse. He has no gun. He has lost contact with his friend. He has no food and no water. He is without devices. He fears death. At this point, where no further action is possible, he makes, Bleyhân insists, a *sign* to God. Stripped of all his devices, the thief can only silently indicate his desperation, or rather his silent sign is itself a further indication of his desperation. But now notice that his sign is curiously explicated as an articulation: "Either feed me *or* take my soul to thyself." At this point his friend rolls down the stone from above, and the message of the story becomes clear. Fearful that even God is against him in such dire circumstances, the thief now cries out: "O Allâh, thou dost not hasten to send food, *but* my soul thou wouldst have at once!" With this cry he moves from a silent sign of desperation to a vocalized, ironic articulation. And following this move, there is a vocal release of tension: "At this his comrade began to laugh . . ." In the worst of circumstances a humble man of action without devices is nevertheless able to respond actively to his situation of desperation. His response is, however, no more than an expression of a man of action who can only vocalize the irony of his being without devices and on the point of death.

The articulations of political strategies by means of devices are at the core of North Arabian Bedouin life. The story illustrates how this is so. Presented with an impossibility, men turn to other possibilities. Bleyhân presses this lesson home in the concluding lines of his tale. He turns to describe the Bedouin life of plunder unfolding on the borders of the Euphrates. I would suggest that this river, which was earlier associated with the articulation of a theft, now figures experience in general as a smooth, silent, and relentless flow of life cutting through the desert scene. Let us see how such an interpretation provides some understanding of the conclusion of this tale.

After the joke played by one thief and the ironic response of the other thief, the two men "luckily reached the Euphrates." We see them concealed and resting in a thicket beside the river. There they observe the movements of the Shammar raiding party. On the margins of the flow of life humble men find protection from a hostile political world. Next we see the Shammar dividing into two equal groups. One group remains on one bank of the Euphrates as the other group fords the river and remains on the other bank. This recalls the division of our four thieves into two pairs and the division of each pair into an active and a passive member. The articulation of the Shammar raiding party on the margins of the flow of life construes the grand life of raiding as another kind of articulation to be contrasted with the more humble strategy of theft by means of simple devices. The story ends with the second pair of thieves successfully approaching the herds of the Shammar, successfully stealing two docile mares, and successfully returning with their booty to their kin. All turns out well in the end. Lacking fellowship and herds, humble men can get by in the desert with simple strategies and simple devices. And even where simple strategies and devices fail, a humble and purely human faculty, the voice, always transcends the problems of desperate circumstances.

There is always something one can do, even if it is no more than vocalizing the irony of one's predicament. Bleyhân feels secure beside the inexorable flow of life in the desert scene as he tells a story about a difficult, but eventually successful theft. Even though the means of life are irrevocably insecure, Bleyhân feels there is a place in the desert for simple humanity.

## 3

In the next tale, the same man reaches still a different conclusion as he thinks over a different experience. The tale which follows does not raise a problem about the relationship of deeds and words. Instead, it suggests that the true meaning and the true reward of a political adventure are in the actual experience itself. There is an insistence in words that it is really deeds which matter. Bleyhân speaks once again:

Once we camped in Iraq near Bradân and al-'Eṣêle. The world was full of pasture. Dry grass stood thickly around all the wells, and of the *qaḍqâḍ* there was abundance everywhere. After our herds had grazed in the neighborhood of the wells, we pitched our tents about a winter day's march from them, *manda.* Then Mashhûr eben Mershed proposed to us to go on a raid with him. Soon a troop of about three hundred riding camels and a hundred riders, *waqm mâye khayyâl,* were accompanying him, first against aẓ-Ẓefîr. We drank at al-Loṣof, then from the 'Aqlat Meshḥen, and soon reached the level country, where we were suprised by the *thrayyâwi* rain. The low-lying land resembled a swamp, *howr.* Our camels could not make any headway there, and so we had to return without success, *menâkîf.* But the Bdûr, who usually encamped on the Euphrates, somehow learned where we were and without delay sent *ṭalab,* pursuers, on camels after us. They overtook us, *laḥeqowna,* compelled us twice to make our camels kneel, *nawwakhowna,* and soon a fight began to rage - may Allâh never bring any true friend of thine into such a fight! *'asa ṣiddîq qalbak mâ yeḥdar hâk al-manâkh.* At first shots were exchanged, then we fought with spears, and finally bare fists were used. We took all their riding camels, attacked their herds, and brought our booty away safely, although they pursued us as far as the Wâdi al-Obeyyeḍ. That year we still call the year of violence, *senet ghaṣbe,* because we drove the captured herds to our camp by sheer force. The commander got thirty camels, the others five or six each.

This story begins with a situation which is quite different from the first story examined. The place and time is one of material abundance. On an occasion when their resources are plentiful, men turn to raiding. They proceed with the belief that they have the adequate means for engaging in a political adventure. And now note the description of the party which is assembled: three hundred camels and a hundred riders. There is an excess of means, not a lack. The adventure which follows, however, is not an easy experience. They must exert themselves as they encounter hard going in the low-lying land. They are discovered and pursued by the enemy. Their progress is stopped as they dismount to resist their attackers. They fight first with guns, then with spears, and then with fists as the enemy closes upon them. But in the end, they are victorious. They steal all the riding camels of the enemy. They are pursued relentlessly, but they nevertheless prevail in bringing their booty safely away. A great reward is secured: "The commander got thirty camels, the others five or six each."

Note how schematic the story is in its descriptions. It might almost be seen as the juxtaposition of a series of symbols: abundance (dry grass standing thickly around the wells), hardship and hard movement (the low-lying land resembled a swamp), submission and arrest (overtook us and compelled us twice to make our camels kneel), a toiling struggle (a fight with guns, then spears, and then bare fists), and, finally, the fruits of violence (plundered riding camels and herds are brought away safely in the "year of violence"). This schematic description of various aspects of an actual experience suggests that it is the actual experience itself which holds a meaning. Bleyhân does not weave his tale around the problem of lending meaning to his experience. The problem of the relationship of the tale to the experience itself does not arise. On the occasion of this raid it is a constant and protracted effort that seems to count: the actual attempt to get through that swamp, the actual struggle with the opponents, and the actual effort to escape with the booty. This was a time of deeds. And significantly, it was also a time when deeds succeeded. Because deeds succeeded, the adequacy of those deeds is not questioned in the tale. When Bleyhân notes that this was the "year of violence," he invokes the primacy of the political struggle itself. He remains secure in the belief that an actual struggle with other men holds some significance.

Much of life among men everywhere consists of strenuous activities, which demand more or less fixed skills. There is no time to think. One must work long and hard. In this last story of a raid we find that a political struggle among men on mounts sometimes took this form. But much of the time, the political life of the camel-herding nomads did not take such a form. Much of the time political life in the desert and steppe involved uncertain procedures and uncertain consequences. And there were long periods of leisure in which these uncertainties could be carefully considered.

These three stories reveal how the North Arabian Bedouins were interested in securing a personal benefit at the expense of other men, but they also reveal a good deal more. In these stories, we see how a personal identity was composed around an investment of resources in strategic adventures with aggressive implications. In the next two parts of this book, we shall consider other kinds of compositions that indicate how the Bedouins attempted to protect themselves from this situation in which men in general were interested in political adventurism.

# Part II

# The narratives of raiding and warfare

An ideological superstructure has been erected on this base of natural and politico-social conditions. This comprises, first, poetry, which is either *l'art pour l'art* or bound up with the interests of the tribes and the poets. This poetry is intertribal, its language is distinguished from classical Arabic essentially by the fact that diptota and triptota are not yet strictly distinguished. Secondly, it includes a prose literature, which, interspersed with verses and speeches, describes heroic deeds in war and peace and tells legends of the ancestors and of the tribal migrations. The language of this prose is likewise not too distant from classical Arabic.

Caskel, *Studies in Islamic Cultural History* (1954), p. 37.

# 4. Cautious and sensible chiefs and the strategic use of aggressive resources

## 1

Among the North Arabian Bedouins a problem of popular anarchy threatened the little herding groups. In response to this, the Bedouins formed protective tribal associations. Within the tribe, the little groups did not raid one another, but joined together to defend themselves from other tribes. At the same time, they recognized tribal leaders who concerned themselves with coordinating the responses of the little groups to threats from abroad. However, the tribe as a political community and the chief as a political authority were not altogether effective. These people shared a general interest in adventurous initiatives. Every step toward their commitment to a political organization was simultaneously a step which restricted the possibility for such initiatives. Putting it in stark terms, we could say that a tribe, such as the Rwala, would have liked their chiefs to have made it impractical for other tribes to raid them, but practical for them to raid all other tribes. Since such an arrangement was not possible, the tribe led by a chief was a marginal political organization to which the Bedouins were committed only when they were faced with the concrete danger of other tribes and chiefs.

This marginality of the tribe and the chief as protective political institutions is the concern of a kind of composition that I have called "the ceremonial narrative of raiding and warfare." With the flow of the tide of politics, tribes and chiefs came to life as institutions. In the midst of such a political life, there was almost always the possibility for some practical alternative. There was almost always something that could be done and someone who would do it. But with the ebb of politics, there was only the memory of it all. And inevitably, these memories were sometimes troubling memories. In real life, tribes and chiefs did not always do what they should have done. In real life, when they did what they should have done the results were not always what they might have been. When this happened, the strategic institutions which were designed to protect and to sustain life seemed limited. A foreboding pervaded the memory of such events. There was a question about whether one could go on as before. This is where the ceremonial narrator set to work. He sat in the camp around the campfire preoccupied with an unsettled recollection. He composed. He recited.

Musil recorded eight tales among the Rwala that could be considered as ceremonial narratives of raiding and warfare. We shall consider four of these. Together with the personal accounts of raiding expeditions, these kinds of tales make up the core of the narrative tradition among the camel-herding Bedouins in North Arabia. These Bedouins, unlike many other peasant and tribal peoples in the Near East, had no tradition of heroic romances. Unlike the settlers among them, they did not tell stories of Abu Zeyd, the hero of the ʻAntar tales. Instead, they only told stories of their own participation in raids and wars or stories of actual raids and wars which had occurred more or less within the memory of living men.[1] Among these men without fiction, we find that fact plays the role of fiction.

In this respect, the ceremonial narrative is simply a weightier version of the personal account of a raiding expedition, which we have considered in the preceding chapter. Like Bleyhân's stories, the ceremonial narrative also raises the question of how a personal identity might be composed in a hostile world where men must struggle to survive, but it poses this question on the level of chiefs and tribes. The ceremonial narrative considers what kind of chiefly character or behavior might be the basis for putting together a tribal domain in which human life might be protected and supported.

The first example of such a narrative is a story about two tribal chiefs. Saṭṭâm, the head chief of the Rwala, is portrayed in the narrative as a reasonable man who attempts only to moderate a dangerous situation, which he knows he cannot entirely control. Turki, the head chief of the Fedʻân, is portrayed as an impetuous hero who, unmindful of the risk, loves to undertake political adventures. This contrast between the two chiefs corresponds quite closely to two stereotypical Rwala views of the character of all chiefs. Here is Musil's paraphrase of these views:

> A chief who is commonly spoken of as a *ṣâḥeb al-marjala* stands in high esteem among the Rwala. Such a one has a brave, strong heart, *qalbeh qawi;* knows how to wrestle with the greatest danger, *maʻeh fetel;* has a broad outlook, *maʻeh ʻerf;* thinks of the future, *shôfteh baʻîde;* and never acts hastily, *leh ṣabr.* He who is merely a daring fighter, *ṣâḥeb al-farse,* is not fit to be either a chief or a leader in time of war. He, too, has a strong heart but lacks calm consideration, *mâ leh ṣabr,* therefore he throws himself into danger recklessly, unmindful of victory or death; *yirmi ḥâleh yâ yiqtel qebîleh yinqatel.*[2]

Saṭṭâm is the man of forethought and forbearance. Turki is the daring and reckless fighter.

In the paraphrase the cautious chief is approved and the heroic chief is condemned. This would seem to be the end of the matter. The persistent appearance of daring and reckless men among the Bedouins, however, reflects an irresolvable dilemma which marks the Bedouin situation. Where the means of life are largely aggressive in their implications, there is a temptation to provoke other men in order to lend life some significance. The paraphrase is a simplistic reaction to this dilemma. It does not reveal that a *preference* for cautious chiefs is actually inspired by the persistent threat of heroic chiefs. Let us turn to the narrative of actual events where we discover a keener insight into political life.

Sometime in the late nineteenth century, the two chiefs, Saṭṭâm and Turki, were drawn into a confrontation. As a result Turki was killed, and the Rwala and the Fed‘ân became engaged in a protracted period of intertribal raiding. We shall be concerned with the interpretation that the narrator lends to this confrontation of two chiefs, which led to such disastrous results. As he tells his tale, the narrator is in the grip of a dread. He is addressing a series of events in which Saṭṭâm, who attempted to moderate a political conflict, failed to accomplish this end, and Turki, who sought to lead a heroic life of political adventure, met his death. Two principal figures in Bedouin political life, that is to say, were thrown into doubt by the course of these events.

As he composes this tale of disturbing events, the narrator uncovers the problem inherent in the very idea of a protective chief and a heroic chief. Saṭṭâm attempts to moderate a political disorder he cannot control. Is he the master or the slave of a political situation? Turki, in order to make something of political life, is obliged to provoke political disorder. Is he a man who plays with the possibilities of political disorder or does he have an instinctive wish for destruction and death? Let us examine how the narrator works over these implications of an actual conflict among the Rwala and Fed‘ân tribes.

### Wars between the Rwala and the Fed‘ân (1877–1900)

The head chief of the Fed‘ân tribe left this world, *dara’;* and his son, Turki eben Mheyd, was recognized as his successor. He was classed with the heroic men, *kân ye‘edd min ar-rajâl al-fursân,* and had great success on his frequent raids, *ṣâr bakhîṭ bel-maghâri.* Therefore he was famous all over the desert, *w-qad ishtahar ṣîteh.* Once he attacked the Rwala. Saṭṭâm eben Sha‘lân, the prince of this tribe, was unwilling to fight him, *mâ hw bâghi qwâmteh,* as he loved him, *kân leh ṭayyeb,* and was related to him, *nasîbeh,* having married his sister, Turkiyye, whom he kept with him all the time, *hi ‘endeh.* But Turki continued to provoke the Rwala incessantly. At one time he fell upon, *ghâr ‘ala,* a clan of the Kwâkbe tribe who were in the act of migrating, compelled them to construct a war camp, *nawwakhhom,* and then fought them from morning until mid-afternoon, *ila-l-‘aṣr w-al-kown ‘âjed bênhom.* After having killed some men and women, *zilm w-ḥarîm,* he robbed them of all he could, *akhadhhom,* and returned with the booty to his kin, *ila haleh.*

Shortly afterwards he undertook a new raid against the Rwala, assailed the herds of the Âl Zeyd kin in the depression of al-Khôr, and took all their camels together with the ʻAlya herd, which consisted only of white she-camels, *maghâtîr,* and which had belonged to them from ancient times; *isemha al-ʻalya w-hi maghâtîr w-qedîme ʻendahom ʻala dawr jdûdhom.* These camels were then entrusted to the special care of ʻArsân abu Qidhle. On his return Turki caught a member of the Rwala tribe, *qaḍab qaḍîb min ar-rwala zelema,* and, after learning from him where the prince was encamped, he let him go on his way but in parting shouted:

"Greet my relative Saṭṭâm and tell him that he should not allow himself to become a chief of nomads raising goats and sheep, because there is grass enough in al-Ḥamâd this year; *lâ yṣir shaykh ash-shikkâra w-al-ʻesheb bel-ḥamâd wâjed.*"

The man gave this message to the head chief Saṭṭâm, *ʻallem saṭṭâm bhâdha-l-jawâb,* who, enraged, instantly exclaimed:

"Oh, that man! Let Allâh decide between us and him. *Hâdha-r-rajjâl yeshûf allâh lena w-leh.* We did not want to fight him, but he provokes us all the time, *w-hw mubtalîna.* O ye Arabs, shoe your horses and get your supplies ready, for tomorrow we shall go on a raid as ordered by our highest commander; *yâ ʻarab eḥdhû kheylkom w-eḥsû zehâbkom w-ḥenna tarâna bâker meddâdeh ghazw bamr al-hâdi.*"

In that part of al-Ḥamâd called al-Heriyyân the Rwala warriors sighted a herd of camels and also caught a man, to whom they said:

"Who are these Arabs? *minhom hal-ʻarab hadhôla.*" His answer was:

"They are the Âl Mheyd, *hadhôla âl mheyd.*"

Saṭṭâm then found a camping place for his men which was well hidden from casual observation and at night sent a special messenger, *nadhîr,* to warn the head chief Turki eben Mheyd in these words:

"We undertook a raid against ye, *jîna ḥenna ʻaleykom ghazw,* not knowing that thou wert encamped on our route. Yet it has already happened, and now I cannot prevent my people from attacking you, *w-lâ atmakken aruddhom ʻan al-ghâra ʻaleykom.* Think it over! If thou believest thou canst beat us, *tanṭeḥna,* behold! here we are, *hâ ḥenna jînâk,* but in my opinion thou shouldst make thine escape tonight, *wa-bshowfṭi ennak tehejj bhâdha-l-leyl,* and keep at a distance from us, *w-trûḥ ʻan wajhana.* If thou dost that, we shall come tomorrow to thy camp, see that thou art gone, stop a while, and then return to our kinsfolk; *nankef w-narjaʻ ila halna.*"

After hearing the message Turki instantly said:

"God will help us against them, *ʻaleyhom maʻûnaten min allâh.* Tomorrow I shall fight them, *bâker lâzem atnâṭeḥ maʻhom.*"

The next day the Rwala came like a whirlwind, attacked the camp, entered it, and possessed themselves of all the herds there, including the one called ʻAlya, which had been captured by Turki some time before. Khalaf âl Idhen killed, as was the will of God, *bamr allâh,* the great chief Turki himself, and took his mail shirt, *dherʻateh,* his saber, and his mare, one of the fleetest of horses, *faraseh kânat min jiyâd al-kheyl.* Khalaf offered this mare to Saṭṭâm as a gift.

After Turki's death there broke out between the Rwala and Fedʻân a war so cruel that rider after rider fell off his horse, *w-'âd aṭ-ṭarîḥ bênhom mâ yeṭîḥ*, and the members of both tribes were bent more on killing a man than on capturing animals, *w-ṣâr 'enda-l-farîqên dhabḥ az-zelema aḥsan min kasb al-ḥalâl.*

The narration begins with a political problem and then recounts how the problem steadily worsens. There is a theme of increasing disruption and constant degeneration. At the opening, the Rwala are attacked by Turki and his band of raiders. The Rwala chief, through his friendship for the hero, hesitates to respond to this attack, and Turki begins "to provoke the Rwala incessantly." As these depredations continue Turki becomes increasingly rash, even extreme. On one occasion, Turki forces his Rwala victims to mobilize for war. This is a far more serious incident than cattle-raiding. Turki has now done more than upset the means of livelihood of the Rwala by stealing their camels. He kills men. He even kills women, a heinous violation of the Bedouin conventions of warfare. On still another occasion he attacks another camp and seizes the 'Alya herd of white camels "which had belonged to them [the Rwala] from ancient times" - a symbol of the Rwala tribe itself. Turki not only threatens possessions. He threatens the family. He threatens convention. He threatens a protective association. He threatens tradition itself. He is destructive to the basis of all life.

On the occasion of the 'Alya theft, Turki sends a message to Saṭṭâm which contains an insult. Just as the acts of this hero are violent, so his very words have the power to unsettle the cautious, sensible, and patient Saṭṭâm, "who, enraged, instantly exclaimed: 'Oh, that man! . . . We did not want to fight him, but he *provokes* us all the time' " [my italics]. Turki finally moves the Rwala chief himself to violence, or so it seems at this moment of chiefly anger. And this is not all. Turki eventually destroys himself, as he engages in a battle with a superior Rwala force and is killed. The instruments of his heroism - his mare, his mail shirt, and his saber - are subsequently scattered among the Rwala. His life is obliterated. The symbols of the character of that life are dispersed. And as if this were still not enough, his death leads to a period of dissension among the tribes, a period when all men are bent upon savagery.

This theme of political order increasingly disrupted and thrown into disorder is most elaborately developed in the contrast of the two characters of the chiefs. The contrast is presented in terms of the sensible Saṭṭâm who is reflective and the energetic Turki who is impulsive.

Saṭṭâm is the cautious and patient chief of forethought. He is not so much hesitating in his response to Turki as wisely reflective. His inaction in the face of Turki's provocation is not really a case of thinking too much and acting too little. He sees how things fit together and work out. He does not run against the current of things. The political disruptions and the outbreak of violence are never attributed to his errors in judgment or to his hesitation, but only to contingencies beyond his control. He works as best he can to forestall and manage events. For example, Saṭṭâm acts against Turki, not precipitously, but only when the disruption of the Rwala tribe becomes too severe. Even when he is momentarily enraged by the insult from the hero, he offers a reason and justification for his anger. And then when he resorts to action, he purposely leads his tribesmen on what he thinks is the wrong route in order to avoid a conflict. It is not his fault that by chance Turki happens to be where Saṭṭâm thinks he is not. Given this turn of fate, Saṭṭâm again attempts to manage the situation. He secretly sends a word of warning to Turki. He even advises Turki of what he will do and what will happen. He counsels Turki to "think it over," just as he, Saṭṭâm, thinks things over. It is not his fault that Turki ignores this good advice, obliging him to attack the hero's encampment.

As the narrative develops, however, Saṭṭâm can be seen from two contradictory perspectives. He comprehends the nature of the political world, its uncertainties and risks. He is a legitimate political authority precisely because he realizes the weakness of authority, the contingency of events, and the riskiness of any project. However, as we see Saṭṭâm working with the disorders provoked by Turki, he begins to appear in a new light. Saṭṭâm attempts to manage the disorders around him, but in doing so he himself begins to be managed by the disorders.

This "splitting" in the character of Saṭṭâm begins, like the theme of disorder, at the outset of the tale and is closely related, like the theme of disorder, to Turki. We learn at the outset that Turki is a relation of Saṭṭâm: the two men are brothers-in-law. The relationship is the oblique tie of affinity rather than a direct tie of blood. Saṭṭâm, who has married the sister of Turki, keeps this woman "with him all the time," and she bears her brother's name in a feminine form, Turkiyye. More emphatically, we learn in the same place that Saṭṭâm loves Turki, an emotion far stronger than the normal one expected of brothers-in-law. Although the cautious and sensible Saṭṭâm is contrasted and opposed to the impetuous and violent Turki, the hero fascinates him and obliquely invests his household. He invades Saṭṭâm's personal emotions and the privacy of his familial life, just as he invades the Rwala tribal territory and Rwala political life.

Subsequently we see a repetitive suggestion that Saṭṭâm's responses to Turki have a questionable value. All his attempts to evade Turki, for example, seem only to bring him closer to a confrontation with the hero. Saṭṭâm attempts to ignore Turki, but he is repeatedly compelled by his presence. Saṭṭâm pretends to move against Turki while in reality seeking to avoid him. As he seeks to avoid him, he comes directly upon him. He then attempts to advise and to control Turki, but the latter seizes the warning of Saṭṭâm's presence to precipitate a battle with him. Eventually all of Saṭṭâm's thoroughly sensible and cautious actions lead to the very things which he most sought to avoid: the death of Turki and political turmoil among the tribes.

We see how Saṭṭâm is *touched* or even tainted by Turki's heroism. As a chief whose function is to moderate political violence, Saṭṭâm's legitimacy is directly tied to the existence of heroes like Turki. This is the implication in the narrator's suggestion that Turki pervades the personal emotions and familial life of Saṭṭâm. This is the implication in the narrator's suggestion that whatever action Saṭṭâm takes to avoid Turki, Saṭṭâm nevertheless comes upon him. As the narrator considers an occasion where a proper policy of moderation failed, he conceives of that policy as commanded and constrained by pervasive political disorder. Saṭṭâm, the man who would control heroism, becomes Saṭṭâm, the man who is the slave of heroism.

Turki's delight in provoking other men, we may conclude, is the cause of the dreadful events in question. But here, too, there is an evolution in his character along with a "splitting" in the implications of a heroic life. At first Turki is not altogether foolhardy and destructive. His life of raiding inspires the admiration of all the Arabs. As a hero he pursues the dangers of raiding playfully and joyfully. This quality of his character can be seen, for example, in the joking insult which he first sends to Saṭṭâm. This is the reason why Turki fascinates. This is why Saṭṭâm loves him. He converts into play what Saṭṭâm bears as a responsibility and what troubles all the other Arabs. Turki demonstrates more clearly than Saṭṭâm, who aims to control political disorder, more clearly than the self-concerned Arabs who fear political disorder, that there is no political life among the Bedouin without disorder and even violence. He is loved and admired as he lives with this problem playfully and joyfully. He makes something interesting out of something that is a burden and a care.

If the development of the narrative is carefully examined, however, we may note that Turki, like Saṭṭâm, can also be seen from two contradictory perspectives. For as Turki plays with and enjoys violence, he comes to pursue the life of violence unthinkingly, even instinctively. This different perspective becomes more important with the description of the increasing violence of Turki's raids. Turki first enlivens the political scene with his cattle-raids, but then he begins to destroy the basis of political life itself. He contravenes its conventions (kills women) and defiles its symbols (steals the 'Alya herd). He enrages cautious men like Saṭṭâm and inflames the Arabs in general. In the final episode of the tale, we see the crucial sign of his problem. As Turki comes to identify with political violence, he can be identified with it. As its agent, he becomes a symbol of the presence of political violence in the North Arabian political world. He represents the source of political life in the desert, but also the problem inherent in that life. Turki, a man who must provoke other men in order to live, becomes Turki, a man intent on provocation for its own sake. A man who plays with other men through aggression becomes a man who wishes to destroy other men.

The decisive scene occurs in the final episode when Turki receives Saṭṭâm's soothing counsel urging him to think things over. Turki here responds unhesitatingly: "After hearing the message Turki instantly said: 'God will help us against them.'" It is as if he had not heard one word of Saṭṭâm's warning and reassurance. Unthinkingly and instinctively he embraces the prospect of conflict. At the moment when Turki fails to make anything out of a life of violence, he will surely and inevitably meet his death; for this is also the moment when Saṭṭâm becomes unable to manage or to evade political disorder any longer. Saṭṭâm is compelled to attack Turki's camp. Consider the last few lines of the tale which recount how the Rwala overcome Turki:

> . . . the Rwala came like a whirlwind, attacked the camp, entered it, and possessed themselves of all the herds there, including the one called 'Alya . . . Khalaf âl Idhen killed, as was the will of God, the great chief Turki himself, and took his mail shirt, his saber, and his mare, one of the fleetest horses. Khalaf offered this mare to Saṭṭâm as a gift.

In these closing lines the narrator seems to suggest that the Rwala reconstitute their tribe as they unify in battle, recapture their herds and their tribal symbol (the 'Alya herd), and finally triumph over the Fed'ân. The passage, however, can be read in a more disturbing way. Do the Rwala decisively suppress Turki, or do they rather take the place of Turki? The narrator suggests this second more disturbing possibility by his description of these concluding events. With the death of Turki at the hands of the Rwala, the instruments of heroism (the saber, the mail shirt, and the mare) are not so much scattered among the Rwala, they are more ominously "inherited" by the Rwala. Note that Khalaf, a man about whom we learn nothing more in this tale, is both the man who kills Turki and the man who offers the mare to Saṭṭâm as a gift. Khalaf, a dark figure in the tale, symbolizes that Saṭṭâm and his Rwala are tainted by the instruments of a way of life that brings the death of men.[3]

We have not quite come to the end of the narrative. A few more lines are appended to this scene of an ambiguous Rwala triumph. Let us read the lines with which the narrator breaks off his tale: "After Turki's death there broke out between the Rwala and Fed'ân a war so cruel that rider after rider fell off his horse, and the members of both tribes were bent more on killing a man than on capturing animals." The Rwala victory over Turki does not lead to peace. There is further political degeneration. The desert is the scene of pervasive and unrestrained intertribal political violence. But let us note the precise character of the two images that describe this violence.

There was "a war so cruel that rider after rider fell off his horse." This image of intertribal violence insists upon the link between men and aggressive instruments which bring men's deaths. In doing so, it recalls the tragedy of Saṭṭâm, a man of peace who lives in a world of violence. It recalls how the private life of this chief was persistently invaded by a man with aggressive instruments. It recalls how every attempt of Saṭṭâm to avoid conflict only drew him deeper into conflict. And finally, it recalls his ominous inheritance of the mare of the hero through the man who killed the hero. Despite his intention to avoid a conflict of any kind, all the efforts of a cautious and sensible chief have led to war, and in the first image of this war, we see the cause of his failure. *Men with good motivations are faulted by their circumstances in the desert and steppe.*

Then, the war is described once again by a second image: "the members of both tribes were bent more on killing a man than on capturing animals." This image of intertribal violence insists that men's worst motivations surface in a situation where they are involved in aggressive actions. In doing so, it recalls the tragedy of Turki, a man of playful heroic actions who was drawn ever more deeply into a senseless wish to destroy other men. It recalls how Turki began with cattle-raiding, but then became involved in the death of men and women. It recalls how he first seized the tribal symbols of the Rwala and then rashly insulted Saṭṭâm, the only man among the Rwala who was his friend. And finally, it recalls how he scorned the cautious and sensible advice of Saṭṭâm as he determined, almost unthinkingly and even instinctively, to engage in a fight with a superior force. Despite his ability to make something interesting of what was a burden and a care for all the other Arabs, he was drawn relentlessly into a wish to destroy other men, and in the second image of the war, we see the cause of this disaster. *Men's bad motivations are fostered by their circumstances in the desert and steppe.*

The tale does not end, like Musil's paraphrase, with any moral about the usefulness of a cautious and sensible chief or the danger of an impetuous hero. It presents more nearly a study of the tragic interrelationship of two great Bedouin political figures.[4] As the narrator thinks over disturbing events in which the characters of two persons representing two Bedouin political institutions were thrown into question, he reveals the values behind these institutions. We learn how chiefs are interconnected with heroes, and we learn of the problem inherent in this interconnection. But the narrator's work has not undermined a Bedouin devotion to protective chiefs and playful heroes. The problems which he raises are attached to specific men and specific events. He is gripped by dread as he recalls the past, but that dread is nevertheless located in the past. There was that time many years ago when rider after rider fell from his horse, when men wished to kill one another more than they wished to rob one another. In the here and now, however, there is still the possibility of going on as before.

## 2

Musil records another narrative which describes the same events as those of the previous one. This second version of the death of Turki does not exactly take the form of what has been characterized as a ceremonial narrative. It more closely resembles Bleyhân's stories in that it is a personal experience told by a man who actually participated in the Rwala expedition against Turki.

It is ostensibly no more than a description of the procedures by which the Rwala sought out and eventually killed Turki. The two versions provide a test of the present approach to the Rwala materials. The ceremonial narrative is concerned with the validity of a political tradition. It is, one might say, an interpretive composition even though it deals with actual events. Let us now read the second version with a question in mind. To what extent do interpretive problems orient a tale which ostensibly does no more than spell out with factual precision a series of events?

Another version of
the death of Turki

It was at the time of abundance, when we set out against Turki eben Mheyd. He was generally called al-Hadhdhâb, meaning omnipresent, as never half a month passed without news coming in of a fresh attack by him on some Rwala camp near or far. Many a warrior was afraid of him, the women frightened their children with his name, and the herdsmen were reluctant to drive the herds out of the camps. Finally Saṭṭâm agreed with other chiefs to undertake a raid against him. Personally he liked Turki, for besides being a brother of his favorite wife, Turkiyye, he was also a man of noble mind and honest. The Rwala, however, threatened to depose Saṭṭâm if he would not crush Turki once for all. We were encamped in aḍ-Ḍreybînât at the time. Saṭṭâm set out for the decisive fight with six hundred riders on horseback and eight hundred on camels, he himself being the commander-in-chief. The Eshâje‘a clan was led by Eben Me‘jel, the ‘Abdelle by Eben Mjeyd, and the Sirḥân by Eben Merdej. Khalaf âl Idhen was Saṭṭâm's chief lieutenant. First we drank from the Khubeyrat ad-Daḥal, then we found water at the head of al-Ghadaf, crossed aṣ-Ṣwâb, and saw a small camp of the Ṣleyb, who told us that Turki was encamped at al-Heri. In al-Ghadaf Saṭṭâm hired a Ṣlubi and sent him at night secretly to Turki. The Ṣlubi overtook the latter on the march to a new camp, made a sign to him to come nearer, and then gave him the message he was entrusted with:

"O Turki! I was sent to thee by thy brother Saṭṭâm. The Rwala are on thy heels, desiring thy life."

This enraged Turki to such an extent that he drew his saber menacingly and commanded the Ṣlubi to be gone, with the words:

"Leave at once! Let nothing of what thou hast now said to me escape thee. If thou utterest a single word before my people, I shall kill thee. Am I, from whom the Rwala have fled so often, expected now to run away from them?"

Turki's slaves wondered not a little why he had his tent erected so far southwest from the camp.

We first sent five of our scouts on horses, *'uyûn,* to examine the country ahead of us, but these turned back as soon as they caught a glimpse of the camp fires. In the morning we sent out others, this time on camelback, *ṣbûr.* One of them soon returned with the report that the enemy was withdrawing in a northerly direction and was being followed by the rest of our scouts. We moved after them in a leisurely manner. Not long after noon a second scout finally came with the report that they had put up their tents and that coffee was being ground at Turki's tent.

At that moment every rider mounted his horse, grasped his weapons and ammunition, and waited for the command. The commanders pointed out the places where the riders of tired or overburdened she-camels, *radd,* were to wait, placed the other camel riders, *ṣâbûr,* between them and Turki's camp, divided the horse troop into two halves, posting one of them on the flank of the *ṣâbûr* to form the reserve, *kemîn,* while with the other they decided to attack, *ghâra.* Then we attacked the camp directly. At that time the Âl 'Awâji clan was also camping with Turki, so we had at once several hundred riders against us. The fight of rider against rider lasted till sunset. Turki exhausted six mares during that time, his slaves changing them at his command. An-Nûri was wounded and many other Rwala, and still the fight was not yet decided. Saṭṭâm was loath to call up the reserve, for he wanted it either to decide the victory or to cover the retreat.

Finally Turki's mare was hit by a shot. In falling she pressed his leg to the ground, and, as he was clad in a mail shirt, he could not free his leg quickly enough and was stabbed by a spear twice. At that moment Gharrâf, Saṭṭâm's slave, sprang to the struggling chief in order to save him, pulled him from under the horse, and the women carried him into the tent, which was at once occupied by four of Saṭṭâm's slaves as guards against the Rwala, inflamed by the battle. Turki's fall having been observed and jubilantly announced by the attackers, the Fed'ân began to retreat but were intercepted by the reserve cavalry, while the camel riders, *ṣâbûr,* sped to the camp to pick up both their dead and wounded friends. Khalaf âl Idhen, who was left in charge of the camel riders, now reached the tent where Turki in the meantime was being cared for by Saṭṭâm himself, and was on the point of giving him the death blow but was prevented by Saṭṭâm, who threatened him with instant death should he lay a finger on his friend. Then Khalaf called on his camel riders to come and get their enemy themselves. In response all the Rwala - and there were some five hundred of them - surrounded Turki's tent, while Khalaf spoke to the prince thus:

"O Saṭṭâm! the Arabs do not fight on such conditions. Behold, we shall not ask thee again. I swear by Allâh, if thou dost not give way, thou wilt roll into thy grave. Canst thou not see that the muzzles of all the rifles are pointing at thee?"

Thus coerced, Saṭṭâm turned to Turki with the words: "Forgive, my brother, and may Allâh also forgive me. There thou seest how my Rwala obey me. O Khalaf, O thou rascal, sell me him whom thou wishest to destroy. I will give thee gold!"

"Away with thee, brother! Knowest thou not that an-Nûri has fallen, that Kurdi, Nâser eben Me'jel, and countless others also have fallen today?"

Nodding to his slaves, Saṭṭâm then with them left Turki's tent, stricken with grief on hearing that an-Nûri and his brother Kurdi were among the slain. Kurdi was dead, but an-Nûri still lived and later fully recovered. After Saṭṭâm's departure the enraged Rwala threw themselves on Turki and beat him to death. They captured all the herds and tents in the camp. Over thirty Rwala had fallen, and about a hundred were wounded. Of the fallen the hero Za'eytel was the most lamented. They also lost twenty-five mares.

The narrator begins with a statement of confident intent: "It was at the time of abundance, when we set out against Turki eben Mheyd." Following this, Turki's attacks upon the Rwala are described as occurring frequently and regularly. But note that Turki's offenses are never catalogued in detail in this version. Indeed nothing more is said of them than this initial remark. And after this, the narrator makes a curious observation: "Many a warrior was afraid of him, the women frightened their children with his name, and the herdsmen were reluctant to drive the herds out of the camp." Instead of dwelling upon Turki's actual deeds, he dwells upon the general fear of those deeds among the Rwala. He suggests, albeit ever so slightly, that Turki was more of a fear in the minds of some Rwala than he was in reality a formidable threat to them. At this point Saṭṭâm's admiration of Turki and his marriage to Turkiyye are mentioned. However, Saṭṭâm here acts against Turki in a decisive manner despite these factors. He acts because of another more important consideration: his own tribesmen are threatening to topple him from power. In this version, the Rwala chief takes an effective practical action for a thoroughly practical reason.

Much of the remainder of the tale describes how the Rwala suppressed the hero Turki without hesitation or doubts by means of superior resources and careful procedures. First, six hundred men on horseback and eight hundred men on camels are brought together. The constitution of this impressive force and its initial movements are precisely set forth. After a brief mention of Saṭṭâm's message to Turki, the preparation for and the conduct of the conclusive battle itself is described. We learn here of the techniques of Bedouin warfare: the sending out of scouts, the withdrawal of transport camels to a place of safety, and the forming of a reserve force in the rear.

Along with this interest in practical resources and procedures, the narrator also mentions a number of improper and even unsavory occurrences. For example, there is no suggestion that Turki might have been killed in a heroic man-to-man contest of riders with sabers as there is in the first version. Instead, Turki's horse is shot with a rifle, and as a result Turki is stabbed twice by a Rwala lanceman. The glory of the Rwala, the tribe of the narrator, also suffers from the bruising realism of his account. Almost all the principal Bedouin customs of warfare described by Musil in other sections of his ethnography are violated by the Rwala in the course and aftermath of the battle. A helpless man is wounded. The law of protection is flouted. A chief is threatened and scorned. A wounded man lying in his tent is beaten to death by an enraged mob. These are outrages, but they are very believable outrages. There is no reason to doubt the authenticity of these events.

Quite probably, this realistic version gives us a more accurate account of some of the precise circumstances that led to Turki's death than the preceding interpretive version. The narrator simply relates the events impartially as they happened. The authority of his account rests upon his respect for the truth. He has the ability to see just what shapes the course of events: adequate resources and careful strategies in the context of a very dangerous world of men with no respect for convention.

Let us now look again at what is said of Saṭṭâm and Turki, as well as just how it is said. The events after all have thrown into question the very basis of political authority. The narrative relates how one chief, even though he may be an enemy chief, brings about his own defeat. The narrative relates how the murder of this chief results from the failure of the Rwala to respect the authority of their own chief. Is the narrator able to describe how men come to grips with political problems in a pragmatic way if the central institution of political authority by which they proceed is somehow in question? How is it that some chiefs are impractical? How is it that practical chiefs are disobeyed? In this regard, there are three points of crisis in the tale: Turki's receipt of Saṭṭâm's message, the fall of Turki in battle, and the confrontation of Saṭṭâm and Khalaf in the aftermath of the battle. Let us look at each of these points of crisis more closely.

When Saṭṭâm's message is delivered to Turki, there is a portrayal of Turki's character. When he learns that Saṭṭâm and his Rwala are near, Turki angrily draws his saber and threatens the Ṣlubi: "Leave at once! Let nothing of what thou hast now said to me escape thee. *If thou utterest a single word before my people,* I shall kill thee. *Am I, from whom the Rwala have fled so often, expected now to run away from them*?" [my italics]. Turki suppresses practical information regarding the presence of a superior enemy force from his followers. This crucial, even fatal suppression is associated with Turki's excessive pride. The narrator, a pragmatic man, is implicitly judging heroism from a pragmatic point of view. He has initially suggested that the hero is an illusory, rather than a real threat. He now attempts to confirm this suggestion by viewing the hero as more concerned with his reputation than with practical considerations. He accurately perceives that a man who looks for adventure in risky provocations values an interesting life over a cautious and sensible life, but then he attempts to discover in such a man, perhaps too wishfully, some fatal flaw. Note a curious feature of this scene. In the preceding version of the death of Turki, there were three symbols associated with Turki's heroism: his saber, his horse, and his mail shirt. Here, in this version, one of these symbols - the saber - appears not in battle but in connection with Turki's prideful suppression of practical information.

Later in the tale, at the second point of crisis, the other two symbols appear in connection with Turki's fall in battle. Here the narrator first describes how Turki and Saṭṭâm behave in the midst of an actual battle. As he does so, the fundamental distinction between the character of an impetuous hero and a pragmatic chief come to light: "The fight of rider against rider lasted till sunset. *Turki exhausted six mares* during that time, his slaves changing them at his command. *An-Nûri was wounded and many other Rwala,* and still the fight was not yet decided. *Saṭṭâm was loath to call up the reserve,* for he wanted it either to decide the victory or to cover the retreat" [my italics]. The narrator describes the battle as a heroic contest: It is a "fight of rider against rider," and in this contest Turki behaves heroically. He does not hold back. He puts everything he has into the struggle. But in doing so, he exhausts himself. In contrast, Saṭṭâm refuses to call up the Rwala reserve despite heavy losses. Saṭṭâm pragmatically gauges the situation, anticipates future needs, and measures out his resources accordingly.

A telling gesture follows these lines as the narrator recounts the very fall of Turki in battle: "Finally Turki's mare was hit by a shot. In falling she pressed his leg to the ground, and, as he was clad in a mail shirt, he could not free his leg quickly enough and was stabbed by a spear twice." The decisive weapon in the fight proves to be the rifle. This is the instrument which brings death at a distance, and therefore the instrument which carries with it the death of all heroism. The saber, the weapon used by heroes at close quarters, is here unmentioned. And now observe just where and how Turki proves to be vulnerable. It is Turki's horse, the second symbol of heroism in the first version, which is shot. It is Turki's horse, the very vehicle of heroism, which pins him helplessly to the ground so that he cannot move. This curious gesture is then emphasized by the narrator. The mail shirt of Turki, the third and final symbol of heroism in the first version, further impedes Turki and leads to his final disablement. A heroic instrument suppresses practical information and precipitates a fatal battle (the saber). Turki exhausts the instruments of heroism in the battle (the six mares). The crucial instrument is unheroic (the rifle). The vehicle of heroism immobilizes the hero (the horse). A heroic instrument proves to be a practical impediment (the mail shirt). The narrator is curiously insistent about the impracticality of the instruments of heroism. As he cites what may have very likely been the actual facts, he chooses and insists upon certain facts which seem to teach a lesson. And suspiciously, this is a lesson which is close to the heart of this narrator.

We are left with a question about the tale. Do the facts offer convincing proof that heroism is impractical and therefore unviable? Or do the facts which are chosen and insisted upon only suggest the narrator's hope that heroism is impractical and therefore unviable? Surely the latter judgment of this tale is the more appropriate one. In so far as it is, this narrator does not quite see that his own devotion to a cautious and sensible politics of pragmatism is actually commanded by the passions of heroism in his world. This narrator does not quite see that heroism, although impractical, persists all the same as men seize upon aggressive political instruments as a tempting means of opening up the possibilities of life.

Let us now examine how the narrator deals with the third point of crisis: the confrontation of Saṭṭâm and Khalaf. Saṭṭâm is the figure of authority without whom pragmatic strategies cannot be put into play. It is with Saṭṭâm that the narrator must identify. But Saṭṭâm does not emerge from these events unscathed. Moreover, the damage done to his authority cannot be attributed to Turki. Unlike the previous narrator, this narrator insists that Turki is not a serious problem, and so he is forced to discover elsewhere the reasons for Saṭṭâm's failure. He finds these reasons among the Rwala themselves.

After Turki has fallen and been wounded, he is saved by Gharrâf, a slave of Saṭṭâm, and carried into his tent by women. This tent is guarded by four of the Rwala chief's slaves. We then see a contrast between Saṭṭâm who symbolizes all that is good in the Rwala and Khalaf who symbolizes all that is bad. As Khalaf comes to the tent seeking vengeance, Turki is "being cared for by Saṭṭâm himself." As Khalaf is on the point of killing the wounded Turki, Saṭṭâm protects the latter by threatening Khalaf with death. And then Khalaf becomes quite explicitly the man who represents the bad aspect of the Rwala. He summons the Rwala warriors against their chief. The latter threaten Saṭṭâm with their rifles and demand that Turki be turned over to them. And then Saṭṭâm becomes quite explicitly the man who represents the good aspect of the Rwala. He asks forgiveness from Turki. He asks forgiveness from God. He tries one more time to buy off Khalaf with gold. Saṭṭâm nurtures. He protects. He values the life of other men, no matter how much trouble they have caused him. He recognizes the existence of a moral authority, which demands a respect for life from all men.

Saṭṭâm, as he is described by the narrator, clearly represents not only the hope that pragmatic political strategies will triumph over heroism; Saṭṭâm also represents the belief that pragmatic men are good men. The description of the Rwala chief suggests that the narrator believes that pragmatic politics represents the possibility for a moral political life. It is easy to see how such a conviction would emerge among the Bedouin given their circumstances. Unfortunately, the events in question have raised a serious problem for such a conviction. Saṭṭâm is a good man but he proves to be a leader of bad men. At the beginning of the tale, the Rwala have threatened to topple their chief from power. The Rwala have attacked a defenseless man pinned beneath his horse during the struggle. Here at the end of the tale, both of these crimes are combined and amplified. The Rwala threaten their own chief with death when he protects Turki, and then savagely beat to death the wounded Turki despite the opposition of their chief. The narrator is too realistic in his approach to life to delete the crimes of his fellow tribesmen from his tale. He recounts them accurately and seemingly unemotionally. Still, as a man who believes that a pragmatic approach to political life is the basis of a good life, he cannot help but color these events and reveal their troubling implications.

Again there is a telling gesture at the point of crisis, as in the case of Turki. Note that Saṭṭâm finally surrenders Turki, that is to say he accepts the failure of his authority, on a point of information that is partly right, but also partly wrong. Khalaf, the dark figure of the first version, offers Saṭṭâm the tainted information:

> "Away with thee, brother! Knowest thou not that an-Nûri has fallen, that Kurdi, Nâṣer eben Me'jel, and countless others also have fallen today?"
> Nodding to his slaves, Saṭṭâm then with them left Turki's tent, stricken with grief on hearing that an-Nûri and his brother Kurdi were among the slain. Kurdi was dead, but an-Nûri still lived and later fully recovered.

Indeed one of Saṭṭâm's first cousins had been killed, but the other cousin, contrary to the report, was still alive. The failure of the good authority, good because he is a pragmatic authority, turns upon real facts which are in part true, but in part false. There are real and proper reasons for Saṭṭâm's acceding to his tribesmen's wishes, but then these real and proper reasons are not all true. Does the correctness of this information explain why Saṭṭâm properly gives in? Does the incorrectness of this information explain why Saṭṭâm improperly gives in? Or rather does the simultaneous correctness and incorrectness of a point of information attach to a pragmatic political authority some ambiguity, inherent in the narrator's approach to experience, which stresses the real facts of actual situations? The tainted information suggests ever so slightly that Saṭṭâm's form of political authority is tainted by these events. This tale of how good men succeed by means of practical procedures is partly right, but also partly wrong. In part, the affair seems to have gone right: the Rwala have confidently overcome and suppressed Turki. In part, the affair seems to have gone wrong: the Rwala have defied their chief and murdered a wounded man.

The closing lines of the tale reveal a lingering anxiety about the course of these events. Here the narrator turns, with a gesture again indicating the kind of man he is, to settle the accounts of the affair: the Rwala "captured all the herds and tents in the camp." A great material reward has been secured, but then: "Over thirty Rwala had fallen, and about a hundred were wounded." Some very real and irreparable damage has been done to the tribe of the Rwala – but the narrator refuses to mention the failure of Saṭṭâm. And then, more poignantly, he continues: "Of the fallen the hero Za'eytel was the most lamented." A hero who was loved and admired is missing – but the narrator refuses to mention the death of Turki, and then calmly and soberly he ends his tale: "They also lost twenty-five mares." Yes, it was rather the loss of something real and concrete. It was surely the loss of those mares that explains the hurtful scar which those events of so long ago, ten years, perhaps twenty, have left upon the memory. This narrator who looks for the good life in a pragmatic approach to experience ultimately attaches a memory of disturbing events to the loss of practical resources.

The second, more realistic version of the death of Turki is no less interpretive than the first version. It is simply less insightful. This narrator believes that the very insights, skills, and instruments of a life of political conflict can be surely used by good men to control political conflict. He does not see the danger of an investment in such insights, skills, and instruments. He sees only the danger of an unpragmatic use of this investment, and he traces the problems of his political experiences on this occasion to two such unpragmatic uses. Men, he believes, are too inclined to value images over reality. This is why Turki takes pride in his heroic actions and why the Rwala initially fear Turki's heroism. Men, he believes, are too apt to lose their good sense and fall prey to their passions. This is why the Rwala rebel against Saṭṭâm and eventually murder Turki. He refuses to recognize the possibility of an irresolvable and therefore dreadful problem at the heart of the Bedouin way of life, which emerged on the occasion of the death of Turki. He only hesitates ever so slightly over an ambiguous point of information. He only admits the possibility of real and concrete damages and losses. The first ceremonial narrator, in contrast, recognizes that the time when Saṭṭâm went out against Turki was a bad time. He dares to think out just how this was an occasion when traditional ideas about a Bedouin way of life are thrown into question.

## 3

The events which led to the death of Turki had disturbing implications for the Rwala narrators. The legitimacy of a concept of correct chiefly behavior was tainted by events even though the Rwala prevailed over the Fed'ân. The next narrative addresses a war with very different implications. The central figure in this tale is Sa'dûn, the leader of a powerful military force making war on the Rwala. Sa'dûn is something more than a tribal chief. He is said to rule over a specific domain and to command a small army. Sa'dûn in this tale will represent a bad form of authority and his eventual defeat by the Rwala will be attributed to his improper behavior. At the same time, the Rwala chief, Prince an-Nûri, will represent a good form of authority and the Rwala victory will be associated with his and his tribesmen's proper behavior. This tale provides an opportunity to see how a specific form of "personal morality" crystallizes in connection with the situation of political uncertainty in the desert and steppe.

There are two crucial features of this morality. Where relationships are unsettled by political uncertainty, one must first realize that one cannot do too much. A measured and cautious behavior is both proper and necessary. Secondly, one must also realize that a respect for other persons must be the base upon which peace and security are established. The distrust born of a situation of political uncertainty can only be overcome by individuals dealing directly and openly with one another while recognizing one another's separate, legitimate interests.

War between the Rwala and
the Muntifeq (1905)

One Sa'dûn al-Ashqar, a member of the reigning kin of the Muntifeq tribe, was known both for his violent temper and stubbornness, *w-kân mejabber ṣâḥeb siṭwaten.* As he was the owner of a large settled territory in Iraq, he was obeyed by a great number of warriors and had a flag of his own which he took with him on his raids, hoisting it over the camping grounds of the Arabs whom he had vanquished and robbed. To show that he was not afraid of revenge, he loved to remain sitting by the flag in such camps for two or three hours after getting possession of them.

Once he attacked, near Rijm 'Aleyye, the camp of the Dughmân and Nṣeyr, containing about ninety tents. After taking them he returned, victorious and without loss, to his kinsfolk. Next year Prince an-Nûri offered him his friendship, which was accepted. This gave the Arabs a feeling of security, *w-'âdat al-'arab ye'minûn.* The chief Sa'dûn al-Ashqar, however, understood little of good faith but much of treachery, *qelîl al-emâne kethîr al-kheyâne,* and paid no regard to the treaty or the friendship, *w-lâ yeqḍobeh al-'ahd w-aṣ-ṣuḥb.* His son Thâmer one day attacked the Sha'lân, who considered themselves friends of the Muntifeq, *mettakhedhîn ṣâḥeb,* near the head of the Feyḥân valley, about sunrise. Before the Sha'lân had shaken off their sleep the Muntifeq were looting the tents on the edge of the camp and beginning to drive the camels away. But the prince, *shuyûkh,* with his sons, the slaves of his household, and other men recovered the herds, pursued the attackers, and defeated them so crushingly that Thâmer barely saved himself with about a hundred riders on horses and camels, *w-lâ yeslam illa' thâmer hw w-ma'eh yeji mâye zelema mâ bên khayyâl w-râʿi dhelûl.* This brave defense naturally pleased the Rwala greatly, filling them also with a sense of security, especially as some of the Ḍana Muslim tribes soon moved into that region and encamped close by.

But then they learned from some merchants that the chief Eben Mejlâd had incited Saʿdûn against them. In order to subdue Eben Mejlâd, an-Nûri eben Shaʿlân assembled his Rwala and made a raid on him and his tribe, the Dahâmshe, who at that time were encamped between Ṭeʿes al-Maʿeyzîle and the *sheʿîb* [watercourse] of al-Khsheybi. But in the meantime something had happened of which the Rwala had not even dreamed. When Thâmer came back with his handful of men and told of his defeat, Saʿdûn al-Ashqar became furious and forthwith began to prepare a war expedition against the Rwala on a large scale, summoning all the tribes which used to help him in his wars, *w-arsal ʿala' min yelumm ʿaleyh,* as well as the Ẓefîr tribe and marching out to punish the Rwala. On the way he also sent couriers to Eben Mejlâd with the message:

"I am going to raid the Rwala. Get ready to join us, for Thâmer's fallen fighters must be avenged. Should any man of the Ḍana Muslim be amongst you, seize and fetter him to prevent him from warning Eben Shaʿlân; *w-elya' mâ kân ʿendakom ḥad min ṭwâref ḍana muslim oqḍobûh w-orboṭûh en lâ tṣîr khabr an-nadhr ʿend eben shaʿlân.*"

By the will of God there happened to be a certain Rweyli in Eben Mejlâd's reach. He was at once put in irons. The following day an-Nûri surprised Eben Mejlâd's camp, capturing thirty-five tents and several herds of camels. In the confusion following the attack the imprisoned Rweyli succeeded in making his escape, still wearing his fetters, of which he was immediately freed by his fellow tribesmen who were plundering the camp. He wished to speak to Prince an-Nûri. When brought before him, he said:

"O an-Nûri, give up all desire for booty, return from this raid, and prepare with both thy kin and thy whole tribe for defense, so that al-Ashqar may not laugh at our expense; for, behold, I listened to what Eben Mejlâd was told by messengers and was therefore put in irons. But today, during your attack, my guards had regard only for themselves, *ballashow bḥâlhom,* and I escaped."

An-Nûri's fighters were very busy just then, *balshânîn.* Some were still attacking, *yehâwesh,* the defenders, others were securing their booty, *yekseb.* However, an-Nûri's mighty voice called them together and made them return to their kinsfolk without delay. Thus a still greater defeat was averted from Eben Mejlâd by the will of Allâh, for, if the prisoner had not informed an-Nûri of what threatened him, all the tents in the camp would have been taken and many more of his men killed.

But no sooner had an-Nûri withdrawn than a messenger came galloping to Eben Mejlâd with the order:

"By Allâh, mount, Eben Mejlâd, thou and thy warriors, your horses and camels, for Saʿdûn with his flag is approaching the Rwala!"

In obedience to the order, Eben Mejlâd and his troop instantly followed the messenger. When he told Saʿdûn about the attack which the Rwala had just delivered, Saʿdûn replied:

"Be comforted with what I shall now tell thee. Ye will get back the long-maned mares which the Rwala have taken from you, *ʿarâyef,* and yet more booty which we shall take from them. Only pray that they will not flee when they sight us. I have sworn an oath on my neck that I must catch an-Nûri even if I should have to pursue him as far as the Ḥawrân. My spear with my flag I shall stick into the ash heap of his fireplace where he makes his coffee, for the accursed an-Nûri thinks too much of himself and brags about the numbers of his warriors; *w-arkoz al-bayraq ʻala nthîla delâleh bann al-malʻûm mestaʻezz wa-mtahaqwi bkithr ejmûʻeh.*"

Saʻdûn led more than three thousand warriors, the majority of them mounted on camels. His son Thâmer accompanied him but did not dare to come near his father, who could not forget his son's recent defeat. The warriors in an attempt to appease Saʻdûn sang the following ditty, *hejêni:*

With us are camels desired by all,
Chosen from among the best riding camels.
On them youths full of pride are sitting,
Who for an-Nûri's tent keep asking.
They follow Saʻdûn, the father of Thâmer,
The darling of her whose shirt-sleeves flutter.
Of Shaʻlân's fighters a small troop will come to us,
And on hearing the Mausers' thunder our camels will stop.

Saʻdûn and his retinue took hunting falcons along with them, and as soon as they sighted a hare or a *ḥabâra* bird (bustard) they urged the falcon, *yeheddûn,* to pursue it and to bring back the game. Once Saʻdûn sent his falcon, *ṭayreh,* to get a hare. The falcon pecked the hare with its beak, and when the latter tried to hide, *tekhawmer ʻanneh,* Saʻdûn said:

"Look, comrades, at that hare! It has crawled into the bush, as did Thâmer, my son, before the falcon which is an-Nûri."

Deeply ashamed, *khajel,* on hearing such words, *jawâb,* Thâmer said: "O God, bring us to the people we are seeking and let us not pass by them or allow them to hide from us! May my father then see them with his own eyes – either to overcome or to send me against them with an army still larger than this!"

When an-Nûri eben Shaʻlân returned to his people he saw that the Rwala had built small camps scattered all over the country. He ordered them to gather together at once. Some days previous the Rwala had been joined by Eben Smeyr and Eben Meʻjel with their Arabs. An-Nûri and his allies moved to the valleys of as-Sweyf and al-Helâli, where owing to good rains there was abundance, *beha rabîʻ,* that year. Of the impending attack Eben Shaʻlân did not say a word in order not to alarm them unnecessarily. The next night an-Nûri and his kin slept on the new camping ground, and with the appearance of the morning star they saw and heard group after group of Arabs fleeing with both tents and herds. On inquiring for the cause of their panic they were told that an unknown enemy was attacking the tents on the southern border of the scattered camps, and as the neighboring Arabs were yet sleepy and ignorant of what was happening they sought safety, not in resistance but in flight. The rifles thundered, and shots were heard on all sides. The confusion grew. At that moment, before the sun had yet risen, Eben Shaʻlân, Eben Smeyr, and Eben Meʻjel with their slaves and warriors sprang to horse, dashing to the place where the sound of rifles and fighting could be heard. On coming near they saw a flag surrounded by a vast throng of men. It seemed as if the Rwala were about to perish, *kharibat qerʻathom.* The enemy were pressing them back by degrees, had taken one camp after another, and had pulled down the tents. The women defended their property as best they could; many had been killed, but none would run away, and all heaped abuse on their retreating husbands and brothers. When the latter finally saw that even their women were resisting bravely, they declared: "We should rather be killed today than let our women by wronged by the enemy," and then a fight ensued compared to which all that happened before was mere play.

It was past noon and the fighting still continued. The victory had as yet inclined to neither side, for each opposed the other with obstinate fury. After noon all the Ḍana Muslim drew together, and at about mid-afternoon in a united body they attacked the enemy. Then it was that Allâh granted victory to the Rwala. Sa'dûn made frantic efforts to stop his fleeing warriors, but in vain. The Ḍana Muslim broke through the enemy's line, and whoever could not flee was killed. Finally the enraged Sa'dûn, who was beating the fleeing men with his camel stick to make them face about, had to flee himself. Besides he himself, his son Thâmer, and Eben Mejlâd only about thirty camel riders and twenty on horseback escaped, *thlâthîn dhelûl w-'ashrîn khayyâl.* All the rest were slain, not one being made captive. The Ḍana Muslim captured all the riding camels, arms, white military tents, and everything of which the enemy had robbed them during his whole expedition. Sa'dûn returned, bowed down with humiliation, would listen to no one, would not speak, and behaved like one intoxicated. He had to recognize his defeat as a just punishment, for, having been a friend, he had turned traitor and was suffering the consequences.

The theme of Sa'dûn's improprieties appears in the initial lines of the tale. He is "known both for his violent temper and stubbornness." He struggles excessively and unreasonably with the world about him. Because he does not accept any limitation on what he might achieve, he is a man who is himself troubled and disturbed. The theme develops in the next line: "As he was the owner of a large settled territory in Iraq, he was obeyed by a great number of warriors." He is a man who possesses a specific territory for himself. He is, more importantly, a man who dominates men and uses men to oppress other men. And now note carefully the crucial description of Sa'dûn as the scourge of the desert: he "had a flag of his own which he took with him on his raids, hoisting it over the camping grounds of the Arabs whom he had vanquished and robbed." Sa'dûn is a man who is obsessed with his own personal power. Because he is so obsessed, he fails to respect the persons of other men as he defiles the moral space of their camps with his flag, the symbol of his power. And then this lack of respect for what is close to other men is associated with a fatal flaw: "To show that he was not afraid of revenge, he loved to remain sitting by the flag in such camps for two or three hours after getting possession of them." Sa'dûn's obsession with his own personal power inevitably takes the form of a fascination with images of power. This is why he has a flag. This is why he incautiously sits in the camps of his victims right beside his flag. This captivation with images of power reveals that Sa'dûn does not recognize the realities of an uncertain political situation. He does not recognize that in the desert and steppe there is no firm basis for the exercise of personal power.[5] The stage is set in these opening lines for a demonstration that respect for other persons is the only proper and effective response to a situation of political uncertainty.

Sa'dûn's successful raid on the Rwala during which he suffered no losses is next mentioned. In response to this raid, Prince an-Nûri exercises a limited, defensive policy. Sa'dûn is powerful, and so an-Nûri does not try to respond with force. He tries instead to make peace by offering Sa'dûn his personal friendship. In doing so, an-Nûri overlooks Sa'dûn's aggression in the interest of peace. This policy fails, however, as a result of Sa'dûn's lack of regard for other persons. The latter makes personal agreements and friendships and then fails to respect those agreements and friendships: Sa'dûn "understood little of good faith but much of treachery, and paid no regard to the treaty." Then Sa'dûn's son, Thâmer, begins to ravage the Rwala in spite of the treaty between the chiefs. He even dares to attack the clan of Rwala chiefs (the Sha'lân), but on this occasion Thâmer suffers a defeat and barely escapes.

Note how the Rwala view their victory over Thâmer: "This brave defense naturally pleased the Rwala greatly, filling them with a sense of security." A similar observation accompanied the treaty between Sa'dûn and an-Nûri: "This gave the Arabs a feeling of security." As they undertake measured, defensive strategies in the interest of peace, which seem to succeed, the Rwala reach measured conclusions about the political situation. They feel slightly more secure, but they are not by any means unmindful of how unpredictable the situation is. They are neither overambitious nor overconfident.

Next the Rwala learn that the chief Eben Mejlâd had incited Sa'dûn against them. An-Nûri again undertakes a limited, but now more offensive policy against this weaker ally of a powerful man. He tries to subdue Eben Mejlâd by a raid upon his tribe and his camp.

Now contrast the responses of an-Nûri with those of Sa'dûn. Sa'dûn hears that his son has been defeated in a skirmish with the Rwala. Neither his son nor many of his followers were killed. Thâmer escaped with his men, even if only barely. Sa'dûn, however, sees this defeat as an *insult* to his person. Furious, he undertakes an unlimited offensive response "on a large scale." A minor affair precipitates a total war. Concerned only with his own personal pride, Sa'dûn egotistically brings down misery, not only upon the Rwala, but also upon his own people.

As Sa'dûn announces that he is setting out to seek vengeance, his true nature surfaces decisively: "Should any man of the Ḍana Muslim be amongst you, seize and fetter him to prevent him from warning Eben Sha'lân." Here we see in a trenchant way Sa'dûn's lack of respect for the persons of other men. He initiates a political policy by treating men like beasts. It is Sa'dûn's order to fetter men, we might also observe, which is associated with his eventual defeat. The warning of the fettered Rweyli tribesman enables an-Nûri to prepare for the onslaught of Sa'dûn's army.[6]

Following this there is one final contrast between an-Nûri and Sa'dûn. An-Nûri and his party are in the midst of plundering the camp of Eben Mejlâd when he learns of the coming attack. Even though the Rwala are about to secure their booty, "an-Nûri's mighty voice called them together and made them return to their kinsfolk without delay." It is the quality of an-Nûri's voice which commands, an intimate feature of his person. And at his command, the Rwala give up their booty even though it is at hand. They hold back. They defensively consolidate.

Following this scene, we find Sa'dûn commanding his followers. Let us observe how it differs from the preceding scene of an-Nûri commanding the Rwala. Sa'dûn announces his intentions and in doing so seeks to reassure his men and allies:

> Be comforted with what I shall now tell thee. Ye will get back the long-maned mares which the Rwala have taken from you, and yet more booty which we shall take from them. Only pray that they will not flee when they sight us. I have sworn an oath on my neck that I must catch an-Nûri even if I should have to pursue him as far as the Ḥawrân.

Sa'dûn entices his followers with images of the fruits of plunder. Sa'dûn, without any qualified reference to the will of God, promises his men that they will succeed by aggression. He only asks from God that the Rwala "not flee when they sight us." Sa'dûn believes unquestioningly in his own personal power, which he asks his followers to believe in too. Sa'dûn also takes an oath on his life that he will catch an-Nûri. He is so self-confident that he is ready to stake his life on his own personal will. He simply refuses to accept that his wishes are in question in a situation of political uncertainty. His vain announcement then concludes with a telling statement: "My spear with my flag I shall stick into the ash heap of his fireplace where he makes his coffee, for the accursed an-Nûri thinks too much of himself and brags about the numbers of his warriors." Here is a decisive association of an image of personal power and a contempt for other persons. Sa'dûn intends to defile an-Nûri's camp, the place where relatives and friends sit sociably drinking their coffee. He will strike at the most noble occasion of desert life. And then, even more trenchantly, he curses an-Nûri's very person as he envies an-Nûri's very person. Sa'dûn has no respect for other persons. Seeing others as a threat to his own fascination with power, he is driven to curse them, to dominate them, and to destroy them.

In the next episode, Sa'dûn and his mighty army of three thousand men are advancing upon the Rwala. To cool his passions, his soldiers are obliged to sing him songs which anticipate a triumph over the Rwala. As they do so, they enchant him with images of power. And now again, Sa'dûn fixes upon one last, crucial image of power: the falcon which seeks out the hare. At this point we see that Sa'dûn not only fails to respect the persons of other men, he even has no respect for his own family. He ridicules and disgraces his own son: "Look, comrades, at that hare! It has crawled into the bush, as did Thâmer, my son, before the falcon which is an-Nûri." Sa'dûn is a man who defiles what is close to his own person just as he would defile what is close to other men. And his son, Thâmer, "deeply ashamed on hearing such words," indicates now that he is tainted by this improper form of paternal authority which victimizes him: "O God, bring us to the people we are seeking and let us not pass by them or allow them to hide from us! May my father then see them with his own eyes - either to overcome or to send me against them with an army still larger than this!" Thâmer, too, only asks God that the Rwala not flee. Believing in the will of his father more than he should, he also assumes that superior forces will prevail.

The next episode describes the conflict between Sa'dûn's army and the Rwala and their allies. We see the Rwala political association contrasted with Sa'dûn's political association almost point for point. While the latter rules a specific domain and commands an army, an-Nûri observes that "the Rwala had built small camps scattered all over the country." Where Sa'dûn personally dominates his force, the Rwala force is a tentative association of several chiefs for transient political purposes: "Some days previous the Rwala had been joined by Eben Smeyr and Eben Me'jel with their Arabs." Where Sa'dûn is moving aggressively and ambitiously out of his home territory, an-Nûri and his allies move defensively and cautiously to a central verdant pasture of their tribal lands. Where Sa'dûn states what his followers will get from the expedition and promises them what he will do, an-Nûri merely "ordered them [the Rwala] to gather together at once." The latter then exercises his authority by a crucial omission: "Of the impending attack Eben Sha'lân did not say a word in order not to alarm them unnecessarily." An-Nûri realizes what he cannot do and what he cannot control. His authority takes the form of a critical omission in contrast to Sa'dûn's assertions and oaths.

With the appearance of the morning star, the battle begins. This is the moment of truth. Here we can understand just why an-Nûri and the Rwala behave as they do. The battle itself is described as a dangerous political situation, which is fundamentally of uncertain outcome:

They saw and heard group after group of Arabs *fleeing with both tents and herds.* On inquiring for the cause of their panic they were told that *an unknown enemy* was attacking the tents on the southern border of the scattered camps, and as the neighboring Arabs were *yet sleepy and ignorant of what was happening* they sought safety, not in resistance but in flight. The rifles thundered, and shots were heard on all sides. *The confusion grew.* [my italics]

The situation is desperate. Sa'dûn's flag appears on the horizon, "surrounded by a vast throng of men." A catastrophic Rwala defeat by a superior force is imminent: "It seemed as if the Rwala were about to perish." The penetration of Rwala territory, followed by the penetration of the scattered Rwala camps, is now followed by a scene of the penetration of the camps themselves. Rwala tents are pulled down. Rwala property is seized. Rwala women are killed. But now, in the camp and close to the family, we discover a spirited resistance: "The women defended their property as best they could; many had been killed, but none would run away, and all heaped abuse on their retreating husbands and brothers." That which Sa'dûn seeks to defile, the sacred moral space of the camp, becomes the source of Rwala resistance. This is where the real battle ensues. It is a battle to defend personal propriety against an unseemly man: "When the latter [the men] finally saw that even their women were resisting bravely, they declared: 'We should rather be killed today than let our women be wronged by the enemy,' and then a fight ensued compared to which all that happened before was mere play." The fight rages. Eventually, the Rwala and their allies draw together and in "a united body" attack the enemy. At this point, God "granted victory to the Rwala." He gives this victory, the narrator seems to hope and to suggest, because the Rwala realize the uncertainty of a political situation. In realizing this uncertainty they have proper respect for a sacred moral space close to the camp, the family, and the person.

As Sa'dûn begins to lose the battle, his improprieties come to the fore. He loses all control. He is enraged. He begins to treat his own followers like beasts as he beats them with a camel stick. There is then a terrible retribution for his improper behavior: "Besides he himself, his son Thâmer, and Eben Mejlâd only about thirty camel riders and twenty on horseback escaped. All the rest were slain." There is likewise a great reward for proper behavior: "The Dạna Muslim captured all the riding camels, arms, white military tents, and everything of which the enemy had robbed them during his whole expedition." And now at the conclusion of this tale we find a disgraced, but also an *inarticulate* Sa'dûn who "returned, bowed down with humiliation, would listen to no one, would not speak, and behaved like one intoxicated." Failing to recognize the character of the world in which he lives, Sa'dûn is unable to hear and unable to speak. His mind is a confused whirl in the midst of events, which he can neither understand nor accept. In the very last line, the moral of the tale surfaces explicitly: "He had to recognize his defeat as a just punishment, for, having been a friend, he had turned traitor and was suffering the consequences." It is above all his failure to respect the person which has led to Sa'dûn's reckoning. A respect for the person is where one begins to listen and to speak among the camel-herding nomads of the desert and steppe. Under circumstances in which men are constantly driven apart, a respect for the person is where one begins to put a peaceful and secure world together.

By a proper recognition of a boundary of political uncertainty, by a proper recognition of the nature of that boundary, a sense of propriety can take shape in the desert and steppe. Propriety takes shape close to home. One must respect a measured and cautious voice. One must respect the integrity of the person. One must respect the sanctity of the family. One must respect the friendly sociability of men who converse around a common fire. While all these qualities may seem vulnerable in the midst of men bent on political adventures, they also conceal a hidden energy, which is provoked at one's peril. Is this not still a familiar sentiment in the Near East today? Can we not still discover there such a theme, long since broken away from the circumstances of pastoral peoples and long since secured as the basis of a Near Eastern popular tradition? Surely this tale of Sa'dûn's improprieties would carry a clear message for peoples all over the present-day Near East, even as they would also sense the strangeness of its idiom rooted in a purely Bedouin time and place.

# 5. Political authority, the metaphor of scriptural signification, and the metaphor of a domestic covering

## 1

In the last narrative, we saw how a distinctive conception of propriety arose in connection with political uncertainty. The idiom of this propriety turned on matters that were close to home: the voice, the person, the family, and the friend. From this, we can understand why the political associations of the desert were largely constructed around such matters. There were no states in the desert. There was instead the power of the voice, the eminence of the person, the sanctity of the family, and the intimacy of companions dealing frankly and sincerely with one another. Beyond these domains there was a world of confusion and even violence.

In the following narrative, a similar problem is carried one step further. This narrative illustrates how a certain kind of formal awareness underlies the chief's deeds and words. Such an awareness is closely related, we shall find, to a metaphor of scriptural signification.[1] The tale begins with an occasion when the head chief of the Rwala is absent from his tribe. As a result of this absence, passions erupt among the Bedouins, an alliance fractures, and the Rwala tribal domain is penetrated by cattle-raiders. The Rwala attempt to deal with this situation by turning to a substitute chief, and this attempt raises the problem of the essential character of a chief's authority.

War between the Rwala and
the Western tribes (1902)

In 1902 the head chief Saṭṭâm eben Sha'lân was invited by the Turkish Government to visit Sultan Abdul-Hamid in Constantinople. When he had left home, the western tribes, seized by a desire for booty, began, although friends, *ṣâḥeb,* to attack Rwala camps. The worst offenders were the Ḥwêṭât, Sharârât, Beni Ṣakhr, and their allied tribes, *w-min yetba'hom.* For instance, they captured herds belonging to the Rwala at al-Khashshâbiyye and al-Ma'âṣer, the particular owners being the Nṣeyr and Der'ân kins of the Âl Mur'aḍ clan; *akhadhow ṭarsh min ar-rwala min âl mur'aḍ min âl nṣeyr w-min âl der'ân.* Finally the owners of the captured herds went in a body to the chief an-Nûri eben

Sha'lân to ask his help. An-Nûri then had the following letters written to the chief Abu Tâyeh of the Ḥwêṭât and to Âl Ḥâwi of the Sharârât:

"Up to this day we and you have been friends. Attacks on each other are not allowed, because we are true friends and comrades. *Benn al-ân ḥenna wiyyâkom ṣâḥeb w-lâ tjûz al-ghâra bênna w-ḥenna ṣiddîq w-rafîq.* We hope therefore that you will return, *te'addûn,* the herds you have taken from the Rwala. Should they attack you and take your herds let the despoiled parties come to us with a letter and we will return their property to them at once; *w-enn lô lann-ar-rwala ghâyerîn 'aleykom w-âkhdhîn lekom ḥelâl w-yejûna-l-manâqîṣ w-ma'hom maktûb minkom ennana ne'addîha bawfa'.* Do not believe that we would attack you treacherously! *naghîr 'aleykom bebawq.* Brave men will not stoop to deceit, *w-al-bawq mâ hw shîmat ajâwîd.* Greetings!"

The letters were handed to the plundered Rwala to deliver. These poor wretches had to wait on the chiefs Abu Tâyeh and Eben Jâzi and on the prominent men of the Sharârât and Ṣkhûr tribes for more than sixty days, imploring that their animals might be returned to them, but they got nothing at all and came back to their kinsfolk much cast down. Not long afterwards these chiefs raided the Rwala again and in an attack on the Kwâkbe camp near Khabra Qraye in al-Khunfa took all their she-camels. Dleymân ash-Shreyfi, one of the Kwâkbe chiefs, *min kbâr al-kwâkbe,* with an auxiliary troop composed of both Kwâkbe and Dughmân warriors, pursued the attackers for some distance but was surrounded by them and killed with all his twenty-one comrades. When this became known to the Rwala camping in the district of al-Khunfa, they tied a piece of black tent canvas to the neck of a riding camel, *dhelûl qalladûha shuqqa,* and sent her to an-Nûri eben Sha'lân who was at that time encamped in al-Ḥamâd.

As soon as the messengers arrived an-Nûri instantly ordered the tents to be loaded on camels and moved with all his people toward the territory occupied by the enemy, who were pasturing their herds near al-Bghêthiyye in the valley of Fejr, northwest of Teyma near the district of al-Ḥâlât. An-Nûri pitched his camp in the district of al-Ḥûl and sent word to the Kwâkbe and Dughmân, who were then dwelling near the oasis of Teyma:

"Stay where you are! We have come to you and will secure your rights for you, *netaqâḍi lekom min qowmkom,* if it be the will of God."

Following this message he approached them with his warriors only, at night found a concealed camping ground between them and the enemy, and issued this order:

"Drive your herds, *sarreḥow ṭarshkom,* in the morning to your right hand, in the direction of the enemy. They will assail them, will then be ambushed by us, and our rights will be secured, *netaqâḍi minhom.*"

In obedience to this order the Kwâkbe drove their herds in the morning towards the place where the enemy was stationed. On sighting them the outposts of the latter reported to their chiefs, who commanded their warriors at once to set out against the herds and to capture them. An-Nûri, who was observing every move of the enemy, fell upon them suddenly from the rear as they passed his hiding place and with his men began to slaughter them, *w-tewallûhom dhabḥ.* Towards noon about five hundred of the enemy had been killed. Only a small troop, *shirdhimaten qalîla,* saved itself by flight but with the Rwala in hot pursuit. The moment the fugitives reached their relatives, the tents were struck and loaded, but the Rwala rushed in before they could remove anything and took many of their tents, besides driving away a number of their herds. At last night covered them all, *ḥâl al-leyl 'ala jamî'*, and the pursuers became separated from the pursued. The Rwala returned home with a rich booty and the satisfaction of having avenged their fallen warriors, *metathârîn bzilmhom alli-ndhabaḥow.*

As a result of this defeat the Ḥwêṭât, Sharârât, and the Rmeyḥ eben Fâyez clan of the Beni Ṣakhr hurried their herds as well as their camels carrying their tents to the Beni Ṣakhr territory. There they explained what had happened to them and begged for assistance. The Beni Ṣakhr, calling upon the neighboring tribes to help them, *fazza'ow kill ḥawâlîhom min al-'orbân,* collected a multitude, the number of which was known to God alone, and erected a war camp between Umm al-'Amad and al-Libben, while in the meantime the territory vacated by them had been occupied by the Rwala. The Rwala tribal symbol, Abu-d-Duhûr, was rocking on a camel ahead of their first column, the rest following in the customary order. The Rwala also erected a war camp, but east of al-Libben. The Beni Ṣakhr, who relied not a little on their great numbers, shouted so as to be heard by their adversaries that they would capture both an-Nûri and his Rwala.

It came to pass, however, that just at that time God directed the steps of the head chief Saṭṭâm from the Sultan in Constantinople to the camp at al-Libben, where the Rwala welcomed him with boundless joy. Defiling before him one after another, *qâmat al-'arâḍât 'endahom,* they vowed to persevere and to revenge themselves. Both sides thus camped for nine days in full view of each other, *w-dâmow 'ala hal-manâkh metanâwakhîn beni ṣakhr w-ar-rwala tis'at ayyâm menawwakhîn al-kill minhom*, exchanging shots all that time. On the tenth day they finally attacked each other and changed their position, and a day ensued for them on which even the hair of a boy just weaned might have turned gray, *yeshîb al-aṭfâl.* The dust whirled up by the horses mingled with the smoke of the gunpowder, and a wild storm raged from early morning till almost the middle of the afternoon, *w-shubek 'ajâj al-kheyl ma' dukhân al-bârûd w-ṣârat 'arṣaten 'aẓîmaten min aṣ-ṣubḥ ila qerîb al-'aṣr*. God gave the victory to the Rwala. They overcame the multitude whose numbers none knew, threw themselves on their tents, and took them with all the furniture and supplies in them. In addition they captured several herds of camels and pursued the enemy till sunset. Then they returned to their tents, rejoicing over the victory. After a further stay of a few days near al-Libben they vacated the Beni Ṣakhr territory and returned to their own lands.

After their defeat at al-Libben the Beni Ṣakhr made continuous raids against the Rwala, oppressing their clans whose pastures were located on the border. Their commander, *'aqîd*, was usually Ṭrâd eben Zeben. Fortune favored him, *misla' w-ḥaqîq*, and he was numbered among the brave men, *w-kân yin'edd min ar-rajâl.* And so it happened after a few years that he collected his fellow tribesmen and the strangers who used to take part in his raids, and surprised a small Rwala camp near a settlement in the vicinity of Edhra'ât. The camp attacked belonged to the Swâlme clan, which was commanded by the chief Eben Jandal. Although he had received information of the impending raid, it was impossible for him to escape, and to get help was also out of the question, as there were no Arabs related to them in the whole wide neighborhood. Ṭrâd eben Zeben approached the Swâlme camp before sunrise, pitched his war tents, and harried the Swâlme till the afternoon. Yet whenever he attacked them, even penetrating into the camp, they ran out of their tents and beat the attackers back until they ejected them completely. Tiring at length of such attacks, *ṭâbat nafseh,* Ṭrâd retreated with shame, but afterwards, whenever he learned of some smaller Rwala camp, he surprised it and drove away all the herds found there. Finally God determined to humble him.

Ṭrâd eben Zeben attacked among others the camp of the al-Qa'âq'a clan of the Rwala, situated near the head of the *she'îb* [watercourse] of Gharâyes. There were about sixty tents there. Capturing all their herds, Ṭrâd hastened with them to his kinsfolk. But at that moment Allâh brought the Sha'lân kin, which was migrating just then, across his tracks. The Sha'lân recognized the tracks as made by a troop of raiders heading east against their fellow tribesmen and at once decided to go in their pursuit, *aṭlabûh.* Following the tracks they kept a sharp lookout on all sides and were finally rewarded by sighting at some distance the raiders, who were returning with a rich booty. Concealing themselves in a place favorable for ambush, they waited for the raiders to come up with them and then attacked with such swiftness that, even before Ṭrâd and his men were aware of it, the Sha'lân both on horseback and on camels were in their midst, *w-elya' mâ ya'lam ṭrâd w-alli ma'eh illa w-al-kheyl w-al-jeysh shâbakathom,* dealing them blow after blow. Ṭrâd soon saw himself compelled to abandon his booty and seek safety in a wild flight to the west. His losses amounted to eight hundred men, while the Sha'lân, besides recovering the stolen herds, also captured many she-camels and inflicted such a defeat on Ṭrâd as he had never met before.

The narrator begins by fixing a specific year during which the head chief of the Rwala, Saṭṭâm, was absent. On this occasion when there was no tribal authority present on the scene, the western tribes, "although friends," are "seized with a desire for booty." They begin to attack the Rwala camps and to plunder the Rwala herds. The tribes responsible for the cattle-raids are all carefully named, but they are also all localized in the west. This is the land where the sun sets, the land of darkness and obscurity.

There is a precise attribution of the absence of the chief to the circumstances of a particular year. There is a precise attribution of the political problem to specific tribes with specific intents. Underlying this precision, however, there is also a vague hint of a figurative fear. The chief is a man whose deeds and words are the basis of peace and security. As the central institution of political authority, his function is to construct a peaceful political world. He must convince men that they must control themselves, deal frankly and sincerely with one another, and recognize each other's differing self-interests. As this institution of political authority disappears, passions erupt in obscure quarters and a political peace is shattered. If we read a little further, this vague hint of a figurative fear becomes a little more specific.

To deal with this situation, the Rwala tribesmen turn to an-Nûri as a substitute for the absent Saṭṭâm. An-Nûri writes letters to the former, now hostile, Rwala allies. In this written communication, he invokes the propriety of true friendship and comradeship as he condemns the attacks of the Rwala allies. At the same time he outlines a formal arrangement for settling intertribal disputes by means of written communications among the chiefs.

Now there is a certain parallel between the relationship of an-Nûri to the head chief Saṭṭâm and the relationship of the letter to an-Nûri. An-Nûri speaks as the representative of the true head chief, just as the letter itself represents an-Nûri's chiefly voice. But the real chief is absent, just as an-Nûri's chiefly voice is absent from the letter. And so the status of the letter as a substitute for an-Nûri's absent voice recalls the status of an-Nûri as a substitute for the absent chief.

And if we examine the contents of the letter, we find that the possibility of such an interpretation is raised precisely because the letter seems specifically designed to suppress such an interpretation. In the letter an-Nûri appeals to true comradeship and friendship as though he were intent on making up for the missing personal warmth of an immediate vocal communication. In the letter an-Nûri confidently outlines a formal arrangement for communications among chiefs as though he were intent on ignoring his own uncertain status as a chiefly substitute. And then there is a final line whose import is far from clear: "Do not believe that we would attack you treacherously! Brave men will not stoop to deceit."

What has an-Nûri done that might lead anyone to believe that he was contemplating some treachery or deceit? The only thing he has done is to compose the letter in question. But is there indeed something treacherous and deceitful about the letter itself? The content of this document appeals to the warmth of a genuine personal relationship and is composed with the assurance of a genuine head chief. But the form of this document announces that it is no more than a device of substitutions. This letter writes an-Nûri's voice in the form of one vocalization substituting for another.[2] While its content cries out, "I am genuine!" its form cries out, "I am a substitution for what is genuine!" And so as an-Nûri concludes his letter, an awareness of some contradiction between the content and the form of his words settles upon him. He tries to ward off this awareness by denying that he intends some treachery or deceit.

The course of events will eventually reveal that the true significance of the letter is just the reverse of these interpretations. The narrator has carefully designed his tale, we shall find, to demonstrate that men of peace, who seem to be vulnerable, are in fact powerful. The substitution of one chief for another and the substitution of a letter for a voice are really a sign of strength, even though at this point they seem to be a sign of weakness. But the affairs of the Rwala will get still worse, before getting any better.

The plundered Rwala take the letters of an-Nûri to the chiefs Abu Tâyeh and Eben Jâzi where "these poor wretches had to wait on the prominent men" of the Rwala allies. They wait for sixty days. They are ignominiously reduced to begging for the return of their herds. They receive nothing. They return to their own kinsfolk "much cast down." The Rwala are shamed and disgraced. Lacking a real chief, the Rwala must sue for peace. And as they sue for peace, the very weakness and vulnerability of their position come to light. Men who bear letters are men who can be ignored. Men who bear letters are shamed and disgraced by their powerlessness.

The western tribes are now convinced that the Rwala are impotent, and they become far more bold. Their plundering of Rwala herds begins again, and at one point, a Rwala chief and twenty-one of his comrades are massacred. The situation has now completely deteriorated. An-Nûri has appealed to comradeship among chiefs as a basis for peace. The former allies have responded by killing Rwala comrades and by killing a Rwala chief. The camel with a black cloth tied around its neck, a sign of death by aggression, reaches the camp of an-Nûri. Having sent a frank and sincere letter proposing a formal arrangement for openly settling differences, an-Nûri receives in reply a dark sign of death from the men of the west. The basis for peace has now been irrevocably destroyed.

At this moment, the situation would seem to be one of complete despair. There is no real chief. Political disorder grows. The world is coming apart. There is no one to put it together again. But at this point, an-Nûri, a man of peace who leads men of peace, has been irrevocably pushed into war. And as this chief and his tribe begin to pursue war, we shall discover a strength concealed within what seemed to be indications of weakness. Men of peace, when pushed into the pursuit of war, we shall find, prove to be formidable opponents.

The remainder of the narrative consists of four separate episodes. They can be summarized as follows:

1. An-Nûri ambushes a group of enemy raiders by means of a formal arrangement. The narration of an-Nûri's strategy illustrates how space and time take on a definition in connection with political conflict.

2. The Rwala are described as a vivid tribal presence, the form of which recalls the letters of an-Nûri. The Rwala triumph over their enemies, who are described as an obscure and disorderly multitude.

3. The wild life of cattle-raiders is contained on the margins of the Rwala tribal domain. One hero who plunders the peripheral camps of the Rwala is surprised and defeated by men who emerge from the concealment of their tents.

4. The wild life of cattle-raiders is decisively suppressed. Adventurers operating away from home in a strange land are dealt a death blow by hidden tribal authorities operating in the familiar space and time of their own tribal domain.

As these episodes progress, the narrator will demonstrate how a secure tribal domain must be constructed around the problem of political violence. Metaphors of scriptural signification and domestic covering, which appear in episodes 2 and 3 respectively, convey the formal qualities of such a construction.

## 2

The first of the four episodes begins with a description of an-Nûri taking the field against the enemy:

> As soon as the messengers arrived an-Nûri instantly ordered the tents to be loaded on camels and moved with all his people toward the territory occupied by the enemy, who were pasturing their herds near al-Bghêthiyye in the valley of Fejr, northwest of Teyma near the district of al-Ḥâlât. An-Nûri pitched his camp in the district of al-Ḥûl and sent word to the Kwâkbe and Dughmân, who were then dwelling near the oasis of Teyma.

Note how the narrator carefully specifies the names of various political groups and their spatial interrelationships. As the Rwala chief moves into action, various groups and the location of these groups become strategically important. In the description of the battle between the Rwala and the enemy which follows, the narrator carefully specifies a series of strategic movements, stationings, and observations. An-Nûri arrives "at night" and conceals himself "between" the two Rwala clans and the enemy raiding party. He tells the former to drive their herds out "in the morning to your right hand, in the direction of the enemy." "On sighting them," the enemy outposts inform their chiefs, and the latter, without reflecting, command "their warriors to set out at once." Meanwhile an-Nûri is "observing every move of the enemy." His party falls "upon them suddenly from the rear as they passed his hiding place." The episode is designed to illustrate how the movements and stationings of groups are crucial aspects of a political conflict. It illustrates how space and time take on a definition as men contest other men. This aspect of the episode is intended to clarify the basis of an-Nûri's political strategy. In advising the two clans to send out their herds in the morning, he contrives a space and time in order to defeat the enemy. And the enemy does not stop to consider that what they see is a contrivance. They immediately accept their sighting of the defenseless Rwala herds at its face value.

An-Nûri fashions a political scene, which is likely to be misinterpreted. He has a sense of form. The enemy does not realize that appearances must be interpreted. They have no sense of form. Let us recall the letter. The letter proposed a plan for peace based upon a formal arrangement – just as an-Nûri now conducts a plan for war also based upon a formal arrangement. The enemy thought that the letters from an-Nûri were a sign of weakness, and they therefore ignored and shamed the bearers of his letters. Similarly now they think the defenseless herds represent an easy prey. Without considering that what they see has been formally arranged, they rush too precipitously to seize the herds they desire. At this point the concluding lines of an-Nûri's letter take on a new significance: "Do not believe that we would attack you treacherously! Brave men will not stoop to deceit." This is actually an assurance that the letter as a formal arrangement is a frank and sincere plan for peace rather than a deception aimed at treachery. The assurance is necessary because an-Nûri, as a man who knows the power of formal arrangements, is able to use them strategically for either peace or war. An-Nûri, who is confidently aware of his political capacities, is seeking to reassure the Rwala allies by renouncing a powerful weapon. The allies mistakenly interpret a sign of a powerful weapon as a sign of weakness and begin to plunder the Rwala herds once again. At this point, an-Nûri *deceives* a group of cattle-raiders with his formal arrangement and then *treacherously* attacks them from the rear. In doing so, he does not contradict the meaning of his letter, he both clarifies and confirms its meaning. He has been pushed unwillingly into war and therefore into a strategy of deceit and treachery. The qualities of a man who understands the formal basis of peace are the same as those of a man who understands the formal basis of war.

The initial political situation which led to the letter as well as the political degeneration which followed appear retrospectively in a new light. There was never a problem of the absence of authority. There only seemed to be such a problem to men who lacked any understanding of the formal dimensions of political experience. As a sign of an-Nûri's recognition of the power of formal arrangements, the letter actually indicated the presence of a potent Rwala authority. The letter did not therefore exacerbate the problem of an absent authority. The political situation grew worse because the western tribes could only respect a real head chief who was visibly on the scene, plainly in command, and concretely backed by men with mounts and weapons. It is the blindness of impulsive men who take things at their face value which leads to political degeneration, and in the final analysis, that same blindness will also lead inevitably to their defeat.

An apparent occasion of weakness proves to be an occasion for the revelation of true strength. An apparent absence of authority (there is a need for a substitute) is an indication of the true presence of authority (there is a formal substitution and thereby the very revelation that authority actually rests on form). This is the message of the story. The three concluding episodes solidify this lesson as they illustrate how the integrity of the Rwala tribal domain is reconstructed in the course of a series of political conflicts. Let us now read the conclusion of the first episode.

As the battle rages during the day, the power of the Rwala is clarified: "Towards noon about five hundred of the enemy had been killed." Then the first of three telling reversals concludes this initial victory: "Only a small troop saved itself by flight but with the Rwala in hot pursuit. The moment the fugitives reached their relatives, the tents were struck and loaded, but the Rwala rushed in before they could remove anything and took many of their tents, besides driving away a number of their herds." It is not really the Rwala camps and herds which are vulnerable, but the camps and herds of adventurous men who impetuously provoke others.

There is one more important feature of this episode. As the narrator describes the conflict, he insists upon the association of political actions with the course of the light of day. The action begins "in the morning." It reaches a climax "towards noon." It ends as "night covered them all and the pursuers became separated from the pursued." This tale does not suggest that a concern with forms is to be preferred to a concern with political experience. This tale suggests that a concern with forms is a potent aspect of political experience, and so there is an insistent association of political actions with the light of day. It is during the actual course of a struggle that the formal dimensions of political experience can be vividly perceived.[3]

## 3

The next episode recounts the great intertribal war. The cattle-raiders return to their home territory and ask their allies and kinsmen for support. The Beni Ṣakhr tribe responds and successfully solicits the help of other neighboring tribes. A great war party is assembled, "a multitude, the number of which was known to God alone." This war party is massive, but obscure in its form and numbers. The Beni Ṣakhr erect a war camp implicitly where the sun sets, west of al-Libben (between Umm al-'Amad and al-Libben). A line or so later, the Rwala will erect a war camp explicitly where the sun rises, east of al-Libben. The Rwala are then described as a clearly limned vision: "The Rwala tribal symbol, Abu-d-Duhûr, was rocking on a camel *ahead of their first column, the rest following in the customary order*" [my italics]. The tribal symbol itself is a striking visual symbol. It consists of a large litter several meters in width and standing several meters high when mounted on a camel. Note how the form of the appearance of the Rwala tribe, the men of the east, differs from the form of the appearance of the enemy war party, the men of the west. We see clearly the Rwala tribal litter high on a camel where it is rocking gently with the animal's movements. We see this litter heading up a string of columns arranged in "customary order."

In the lines which follow, the Beni Ṣakhr and the Rwala tribes are compared as two different kinds of tribal entities: "The Beni Ṣakhr, who relied not a little on their great numbers, shouted so as to be heard by their adversaries that they would capture both an-Nûri and his Rwala." The enemy relies upon its massive numbers, rather than a form of strategic procedure. The enemy shouts out its hostile intentions, rather than reflecting and considering. And the enemy again misperceives an-Nûri and his Rwala as weak and vulnerable. Now let us turn to the parallel description of the Rwala which follows. At this critical moment, when a great war is imminent, the Rwala head chief, Saṭṭâm, by the grace of God, reappears upon the scene. The chief is now present and visible once again, and the Rwala tribe is whole once again. Here as the chief reappears on the field of battle, the form of the Rwala tribe is displayed: "The Rwala welcomed him with boundless joy. Defiling before him *one after another*, they vowed to persevere and to revenge themselves" [my italics]. The Rwala tribe has been previously described as defiling in columns across the landscape in an orderly way. Now each member of the tribe is described as defiling individually one after the other before their chief.

These descriptions not only contrast the disorderly enemy party with the orderly Rwala. The two formal descriptions of the Rwala ever so slightly suggest in turn a metaphor of scriptural signification. A visible string of orderly columns moves across the landscape. The moving Rwala war party takes the form of a textual line. Before their chief, the Rwala pass in succession and visibly display their hostile intentions. The signifiers of this orderly text are warriors. Here on the field of battle, the Rwala tribe is visible. And as the tribe becomes visible, we see a form which is reminiscent of the appearance of the text of an-Nûri's letter. When the chief is present, when the tribe is assembled, we see the manifestation of a certain kind of "formal arrangement." It is as though the form of a chiefly voice has appeared in the shape of a party of hostile warriors. Now, the Beni Ṣakhr and their allies might well wish that they had respected the seemingly impotent letters of an-Nûri as they perceive the manifestation of these formal devices in a visibly strong and energetic form.

In the following lines the narrator describes the great intertribal war and emphasizes once again how political space and time take shape around political violence. As he insists upon the importance of form, he also insists upon the connection of form with political violence. In the midst of a great intertribal war, we see how space and time are articulated around a confrontation of the tribes. First, there is an articulation of time. As the two war parties face one another, the days are marked. As the two war parties exchange shots, the time of day is marked: "Both sides thus camped *for nine days* in full view of each other, *exchanging shots all that time*" [my italics]. Next, as serious hostilities commence, there is an articulation of space: "On the tenth day they finally attacked each other *and changed their position*" [my italics]. And next, as the battle reaches a climax, there is a scene so charged with articulations that it ages its witness: "and a day ensued for them on which even the hair of a boy just weaned might have turned grey." So much happens in the midst of this battle that a newborn child would grow old in the course of his experience of that single day. And next, the telling phrases which describe the very climax of the battle follow: "The dust whirled up by the horses mingled with the smoke of the gunpowder, and a wild storm raged from early morning till almost the middle of the afternoon." This is a clouded, wild, and raging scene of violence. It encapsulates and contains within itself a great disorder. It cannot be sorted out. One cannot make sense of it.

In this description of a great intertribal war, we see how space and time are articulated around the problem of political violence. But then we also see that the very climactic moment of political violence is a clouded moment of spatial and temporal disorder. The world is put together around the problem of political violence. The world comes apart at the very moment of political violence. This is the perception of men who appreciate the value of formal arrangements. They know that a world of peace and security rests upon constructing a political space and time so that political violence is contained. They know that the world must take shape around the problem of violence just as they know that the moment when passions emerge and violence ensues is a moment of uncontrollable disorder.

In the end, "God gave the victory to the Rwala." The Rwala chiefs and warriors cannot by themselves triumph. No men can decisively triumph over political violence in the desert and steppe. Nevertheless, a conclusion follows from the implications of the design of this tale. The narrator suggests that God gives the victory to those who recognize the proper forms by which one must respond to political violence. In the final analysis, an awareness of the importance of formal arrangements for the construction of a political peace is a moral quality. And so following the battle, the good are rewarded and the bad are punished. The Rwala overrun the camps of the numberless multitude, seizing their tents, along with their furniture and supplies, and several herds of camels. The enemy is the "pursued . . . until sunset" when darkness once again settles over the desert scene.

## 4

After the victory of the Rwala, the Beni Ṣakhr, nevertheless, make "continuous raids against the Rwala, oppressing their clans whose pastures were located on the border." With the decisive defeat of the former Rwala allies, conflict persists, but only in a marginal area. For the first time, we have the suggestion of a Rwala tribal domain of peace that is set apart from an external world of war. This domain is bounded by a zone of political uncertainty. In this zone the heroic life flourishes as Ṭrâd raids the Rwala for years. Eventually, however, this hero suffers a setback. Note well the design of this account of a decisive conflict. Almost no details of a battle strategy are given. The dimensions of Ṭrâd's defeat do not seem to be of impressive proportions. What is the significance of this episode? Why is it included in the narrative?

Let us first pick up the theme of marginality which colors the description. Ṭrâd's group is itself a marginal group of men. It is composed of "his fellow tribesmen" as well as "strangers." This is the sort of motley band of adventurers one discovers in the tribal marches rather than at the center of tribal life. And now compare the narrator's description of the Rwala victims of Ṭrâd's raid. The Swâlme camp, which Ṭrâd attacks, is only a small group of Rwala allies. They are located on the border of the Rwala tribal territory. They have no close relations in the vicinity to whom they might turn for help. Their escape route back to the center of the tribal domain is cut off. They represent a borderline case where a tribal domain becomes vulnerable. Yet unlike the motley band of Ṭrâd, they are nevertheless on home ground. They have received information of the impending raid. They move in a familiar space and time, even if on its margins.

Ṭrâd attacks and harries the Rwala camp through the day, but encounters unexpected resistance. The actual basis of this resistance is never really explained. Instead the following description of his aggressions is given: "Yet whenever he attacked them, even penetrating into the camp, they ran out of their tents and beat the attackers back until they ejected them completely." Ṭrâd and his raiders penetrate into the very midst of the Rwala camp. There seems to be no one to defend it, and victory seems near. But suddenly, men appear from their domestic coverings: "they ran out of their tents and beat back the attackers." Ṭrâd and his raiders are mysteriously ejected by an initially unseen force.

The deserted tents suggest a domestic scene vulnerable to aggression, but instead the tents conceal a protective energy. This takes us back to the beginning of the tale. The letters of an-Nûri were a sign of an *inapparent* power. Seemingly, they revealed a condition of weakness, but in fact they revealed the presence of a real strength. Now the image of tents, which conceal a protective energy, associates an inapparent power with a domestic scene. This suggests that a recognition of the power of formal arrangements, the source of an-Nûri's unseen strength, is somehow characteristic of men who are on their home ground in their home camps.

At the conclusion of the episode, the second of three telling reversals occurs and this minor battle is explicitly connected with the initial events of the tale. Ṭrâd, the man who leads the heroic life of raiding, exhausts himself in this struggle with a concealed domestic energy: "Tiring at length of such attacks, Ṭrâd retreated with shame." As heroism exhausts itself in wild and desperate actions, heroism is personally touched and disgraced. It is really these cattle-raiders who are shameful, not those peaceloving Rwala who carried an-Nûri's letters to the chiefs of the western tribes. This accomplished, the narrator has only to illustrate how the Rwala tribal domain solidifies against a threatening external world. As he does so, we see more clearly how the tribal domain itself conceals a potent, domestic energy.

## 5

Ṭrâd continues to raid the Rwala. He tries to surprise some small defenseless Rwala camp and to drive away its herds. The last episode begins with the conclusion of such a raid. Ṭrâd has plundered the herds of the al-Qa'âq'a clan and is returning to his kinsfolk. In the meantime, the Sha'lân kin, the kin from whom the Rwala chiefs are chosen, happen to cross the tracks of Ṭrâd and his raiders. As the representatives of a Rwala protective authority enter the scene, we are presented with a description of men moving surely within a familiar space and time, clearly recognizing the features of their surroundings, and accurately interpreting their significance. The Sha'lân are aware that the tracks heading east are the tracks of raiders coming from the west, and they set out in pursuit of Ṭrâd:

> Following the tracks they kept a *sharp lookout* on all sides and were finally *rewarded by sighting* at some distance the raiders, who were returning with a rich booty. *Concealing themselves* in a place favorable for ambush, they waited for the raiders to come up with them and then attacked with such swiftness that, *even before Ṭrâd and his men were aware of it*, the Sha'lân . . . were in their midst, dealing them blow after blow. Ṭrâd soon *saw himself compelled* to abandon his booty and seek safety *in a wild flight to the west*. [my italics]

The Sha'lân kin are able to hide themselves strategically within a familiar space. Ṭrâd and his men are caught out in the open and offguard in a strange territory. The description of the rout of Ṭrâd's party turns, as in the first episode, upon the awareness of space and time by one party and the lack of awareness of the other party. In this final episode, however, the crucial theme is the contrast between the Rwala protective authorities operating surely and swiftly in familiar space and Ṭrâd's political adventurers taking extreme risks as they look for opportunities in a strange land. As the Sha'lân triumph over the raiders, their victory demonstrates that the formal dimensions of political experience are on the side of peaceful men. These are men who do not go abroad in order to plunder other men, but who stay at home in the familiar space and time of their own tribal domain.

Ṭrâd suffers a final terrible defeat at the hands of protective domestic authorities and is forced to "seek safety in a wild flight to the west," the land of darkness and obscurity. The narrator then concludes his tale with the last of three telling reversals. He attributes eight hundred dead to the enemy on this occasion, the largest, and surely the most exaggerated, number of casualties cited in the entire tale. The stigmas of obscurity and death are added to the loss of herds and tents and the shamefulness of a life of heroism. The bad situation which followed upon an-Nûri's letter-writing has now been completely reversed, and with this the narration comes to an end.

## 6

As he begins his account, the narrator fixes his attention on the absence of the head chief Saṭṭâm. This absence raises the question: "Is the authority of the Rwala chiefs substantial or insubstantial?" Each of the ceremonial narratives of raiding and warfare that we have considered could be said to deal with such a question. Each tale addresses, more or less successfully, a train of events that has raised a doubt about whether the Rwala chiefs were effective or ineffective. As in the other narratives of Chapter 4, here we learn how the Rwala chiefs follow certain kinds of practical procedures, which are designed to cope with a situation of political uncertainty. All of the ideals and values which were associated with the behavior of Rwala chiefs in the other narratives are either explicitly or implicitly a feature of this narrative too. However, the narrator of this tale carries this problem to its very limits. He attempts both to generalize these ideals and values of chiefly behavior and to ground them in the very setting of a Bedouin way of life. The letters of an-Nûri, a metaphor of scriptural signification, are the key to this effort.

In the world of the North Arabian Bedouins, intertribal peace could sometimes be based upon frank discussions and sincere agreements among chiefs. Initially, the letters of an-Nûri are simply the instruments of this specific practical procedure. An-Nûri proposes a formal arrangement for regular communications among the chiefs by means of an exchange of letters. He attempts to institutionalize a basis for discussions and agreements. In the course of events, however, this attempt fails, and the letters are reinterpreted. They are seen as an image of chiefly authority. They stand for and make visible general qualities of behavior which are attributed to the Rwala chiefs. In this respect, the letters of an-Nûri reveal the shape of a chiefly voice that speaks for peace. This is a voice that mirrors a recognition of the *formal dimensions* of experience precisely because it is a voice that consists of a *formal arrangement* of inscribed signs upon a piece of paper. A metaphor of scriptural signification, we find, suggests how a kind of relationship between behavior and experience is the basis of peace in the desert and steppe. This relationship of behavior and experience is generally characteristic of thoughtful and realistic men who consider how the setting of political experience favors a strategy of peace.

On the occasion in question, events proved that the formal dimensions of experience *were* decisively on the side of men of peace. Impulsive adventurers who repeatedly took extreme risks by going abroad into strange lands were defeated in the end by men who remained in the familiar space and time of their own tribal domain and obeyed the strategic instructions of their reflective chiefs. The train of events provided the narrator with an opportunity to substantiate the authority of chiefs who stand for peace. In seizing this opportunity, he comes to see a minor feature of an intertribal conflict which lasted several years, the letters of an-Nûri, as a general symbol of a peaceful chiefly authority, and he comes to see the very setting of a Bedouin way of life, the familiarity of men with the space and time of their own tribal domain, as the solid ground of such a peaceful chiefly authority.[4] And so the narrator works his magic. His listeners forget that many of the Bedouins were interested in the rewards of adventures abroad. They forget that most of the Bedouins were persistently afflicted by insecurity and threatened with violence because of this interest. They forget, in other words, that tribe and chief were at best only a marginal basis of peace in the desert and steppe.

Curiously, however, the marginality of tribe and chief is clearly revealed by the very metaphor which stands for and makes visible a peaceful chiefly authority among the Bedouins. The crucial feature of the letters of an-Nûri, as an image of chiefly authority, is their apparent *insubstantiality*. They are nothing but pieces of paper with markings upon them. What indeed is the significance of such a flimsy device among wild men with mounts and weapons? Who might listen to this silent voice of peace amid the pounding of hooves, the clatter of swords and lances, and the explosions of rifles?

Initially, the narrator insists upon the ephemeral quality of a peaceful chiefly authority, but he does so for tactical reasons. As his account develops, he is able to suggest that a peaceful chiefly authority, which at first seemed to be an evanescent feature of a Bedouin way of life, was in fact a substantial center of such a life. By admitting the worst at the outset of his tale, he can thereby make the most of a favorable train of events. In this way, he is able to conceive of the letters of an-Nûri, mere pieces of paper with markings upon them, as a symbol of very real power. The Rwala tribe is portrayed as the transformation of a flimsy device into a potent political instrument. Moving across the landscape, the Rwala tribal columns are imaged as a vivid textual line. Parading before the head chief, the Rwala warriors are imaged as the signifiers of this textual line. And so tactically the narrator is able to dispel, with the magic of a tale, all doubts about how tribe and chief could be a basis for peace, even though his very images reveal the marginality of these Bedouin political institutions.

Among the North Arabian Bedouins, the tribe could not be convincingly conceived as a society in which personal relationships were determined by the norms of a tradition and group relationships were coordinated by institutions. The tribal chief was therefore not conceivable as the representative of a religious cosmology nor as the administrator of a political regime. Instead, the tribe was more nearly a strategic construction, while the chief was more nearly its reflective architect. In this regard, the Bedouin narrative provides a more insightful analysis of the character of tribe and chief than can be found in the writings of anthropologists. However, the narrative also reveals more than the precise mechanisms of a marginal Bedouin polity. Even though the North Arabian Bedouins had no communities based upon religious traditions and political institutions, we find the elements of a peculiar politico-religious idiom in the narrative. Whenever and wherever the problem of insecurity and violence diminished in intensity, we might well presume, this idiom could have become the foundation of a religious cosmology and a political regime.

As a form of metaphor, for example, the letters of an-Nûri are akin to the notion of sacred scriptures in Arabia. Among the townsmen and villagers, scriptures are typically conceived of as the revelations of a merciful divinity who is immanent in the shape of the world at large. In a similar way, the letters of an-Nûri suggest that peace among men is favored by the formal dimensions of political experience. Among the townsmen and villagers, scriptures are also associated with a politico-religious code of personal behavior by which social iniquity and political disorder can be suppressed. Again in a similar way, the letters of an-Nûri suggest that a personal recognition of the formal dimensions of political experience is the source of a power by which good men overcome bad men. Indeed, the Arabian notion of scriptures can be viewed as an intensification and solidification of the Bedouin metaphor of scriptural signification. Scriptures call for a personal moral response to problems of social iniquity and political disorder by announcing the presence of a transcendental authority behind the design of the world at large. This notion of scriptures, one might say, is a more substantial metaphor of scriptural signification, which reflects the more substantial possibility of conceiving, if not realizing, a secure community of peace in the settlements of Arabia.

These parallels indicate how a background of pastoral nomadism lies behind some of the central motifs of religious traditions and political institutions in the Near East. Thus a vision which took shape among pastoral peoples of the Near Eastern hinterlands eventually became a fundamental element of Islamic civilization. It even seems possible that the invention of phonetic writing may have also been in some way associated with an even more archaic form of this same vision. In the narrative that we have just considered, a written document is seen as a symbol of a voice which speaks for peace. The narrator therefore draws upon the idea of phonetic writing in order to convey the general features of a peaceful chiefly authority. However, it is at least plausible that historically this association of a written document and the qualities of a chief was reversed. That is to say, the vision of a voice of peace, as a formal arrangement, could have inspired the idea of a representation of the voice as a formal arrangement. If so, the invention of phonetic writing could in some way be linked with the politico-religious idioms of Near Eastern pastoral nomadism. In so far as this might have been the case, the political experiences of pastoral peoples in the eastern Mediterranean also played a part in the history of Western civilization; for the modern Western world is almost inconceivable apart from the democratic, egalitarian, and technical implications of the alphabet, which originated among the Semitic peoples of the Near East.

In any case, it is clear that the Bedouins could have understood the significance of the Koran when it first appeared on the scene, even though they would have certainly understood it differently from the Arabian townsmen and villagers. In the Bedouin narratives of raiding and warfare, the letters of an-Nûri represent an image of chiefly authority; nevertheless, these letters are devices which have a concrete place in the conduct of a political affair. The Bedouins are necessarily men of action, given their situation as camel-herding nomads. They may sometimes insist that an active response to political problems must take a certain form, but they are not inclined to consider a purely formal response to political problems. They are therefore only fascinated by forms which refer to the properties of active responses. The Bedouins, in other words, could perhaps understand the Koran as a book that was the basis of a politico-religious community, but they would be inclined to stress all those ways in which the Koran prescribed political actions rather than religious rituals.[5]

**7**

Another feature of the tale - the tents that conceal energetic men capable of resisting Ṭrâd and his adventurers - also touches upon this problem of how the politico-religious conceptions of the Bedouins were different from those of the townsmen and villagers of Arabia. The metaphor of a domestic covering is one of the most important and distinctive themes of kinship and marriage in traditional Arabia. Let us consider only the veiling of women as one example of an Arabian concern with the seclusion of women from public life. Like most tribal peoples in the Near East, the Arabian Bedouins frequently despised the veiling of women, and they were not normally preoccupied with the seclusion of women. The practice of veiling was, instead, a more typical feature of the Arabian settlements, where the seclusion of women was often one of the fundamental principles of social morality.[6] If we compare the significance of the veil and the significance of the tent in the last tale, we can see how these two metaphors reveal a contrast in the social norms of pastoralists and those of settlers in traditional Arabia.

In episode 3, the tents that conceal energetic men suggest that peaceful men in their camps have the power to come to grips with a threat from abroad. Similarly, the tale as a whole is designed to demonstrate that a tribal chief has the power to defend a tribal domain in the face of threats from abroad. The exact form of a peaceful life in the camp itself or in the tribal domain is of no concern, just as it was of no concern in any of the narratives we have read. Instead the concern of all the narratives is the possibility of defending a peaceful life within the camp or the tribe, *the precise shape of which remains obscure.* With regard to the practice of veiling, however, the emphasis is just the reverse. The veiling of women insists upon the form of a life at home; a life at home has a moral design which consists of the precise way in which it is separated, protected, and concealed from the outside world.

The settlers of Arabia were also faced with the problem of political adventurism. In this respect there was no clear boundary between pastoral and settled life in traditional Arabia. The problem of political anarchy originated in the conditions of pastoral life, just as it was also sustained by those conditions, but the settlers were in no way insulated from a popular investment in the use of instruments of aggression.[7] They were in the midst of Bedouins and had even, in many cases, once been Bedouins. However, unlike the pastoralists, they were involved in commerce and industry. That is to say, they were highly dependent upon political stability, even though they were troubled by political anarchy. As a result, the settlers, far more than the pastoralists, were devoted to the elaboration of a set of social norms as the necessary conditions for a communal way of life.

The settlers could not base the conventions of their communities upon an ideal of productive cooperation in the public domain. Such a feature of communal life was manifestly in question in their settlements, which were threatened externally and internally by political anarchy. Instead, the elaboration of social norms took shape in those areas that could be securely wrested from political anarchy, such as the domain of familial experience. Among the settlers we therefore find an impressive elaboration of the institutions of kinship and marriage in an idiom which reveals the very problem of uncertain political relationships within the community.

The patriarchal family and the strict seclusion of wives and sisters are two distinctive Near Eastern institutions of kinship and marriage, which reveal the circumstances of their historical origins plainly enough. The male is conceived as a protective moral authority who represents the family in public life. The fragile chastity of the female stands for the integrity of this protective moral authority. Why would there be such an emphasis on the moral will of the head of a household unless public life raised the problem of moral disorder? Why should the head of a household be so resolutely conceived as a male role unless the moral disorder of public life placed a premium on physical strength? Bizarrely, however, the elaboration of the status of males as patriarchal authorities was closely associated with the chastity of women. There was no realm of experience where the moral will could be surely exercised in a routine and systematic way, save in the realm of domestic experience; for in the world abroad there was moral disorder.

Only within the domestic domain of male control of the female could the social norms of the community be intricately developed, for there was no possiblity of conceiving that the relationship of males in the public domain was regulated by social norms.[8] Men had to base the possibility of dealing with one another on an intricate normative regulation of a private life they did not have in common, rather than a public life they did have in common. Strangely, the social norms of a community took shape as an elaborate set of rules by which men separated, protected, and concealed the most intimate feature of their lives from one another.

Another peculiar social norm of traditional Arabia illustrates how institutions of kinship and marriage, which stress the integrity of a familial interior threatened by a political exterior, can nevertheless become the basis for generalized ties. This is the social norm of preferential father's brother's daughter marriage which has been discussed at great length by anthropologists. A man is given the right to take his first female cousin in marriage if he so chooses.[9] By such a right, kinship and marriage are potentially restricted to the field of the closest relationships among males. It therefore expresses the principle of shoring up a domestic interior against a threatening political exterior. This right is extended by degrees. If the first male cousin foregoes his right, the second male cousin must be consulted about the marriage of the girl. If the second male cousin foregoes his right, the third must be consulted, and so on. This idiom of kinship and marriage as an expression of the integrity of an inside against an outside is extended indefinitely by securing the collective agreement of "close" kinsmen to give a woman in marriage to "distant" kinsmen.[10]

The settlers of traditional Arabia lived by commerce and industry in a political situation, which was troubled by a popular readiness to resort to force. In lieu of a norm of productive cooperation, the settlers elaborated norms which suggested that the most intimate features of human experience were reserved from public life. Nevertheless, these social norms were the basis of communal conventions of personal behavior, and therefore were also the basis of the pursuit of commerce and industry.[11]

This dilemma of the settlers explains why communal conventions are typically attributed a powerful practical efficacy in this part of the world, regardless of whether these conventions are or are not a realistic basis for dealing with the social problems of the moment. For historically, townsmen and villagers could only respond to a concrete problem of anarchy by invoking ever more insistently a formal code of personal and familial morality. To resort to a practical response to the problem of anarchy would have brought about an intensification of the problem itself, which was caused precisely by a readiness to take up instruments of violence as a means of dealing with political experience. The insistence of the townsmen and villagers upon the efficacy of communal conventions as the basis of personal health and public prosperity is therefore an attitude inspired by a situation in which a response to concrete political problems was limited to the fervent invocation of a moral code. As a result, the problem of political adventurism in the desert and steppe, an absence of morality, often became the very reverse problem in the settlements, a fanatical excess of morality.[12] These are the unpleasant tendencies of a situation in which men had been drawn into the exercise of power. There were more admirable tendencies, however. Among the pastoralists, more thoughtful men were ready to take up arms in a constructive way for peace. Among the settlers, more realistic men were concerned with the way in which a set of social norms might effectively provide the basis for the general prosperity of all men.

The last tale enables us to understand how a metaphor of scriptural signification and a metaphor of domestic covering are closely related to the problems of pastoral political experience. With this understanding, we have briefly considered the traditional towns and villages of Arabia where there was a similar political problem, but a much deeper interest in commerce and industry. In this way, it has been possible to glimpse how certain key political metaphors among the pastoralists eventually became elaborated as concepts of religion and society among the settlers.[13]

# 6. Rwala monotheism and the wish for authority

## 1

Although there was an interest in an aggressive way of life among the North Arabian Bedouins, these peoples were concerned about the value of human life, or rather just because there was this intense interest in an aggressive way of life, they were also deeply concerned about the value of human life. Some men were, in Doughty's words, "wild men" of "squalid ignorance and extreme living"; other men were, again in Doughty's words, "men of ripe moderation, peacemakers of a certain erudite and subtle judgement." In the ceremonial narratives, we have been examining the reflections of this last type of individual. Inspired by the threat of political anarchy, the ceremonial narrator was preoccupied with a wish for a moral authority as he considered the chief's construction of a secure domain of peace. As the ceremonial narrator pursued such a project, he relied upon two central concepts – one within the sphere of human relationships and another more awesome one beyond this sphere. First, he conceived of the tribal chief as a vehicle of a general human concern for peace and security. Second, he conceived of a natural order in the world at large, which favored a human concern for peace and security. Let us consider how this is so.

The ceremonial narrator was involved in developing interpretations of the strategic possibilities of actively dealing with political experience, but he was not exactly interested in strategy itself as a basis for dealing with an actual political situation. Rather, he was interested in discovering in the general properties of strategies a sign of a moral authority, which was on the side of peace. As he pursued this interest, the narrator turned directly to the popular Bedouin investment in political procedures and resources in order to discover just how such an investment might favor peaceful men over adventurous men. And the narrator was able to demonstrate that the basic design of a Bedouin life experience indeed favored the employment of such an investment in the interests of human welfare rather than at its expense. By the measured use of aggressive resources, cautious and sensible men could triumph over impetuous men who were ready to take extreme risks. Peaceful men in the familiar space and time of a tribal domain could triumph over adventurers who went abroad into strange lands.

So the very design of camel-herding nomadism as a way of life which demanded, to some degree at least, a routinized human association, a systematic management of resources, and an intimate knowledge of the environment, was on the side of peace. Fixing upon these dimensions of a Bedouin way of life, the ceremonial narrator could insist that whatever men's character might be, the very setting of life itself, the design of the world at large, was on the side of peace. The narrator adopted this moral principle as he provided an account of how a central moral authority among the Bedouins, the tribal chief, worked for peace. As he illustrated how such a chief responded to political threats by formulating strategic policies, he could demonstrate how a natural order was on the side of such policies. And as he revealed how this was so, he could conceive of the existence of an ultimate moral authority which lay behind this natural order. The concept of a Supreme Authority, therefore, expressed a Bedouin conviction that human life was protected and supported by the design of the world at large.

The difficulty which troubled this perspective, however, was that the very real advantages which peaceful men had over heroic men were not decisive enough to prevent men from going abroad and taking risks. Indeed, there were certain features of life which even tempted men to go abroad and to take risks. And even worse, the very basis of a measured, pragmatic effort itself, the knowing and using of the world in the interest of peace, involved an investment in aggressive resources that threatened human life.[1] The ceremonial narrator adopted what was only a possible, not a necessary approach. His insistence that the design of the world at large was on the side of peaceful men and against adventurous men was therefore only a marginal moral principle.

The Rwala God was humanistically merciful. He reflected a devotion to an authority which protected and supported human life where men were threatened by political adventurism. The Rwala God was all-knowing and all-powerful with regard to the unfolding of political events. He reflected the conviction that the design of the world at large lay decisively beyond the will of men at the same time as it favored the welfare of humanity in general. The Rwala God, however, was also a transcendental authority. He reflected the marginal possibility of actually realizing moral ends, which were in principle fully realizable.

Every aspect of Rwala monotheism was so much a part of the peculiar pattern of motivations and circumstances that we find among the North Arabian Bedouins that it seems appropriate to link the traditional Arabian concept of a uniquely severe form of monotheism to a background of camel-herding nomadism.[2] As a life of political adventurism developed among the North Arabian Bedouins, they devised political procedures and resources in reaction to the threat of this political adventurism. And as the forms of a strategic response to protect and support human life were routinized and systematized, a severe conception of a monotheistic God crystallized. Among the Bedouins, a strategic effort to protect and support human life was the basis for a practical political ethic. Here in the circumstances of life among the camel-herding nomads we find the origins of a religion based upon worldly political performances.

Such a religious tradition was first born among the pastoral nomads of the central Near East. Here long before the pastoral nomads had mounts, there was the combination of vulnerable resources (herds), independent scattered groups (nomadism), and dangerous political instruments (as a result of the technological developments in the nearby early centers of civilization). However, it was much later, among the camel-herding nomads, that the crucial interconnection of these conditions became clearly apparent. As a result of the extreme character of their pastoral life, their traditions reveal in an especially striking way certain forces that were at work throughout the arid zone, from western North Africa to eastern Central Asia, from very early times. Let us now return to the ceremonial narratives already discussed in order to examine how the mention of God is consistent with the preceding analysis of Rwala monotheism.

## 2

The narrative of the conflict between the Rwala and the western tribes best reveals how God is invoked as an authority which would protect and support human life. God is first mentioned in the second episode of this tale, where he acts at the beginning and at the end of the great intertribal war. First, God directs "the steps of the head chief Saṭṭâm from the Sultan in Constantinople to the camp at al-Libben." The restoration of the visible presence of Rwala political authority, a chief who is interested in peace but has been pushed into war, is attributed to the more ultimate authority of God. Then, as the intertribal war reaches a climax in a clouded moment of chaos, it is God who gives victory to the Rwala. The Rwala triumph is not a direct product of Rwala capacities, since victory in war is not surely within the grasp of any men in a situation of political uncertainty. Their triumph is instead a sign that they have proceeded in a proper way. They have recognized the power of formal arrangements. These formal arrangements are on the side of peaceloving men committed to a domestic life that values what is close to home. And it is a merciful God who stands behind this design which favors peace. So as the Rwala recognize the power of formal arrangements, they recognize the authority of God, and God in return gives them victory.

After a decisive act of God is mentioned at the beginning and end of the great intertribal war, an intention of God is explicitly aimed at the suppression of the life of heroism. The episode begins by describing the continuing raids of the hero Ṭrâd. The narrator then remarks: "Finally God determined to humble him." A line later, the enactment of this intention is associated with a "chance" discovery: "Allâh brought the Sha'lân kin, which was migrating just then, across his tracks." This sets the stage for the Sha'lân ambush of the cattle-raiders. The narrator sees in these events, which have proved to favor peaceloving men, the intention of God. He sees the peaceloving men themselves as the instruments of God's intention. God himself appears as a transcendent political actor. He intends and acts, and as he does so, he favors the security of human life. Still, he is necessarily removed from the political scene, which is charged with too many uncertainties. His presence can be detected only in connection with those events which seem to be crucial for the ends of good men. Where events raise a question about the protection and support of human life, such a question must be associated with men's clouded vision or men's turbulent passions.

In so far as the concept of God arises in connection with a certain kind of interpretation of political experience, the concept of God among the Rwala must also be implicated in the very problems of such an interpretation. To see how this is so, let us examine a philosophical implication of Rwala monotheism as it appears in Rwala expressions.

In the first version of the death of Turki, Saṭṭâm invokes God as he decides to move against the hero:

Let Allâh decide between us and him.
*Hâdha-r-rajjâl yeshûf allâh lena w-leh.*

In another account of a war between the Rwala and the Beni Ṣakhr, Saṭṭâm makes a similar statement as he decides to go to war:

Let Allâh judge between them and us! Up and at the Beni Ṣakhr!
*Yeshûf allâh lena w-lehom 'ala beni ṣakhr.*[3]

These are two expressions of the form of God's authority which emerge in connection with a struggle among men. However, both are translations of the same Arabic root whose literal meaning among the Rwala is "to see," not to decide or to judge. There is no reason to dispute Musil's translations. Rather, his glosses of the verb which literally means "to see" are quite significant. They indicate that the Rwala interpret the outcome of a struggle as indicating the intention of an authority behind political experience. They also indicate that the conception of this authority is associated with visual perception. But why do we find this curious association of decision and judgment with vision? Look at the world about you, a Rwala might urge. See how you can interpret it and sort it out. The world about you is a familiar world, it reflects your secure place within it. We are among men who are pressed to make a strategic sense of space and time. The enemy lies concealed in the landscape. One must know one's surroundings well. One must know the way the land lies and the way groups lie within the land. One must be prepared to act with this knowledge in mind. By visually perceiving a political space and time in a decisive and judicious way, cautious and sensible men may make a haven for themselves within this world. The familiar comprehensibility of a visual space and time is therefore an indication that a merciful authority lies behind the design of experience.

The possibility of a visual interpretation of experience is an indication of the existence of God's authority. Therefore, God's acts of visual perception are a suitable metaphor for the manifestation of God's authority. As God decides and judges in connection with a political struggle, he looks from one man to the next or from one tribe to the next. We can now begin to understand just how the Bedouin conception of God's authority is problematic in a peculiar way. If God decides and judges *as he sees*, then the character of authority cannot be elucidated in the form of a systematic political theory. God's authority, just like the authority of the Rwala chiefs, is not quite dissociable from the actual process of a strategic response. The Rwala interpretation of political experience, an interpretation that is indissociable from their political circumstances, raises a peculiar problem of political philosophy. In glimpsing this, we also glimpse how the problems of political philosophy in general are embedded, like all human experience, in an historical epoch.

Let us now turn to the three invocations of God, which appear in the first version of the death of Turki, with a question in mind. Is it possible that God, too, like the cautious chief and the impetuous hero, is touched by the sense of dread which pervades this tale? The first invocation of God in this tale is the most elaborate. It occurs in the speech of the chief Saṭṭâm when he receives the insulting message from Turki: "Oh, that man! Let Allâh decide between us and him. We did not want to fight him, but he provokes us all the time. O ye Arabs, shoe your horses and get your supplies ready, for tomorrow we shall go on a raid as ordered by our highest commander." In this invocation, God will decide, much as the sensible Saṭṭâm decides in his capacity as a protective chief. Moreover, God is conceived as a military commander who orders a strategic effort, much as Saṭṭâm himself orders the practical preparations for this effort. We see something of Saṭṭâm in Saṭṭâm's conception of God, but God is nevertheless not a divine glorification of Saṭṭâm. God suggests the metaphysical sufficiency of Saṭṭâm's point of view, but this point of view is more than a personal whim. Saṭṭâm sees in the nature of political experience the possibility of dealing with it in a morally pragmatic way. It is not exactly his narrow self-interest that he idealizes with the name of God; it is a moral pragmatism that he idealizes. Given the circumstances in which he finds himself, such an ideal does indeed have a weighty authority and is far more than a personal whim.

Turki conceives of God differently, although the relationship of Turki's self-conception to God is similar. When Turki receives the secret message from Saṭṭâm, he invokes God in connection with his unthinking and instinctive statement of intent: "God will help us against them. Tomorrow I shall fight them." For Turki, God is a companion in political adventurism. Turki sees in God a support for his life of heroism. Turki, in other words, sees the authority of political experience, its possibility of meaningfulness, as a political adventurist. He locates behind a life of provocation the presence of an authority who aids him in a friendly way rather than an authority who commands him to undertake a moral struggle on the side of human life.

And finally there is a third invocation in this first version of the death of Turki. It occurs almost, but not quite, at the end of the narrative. It is the invocation of the narrator himself who observes at the moment of Turki's death: "Khalaf âl Idhen killed, as was the will of God, the great chief Turki himself . . ." For the narrator, God is the author of the events which he describes. He sees the possibility of composing his tale of political events as an indication that political experience has a design that men can clearly understand. He sees the outcome of these events as manifesting the intentions of a divinity who is the author of this design of political experience.

In each case, God is conceived somewhat differently, but in each case God figures as the authority of a certain kind of response to experience. And similarly God is necessarily implicated in the sufficiency of the kind of response which is in question. In this respect, we can examine just how God is implicated in the very dread that pervades this first version of Turki's death. When Saṭṭâm invokes the authority of God, he says that God has ordered a raid, but then Saṭṭâm does not really intend to undertake a raid. He really intends to evade Turki. Saṭṭâm thus proceeds correctly and properly as a cautious and sensible political authority on the side of peace. At the same time, the event which does come about by the order of God does not seem to be on the side of peace. This implies a rupture between Saṭṭâm's cautious and sensible self-conception and the events which cannot be evaded. This implies, that is to say, that God's design, the necessity for a battle and the necessity for Turki's death, has dreadful implications for moral men.

Turning to Turki, we find that the hero says that God will help him, but God does not help him. Turki is killed in the raid. God is not the friendly companion of the political adventurist. Yet Turki, unlike Saṭṭâm, proceeds to do exactly what he says he will do: "Tomorrow I shall fight them." The Arabic might be translated here: "Tomorrow it is necessary to fight them." While Turki's political adventurism does not receive God's help, Turki does act in accordance with God's will. Again there is a rupture between a self-conception and a necessity inherent in events. But it is a different kind of rupture, just as Turki is a different kind of man. Saṭṭâm is helped by God (he defeats Turki) even though he attempts to evade God's dreadful will. Turki is not helped by God, even though as the impetuous hero he is the instrument of his dreadful will.

A few lines later the narrator observes at the moment of Turki's death that the hero dies as God intended. Like Saṭṭâm and like Turki, the narrator sees an authority behind the necessity of events. But now let us note that Khalaf âl Idhen, a dark figure about whom we are otherwise told nothing, is God's instrument in connection with two acts: "Khalaf âl Idhen killed, as was the will of God, the great chief Turki himself, and took his mail shirt, his saber, and his mare, one of the fleetest of horses. Khalaf offered this mare to Saṭṭâm as a gift." God wills that Khalaf should kill Turki. Does God also will that Khalaf should pass Turki's mare to Saṭṭâm? Does God will that the authority of Saṭṭâm should be tainted with the dreadful implications of this instrument of heroism? Again we find that the inheritance of the mare is a crucial point in the narrative. Here we see not only that the events in question have an ambiguous value, but that the authority of the God who stands behind these events also has an ambiguous value.

The issue of the character of God's transcendant authority is never resolved in this narrative, but another issue, the real and concrete cause of these dreadful events, is quite decisively resolved. The narrator follows his account of the death of Turki with the description of the terror following his death. He observes that "the members of both tribes were bent more on killing a man than on capturing animals." The line which was emblematic of the entire course of the confrontation of Saṭṭâm and Turki suggests that human passions are the real and concrete roots of these dreadful events. Just what relationship God might have with these passions remains obscured by the gesture of a dark figure, Khalaf.

## 3

In Chapter 1, the North Arabian Bedouins were compared with other Near Eastern tribal peoples, and the lack of any important religious myths or rituals among the North Arabian Bedouins was noted. In the course of reading the political narratives, we have encountered religious conceptions, but they are quite distinctive conceptions. Rwala religious traditions are linked with practical political policies and procedures, not with myths and rituals. Not surprisingly, there is no extensive Rwala cosmology which stands behind and legitimates political life. As political events move along, the Rwala chiefs attempt to come to grips with them, and the Rwala narrators attempt to make sense of them. Their narratives of raiding and warfare only refer to events more or less within the memory of living men.

There are, however, a number of Rwala reflections which might be called "myths." These myths were apparently so informally offered that Musil did not go to the trouble to record them verbatim. Here, for example, is Musil's paraphrase of the Rwala view of paradise and hell:

> Paradise is somewhere below ground. There it rains regularly, there is always *rabî'*, abundance, good pasture, *kheyr*, and there also the moon shines all the time. In paradise all the Rwala live together, are young, and never grow older. They can marry there and have grown children at once. Every one has a big tent, big herds, and many children. They raid hostile tribes which have been condemned to hell, where all enemies of the Rwala are sent.
>
> Hell is situated either on the sun or in some other place above the earth. There the sun scorches by day and night, rains are very rare, the breeding of camels meets with no success, the soil has to be irrigated artificially - and the Bedouins there must work long and hard. They serve the *fellâḥîn*, have to obey the government, are conscripted, perform military duty, and Allâh himself knows all their torments. Some call hell *dhalfât* and think that in that place neither the moon nor the stars ever shine.[4]

Paradise and hell are not populated with those who have done right and those who have done wrong. They are seen in purely tribal terms. All the Rwala are in paradise. All their enemies are in hell. In this respect, this myth clouds the dilemmas of Rwala political experience by resolving the contradiction between a moral life and an interest in political adventure. In paradise we find a fully formed and exuberant domesticity. There is an abundance of pasture. All the Rwala live together in harmony. Everyone is perpetually young. Everyone can marry. Everyone has many children. Children grow up at once. The tents are big. The herds are large. Each of these features suggests a high valuation of domestic life, and such a high valuation is the basis on which peace must be built among the camel-herding nomads. At the same time, all the Rwala in paradise are free to raid their former, worldly enemies at will. In paradise one can enjoy all the pleasures of peace while preserving all the excitement of adventure.

The love of free political action, which is implicit in the vision of paradise, appears more emphatically in the vision of hell. Unlike paradise, a covered and therefore protected place, hell is an uncovered and therefore exposed place. Scorched by the sun and without rain, there is no basis for a domestic life. But worse than this, the Bedouins must labor to survive. Camels do not breed, and so the Bedouins must farm, and for lack of water, their farming involves a great deal of work (irrigation). And worse than this, these Bedouins are the political subjects of the peasants (*fellâḥîn*). They even have to obey the government. And misery upon misery, they are even conscripted. Indeed, only God does know "all their torments." In hell there is neither the pleasure of domestic abundance nor the excitement of political adventure. In hell there is only a tedious, domestic labor and a demeaning political subjugation. Surely this self-serving myth, when compared with the insights of the ceremonial narratives and the playfulness of Bleyhân's tales of raiding, should raise some questions about the idealization of myth as a vehicle for cultural truth. A literature divorced from the reality and concreteness of events is quite possibly, even if not necessarily, a literature that is wishfully self-serving.

There are other features of this paraphrase which suggest the more interesting side of myth. They might be characterized as a fascination with the life of forms. Paradise is illuminated by the cool half-light of the moon. Among the Bedouins, the nighttime is a time of repose. This is the time when the affairs of the day have come to a stop. This is the time when one can consider at one's ease just what it all might have meant. In hell there are no moon and no stars, no light for the work of the imagination. The shape of life must remain unclear among the damned. Men are condemned not to be able to consider who or where they are. Hell is a place where there is a poverty of imaginative forms. This brings us to the name of hell which "some call" *dhalfât*. Musil has probably mistranscribed *ẓalfât* as *dhalfât*. In classical Arabic, *ẓalfât* is glossed as a high, rugged land that will not show a footmark. This is consistent with Musil's paraphrase of the Bedouin view of hell in the above passage. It is a place which is exposed to the elements and which is lacking in shapes and forms.

Similar themes appear in another myth about God:

> In the belief of the Bedouins and the Ṣleyb there is somewhere far beyond the horizon a tall mountain on each side of the earth. One half of each mountain rests on *terra firma*, the other half in the sea, into which it sinks abruptly, while towards the land it sends out a sharp spur called *khashm*. These four mountains carry the whole firmament. During the rainy season the spirits and even Allâh himself prefer to dwell near the southern mountain, which the Arabs call *ash-sherq*, as it is supposed to be situated in the inner desert. In summer, however, Allâh moves with all the spirits to the northern mountain *yegharrebow*.[5]

Here is a vision of a cosmological "domestic structure." The House of God has the earth as its foundation. Its four walls are sharply delineated by the seas. It has four mountainous supports upon which rests its roof, the entire firmament. God moves regularly and customarily within his house with the seasons, just as the Bedouins move. God has in his company a host of companion spirits, just as the Bedouins have companions. A merciful God is associated with a geographical space and time which is portrayed as a domestic structure, just as hell is conceived as an exposed terrain lacking shapes and forms. Among the Bedouins, the hope for the existence of a moral authority, which would protect and support human life, is linked with the possibility of perceiving an order in the world at large, which favors a domestic way of life.

# Part III

# The poems of raiding and warfare

But in their idle lives, the Beduins have a surfeit of the bibble-babble in the byût, where they find not other business than the clapping of tongues in all their waking hours; their heads ache of weaving cobwebs in their very emptiness. They are cloyed with a new-made song, with the sententious ditties of the desert poets, that search a man's wit, and that raise his blood, that counsel his life. Hard to please, they find but one barren artifice in them all; I have heard the Beduins mocking that irksome, because never changed, and solemn yawning stave, in the Muse of their desert Nature, which must bring in all riding, *ya ent râkabin*, 'Ah! thou who sittest mounted' (upon a thelûl). – The mind is a kind of corroding mobility.

Doughty, *Travels in Arabia Deserta*,
vol. 1 (1921), p. 467.

# 7. Heroic skills and beastly energies

## 1

The ceremonial narratives of raiding and warfare illustrate how the tribal chief was conceived as a leader who worked to control a threat from abroad. In this regard, the tribal chief was only marginally effective. His agreements with other tribal chiefs were disrupted by his own tribesmen's interest in adventurous initiatives. Likewise, the tribal chiefs with whom he made agreements were unable to command their own tribesmen who also retained an interest in adventurous initiatives. Therefore the Bedouins remained exposed to a threat from abroad, despite the efforts of their chiefs. This situation drove them to take whatever measures they could, and the principal measure was a resort to the use of weapons in self-defense. As we read the ceremonial poems of raiding and warfare, we find expressions of a Bedouin devotion to the use of aggressive resources, but more interestingly, we also find eloquent statements of the disturbing implications of such a devotion. The ceremonial poems of raiding and warfare raise a question about whether any way of life is altogether possible in the desert and steppe, if it limits the readiness of men to resort freely to deadly instruments.

In his chapter "War and Peace," Musil records fifteen poems which are associated with the same events as those in the ceremonial narratives. Musil includes a text in Arabic of each poem, an English translation of the Arabic, a general commentary on the poem, and a verse by verse commentary. He cites the names and origins of the poem's author, and he cites the names of the reciters from whom he heard the poem. Of these fifteen poems, only eight are of immediate interest for the present analysis.[1] Each of these eight takes the form of a ceremonial poem of raiding and warfare. They all begin with an image of riders on mounts or a reference to such an image. They are all composed in accordance with certain rigid prosodic rules.

Poetry is the principal form of popular artistic expression among the North Arabian Bedouins. Musil's ethnography includes scores, if not hundreds, of poems which touch upon almost every aspect of Bedouin life. An examination of this collection of poetry, however, indicates that the ceremonial poem of raiding and warfare holds some special significance for the North Arabian Bedouin poetic tradition. The structure of other Bedouin poems appears to take the form of a relaxation from the more rigid structure of the poem of raiding and warfare. For example, the image of riders on mounts is often retained in the longer Bedouin poems, even though the political implications of such an image are dropped. Similarly the prosody of all Bedouin poems is much like the prosody of the poem of raiding and warfare, but the rigidity of prosodic rules tends to be weakened. This pattern suggests that as the Rwala poets turn their attention to a certain realm of political experience, there is a necessity to express themselves in a certain way. In this realm, a poetic form crystallizes and solidifies to an extent that it does not in any other realm of Rwala experience. The result is that the poem of raiding and warfare has come to serve as the very basis for poetic conventions in general.

In his first book on the Bedouins, Musil describes the recitation of poems around a campfire as follows:

> The *qaṣîde* is a poetic story in verse and its author is usually a well known poet. It usually glorifies the famous deeds of the lineage or tribal leaders or represents a day of battle. Most of the *qaṣâyed* are of interest only to contemporaries and are no longer remembered after they have died.
>
> Often such poems are quite long and the poet almost never composes them all at once. Usually he only makes a few verses, repeats them to his friends and children in order to prevent his forgetting them. Later he adds on new verses. The friends or other listeners call to his attention one or another deed which he has passed over; and then he must mention it and add corresponding verses at the appropriate place.
>
> Thus it often happens that those acquaintances who came to know the poem in its original form hear other verses in another camp which they do not know and do not want to accept until they have asked the poet himself about them. Often the poet himself replaces a few words. Yes, even entire verses are replaced by other verses which he prefers; however, others do not know them and often never accept them. Thus one hears several versions of a *qaṣîde,* not only of a dead poet, but also of a living one. Yes, even of a poet present at the recital, which the reciting poet accepts as all his own, although they often differ markedly with respect to length and order (of arrangement). When such poems are recited at the campfire and the poet is not present, those attached to specific versions fight among themselves, criticize this or that verse of the poet, and add others. A fusion of verses of different poets happens especially easily if they have the same number of syllables and the same rhyme, although they sing about entirely different events. At the same time the names of people and places are changed and the theft is complete.[2]

These comments must be viewed with caution. Very few of the poems which Musil collected can be accurately described as a story in verse. Those few that do take such a form are attributed to townsmen or villagers, even though Musil may have heard them from Bedouin reciters. And when Musil judges some poems to be quite long, he is probably thinking in terms of poems ranging in length from ten to twenty verses. These poems are long only in comparison with the usual Bedouin ditty of two verses. The North Arabian Bedouins did not compose epic poems of hundreds or thousands of verses in length. Finally, the comments on the Rwala poets' indulgences in artistic theft are not to be doubted. However, they should not create the impression that Rwala poetic composition is haphazard. Unlike the formulaic character of some oral epic traditions, Rwala ceremonial poetry is not extemporaneously composed. It is first patiently and diligently constructed; then it is scrupulously memorized word for word.

Shortly after his general description of Bedouin poetry, Musil describes the fundamental musicality of Rwala poetry:

> The *qaṣâyed* poems are usually delivered in accompaniment with the *rbâba.* The singer recites one verse in such a way that he slurs over several syllables, shouts out and emphasizes the most important names, and lifts the last words into a falsetto and lengthens them, while fitting them to the tones of his instrument. The listeners usually repeat the last word. One is so used to this manner of presentation of the *qaṣâyed* that one is not capable of presenting a *qaṣîde,* which after all is known by heart, in an ordinary monotone. I often observed this when I wanted to record a poem and the singer therefore had to pronounce the single verses slowly, word for word. While doing this he often got stuck and repeatedly had to begin the singing recitation from the beginning if he wanted to recall the continuation.[3]

This passage makes it clear that Rwala poetry has a musical value of a high order. Let us turn to examine the prosodic features of Rwala poetry, the sound patterns upon which its musicality is based.

One of the most striking features of Rwala poetry lies in its severe restrictions on prosodic form. Almost all of the poetry recorded by Musil consists of a series of verses of two hemistichs. All the first hemistichs of each verse end with an identical rhyme, and all of the second hemistichs of each verse end with an identical, but contrasting, rhyme. Musil records scores of Rwala ditties and songs, dozens of longer poems from four to twenty or so verses, and a few poems of about fifty verses, all composed on these principles. Here is his brief explanation of the principles of poetic composition:

> The Rwala love to hear, recite and compose poems, which they call *qaṣâyed* (sing., *qaṣîde*). A verse is called *qâf.* It usually consists of two halves, the first being *nuṣṣ al-qâf* and the second, which is always rhymed, *âkher al-qâf,* being *qâf at-tâli.* The poet says of himself: "I composed a poem, *qaṣatt* or *qilt al-qaṣîde.*" Sometimes a poet will not say that he composed (a poem), *qaṣad,* but merely that he uttered (a poem), *qâl.* The audience say to the poet: "Reveal us thy poem, *ebdaha 'aleyna.*"[4]

His failure to mention the rhyme of the first hemistichs (*nuṣṣ al-qâf*) stems from the occasional tendency for this rhyme to be dropped. In all the poems of raiding and warfare, however, the first hemistichs all rhyme.

The rhyming patterns of the eight ceremonial poems of raiding and warfare in Musil's chapter on "War and Peace" suggest a connection between the musical value of rhymes and the conceptual structure of a verse. These patterns are as follows:

| First hemistich | Second hemistich | Length of poem |
|---|---|---|
| 1 . . . âb | . . . îd | 9 verses |
| 2 . . . îb | . . . ûj | 17 verses |
| 3 . . . âd | . . . âni | 20 verses |
| 4 . . . îd | . . . âḥi | 10 verses |
| 5 . . . âj | . . . arha | 13 verses |
| 6 . . . îs | . . . ûmi | 13 verses |
| 7 . . . ow' | . . . âwi | 11 verses |
| 8 . . . âyel | . . . îd | 5 verses |

In these examples, the rhyme of the first hemistich tends to end in a stop (*b, d, j*) or a fricative (*s,* '). The rhyme of the second hemistich on the other hand tends to be unstopped and of a longer, more songlike duration. This suggests that the rhyme of the first hemistich "cuts" the first hemistich from the second, whereas the rhyme of the second hemistich lends a songlike value to the completion of each verse. Numbers 1 and 2 are exceptions to this general pattern in that the final rhyme of the verse is also a stop. Number 8, on the other hand, reverses this general pattern. This last example, however, tends to confirm that there is some connection between the musical and conceptual structure of a verse. This poem is a parody of a poem of raiding and warfare which "inverts" its principles of composition.[5]

Turning to the question of Rwala meter, we encounter a difficulty. Musil's transcriptions of Rwala poetry are inadequate. The Rwala poets were unable to provide Musil with a simple spoken version of their poems for the convenience of transcription. When they tried to speak their poems instead of singing them, they tended to break the meter. The result is the texts recorded by Musil. An exact scansion of these texts is not therefore possible, although a fluent speaker of the Rwala dialect might well be able to recite them properly.

Landberg, by employing a painstaking method of repeated transcriptions and corrections, recorded similar poems from the Rwala and their neighbors. As in classical Arabic poetry, the meter of the poems recorded by Landberg is based upon quantity rather than accent. This means, for example, that a poetic recitation changes the accentual emphasis which a word might have in a normal prose recitation. That is to say, the poetic recitation lends words a musical value that they do not ordinarily have. A poem recorded by Landberg, and attributed to a Rwala source, provides a good example of the deformation of the normal prose reading of words by the musical poetic recitation:

6. Ma hî' ḥalâl ejdudna lauwalîni — *Prose recitation*
   Ma hî ḥalâ lejdûdinal auwalîni — *Singing recitation*
   – – ⏑ – | – – – ⏑ – | – ⏑ – – – — *Scansion*

   Kesban ladeyna min ḥalâib ʻadâna
   Kesban ladeyna min ḥalâib ʻadâna
7. Wilya aʻtaleyna ṣufr lôn es-sanîni
   Wilyaʻ-taleyna ṣufre lônis-sanîni
   Umin eṣ-ṣaḥâba maʻ-taraḏhin aḥṣâna
   Um neṣ-ṣaḥâbah maʻ-taraḏhin eḥṣâna
8. Win ṣâr ʻand iqṭîihin win eḥdina
   El-môte ʻandiq-tîyihin win eḥdîna
   Ya suraʻ rodd unḥûrehin maʻ jafâna
   Ya suraʻ roddin-ḥûrahin maʻ jafâna[6]

While the second hemistich of verse 6 is read and sung identically, the other hemistichs are read and sung differently. Note that when the informant does not sing, but merely speaks the poem, he even tends to change the words of the poem, as in the first hemistich of verse 8. This again implies some close structural connection between a poem's musical values and its conceptual values.

Landberg's work suggests that many, and perhaps even most, of the poems recorded by Musil are based upon one of two metrical forms. One of these forms has eight syllables in each hemistich of a verse. Many of the ditties recorded by Musil seem to be based on this form. The other form has twelve syllables in each hemistich. Many of the longer poems recorded by Musil, including the poems of raiding and warfare, seem to be based on this form. There is a specific comment by Landberg on one kind of eight-syllable ditty recorded by Musil in *Arabia Petraea.* These are short "songs of war," called *ḥedâwi* by the North Arabians. Landberg claims that the meter of all these poems is a form of *rajaz,* the meter of the oldest known poetry in the Arabic language.[7] He provides two examples of such a meter:

1. – – ⏑ – | – – ⏑ –
2. – – ⏑ – | – ⏑ – –

Landberg also states that the meter of the so-called "marching songs" collected by Dalman in North Arabia is also a form of *rajaz.*[8] In another place, Landberg has provided us with five examples of the longer twelve-syllable poems which are found among the North Arabian Bedouins.[9] All these poems are similar to those collected by Musil. Three of them are attributed to a Rwala reciter. The meter of all of these poems is also a form of *rajaz:*

– – ⏑ – | – – ⏑ – | – ⏑ – –

It is possible then that the meters of almost all the poems to be considered, and perhaps the meters of almost all the poems recorded by Musil, are based upon one of the above forms of *rajaz.* However, at least one poem recorded by Musil offers good internal evidence that it is recited to a beat of ten, not twelve, and it may even be that there is no strict quantitative value to this beat. Landberg would not have been very happy with such a form of poetry. He had very precise views about Arabian meters, and he devoted an immense amount of attention to the problem of transcribing Arabian poetry. His work, together with Musil's work, does indicate that there is a great deal of North Arabian poetry that is based upon some form of what he considered to be a *rajaz* meter.

If we assume then that Landberg is largely right about North Arabian prosody, this poetry has a peculiar feature. This is the high redundancy of the prosodic rules that govern its composition. Each verse of a Rwala poem tends to have the same two contrasting rhymes for each of its hemistichs. In addition, each hemistich is also a metrical repetition of its associated hemistich in the same verse. Only the final rhyme changes. And although we do not know how any of the poems to be analyzed were sung, all the poetic melodies recorded by Musil in his study *Arabia Petraea* involve the exact repetition of the melodic line in each hemistich.

This extreme form of melodic and prosodic repetition becomes more interesting when one notes the relationship of prosody and syntagmatic continuity. Each hemistich tends to be a syntagmatic unit, and each verse tends to be a whole thought. This means that the two explicit points of conceptual articulation are marked by a recurrent sound value (the two rhymes). The point where two thoughts are brought into some relationship, the termination of the first hemistich, is always marked by the same recurrent rhyme. The point where the resulting whole thought comes to an end (the termination of the second hemistich) is always marked again by a recurrent, but contrasting rhyme. This is still another indication of a connection between the musical and conceptual structure of a verse. It raises the question of whether one might be able to understand what is said apart from the musical form in which it is said.

A fuller elaboration of the significance of Rwala poetic structure must rely upon the reader's familiarity with the material. As a means for gaining this familiarity, we shall first view musicality, meter, and rhyme as no more than arbitrary esthetic conventions. We shall then attempt a discursive reading of the poetry and determine what difficulties arise.

## 2

Provisionally setting aside all that we have learned from the narratives, let us suppose that the Rwala are simply historically minded. They have wars. The wars have important effects upon their way of life. They therefore remember the wars and tell stories about them. From this point of view, the narratives could be viewed as documentaries of political cataclysms in the desert, and the poetry could be viewed as a verse-narrative. The poems inscribe the events of war in the collective consciousness by adding to them a more or less arbitrary esthetic element and by interpreting the events of war in terms of the normative values of Bedouin society. Such a perspective is not too different from the one which Musil adopts in his descriptions of the narrative recitations and poetic performances around the Bedouin camp fire.

The poem which might best lend itself to such a reading is one that refers to events which Musil labeled "Wars between the Rwala and the Beni Wahab (1850–64)." In the course of this conflict, the opponents of the Rwala were led by Muḥammad eben Smeyr (see v. 2), who was chief of the Weld ʻAli tribe for almost half a century. On one occasion, Muḥammad led the Beni Wahab confederation together with a contingent of Ottoman troops composed of Druse, Turcoman, and Kurdish volunteers and a regular cavalry corps. Ḥasan (v. 5) was the Ottoman commander. Sbeybekh (v. 18) was the chief cavalry officer and al-Yâqîn (v. 19) was his subordinate. Here is Musil's translation of the poem:

1. O thou who ridest, when starting on a journey, a thoroughbred camel
   With bulging hips, one that shies and is used to journeys hither and thither,
2. When thou comest to Muḥammad, the heir of noble heroes,
   I desire thee to shave his chin with a razor.
3. He has refused our friendship while we were willing,
   For he was dazzled with the flash from soldiers' rifles.
4. He brought soldiers from far away
   With the dwellers in Hermon and the Turcomans,
5. And then near them assembled a throng of people burning with rage,
   And both he and Ḥasan forbade pardon.
6. Sons of men of counsels, a fighting troop of prudent observers
   On sterile she-camels, famous and fat,
7. Before witnesses drove back the protectors of Jedhʻa
   As soon as their troop came into view.
8. They returned to the attack, but the return did not maintain its course,
   So that the Ḥajjâj and Ḥamâmde kins yielded themselves.
9. Thou wouldst say that Jamʻân's sons were Kurdish soldiers,
   So have they besprinkled scorched stone heaps with blood
10. By their steel rifles, each shot of which reaches its goal;
    If not some agha's head, then it is his stud horse.

11. When their rifles' load is once fired, it will not depart from its course.
For they first weigh each bit of powder.
12. In quick flight Eben Smeyr's troop vanished,
So that he gathered them up one by one as the tent poles tied with ropes are picked up for migration.
13. Those of our men who fell far beyond the creek,
Their death is atoned for, their pastures now are in Paradise.
14. For blood price we took two thousand lives,
A half of whom understood us, while half were barbarians.
15. Woe to their chief for his reign! Long has it endured in his kin,
And he might peacefully rest in the irrigated depressions.
16. Thou hast begun a war with a tribe that can strike thee from afar,
As even the hardest iron yields when thou takest pains to bore it.
17. The chief, Akhu Dinya, is accustomed to heroic deeds,
And the bone he grinds will change into flour.
18. As soon as the rutting she-camels dashed out, Sbeybekh fled, not to return,
And like an 'Omân camel forgot all prudence.
19. Al-Yâqîn, too, hurried, though longing for our supplies,
And in his flight loosened both rope and rein.
20. On war tents they trod, O Jdê'! when fleeing
From our face, just as the followers of the leader with the wild poppy-red tarbush.

Musil transcribed the original oral version as follows:

1. Yâ râkeben ḥorren elya' ṣirt maddâd
nâb ad-defûf w-jâflen muṭrashâni
2. yelfi lamḥammad mwârîth al-ajwâd
waddak teḥûf leḥyeteh bel-ḥsâni
3. 'ayya' 'an aṣ-ṣuḥbe yowm hiye bel-awdâd
w-haqwah kethr melâṣef ash-sheyshekhâni
4. jâb al-'asâker min wara min ghâd
w-ahl ṭwîl al-felj w-at-turkmâni
5. w-lammaw bihom rab' min al-gholl zahhâd
w-mḥarremîn al-man' hw w-al-ḥesâni
6. awlâd mejles surbat al-ḥarb w-an-naqqâd
min fowq ḥîlen mukrammâten asmâni
7. ekharaw hal al-jedh'a 'ala 'uyûn al-ashhâd[10]
elya' mâ tebayyen jam'ahom bel-bayâni
8. raddaw 'aleyhom raddeten mâ beha snâd
wa-tsallemaw ḥajjâj w-al-ḥammadâni
9. w-awlâd jam'ân teqel 'askar akrâd
min ad-damm bellaw yâbs al-murjumâni
10. bemqarrarât ramîhen ṣowb beṣmâd
brâs al-agha w-en akhṭateh bel-ḥṣâni
11. w-elya' qba' neqdaha tesned asnâd
w-mzayyenîn melḥahen bel-wazâni
12. w-jmû' eben smeyr râḥat sharrâd
yilemmahom lemm al-'amad besh-shebâni
13. alli dhubaḥ minna min wara-s-seyl min ghâd
w-mowteh ḥaqîq w-malfâh al-jenâni

14. akhadhna meddâhom elfên ba'dâd
naṣfen fehîm w-naṣfehom ṭurṭumâni
15. wêleh 'ala ḥokmeh mabṭi w-al-ajdâd
w-endeleh ber-riyâḍ al-amâni
16. ḥârabt rab'en yeqtelûnak bel-ab'âd
jâsi-l-ḥadîd elya tma''enûneh lâni
17. ash-sheykh akhu dinya furûsen w-mu'tâd
w-'aḍm alli yeṭḥaneh yowda' marmahâni[11]
18. elya' ṣiyyijen harab sbeybekh w-lâ 'âd
wa-mtadhayyeren teqel qa'ûden 'omâni
19. al-yâqîn 'ajlen w-en bagha minna-l-afwâd
w-yowm enhazam erkha-r-rasan w-al-'enâni
20. dahqaw buyût al-ḥarb yâ jdê' sharrâd
'an wajh mithl ma'âqeb ad-deydekhâni.

Setting aside the opening image of riders on mounts as an artificial convention, the poem does seem to be a verse-narrative, at least from verses 1 to 12. Verses 13 through 17 then appear to be evaluations of the Rwala victory which attribute a normative significance to the events in question. Verses 18 through 20 take up the war again, this time referring to the Ottoman military contingent rather than the opposing Bedouins. The last line knits together the two "narrative" sections by referring to the opposing Bedouins in the first hemistich and the Ottoman regulars in the second.

Upon still closer inspection and with the aid of Musil's verse by verse commentary, however, the narrative continuity of the poem is seen to be illusory. It is more a product of an initial ignorance of the relations between the participants of the battle and the events of the battle itself. In addition, the evaluative verses have curious structural features.

Let us begin with the narrative continuity. Verses 3 to 5 do indeed describe the prelude to a general conflict, but the next set of verses (v. 6–8) shifts discontinuously to specific events within this general conflict. The "sons of men of counsels" were a party of the Sha'lân clan, the reigning kin of the Rwala. However, they do not exactly stand for the Rwala in general, as in the case where the chief stands for the tribe in the narratives. For example, their opponents in this scene, the Ḥajjâj and Ḥamâmde clans of verse 8, do not refer to the reigning kin of the opposing Bedouins. On the contrary, they are only particular groups within the Weld 'Ali tribe. In other words, the scope of the general introductory verses has been precipitously reduced. Particular groups and particular events are described in these verses.

In the next set of verses (v. 9–11), the scene changes again. "Jam'ân's sons," according to Musil, are three heroes among the Sha'lân clan. It is not clear whether these three men are part of "the sons of men of counsels," or whether their depicted heroism was part of the conflict of verses 6 to 8. It is clear that another discontinuity has occurred in the account.

For either the poem has shifted entirely to a new scene, or it has backed up in time to describe a particular event within the battle that was concluded in verse 8. Moreover it is now clear that the scope of the battle is narrowing with each set of verses: the general conflict (v. 3-5), a major battle within the conflict (v. 6-8), and three men firing their rifles (v. 9-11).

In the next verse (v. 12), the perspective shifts again to the general level of verses 3 to 5 with a concluding description of the Rwala rout of the enemy. This conclusion is followed by a series of evaluative verses (v. 13-17), and the final verses again depict scenes of battle (v. 18-20). However, the rout of the Ottoman regulars, which is described in the final verses, stands in no clear relation with the events of verses 3 through 12. There is even a hint that these last verses may refer to a different battle altogether. Musil notes that the phrase "though longing for our supplies" alludes to the plan of al-Yâqîn to ambush the supply camels of the Rwala which carried foodstuffs to their refuge in the inner desert. This indicates that these verses may well refer to events which were not part of the general conflict of the verses 3 to 12, or even that they refer ambiguously to two or more battles.

This more detailed analysis demonstrates how very little we learn about the course of the battle from the poem. We do not know if the war to which the poem refers involved a single battle on a particular day, an extended battle over several days, or several battles over a period of months. The Rwala of course do not share our ignorance since their narrative tradition fills out the details which are missing from the poem. However, this is just the point. The necessity of knowing the narrative tradition in order to place the scenes in context only emphasizes how discontinuous, fragmentary, and unstorylike the poem is.

If the attempt to interrelate the verses discursively is given up, the poem divides neatly into disconnected blocks of verses: the prelude to the battle (v. 3-5), an isolated depiction (v. 6-8), and a second isolated depiction (v. 9-11). The conclusion to the first depiction (v. 12) then seems to trigger off a series of evaluative verses (v. 13-17) which however do not seem to be sufficient for ending the poem. A third isolated depiction of battle follows these evaluative verses (18-20). The poet has, it seems, felt it necessary to end the poem with an event rather than an evaluation. The final verse links together the two most decisive events of the war: the rout of the opposing Bedouins and the rout of the Ottomans.

The possibility of dividing this poem into disconnected blocks of verses is a characteristic feature of the poems which Musil collected from Bedouin authors. Rwala poems other than the poems of raiding and warfare often have similar qualities. In this regard, consider the following description of poetic composition that Musil gives in his book *Arabia Deserta:*

Our omnivorous poet Miz'el akhu Za'êla was composing a poem in my honor. Since a roving versifier must earn his living by his art, he apparently thought I would pay him well for a poem I liked. It was interesting to watch his procedure. He would ponder for several minutes and then recite two verses twenty or thirty times, substituting for some of the expressions new and better ones - *azyan,* as he called them. Then he would bid Ṭaresh pay attention and remember these verses. After Ṭaresh had learned them, Miz'el would be absorbed and silent again, and after a while would sing the first two verses and add the third to them. Having sung them to Ṭaresh innumerable times in his shrill voice, he would ask me to write them down while he composed the rest. When I found that he depicted me in his poem as sitting upon a *hejîn* (mount camel) I demurred, saying that I rode a *dhelûl,* that the Rwala do not say *hejîn* but *dhelûl.* The poet acknowledged this, but said he could not employ such a common word as *dhelûl* in his poem, for in a poem one has to use the word that is more graceful even if less familiar.[12]

This description of poetic composition suggests that dividing a poem into blocks of two and three verses might well be an appropriate first step in the analysis of any Rwala poem.

Once this new perspective on the poem as a series of disconnected blocks of verses is taken, the internal narrative structure of each block also becomes questionable. This is best seen by a schematic diagram of the subject matter of each verse:

*Block 1*

Verse 6: A fighting troop on mounts.
Verse 7: They drive back an enemy contingent.
Verse 8: The enemy attacks again and is driven back.

*Block 2*

Verse 9: The sons of Jam'ân firing their rifles.
Verse 10: Repetition of the same scene.
Verse 11: Repetition of the same scene.

*Block 3*

Verse 18: The Rwala charge and rout the enemy.
Verse 19: Repetition of the same scene.
Verse 20: Repetition of the same scene.

Each of the verses of any one block tends to describe the recurrence of one particular scene in the course of the battle (Block 1) or to describe one particular scene of battle again and again (Blocks 2 and 3). At the same time the interconnection of the scene described in any one block is not related in a continuous way with the scene described in any other block. The poem is very poorly described as a verse-narrative. One would expect to find in a verse-narrative a description of a series of events, not a discontinuous repetition of events.

If we turn to the evaluative verses (v. 13–17), a different kind of problem arises. All these verses have a common theme: the idealization of a Rwala performance in battle. Still these verses are not altogether consistent with one another. The basis of the idealization of the Rwala seems somewhat uncertain. The first of these verses refers to the fallen Rwala and idealizes their deaths. Having proved themselves in battle, the Rwala dead gain their reward in paradise. The second verse then refers to the men among the enemy whom the Rwala killed and describes them as a payment for the Rwala dead. We might cynically observe that the Rwala poet sees his own dead as heroes who gain a divine reward, while he sees the enemy dead merely as payment for the Rwala dead. The important point is, however, that the poet in some curious way seems to recognize and even to insist upon this moral inconsistency. Note the description of the enemy which follows the mention of the blood price in verse 14: "A half of whom understood us, while half were barbarians." Here an important basis of a moral community among the Bedouin, a common language, is specifically mentioned, but attributed no importance. It did not matter, the poet implies, that some of the enemy were like the Rwala and some were not.

Once we have noted that these two verses are purposely designed to contradict one another, we can understand what the poet is saying. The poet idealizes the Rwala performance in battle as a religious act: after a heroic death in battle (h. 13a), they live on in paradise (h. 13b).[13] The poet then undercuts the implication that the Rwala performance in battle was part of a struggle of good against evil: the Rwala take an impressive vengeance (h. 14a) upon a morally neutral opponent (h. 14b). The tribal poet is neither morally obtuse nor cynical. He is amoral. He intentionally *withdraws* the moral implications of a religious idealization in verse 13 with the mention of a blood price reckoned upon a morally neutral opponent in verse 14. He thereby leaves us with the understanding that the very performance of a heroic act is in itself a religious ideal, rather than one element in the struggle of good against evil.

The poet metaphysically idealizes a Rwala heroic act in battle. He then undercuts the implication that it is the metaphysics which is of importance. In this way he underlines the importance of the heroic act itself. A similar strategy continues in the three remaining "evaluative verses." In the initial line of verse 15 the poet first refers to the defeat of the enemy chief Muḥammad, but in doing so he also praises him: "Woe to their chief for his reign (*ḥokmeh*)! Long has it endured in his kin." It is precisely Muḥammad's rule as a hereditary chief that receives praise. This sets the stage for an ironic comparison of the notion of chiefly authority, which is based upon a rule (*ḥokmeh*), with the notion of heroic authority, which is based upon a performance in battle. In the second hemistich of verse 15, Muḥammad's enduring rule is described as confined to the precincts of an agricultural settlement: "And he might peacefully rest in the irrigated depressions." The impressive temporal measure of Muḥammad's rule has been confined to a peaceful agricultural domain as a result of a Rwala heroic performance. In the next verse (v. 16) Muḥammad is addressed again as the Rwala capacity for action is explicitly evoked: "Thou hast begun a war with a tribe that can strike thee from afar." The suggestion of the spatial restriction of Muḥammad's hereditary rule is followed by a suggestion of the spatial extension of Rwala heroic actions. The second hemistich of this verse then evokes the effectiveness of actions against a rule which endures: "As even the hardest iron yields when thou takest pains to bore it." Actions triumph over the enduring qualities of Muḥammad's hereditary rule.

The last of the evaluative verses associates an ancient Rwala chief, the mythical founding ancestor of the Rwala tribe, with the consistent Rwala performance of heroic actions: "The chief, Akhu Dinya, is accustomed to heroic deeds." This verse then concludes with a description of the authority of this ancient chief as a performance of actions which result in death: "And the bone he grinds will change into flour." Here is a final ironic echo of the restriction of Muḥammad's hereditary rule to an agricultural domain. The deaths which result from the ancient authority of heroic actions are attributed an agricultural quality.

The interesting aspect of these evaluative verses is not that they advance a moral, which is confirmed by the results of a battle. Instead, these verses validate a Rwala performance in battle by suggesting that such a performance throws into question the ideas of religion and authority, except in so far as they might reflect the value of a performance in battle. Having asserted that the values of life lie in a performance in battle, the poet appropriately ends his poem with a description of the results of this Rwala performance in battle. Unlike the first verses of the poem, these final verses stress the flight of the enemy instead of describing the Rwala performance that precipitated this flight. The final verse links the rout of Muḥammad and his Bedouins ("On war tents they trod . . . when fleeing") with the rout of the Ottomans ("just as the followers of the leader with the wild poppy-red tarbush").

If we consider the curious structure of the first twelve verses, their intent now becomes somewhat clearer. The first two verses are a conventional poetic opening. Verses 3 to 5 then describe the circumstances of a great intertribal war. Verses 6 to 8 describe a major battle in that war as a Rwala performance. Verses 9 to 11 describe even more specifically the particular performance of particular Rwala. The reduction in scope of the verses is aimed at isolating a Rwala performance as the matter of principal importance. After this, the poet describes the general rout of the enemy (v. 12) as though it were a direct product of a particular performance. The evaluative verses (v. 13-17) then insist on the very value of a Rwala performance, and the closing verses (v. 18-20) link this value with its immediate, concrete result, the rout of the two enemy contingents.

As the poem is examined in detail, we find that the description of the battle is implicated in the structure of a verse: A central act of violence is repetitively described in each block of verses. We also find that the relationship of one verse to another and the relationship of one hemistich to another is associated with an ironic expression. In this way the poet focusses attention upon the centrality of an act of violence which throws religion and authority into question. A discursive reading of the poem fails, and poetic structure emerges as a decisive problem for understanding a Rwala poem. At the same time we see how the failure of a discursive reading is a result of the poet's concern with a heroic performance at the center of a struggle rather than his concern with the significance of that performance within a larger context of political experience.

## 3

The last poem seemed to be one of the more discursive poems of raiding and warfare and therefore one of the most easily understood of all these poems. In fact, it is one of the most difficult. We shall consider a few of the key verses of this poem in the next chapter. For now, another poem is better suited as an introduction to a reading which takes into account poetic structure. The poem in question refers to the events which led to the death of Turki. It is attributed to Khalaf âl Idhen, Saṭṭâm's lieutenant on this occasion. In his poem, Khalaf insists that intertribal conflicts turn upon a principle, very much as the narrators insist that these conflicts turn upon moral principles. For this reason, his poem provides an especially vivid illustration of how the work of poets differs from the work of narrators. Khalaf's principle, we shall find, inverts the narrators' commitment to measured, pragmatic strategies, which protect and support human life. Instead it asserts that men should abandon themselves without restriction to the use of instruments of aggression that have the potential to destroy the basis of human life.

In verse 3, a poet among the Fed'ân, Meḥda' al-Hebdâni, is mentioned. Ḥzeyl and Qâyem (v. 7 and 12) were two Fed'ân heroes. The word *rûthe* in the last verse refers to a kind of pasture on which camels tend to grow fat. Here is Musil's translation of the poem:

1. O thou who ridest a she-camel with a regular pace,
   A sterile one, whose back has borne no burden for eight years!

2. Over the plateau towards the evening she quickly trots,
For, being fleet of foot, throughout her life she has never been urged on by any rider.
3. Reaching that babbler, Meḥda' al-Hebdâni,
Relate the tidings that he also well knows.
4. I said that the sisters of Quṭne attacked us, though not at feud,
And their riders came back with our fair camels from where the herds spent the winter.
5. That news was true, and men shook their heads about it,
And whoever had a wife ceased to press her breasts.
6. The throwers from the saddles would not obey Saṭṭâm
And rushed upon you like a rolling flood.
7. O Ḥzeyl! by Allâh, Qâyem was like a rutting camel
And led a troop of fleet-footed mares in the wake of the captured she-camels.
8. Then when the dew had evaporated they prepared red dyestuff for your chief
In a cloud of dust, dripping with blood and amid the thunder of costly weapons.
9. A blow was dealt to Turki by the throwers from saddles,
By the hand of a hero who rolled him from the mare's back;
10. And it is this deed which brought glory, not the capture of she-camels in a rolling land;
This deed drove your families from the shelter of their tents.
11. Oh, shame on him whose followers were like Haddâj
For our sabers! and how glorious the dripping of their blood!
12. Our young camels, O Ḥzeyl! grew gay with pasture which no one has touched,
And your young camels, O Ḥzeyl! are eating off their own hair.
13. Your herds must not come near the *rûthe* in al-Khôr
Whilst our young camels move thither.

The meter of the Arabic seems to be a form of *rajaz* in the sense that Landberg understood the term. I cannot strictly determine it from Musil's transcription:

1. Yâ râkeb alli mashîha rowj w-arwâj
ḥâyel themân sinîn makhlan ḍaharha[14]
2. ma' al-beyâḥa mashîha al-'aṣr diflâj
wa-hmîme mâ 'omr al-mu'anna nazarha
3. telfi 'ala meḥda' al-habâdîn ma'âj
w-eḥki-l-'elûm alli bqalbeh khabarha
4. qelt ekhwât quṭne ḥârabûna belâ ṣwâj
w-eqfow bshiqḥen 'an meshâti diyarha
5. w-al-'elem ṣâdeq w-ṣâr len-nâs nejnâj
w-mel leh khalîle 'âf raṣṣat thamarha
6. w-saṭṭâm 'ayyaw beh makhlîn al-asrâj
w-kattaw 'aleykom bijmû'en ḥadarha
7. yâ ḥzeyl w-allâh qâyem teqel ṣeyyâj
w-tqawwedû serd as-salâyel betharha

8. w-ḥîn aḍ-ḍaḥa sawwaw ʻala-sh-sheykh semâj
 bsaḥâbaten qeshṭ al-jwâher maṭarha
9. w-turki shallawh mukhlîn al-asrâj
 min kaff qarmen shaqlabeh min ḍaharha[15]
10. w-hâdha-l-fakhar mâ hi bʻârîn behbâj
 alli ʻazal ʻeylâtakom ʻan khadarha
11. yâ ḥeyf yâ-lli rabʻateh mithl haddâj
 bisyûfena w-ḥelw manthar ḥemarha
12. abkârana yâ ḥzeyl min raʻyet al-qafr ṣeyyâj
 w-abkârakom yâ ḥzeyl terʻa wabarha
13. eqtâʻakom ʻan rûtht al-khôr tinʻâj
 w-abkârana teḥoṭṭaha binaḥarha.

The prose narrators were concerned with demonstrating how cautious and sensible men responded to Turki's political adventurism. They began by describing Turki's heroism as a problem which disrupted the Rwala tribe. They then described how the Rwala chief pursued a strategy that was designed to moderate or to suppress Turki's provocations. In contrast, Khalaf's poem begins with the very source of a Bedouin heroic self-expression, the relationship of a man and a beast. Musil's translation of the first hemistichs of the first two verses is inaccurate. Here is a more literal version of these verses:

1. O rider who trots her with a regular pace,
 A sterile one whose back has borne no burden for eight years.
2. Over the plateau he trots her toward evening quickly,
 For, being fleet of foot, throughout her life she has never been urged on by any rider.

Typically the first verse of a poem sets forth a theme which is clarified in the course of a description of a particular conflict. This is the case with this poem. The first hemistich of the initial verse can be glossed as a description of a heroic skill which involves the use of an instrument, a rider trots his mount. The second hemistich can be glossed as a description of the heroic instrument which is the means of this skill. The beast in question is particularly suitable as a mount. A she-camel which has never been bred is especially hardy and durable, and a camel which has not been ridden in a long time is especially spirited. The structure of the initial verse, therefore, insists upon the interconnection of a feature of a man, his skill as a rider, and a feature of a beast, its energy as a mount.

With this basic structure of the verse in mind, we can examine the form of each hemistich in more detail. The first hemistich is not exactly a description. It is a poetic evocation: "O rider . . ." As a poetic evocation, the hemistich does not exactly describe the skill of a rider. Rather it describes how a man with a skill (rider) performs an action (who trots her) which evokes the formal movement of a beast (with a regular pace). There is implicitly a parallel between poet and rider in the design of the hemistich.

The poet by his *speech* evokes a formal image which consists of a man in control of a beastly instrument. The rider by his *actions* evokes a formal movement of a beastly instrument. This initial hemistich announces a poetic evocation that will consist of a clarification of the form of a heroic life abroad.

The second hemistich then adds to this poetic evocation a description of the beast itself. As such, the poetic evocation of a human skill in the first hemistich is qualified with an insistence upon the instrumental means of this skill. If we examine the description of the beastly instrument quite closely, we find that it indicates the constraint of human speech and action by the properties of the instrument itself. While the sterility of the she-camel indicates a hardy and durable mount, this quality also implies that the beast in question has been reserved for heroic purposes, rather than bred for domestic purposes. This quality of the beast, in other words, suggests the priority of the heroic life abroad over a domestic life within the camp. The proper form of a poetic evocation in the camp, we shall find, must recognize the priority of a life abroad over a domestic life in the camp. The second quality of the beast, its not having been ridden in many years, also implies that it has been reserved for heroic purposes. However, it is more exactly an insistence upon the energy of the beast as a thing completely apart from the rider: "whose back has borne no burden . . ." Such an insistence suggests that *the priority of a heroic life abroad is derived from the energy of beasts themselves.* A human action by means of a beastly instrument in a life abroad, we shall find, properly turns upon a self-abandonment to beastly energies.

Speech matters only in so far as it clarifies that it is really heroism which matters, and so the poet must recognize the form of a heroic life abroad. Human actions in a life abroad matter only in so far as they recognize the priority of beastly energies, and so the hero is a man who abandons himself to the use of a beastly instrument. Behind a poetic evocation, there is skillful use of an instrument in a life abroad. Behind the skillful use of an instrument, there is a priority of a heroic life abroad. Behind the priority of a heroic life abroad, there is the energy of beasts. These are the implications which the poet will uncover in the circumstances of the conflict between the Rwala and the Fed'ân on the occasion of Turki's death.

This analysis of the initial verse enables us to understand something more about poetic musicality. As the poet sings a hemistich, the *rajaz* meter of the hemistich imitates the rhythm of camel hooves. The final rhyming phrase of the first hemistich, "with a regular pace (*rowj w-arwâj*)," very likely consists of one foot of the *rajaz* meter ( – ⏑ – – ). This association of a metrical unit and a term for a formal camel pace emphasizes that poetic form is intended to evoke and to clarify the form of a heroic life abroad. What the poet says is regulated by the formal pattern of a movement of a man on a beast, just as what the hero does is regulated by the formal pattern of the movement of a man on a beast. In part, the poet reveals the form of a heroic life abroad. As he constructs his words, he plays with the formal implications of heroism. But in part, he does so in such a way as to suggest that his play is constrained by the forces inherent in a heroic life abroad. His play insists upon the priority of beastly energies.[16]

We have also just seen that the very structure of the initial verse, as a relationship between two elements (two hemistichs), reflects a relationship between two elements at the heart of a life abroad, the skill of a man and the energy of a beast. So it is not only the meter of a hemistich, but also the structure of a verse which both evoke and clarify the form of a heroic life abroad. And finally, if we examine the second hemistich, we find a third feature which suggests that the structure of the poem itself evokes and clarifies such a life abroad. The phrase "eight years" implies that the camel in question is just the right age for riding. This particular time span, however, also has a purely formal function. It is a signal that the instrument of the poet (his poem) has eight temporal parts. This signal is communicated by suggesting that the instrument of the hero (the camel) has an age of eight temporal parts. A block of four verses consisting of eight hemistichs, we shall find, is a basic unit of the poem's composition. Specifically, the poem divides into three sets of four verses together with a concluding verse (v. 13).

The conceptual design of the initial verse implicitly reveals the significance that will arise in the course of a political conflict. The music of a poetic evocation determines the form of a poetic line as the voice is constrained by the rhythm of camel hooves. A two-part structure determines the form of a verse as it is constrained by a heroic relationship. An eight-part structure determines the form of a composition of verses as it is constrained by the nature of beastly energies. This initial verse, in other words, is a formal generalization of what will come to light in the course of events on the occasion of Turki's death. This verse illustrates in a remarkable way just how a poem is constituted as a play upon the formal implications of the relationship of men and beasts in the midst of a struggle among men. Its form is a crystallization of a self-expression by means of beastly energies among the camel-herding nomads. An understanding of their poetry, therefore, is a means of understanding the political experience of these peoples, just as an understanding of their poetry would hardly be possible apart from some consideration of their political circumstances.

This is a detailed and lengthy analysis of a single verse. Each of the successive verses of the poem can be more readily understood, since they are generally a variation of the opening themes. The structure of the second verse, for example, is similar to the structure of the first. Now, however, the poet is explicitly insisting upon the *separation* of a poetic occasion in the camp from a heroic life abroad of riders on mounts. As he does so, the priority of a heroic life abroad, which is based upon beastly energies, begins to become explicit. In the first hemistich, for example, the poetic evocation has vanished, the rider is no longer explicitly mentioned, and the movement of the mount is no longer described as a formal movement. Instead, we see only the action of the rider's control, which produces the action of the mount's fast movement: "he trots her (*mashîha*) . . . quickly (*diflâj*)." At the same time these actions have become dimly perceived images in the twilight of a faraway landscape: "Over the plateau (*ma' al-beyâḥa*) . . . toward evening (*al-'aṣr*) . . ." In the second hemistich, the energy of the mount is now described in terms of the absence of any effort on the part of the rider to evoke its movement: "For, being fleet of foot . . . she has never been urged on by any rider." As the poet insists upon the separation of a heroic occasion from a poetic occasion, questions of poetic intent ("O rider") and poetic form (the rhythms of the voice and the pace of the camels) vanish as we move into the heroic occasion itself. Here, a man lets himself be effortlessly carried away by the energy of a spirited mount, and a heroic intent reduces to a self-abandonment to beastly energies. The heroic relationship of rider and mount is now situated in the desert and steppe and derived from the energy of the beast, which is the feature of the desert and steppe.

The second pair of the initial block of four verses can now be analyzed together and contrasted with the first pair. In verse 3, the rider, who abandons himself to the energy of his mount, figuratively comes to an enemy poet and confronts him: "Reaching that babbler, Meḥda." In the second hemistich we learn why Meḥda is a babbler: "Relate the tidings that he also well knows." The words of the enemy poet are babble (crooked, *ma'âj*) because they do not recognize the truth of events. By implication, his speech does not properly reflect the form of a life abroad. The Rwala poetic evocation in the first pair of verses "confronts" a Fed'ân poet whose speech is improperly constructed and therefore babble.

Just as verse 3 evaluates a Fed'ân poet's speech, so verse 4 now evaluates Fed'ân actions abroad. The initial principle which links speech with the form of a life abroad is here fulfilled as the Rwala poet follows his evaluation of Fed'ân speech with an evaluation of Fed'ân actions. In the first hemistich of verse 4, he announces this evaluation: "I said that the sisters of Quṭne attacked us, though not at feud." The Fed'ân plunder of the Rwala herds is evaluated as an improper action because it was not connected with a Rwala offense against the Fed'ân. The phrase which Musil translates as "though not at feud" literally means without provocation or incitement (*belâ ṣwâj*). In the second hemistich of verse 4, the poet links this evaluation with the description of a Fed'ân action: "And their riders came back with our fair camels . . ." The construction of the verse also demonstrates the proper form of poetic speech which the enemy poet's crooked words do not recognize. The Rwala poet ties his evaluation of Fed'ân actions to a description of events involving those very actions.

But why would a heroic poet evaluate the Fed'ân plunder of Rwala herds as an improper act? Is not plunder itself a form of heroic action? In the next block of verses, we will find that the plunder of the Rwala herds is not seen as a sign of Fed'ân heroism, but as a sign of a Fed'ân desire for herds. It is an act, that is to say, which places a human desire for beasts before the priority of a self-abandonment to the use of energetic beasts. This Fed'ân desire for beasts ignores, therefore, the problem of intertribal political hostility (attacked us, though not at feud). It is precisely a threatening situation of intertribal hostility, which demands a self-abandonment to the use of energetic beasts. And ironically, it is precisely the possibility of a self-abandonment to the use of energetic beasts that makes such a situation so threatening. Khalaf, however, will insist only on the principle of a self-abandonment rather than on the irony of such a principle. Khalaf, we shall discover, identifies a heroic life abroad not with the play of political adventurism, but with the total dedication of men to instruments of aggression in the course of intertribal conflicts.

This anticipation of the poet's interpretation of the events leading to the death of Turki enables us to understand a curious feature of verse 4. The first hemistich announces the Fed'ân attack as follows: "The sisters of Quṭne attacked us . . . ," and follows this with a description of the event: "And their riders came back . . ." The "sisters of Quṭne" are a herd of Fed'ân riding camels. The Fed'ân attack is announced as an improper use of mounts by riders. They take up their beasts to fulfill their personal desires for beasts. The Fed'ân speak differently from the Rwala (v. 3). The Fed'ân use their mounts differently from the Rwala (v. 4). This difference has brought the two tribes into conflict, and this difference will also result in the victory of the Rwala over the Fed'ân. With the completion of verse 4, we have moved from the evocation of the form of a heroic life abroad (h. 1a) to the very event which inspired this evocation (h. 4b). At the same time, we have also moved from a concern with the proper form of speech and action in connection with a life abroad (the theme of the initial pair of verses) to a concern with the specific form of human intents on the occasion of the intertribal conflict (the theme of the second pair of verses). All of the successive verses of the poem will take the form of verse 4. An action or reaction of men (or beasts) will appear in the first hemistich. An event associated with this action or reaction will appear in the second hemistich. This will satisfy the principal of the opening verses whereby speech and action must be derived from the properties of a life abroad.

The next four verses (v. 5–8) can also be analyzed by dividing them into two successive pairs. The first pair describes how the Fed'ân plunder of the Rwala herds evoked a reaction from the Rwala. First the internal state of the Rwala is described as the news of the attack arrives in the camp: "That news was true, and men shook their heads about it." The shaking heads suggest a purely personal and largely internal response on the part of individual Rwala. The second hemistich then relates this personal and internal response to an overt action: "And whoever had a wife ceased to press her breasts." The action clarifies the value of the response. The Rwala repress their personal sexual desires, which are characteristic of a domestic scene, as they turn to pursue a life abroad. The purely personal response of the Rwala takes the form of setting aside purely personal desires. In the next verse (v. 6), the shaking heads are transformed into the rebellion against the authority of the tribal chief: "The throwers from the saddles would not obey Saṭṭâm." As political authority disintegrates, men on mounts with dangerous instruments appear upon the scene. The image of heroic events follows: "And rushed upon you like a rolling flood." Here we see a powerful release which flows not from human, but from natural energies. This charge of riders on mounts is figured as an orgasm not of men, but of nature. As men take up mounts, they become a destructive force in the natural world at large.

Note that the relationship of these two verses continues the theme of the opening pair of verses. We begin with a disturbed personal response to an event abroad (the shaking heads), which is reflected in a distancing of personal concerns from the domestic scene (men turning away from their wives). The disturbed personal response then becomes a disturbance of tribal polity (rebellion against Saṭṭâm), which results in the release of destructive energy in a life abroad (the charge of mounted riders imaged as a natural event). This interpretation is confirmed by a comment of one of Musil's informants. This man interpreted the shaking heads of verse 5 as an indication of the criticism of Saṭṭâm, which foreshadowed the rebellion of verse 6.

In the next pair of verses (v. 7 and 8), we see the result of a collision between a Fed'ân desire for herds, which leads to a provocation, and a Rwala heroic response to this provocation. In verse 7, Fed'ân actions abroad are evaluated as a personal lust for cattle: "Qâyem was like a rutting (*ṣeyyâj*) camel." The description of the Fed'ân action follows: "And led a troop of fleet-footed mares in the wake of the captured she-camels." We have just seen in the preceding pair of verses how the Rwala set aside personal desires as they respond to provocations abroad. In contrast we now see how a personal desire (the cattle lust of Qâyem) gives rise to a careless provocation of the Rwala. The desire to possess more herds for themselves is what impels the actions of the Fed'ân.

Here the poem takes an ironic turn. The word for Qâyem's "rutting (*ṣeyyâj*)" in verse 7 is derived from the same root as the word for "provocation (*ṣwâj*)" in verse 4. The Fed'ân are incited (*ṣeyyâj*), they lust for Rwala cattle, even though they have not been incited (*belâ ṣwâj*) by the Rwala. The source of this irony lies in Fed'ân actions. Their personal desires are out of place in a life abroad. In the final verse of this block, the poet clarifies just how out of place they are by means of another irony. It takes the form of a grotesque metaphorical description of the Rwala response to the impropriety of Fed'ân actions. The Rwala perform a marriage ceremony for Turki, the Fed'ân chief who leads his men in cattle-raids: "they prepared red dyestuff for your chief." The Fed'ân pursue their personal desires in a life abroad, rather than restricting these desires to a domestic scene. Here the Fed'ân discover just how a life abroad resembles the domestic scene. The Fed'ân lust will be satisfied by a dreadful marriage ceremony. The body decorations for this ceremony are prepared from blood, not henna. The description of the marriage festival follows: "In a cloud of dust, dripping with blood and amid the thunder of costly weapons." The finery of this ceremony consists of costly weapons. The music of this ceremony is the shots of rifles and the pounding of hooves. The spectacle of this ceremony takes the form of a destructive storm in the world at large. Behind the clouds, lightning, and thunder of this storm, we glimpse the dreadful energy of instruments of aggression.

The second block of verses describes how the manifestation of a Rwala response (v. 5 and 6) converts a Fed'ân lust for cattle (v. 7) into a marriage festival of blood and death (v. 8). In this respect the final verse of this block is not an attempt by a Rwala poet to glorify Rwala heroic actions by means of an imaginative metaphorical description. Rather, this charge of riders and mounts which is figured as a dreadful marriage festival is derived from the inappropriateness of a Fed'ân life abroad. It is a grotesque metaphor, which suggests just how grotesque the Fed'ân lust for cattle becomes when the true nature of a life abroad surfaces as a self-abandonment of men to the use of instruments of aggression.

The last block of four verses addresses the results of Rwala actions and in doing so clarifies their significance. The initial pair of verses in this block evaluates the personal implications of these actions. In the first hemistich of verse 9, a decisive event which occurred during a struggle of riders on mounts is described: "A blow was dealt to Turki by the throwers from saddles." A Rwala heroic performance is here aimed against a specific person, the chief of the Fed'ân. The second hemistich then describes this heroic performance as a specific personal action: "By the hand of a hero who rolled him from the mare's back." As we see that hand which strikes a man, we see the heroic identity that lies behind the flood and the storm. It is the identity of a man which can be reduced to his employment of an aggressive instrument. Such an identity is conveyed by that part of the body which figures a practical accomplishment - the hand. As the hand acts, it separates a rider from his mount. A Rwala heroic performance, which consists of self-abandonment to the use of an aggressive instrument, is itself a response to the investment of men in the use of beastly energies.

In the next verse of the initial pair (v. 10), the unhorsing of Turki is first interpreted as a sign of the difference between the personal actions of the Rwala and the personal actions of the Fed'ân: "And it is this deed which brought glory, not the capture of she-camels in a rolling land," a reference to events in verse 7. In the next hemistich, the results of this difference are described: "This deed drove your families from the shelter of their tents." The Rwala set aside their personal desires as they turned their attentions from a domestic setting to a life abroad (v. 5). As a result, the domestic setting of the Fed'ân, who pursued their personal desires in a life abroad, is now disrupted by a Rwala action. Where there is a threat of intertribal conflict, putting personal desires before self-abandonment to the use of instruments of aggression leads to the disruption of the very scene of personal desires: a domestic setting.

The final pair of verses in this last block evaluates the political implication of Rwala actions. In verse 11, a description of the slaughter of the Fed'ân polity parallels the description of the fall of the Fed'ân chief in verse 9: "Oh, shame on him whose followers were like Haddâj." The flow of blood from the Fed'ân tribesmen is likened to the flow of the great spring of Haddâj. The clarification for this comparison follows in the second hemistich: "For our sabers! and how glorious the dripping of their blood." The hand of a person, which unhorses a Fed'ân chief (h. 9b), here becomes the use of a personal instrument of aggression (by means of our swords, *bisyûfena*), which slaughters the Fed'ân polity. This verse clarifies the true nature of political authority in the desert and steppe. It is not the authority of a chief, but the authority of personal instruments of aggression. The Rwala rebelled against their chief as they abandoned themselves to the use of aggressive instruments and became a powerful polity (v. 6). The polity of the Fed'ân is now slaughtered as a result of the faulty leadership of their chief (v. 11). Where there is a threat of intertribal conflict, putting the authority of a chief before the use of personal instruments of aggression leads to the slaughter of the polity.

The figure which describes the results of the actions of the Rwala in verse 11 can be compared with the flood and the storm in verses 6 and 8.

As the copious flow of Fed'ân blood is compared with the flow of the great spring Haddâj, Rwala political violence is imaged as a natural feature of the desert landscape. It is the use of personal instruments (by means of our swords) and a delight in the results of using them (how sweet the scattering of their blood), which lies behind the fact that political violence is a natural feature of the desert landscape.

In the next verse of the final pair (v. 12), the political implications of Rwala actions, described in the previous verse, result in a decisive difference between the tribal polities of the Rwala and the Fed'ân:

> Our young camels, O Ḥzeyl! grew gay (copulated, *ṣeyyâj*) with pasture which no one has touched,
> And your young camels, O Ḥzeyl! are eating off their own hair.

The Rwala herds multiply as their beasts freely exercise their natural sexual desires. Cattle wealth is a result of heroic actions, even though it is not properly the end of those actions. At the same time, the herds of those men who have a lust for cattle diminish, as their animals are constrained to feed unnaturally upon their own bodies. In this result we see the final irony of Fed'ân improprieties. The free expression of desires by beasts (*ṣeyyâj*) is a natural feature of beasts and the productive results are pleasing (h. 12a). But the free expression of a desire to possess beasts is an unnatural feature of men, which leads to an unnatural constraint upon their beasts, and the unproductive results are grotesque (h. 12b).

In the concluding verse (v. 13), the Rwala poet first commands the Fed'ân not to come near (*tin'âj*) the pastures of al-Khôr: "Your herds must not come near the *rûthe* in al-Khôr." Men of crooked (*ma'âj*) words must now perform crooked (*tin'âj*) movements with their mounts, while men who recognize the realities of a life abroad can command, by virtue of their recognition that the energies of beasts come first. And then the Rwala poet once again suggests the linking of human speech and action with beastly energies. He confirms his command that the Fed'ân turn aside from al-Khôr with an image of the movement of Rwala herds toward that pasture: "Whilst our young camels move thither." In the desert and steppe, human intents prove powerful when they are attached to beastly energies.

The principle of this poem might at first seem to be akin to the principle of the narratives. There was an insistence in the tales that one must speak the truth and in doing so recognize the reality of a political situation. However, there is an important difference in the way in which this poet conceives of a truth that is derived from the reality of a political situation. In the narratives, some concept of a form of articulated response was always implicit in the description of how men attempted to deal with political anarchy. In the first version of the death of Turki, Saṭṭâm tried to control or to evade Turki by means of cautious and sensible policies that were on the side of peace. In the second version, the narrator was committed to pragmatic strategies by which heroes like Turki might be effectively suppressed. Similarly, as an-Nûri and his Rwala struggled with Sa'dûn, their behavior was shaped by their recognition of a form of personal propriety. And, of course, in the tale about the wars with the western tribes, the very power of an articulated response to anarchy was an explicit concern.

The poet Khalaf interprets the Bedouin political situation in a very different way. For him, the fundamental principle of a political response must involve a self-abandonment to the use of destructive resources. He justifies such a principle by invoking the destructive potential of aggressive instruments and beastly energies. These political resources have the power to kill chiefs, disrupt the family, slaughter followers, and reduce men to poverty. That is to say, the character of political resources raises a question about polity and society as formal arrangements. Indeed, the character of political resources raises a question about the possibility of any articulated response to the political situation whatsoever. Khalaf insists instead that men must abandon themselves to the use of mounts and weapons, because there is no other way that one might conceive of living where men possess mounts and weapons.

The hero in war is a man who lets himself be carried away by destructive resources. The hero in peace is a man who insists upon the principle of the unrestrained use of destructive resources in war. Let us recall once again that it is Khalaf who speaks. It is Khalaf, the man who killed Turki and presented the mare of the dead hero to Saṭṭâm. It is Khalaf, the man who sponsored the rebellion against the merciful Saṭṭâm and led the enraged mob that murdered Turki. This poem, however, is a sign of something more than the character of an individual who was especially devoted to the use of a destructive means as the basis of political life. The poem illustrates how easily a fascination with the playful use of destructive resources in the desert and steppe could degenerate into an unrestrained dedication to such instruments. Such a degeneration was just what the first narrator of the death of Turki dreaded when he concluded his tale: "there was a war so cruel that rider after rider fell off his horse, and the members of both tribes were bent more on killing a man than on capturing animals." This was more than the problem of the character of a specific individual. This problem was inherent in the political circumstances of the desert and steppe.

## 4

The author of the next poem, like Khalaf, believes that intertribal conflict is the central fact of political experience, but he does not insist that men should abandon themselves to the use of mounts and weapons. Instead, he suggests that the interconnection of men and instruments of aggression has an esthetic value. As he describes the Rwala in war, he not only conveys the terrible power of their commitment to an aggressive means; he also conceives of a Rwala tribal authority and a Rwala tribal association in terms of this esthetic value.

This illustrates a feature of the poems of raiding and warfare that was not so evident from Khalaf's insistence upon a principle of heroic speech and action. The poems, as esthetic constructions, reveal the expressive implications that touch the lives of men who are committed to the use of personal instruments of aggression. They are men who come to see the world around them from a certain perspective. They value a kind of "clarity" in their relationships with one another and in their interpretations of political events. They look upon formal political arrangements with suspicion and distrust, as the complex constructions of men who are essentially interested in their purely personal welfare. They take this point of view, we shall see, as they consider the awesome power of personal instruments of aggression in the desert and steppe. When men believe that there is a single feature of political experience that shapes and commands all life, then they believe that human responses have been determined in a clear and self-evident fashion.

The poem refers to the events which Musil labeled "Wars between the Rwala and the Beni Wahab (1850–64)," the same conflicts touched upon by the poem in section 2 of this chapter. The leader of the Beni Wahab is Muḥammad eben Smeyr, mentioned here in verses 4 and 5. Here is the poem:

1. O ye who ride in the saddles of stubborn she-camels,  
   On four young sterile she-camels, slender ones from al-Hûj –
2. Like an ostrich they run, moving their upper parts;  
   The heroes can rest when their saddlebags are raised like wings by the riding camels!
3. In the spring they grazed southwest of at-Tinf,  
   But in midsummer at al-Mrûj, far from the heat which brings bone diseases.
4. They will come to Farḥân's father, that tormentor of the wounded,  
   In a struggle of riders, when one vanquishes and the other is vanquished,
5. To the protector of loads, freighted for al-Mzêrîb,  
   When the redcaps fix the day of complaints.
6. Say: "O Ḥmûd! he surely will reward thee with cuffs and kicks,  
   And, if victorious, will tread on thee as on a slipper.
7. Thou must know what it means for thee to be far from the chief and what to be near him,  
   Also that the spittle of anger has long ago been spat out between the fighters."
8. Feyṣal bought al-Jeydûr with the help of those with worn teeth  
   And of a few rutting stallions with their square heads.

9. Firmly did Feyṣal grasp his sword by the handle,
 Oh, how terrified was the heart of the cautious and the incautious too!
10. We are entitled to al-Jeydûr both by right and by possession.
 And the Jlâs think one who seeks his right is already vanquished.
11. 'Abdallâh's descendants, behold! have recovered from their illness,
 Their young mares obey and their men turn round [on the command].
12. Oh, shame! that solver of the most intricate disputes
 Was wounded between his left shoulder blade and his first rib!
13. He that protected the bent [fleeing] riders
 Was deserted like a wether left behind by the flock and dying of the *rowje* disease.
14. They fled through those narrow gullies yonder
 And today keep their horses, fed only from food bags, tied up at al-Jûj.
15. 'Eyfe with his old she-camel searches for a host,
 And in the land of al-Belqa hands around pots of whey diluted with water.
16. Oh, shame! 'Eyfe goes no more near the flames of war!
 His throat is so widened that his mouthful is like a bundle meant for a camel.
17. Concerning Eben Sha'lân's market place I declare that it is ours by right and possession;
 He who denies it is for his babble justly despised by all.

The cast of characters is as follows:

v. 4, Farḥân's father: Muḥammad eben Smeyr.

v. 5, Redcaps: Ottoman officials.

v. 6, Ḥmûd: Originally an ally of the Rwala who was staying with Muḥammad eben Smeyr when the poem was composed.

v. 8, Feyṣal: The war chief of the Rwala at the time of the conflict over the territory of al-Jeydûr.

v. 10, Âl-Jlâs: The Âl-Jlâs and the Beni Wahab, who are here at war with one another, are the two major groupings of tribes within the Ḍana Muslim. The Rwala, led by Feyṣal, are in the Âl-Jlâs grouping. The Weld 'Ali, led by Muḥammad, are in the Beni Wahab grouping.

v. 11, 'Abdallâh's descendants: A section of the Rwala tribe originally allied with Muḥammad, but who rejoined their kinsmen when the two tribes went to war.

v. 12, solver of the most intricate disputes: a celebrated judge among the Weld 'Ali who was wounded by the Rwala.

v. 15 and 16, 'Eyfe: A relative of the poet who joined Muḥammad in the war against the Rwala and was subsequently unable to reconcile himself with his own kinsmen.

I cannot determine the meter of the poem with certainty. Here is the Arabic:

1. Yâ râkebîn kwâr ḥeylen meṣâ'îb
 arba' abkâren ḥîl min ḍummar al-hûj
2. heyqen hajjât heyqen yesîjen al-maṣâlîb
 keyf an-nishâma zaffat al-hejen bel-khrûj

3. mirbâ'hen mâ ḥaddar at-tinf taghrîb
wa-mqîḍahen 'an ḥerwat al-ghoshsh bel-mrûj[17]
4. yelfen labu farḥân 'aṭb al-aṣâwîb
en ṣâr bel-fersân zâ'ej w-maz'ûj
5. zeyzûm ḥamlât wariden al-mzêrîb
en tarramow ḥemr aṭ-ṭwâqi 'ala-ṣ-ṣûj
6. qil yâ ḥmûd lâ yejzâk ṣafq w-'arâqîb
en entaṣar yeṭâk ber-rejel bâbûj
7. 'endak khabar ba'adak 'an ash-sheykh teqrîb
w-rîq az-za'al bên al-ḥarîbên mamjûj
8. feyṣal shara'-l-jeydûr bemfâṣel an-nîb
w-khaṭwa'-l-ḥṣân mrâba' ar-râs hâyûj
9. feyṣal elya' naṣṣab 'ala-s-seyf tenṣîb
w-mâ faḍaḥ min qalb 'âqel w-khajkhûj[18]
10. ḥenna 'ala-l-jeydûr ḥaqq w-teqâḍîb
w-'enda-l-jlâs mudawwer al-ḥaqq maflûj
11. awlâd 'abdallâh balâhom tarow ṭîb
emhârahom ṭow'ât w-arkâbahom 'ûj[19]
12. w-yâ ḥeyf yâ fakkâk 'ûj al-meṭâlîb
bên al-khwêlef w-as-serâjîf mar'ûj
13. yethni qafa'-hla-ḍ-ḍhûr al-maḥâdîb[20]
w-khulli kema kabshen wara-ḍ-ḍân maryûj
14. aqfow ma' hâk at-tlâ' aḍ-ḍanâbîb[21]
w-kheyl al-'alîq murabbaṭâten 'ala jûj
15. w-'eyfe yeṣadder fâṭereh lel-ma'âzîb
yedûr bel-belqa' mqâṣîd marjûj
16. yâ ḥeyf 'eyfe mâ yedâni-l-lwâhîb
ḥalqeh wasî' w-laqmeteh teqil daḥrûj
17. w-'an sûq eben sha'lân ḥaqq w-teqâdîb
w-harrâj tara min kathar al-herj masmûj.

This poem exhibits the well-known features of traditional Arabian poetry in a remarkable way. It is difficult to read the poem discursively, and various references in the poem are obscure. Eight different persons or groups are named in the course of thirteen consecutive verses (v. 4–16) and the relationships of these various persons and groups is not set forth in the poem itself. Fortunately, Musil provides a detailed explication of these references and the various circumstances that link them to the events in question. This explication is summarized above in the list of characters.

The poem can be provisionally broken down into blocks of verses. There is an opening image of riders on mounts which includes verses 1 to 3. In verses 4 and 5, these riders arrive at the camp of the enemy chief, Muḥammad eben Smeyr, and challenge him. The enemy chief is addressed by various epithets: "Farḥân's father," "that tormentor of the wounded," and "the protector of loads." In verses 6 to 7, these riders also warn a former Rwala ally who was staying with the enemy chief when the poem was composed.

The next block of verses (v. 8–10) describes the intertribal war in terms of Rwala actions. Verse 11 is a transitional verse which depicts a section of the Rwala, who were at first inclined to support Muḥammed, but who later rejoined their tribal kinsmen at the outbreak of hostilities with the Beni Wahab. The block of verses which follows (v. 12–14) describes the intertribal war in terms of the actions of the Beni Wahab. In verses 15 and 16, a relative of the poet who went over to the enemy on this occasion is ridiculed. Verse 17 concludes the poem.

Certain blocks of verses in the poem parallel one another. The block which describes the Rwala victory (v. 8–10) parallels the block which describes the Beni Wahab defeat (v. 12–14). Similarly, the pair of verses which warns an ally who was staying with Muḥammad (v. 6–7) parallels the pair of verses which ridicules a relative of the poet who joined Muḥammad in the recent war (v. 15–16). Verse 11 is a transitional verse between these parallel structures. It includes a theme of "a reversal" in its description of a section of the Rwala turning about on their mounts. Now let us examine the poem verse by verse.

The initial verse is similar to the initial verse of the preceding poem. A skillful action by means of an instrument is described in the first hemistich. The instrument itself is described in the second hemistich. The only obvious difference is that this verse mentions a group of riders and mounts instead of one rider and one mount. However, let us examine a literal translation of the initial verse of this poem:

> O riders who are saddled on sterile she-camels who are stubborn,
> Four young sterile she-camels, from the slender ones of al-Hûj.

In the first hemistich of this verse, there is a poetic evocation of men with a heroic skill (riders) who are attached to (saddled on) heroic instruments (sterile she-camels) who have an untamed energy (stubborn, unbroken). Another difference between the initial verses of the two poems is now apparent. The first hemistich of the above verse evokes the very attachment (saddled on) of skilled men and energetic beasts. In doing so, it also describes the energetic beasts as not fully under the control (stubborn, unbroken) of men with a skill.

In the second hemistich of the above verse, beasts are described whose qualities make them suitable for heroic purposes. They are sterile females, and they are of a special breed from al-Hûj. Both of these qualities indicate a mount of great endurance. Now, however, the poet explicitly mentions four camels. In doing so, he indicates that the group of riders on mounts has a certain structure. It is a form of association of both men and beasts. In addition, the breed from al-Hûj is known not only for its endurance, but for its esthetic qualities as well. This aspect of the camels is emphasized by the remark that the camels are "from the slender ones of al-Hûj." This description of the beasts suggests that both a structure and an esthetic value arise out of the very properties of the beasts themselves.

Now we can see quite clearly how this initial verse differs in its implications from the initial verse of the last poem. As men attach themselves to beasts, they come together to form a structured association because of the properties of beasts. As men attach themselves to beasts, an esthetic value appears and is derived from the properties of beasts. The stage is being set in this initial verse for the conception of a tribal polity, which is derived not from the character of the relationship of human skills and beastly energies, but more curiously from the "esthetic value" of the attachment of men to beastly energies. This feature of the polity will become manifest in the midst of the violence of an intertribal conflict.

The poet has signaled that the heroic association of riders and mounts has a structure of four parts (four young she-camels) in the initial verse. This four-part structure now appears in the four hemistichs of verses 2 and 3. The first of these verses will reveal how an esthetic value arises in connection with the energy of beasts. The second of these verses will reveal how a pastoral society takes shape around human recognition of this esthetic value. These verses can be more accurately and literally translated as follows:

2. Ostriches have started, ostriches moving their shoulder muscles,
   The easy pleasure of the heroes is the raising of the wings of the riding-camels with saddlebags.
3. For their springtime pasture, they did not descend the southwest of at-Tinf,
   And for their summertime pasture, far from the heat of bone-diseases, they were at al-Mrûj.

In the first hemistich of verse 2, we find a simile which compares running camels with running ostriches. The structure of this hemistich takes the form of a relationship between the active appearance of a poetic image (ostriches have started) and the source of energy behind this image (ostriches moving their shoulder muscles). This hemistich, that is to say, insists upon the esthetic value of the properties of beastly energies by means of a poetic image of running beasts at the same time as it derives this esthetic value from beastly energies.

The second hemistich of verse 2 can be understood as an analysis of the esthetic value of the poetic image in the first hemistich. First, we find that the image of running ostriches, as a representation of running camels, depends upon the very attachment of men and beasts: "the raising of the wings of the riding-camels with saddlebags." The wings of the ostriches are not an anatomical feature of camels' bodies. They are not the waving arms of the riders, nor are they the fluttering clothes of the riders. The wings are the saddlebags, the very article by which men attach themselves to beasts. The esthetic value of the poetic image is precisely that it makes visible the attachment of man and beast.

When this verse begins with the phrase, "Ostriches have started," it is referring to the poetic evocation of the attachment of riders and mounts in the initial verse. It has transformed this evocation into an esthetic conception of a heroic life abroad. In the second hemistich of the second verse, we discover as well that the esthetic form of such a life has an effect upon the riders of mounts: "The easy pleasure of the heroes is the raising of the wings . . ." The appearance of an esthetic form, which is derived from the very attachment of men and beasts in a life abroad, has the effect of putting these men at their ease and satisfying their desires.

The poet insists upon the atomistic relationship of rider and mount as a central feature of political experience, just as Khalaf insisted upon this atomistic relationship in the last poem considered. However, this poet construes the relationship as an esthetic form rather than a principle of behavior. As a result, he lays the ground for conceiving of a Rwala polity not as a formal entity, which is disrupted by a self-abandonment to the use of aggressive instruments, but as a form of heroic association, which reflects the esthetic value of its members' attachment to their beasts. He takes this step in the next verse, which completes his four-part structural analysis of men's attachment to energetic beasts.

The third verse is a description of the space and time of a pastoral nomadic society. Men and beasts occupy different territories as the seasons change. The first hemistich of this description takes the form of an intentional occupation of a mountain pasture: "they did not descend the southwest of at-Tinf." This determined occupation of an elevated landscape will eventually be associated with the esthetic value of clear visibility. The pastoral society, which occupies a mountain pasture with determination, we shall find, reflects men making visible their attachment to aggressive instruments by means of a determined gesture. The second hemistich of this description of a pastoral society suggests it is free of the affliction of a disease: "far from the heat of bone-diseases, they were at al-Mrûj." This healthy occupation of a pasture by men and beasts is marked by the vigor of beasts themselves. However, the health of the Rwala beasts is described in negative, rather than positive terms. The pastoral society which occupies a pasture free from disease, we shall find, suggests another kind of pastoral society which is beset by an affliction, precisely as a result of a failure to recognize the priority of men's attachment to beastly energies.

In the next two verses, the Rwala heroic polity arrives and confronts not an enemy poet as was the case in the last poem, but an enemy chief, Muḥammad eben Smeyr. Unlike Khalaf, this poet does not contrast the personal behavior of the members of two tribes in terms of a principle. He contrasts instead the esthetic form of two tribal polities. In doing so, he addresses a chief whose personal authority represents the form of a tribal polity. Let us see how this is so.

Muḥammad is characterized in each of the two verses in two very different ways. In the first hemistich of verse 4, he is described as the father of Farḥân and as "that tormentor of the wounded." We see Muḥammad as a man of authority (a father) and we see the form of his authority in terms of his actions in war (a tormentor). Musil's informant explained the second epithet as a reference to the fact that the wounds inflicted by Muḥammad were said to take an inordinately long time to heal. In the second hemistich of this verse, the confrontation of the Rwala and the Beni Wahab is described as a decisive struggle of riders on mounts: "when one vanquishes and the other is vanquished (*zâ'ej w-maz'ûj*)." Note that the Arabic expresses this very quality with a certain poetic decisiveness.

To understand verse 4, we have to compare it with the verse which follows. In the first hemistich of verse 5, another epithet for Muḥammad appears: "To the protector of loads, freighted for al-Mzêrîb." This epithet refers to Muḥammad's contracts with the Ottomans to provide protection for some of the caravans of pilgrims and supplies, which were destined for Medina and Mecca. Here Muḥammad is not exactly described in terms of his actions in warfare. He is described in terms of his paid services as a mercenary for the Ottomans. In the second hemistich of this verse, we find a kind of confrontation, which is not at all like the struggle of riders on mounts described in the preceding verse: "When the redcaps fix the day of complaints." This refers to the haggling between Muḥammad and the Ottomans about whether the former had performed his services properly and how much he was to be paid. Muḥammad then is not simply a chief who leads men in war. He is a chief who leads men who perform military services for money. These are not heroes, but self-interested men who are involved in contracts and litigation.

The last verse has clarified the implications of the preceding verse. When Muḥammad fights in war, there is something esthetically indecisive about the blows he delivers. He is the tormentor of the wounded. Now verse 5 reveals that this quality is actually a subtle reflection of his involvement in contracts and litigation. These are covert, complex agreements of self-interested men who bargain and deal with other men. They do not have the decisive quality of a struggle of riders on mounts in which there are those who win all and those who lose all. Muḥammad and the men he represents are men of mixed motivations. They fight like the Rwala, but they fight as self-interested men who are involved in contractual agreements with other men. The clarification of verse 4 by verse 5 is a theme which runs through the remainder of the poem. Note that the suggestion of a poetic clarification of one verse by another is related with the "decisive" quality that the poet attributes to a struggle of riders on mounts in verse 4. Eventually we shall see that this theme of a poetic clarification is connected with the theme of the esthetic value of the clearly visible attachment of skilled men to instruments of aggression.

These last two verses complete the formal opening of the poem. In the verses which follow, these themes begin to be developed in connection with a specific situation. In verse 6, the poet commands his riders on mounts to address this specific situation: "Say: 'O Ḥmûd! he surely will reward thee with cuffs and kicks.'" Ḥmûd eben Me'jel, originally an ally of the Rwala, was staying with the chief Muḥammad eben Smeyr when the poem was composed. Here this ally is warned about the character of personal relationships among self-interested men. In the second hemistich, the poet suggests that the character of these personal relationships will be clarified by the outcome of a war: "And, if victorious, will tread on thee as on a slipper." Muḥammad, who is self-interested, only uses men so long as he needs them. Once danger is past, he abandons them. Verse 7, which is also addressed to Ḥmûd, can be literally translated as follows:

> Thou art aware of thy separation from the near chief,
> And the spittle of anger between the fighters has been spat.

Ḥmûd is separated from the more natural and genuine form of authority of the Rwala head chief (h. 7a). This is a form of authority which arises from the threat of men's passions which lead to war (h. 7b).

These last two verses, like the preceding two, have described two forms of authority, one linked with the properties of men who seek their self-interest and one linked with the properties of intertribal conflict. However, these two verses have explicitly suggested that intertribal conflict itself confirms the faultiness of one of these forms of authority and the validity of the other. At the same time, these last two verses illustrate just how men should have relationships with other men. Where men with aggressive instruments are impassioned, they should set aside their concern for their own self-interest in consideration of the overriding threat of political conflict. They should instead be loyal to those who are closest to them. We glimpse just how a situation of political turmoil makes men attentive to their relationships with one another. We glimpse how the virtue of loyalty is forged by the threat of political violence.

The next three verses describe the war between the Rwala and the Beni Wahab, which involved a dispute over the territory of al-Jeydûr. The first of these verses (v. 8) can be literally translated so that the position of each of the English words reflects the position of the Arabic words:

> Feyṣal bought al-Jeydûr by means of those with worn teeth,
> And a few stallions, square-headed and rutting.

In the first hemistich, Feyṣal, the Rwala war chief at the time, "buys" the territory in question, just as Muḥammad buys men and is a bought man. However, the currency of the Rwala chief is not money, but a type of beastly instrument. In the second hemistich, the form of this purchase is again emphasized by linking it with a second type of beastly instrument. Musil's informant interpreted each of these phrases as referring to both a kind of man and a kind of beast. "Those with worn teeth," he observed, were older prudent warriors on older hardy camels. "A few stallions, square-headed and rutting" were younger impetuous warriors on highly spirited horses. This interpretation is derived in part from the structure of these images. Unlike the opening verse of a poem, they do not refer directly to the energy of a beast in terms of its breed, its sex, its sterility, its having been newly broken, or its having never been ridden. They refer to the energy of the beast indirectly through its "facial" features. The idea of a face is immediately interpreted by the Bedouins as a reference to men. This part of the anatomy is a primary feature of humans but only a secondary feature of beasts. And yet the poet is literally describing beasts and so the result is a kind of man seen through the features of a beast.

Note that each of these images receives peculiar emphasis. The part of each phrase that refers to a beastly face ends the hemistich and constitutes both the internal and terminal rhyme of the verse. As this verse describes the appearance of the Rwala chief, we see him in connection with these beastly faces. These beastly faces moreover are esthetic constructs. They convey a unity of men and beasts in terms of the skill of the first and the energy of the second. These phrases, that is to say, are an echo of the initial theme of the attachment of man and beast as an expressive form. They are poetic images, like the running ostriches. But now we see that the true import of this expressive form appears in the context of an intertribal war.

In the next verse, the significance of this expressive form becomes clear. Verse 9 can be translated so that the position of the English words matches the position of the Arabic words:

> Feyṣal when he raised the sword firmly grasped,
> Oh how confused (disordered) the heart of the cautious and the reckless.

In the first hemistich, the Rwala chief grasps and elevates a sword so that it can be seen. The image of the raised and grasped sword appears at the emphatic point of the poetic line and constitutes the rhyme phrase (*naṣṣab 'ala-s-seyf tenṣîb*). Here is the true authority of the desert and steppe.

Here is the true significance of the attachment of men and beasts. It is the image of a man who is attached to an aggressive instrument. Feyṣal, the Rwala war chief, makes this authority visible as he raises the sword firmly grasped. Chiefs must act, men must come together, the poet suggests, around this central fact of Bedouin political experience.

In the second hemistich, we see that this raised sword firmly grasped impinges visually upon the enemy. Now we can understand why the expressive form of an attachment of men and aggressive instruments is represented as a visual image (the running ostriches, the beastly faces, the raised sword firmly grasped). The visual aspect of these expressive forms suggests the clear and self-evident quality of the attachment of men and aggressive instruments in the desert and steppe. The esthetic value of the attachment of men and aggressive instruments is intended to convey the esthetic quality of a life experience which is constructed around this attachment. For in verses 6 and 7, we have seen that relationships themselves have a clear and self-evident quality as the tribes are drawn into a conflict. And now let us note another curious feature of this second hemistich of verse 9. As men perceive the raised sword firmly grasped they are thrown into confusion. Two types of men are described, "the cautious and the reckless." These two types are the same types represented in the beastly faces of the preceding verse, older more prudent men and younger more impetuous men. As the attachment of men to aggressive instruments becomes clearly visible, it is no longer a matter of just how men use these instruments. The precise quality of the skill of men is of no consequence. It is rather the very link of men with aggressive instruments that is the central fact of political experience.

The final verse of this block, verse 10, can also be literally translated so that the position of the English words matches the position of the Arabic words:

> We are over (in possession of) al-Jeydûr, Truth and Seizure,
> And near the Âl Jlâs, he who seeks (in a circuitous manner) the Truth (his rights) is Vanquished (split).

This verse is an announcement of the Rwala victory over the Beni Wahab. It conceives of this victory as a moment when the difference between the Rwala and Beni Wahab is clarified.

The first hemistich is an evaluation of the Rwala possession of al-Jeydûr. This evaluation takes the form of a concise phrase which appears at the emphatic point of the poetic line: "Truth and Seizure." The word for Truth (*ḥaqq*) connotes a clear, self-evident reality, the very quality of a here-and-now perception of an object before one's eyes. The word for Seizure (*teqâḍîb*) connotes an act of taking by cutting away. The possession of al-Jeydûr, this phrase suggests, is a confirmation of the transcendent value of men's attachment to aggressive instruments. A Truth is associated with the concreteness of a forceful seizure by means of an instrument. And at this transcendent moment of Truth, we hear an echo of the determined occupation of a mountain pasture by men and beasts in verse 3. For the announcement of the possession of al-Jeydûr literally states that the Rwala are "over" al-Jeydûr. An elevated pastoral society conceals within it the lofty Truth of men's attachment to instruments of aggression.

The second hemistich of this verse describes how the Rwala (the Âl Jlâs) approach to political experience differs from the Beni Wahab approach, and suggests that this difference is clarified by the results of war. This is accomplished by an ironic play upon the concept of Truth (*ḥaqq*). In the first hemistich, the Arabic word *ḥaqq* suggests a clear and self-evident reality, a matter beyond dispute. In the second hemistich, the word *ḥaqq* suggests a claim against another that is advanced through litigation, a matter which is the subject of a dispute. The transcendent values of the Beni Wahab involve suppositions and arguments about their legitimate self-interests, rather than the reality of concrete facts. When such men encounter the Rwala, they are vanquished or more literally "split apart (*maflûj*)." The Beni Wahab who attempt to bargain and to connive for their advantage are ultimately the victims of the clear and self-evident reality of the upraised sword firmly grasped.

The next verse (v. 11) is a transitional verse. It refers to a section of the Rwala, the descendants of 'Abdallâh, who were initially inclined to support Muḥammad, but who rejoined their kinsmen upon the outbreak of hostilities. In the first hemistich, the poet describes the return of the descendants of 'Abdallâh as a recovery from a disease and insists upon the visibility of this event (behold!). In the second hemistich, the poet images the actual event of this return as mounts responding to their riders and riders turning about (*'ûj*) their mounts. A state of vigor and health is presented as the visible event of men commanding and redeploying their instruments of aggression.

The "turn about" by the descendants of 'Abdallâh is also a signal of a formal reversal in the poem itself. We have just seen the Rwala achieving a victory in the war. We shall now see the Beni Wahab suffering defeat. This shift in perspective is also coordinate with a shift from a lofty tribe, whose behavior is in accordance with a clear and self-evident reality, to a base tribe which proves to be afflicted with the disease of disloyalty. The first verse of the following block of verses (v. 12–14) begins where the preceding block of verses (v. 8–10) ended:

> Oh, shame! that solver of the most intricate disputes
> Was wounded between his left shoulder blade and his first rib!

The man of the Beni Wahab who is mentioned here was famous for his abilities as a native judge or mediator (*'ârefa*). Here we see how the Beni Wahab, as men who seek out their self-interests, are literally split apart. The fate of men of litigation and disputation, which was announced in verse 10, now appears as an actual event in the course of the intertribal war. However, these verses are not simply a continuation of the account of the war. This block of three verses parallels the structure of the preceding block of three verses. To see how this is so, let us begin by noting the curious anatomical detail with which the wound of the judge is described. In verse 8, we saw the images of powerful men through the heads of energetic beasts. In verse 12, we catch a glimpse of the image of a vulnerable beast through the anatomy of a weak man. For as the poet previously invoked the head of a kind of beast and thereby suggested the face of a kind of man, he here invokes the anatomy of a kind of man near the seat of energy of a beast (recall the moving shoulder muscles of the ostrich in verse 2) and thereby suggests the body of a kind of beast.

Verse 13 clarifies the significance of this human metaphor of a beast in verse 12, just as verse 9 clarified the significance of the beastly metaphor of a man in verse 8:

> He that protected the bent [fleeing] riders
> Was deserted like a wether (a castrated male sheep) left behind by the flock and dying of the *rowje* disease.

As Feyṣal raised the sword in the first hemistich of verse 9, it became clear that the representative of the Rwala in battle was a man attached to an aggressive instrument. In the first hemistich of this verse it becomes clear that the representative of the Beni Wahab in battle is a man of litigation and disputation who protects their retreat. And while Feyṣal's representation was associated with raising and making visible the sword, the judge's representation is associated with men lowering themselves over their mounts (the curved ones, *al-maḥâdîb*) as they flee the Rwala onslaught. In the second hemistich of verse 9, the value of the upraised sword firmly grasped was described as a terrible power whose perception disordered men's responses whatever their quality. Now in the second hemistich of the above verse, it becomes clear that those men who are represented by a man of litigation and disputation are like vulnerable beasts. Like a diseased sheep, the judge is dying. Like a fearful flock, his companions desert him. And while previously verse 9 revealed that the beastly faces in verse 8 were a metaphor of the attachment of men and powerful beasts, verse 13 now reveals that the human anatomy in verse 12 is a metaphor of the resemblance between men and vulnerable beasts. Men who live in a pastoral society cannot escape their connection with beasts. Failing to be cognizant of the reality of a powerful, instrumental connection with beasts, they come to resemble vulnerable beasts.

Verse 14 now confirms the significance of the Beni Wahab performance in battle, just as verse 10 confirmed the significance of the Rwala performance:

> They fled through those narrow gullies yonder
> And today keep their horses, fed only from food bags, tied up at al-Jûj.

In the first hemistich of verse 10, the Rwala possession of al-Jeydûr was evaluated as a confirmation of the transcendent value of men's attachment to aggressive instruments. In the first hemistich of the above verse, we see the fall of the Beni Wahab as a result of their affliction by the disease of disloyalty. The Beni Wahab descend into the twists and turns of the gullied landscape as they seek safety from the Rwala. And the very form of this descent reveals that they are conniving, self-interested men. In the second hemistich of verse 10, the power of the Rwala over men of litigation and disputation was clarified. In the second hemistich of the above verse, the Beni Wahab appear as powerless men who are unable to range their herds freely. This is the completion of the "turn about" in verse 11. A lofty pastoral society which is free from disease has appeared in connection with the clear visibility of its members' attachment to aggressive instruments. Here a base pastoral society, whose members must tie up their aggressive instruments, has appeared in connection with the disease of disloyalty which afflicts self-interested men.

In the next two verses (v. 15–16), the poet confirms his warning to Ḥmûd (v. 6–7) by describing the fate of 'Eyfe after the defeat of the Beni Wahab. 'Eyfe, having been disloyal, is deprived of a life of fellowship and herds. He wanders in search of a patron (h. 15a), and subsists upon the diluted fare of agriculturalists (h. 15b). In the verse which follows, we see how his fate reveals the grotesque feature of his character. Deprived of fellowship and herds, 'Eyfe cannot approach "the flames (*lwâhîb*) of war" (h. 16a). This pun on the name of the Beni Wahab suggests that 'Eyfe can no longer pursue his self-interests as a mercenary in the service of Muḥammad. His desires go unfulfilled and his appetite resembles that of a camel (h. 16b). The vulnerability and weakness of the Beni Wahab in battle were construed in terms of their metaphorical resemblance to weak and vulnerable beasts. The insatiable appetite of the self-interested and therefore disloyal 'Eyfe is now construed in terms of his metaphorical resemblance to a hungry beast. Men cannot escape their interconnection with beasts in the desert and steppe. They must come together around the use of their beasts as aggressive instruments. This is because there is a powerful force inherent in their instrumental connection with beasts, which unsettles every other human response. To fail to recognize this instrumental connection is to have a grotesque metaphorical connection with beasts.

The final verse (v. 17) is the poet's announcement of the significance at the heart of the conflict between the Rwala and the Beni Wahab. This verse can be more literally translated as follows:

> And as for the market place of Eben Sha'lân, Truth and Seizure,
> And he who disputes it, behold! for all his disputation (incoherence, factiousness) is grotesque (ugly, hideous).

In the first hemistich the poet characterizes the territory of al-Jeydûr as "the market place of Eben Sha'lân (the clan from which the Rwala chiefs are chosen)." A battlefield is the place where the Rwala deal with other men (by fighting them) and purchase their livelihood (by means of weapons). The poet then concludes this hemistich with the clear and self-evident phrases of such men: "Truth and Seizure." In the second hemistich the poet compares these men with men of disputation whose very manner of living (incoherence, factiousness) makes them grotesque (they resemble beasts). With the Truth of a dispossession by force of arms, this is now clearly and self-evidently (behold!) the case.

This poem, like the last, stresses that the relationship of men and aggressive instruments must come first in political experience. However this poet, unlike the last, does not suggest that such a priority requires a self-abandonment to the use of destructive resources. He conceives that the priority of men's attachment to destructive resources has esthetic implications. He thereby suggests that Rwala political responses, as well as the polity itself, take a form which reflects a Rwala recognition of this priority. Just as the power of men with aggressive instruments is a clear and self-evident reality, so men must deal forthrightly with one another as they join in recognition of the priority of this manifest reality. As for those who deviously seek their self-interest, an occasion of intertribal conflict must inevitably reveal that disloyalty inspired by self-interest is an affliction which makes men weak and vulnerable.

But there is another side to the implications of the esthetic features of Rwala political responses and the Rwala polity. These features are based upon an external truth, a clear and self-evident reality. This external truth consists of men's "attachment" to destructive resources. Whether they like it or not, men are attached to a power, and they can do no more than recognize their attachment. There is no description of a Rwala political response as a skillful use of mounts and weapons. There is only a suggestion that a political response esthetically reflects the visibility of a Rwala attachment to such resources. Feyṣal raises the sword firmly grasped. There is no description of the Rwala polity as a form of political association, which involves communication or cooperation. There is only a suggestion that the polity esthetically reflects the form of its members' recognition of their attachment to destructive resources. A pastoral society which occupies a high mountain pasture reflects the lofty truth of the raised sword firmly grasped. Such an esthetic conception of a polity suggests that men are constrained by an external reality which they can at best only recognize. This conception therefore raises a question about any formal articulation whatsoever of political responses or of political structure. All that is possible is a recognition of the constraint of a self-evident reality.

Each of the poems of raiding and warfare that we have considered in this chapter focuses upon the relationship of men and their aggressive resources. All three poems, moreover, suggest that this relationship raises a question about the possibility of a formal political life. And in all three poems, poetic structure is the basis of a remarkably eloquent statement of such an implication.

# 8. Poetic structure and the pressure of heroic interests

## 1

The poems of raiding and warfare presented in the last chapter reveal how the relationship of men and personal instruments of aggression was a central feature of North Arabian Bedouin political experience. The role of the motivations and circumstances of pastoral nomadism among these peoples is therefore confirmed by a reading of their popular artistic expressions, just as it was confirmed by an examination of ethnographic and historical materials in Chapter 2. However, a reading of the poems of raiding and warfare can potentially accomplish more than a study of Bedouin ethnography and history with regard to this problem. The forms of popular artistic expression are a residue of a historical process. As such, they potentially provide some indication of the way in which popular motivations took shape within a pattern of circumstances. In so far as they do, they tell us something about the general character of a people's historical experience.

One striking feature of this artistic expression among the North Arabian Bedouins is its strict limitation to a rigidly defined form of poetic expression. Such a severe limitation might be mistakenly seen as a typical feature of any society whose way of life was both tribal and archaic. A tribal and archaic way of life, however, is not necessarily associated with a poverty of expressive forms. On the contrary, there are many examples in the ethnographic record of the impressive variety of artistic accomplishments among such peoples.[1] Men living by the same more or less simple means over several millennia, it seems, are normally drawn into the development of every expressive possibility open to them. Over the centuries, the forms of a tradition proliferate as a result of this effort. The relative absence of such an expressive evolution among the North Arabian Bedouins suggests that some force was at work that restricted a differentiation of their expressive interests.

The general pattern of North Arabian Bedouin poetic forms indicates the presence of such a force in the field of their political experience. In section 1 of the last chapter, we saw how the poem of raiding and warfare – the most ambitious form of popular artistic expression among these Bedouins – is the source of the rigid canons of poetic composition. Men feel that these artistic expressions, which are a response to political experience, must take fixed forms and deal with fixed themes. Men feel that these forms and themes provide the criteria for all their artistic expressions. Moreover, a reading of a few poems of raiding and warfare has provided more than a glimpse of the force in political experience which was behind these feelings. These poems insisted that the use of personal instruments of aggression was the source of a disruptive power. They suggested that other forms of human life were unviable in the face of this power. Indeed, they suggested that this power was so formidable that it demanded that men abandon themselves to the use of such instruments as the only means of responding to the threat of their use. The poems, that is to say, reveal an interest in the use of aggressive resources, which in itself *unsettled the possibility* of any response that was not concerned with such an interest.

We might therefore reach the following conclusion. The force that restricted the evolution of artistic expression among the North Arabian Bedouins was a popular interest in personal instruments of aggression. And if artistic forms, the forms of speech and action which are potentially most isolated from the pressures of political experience, were limited by the force of a political passion fostered by historical circumstances, then the forms of social and political speech and action were surely all the more crucially limited by the same force.

Such an extreme conclusion is surely unjustified. A few Bedouin poems collected around the turn of the century might well indicate that a certain pattern of political motivations and circumstances was from time to time of considerable importance among the North Arabian Bedouins. This does not mean that such a pattern could always be seen as a central determining factor of a Bedouin way of life. However, should we be able to show that the very form of Bedouin poetic expression is an articulate crystallization of a popular interest in aggressive resources, then we would indeed be able to confirm that such an interest was a dominant feature of North Arabian Bedouin history which had a decisive influence on the artistic, social, and political traditions of these peoples. From a reading of popular artistic expressions, we might learn of the pressures in Bedouin historical experience which shaped the formation of these expressions. Popular artistic expressions are therefore a window through which we might see the character of a Bedouin past. They reveal a certain pattern of motivations and circumstances within which Bedouin expressive forms, as well as Bedouin social and political forms, were obliged to take shape.

Some close connection between poetic structure and the relationship of men and aggressive resources is evident from the discussion of the poems of raiding and warfare in the last chapter. The rhyme scheme of a poem suggests that each verse consists of the formal statement of a relationship. The same internal rhyme marks the division of each verse into two parts. The same terminal rhyme marks the completion of each verse. A poem, that is to say, seems to be composed as a series of formalized two-part statements that touch upon the implications of a relationship. In the conventional openings of the poems, this form of verse structure is explicitly employed to portray the relationship of men (riders) and one of their instruments of aggression (mounts). In the remaining verses of the poems, an intertribal conflict is described which turns almost entirely upon the way men use instruments of aggression. Here again, the two-part structure of a verse is an important feature of these descriptions. The forms and themes of the poems of raiding and warfare are therefore clearly implicated in the relationship of men and their aggressive resources. But just why should such a relationship result in an art form which consists of a lyric that is composed as a series of two-part relationships?

The detailed analysis of the poems in sections 3 and 4 of the last chapter provides the basis for resolving this question. These poems evoked a human interest in certain resources (beasts and weapons) where the very nature of the resources (beastly energies, instruments of aggression) raised a question about the various forms of a response to life in general. Such a human interest involves an inherent tension, almost a contradiction. It consists of a relationship with the world, which provokes a question about one's own relationship with the world. The rhetorical evocation of such a form of life therefore requires a statement which itself suggests a tension, if not a contradiction. We have seen how such a rhetorical evocation was accomplished in the conventional openings of the poems by employing the two-part structure of a verse. An initial hemistich suggested a performance by men (riders) who used a means (mounts). A final hemistich insisted that the nature of beastly energies, not the interests of men, was the crucial feature of this performance. But such a rhetorical evocation need not involve a two-part structure. Consider, for example, a single hemistich of an opening verse in one of the poems cited: "O riders who are saddled on she-camels who are stubborn (unbroken)." Read one way, the hemistich describes men who are characterized by their control of the beasts which they ride. Read another way, it suggests that the men are not altogether in control of the beastly energies to which they are nevertheless attached. However, in so far as a speaker might wish to insist upon recognizing and clarifying tension between an interest in a means and the implications of the nature of this means for the forms of human life in general, then a two-part structure would be a convenient and appropriate form. Or in so far as a speaker might wish to suggest that such tension was a central feature of human experience, then a two-part structure would become something more than simply convenient and appropriate. As a form of speech it would symbolize the voice of a man who had been shaped and marked by that tension.

But let us suppose that men felt that they could not altogether choose what they wished to say. Let us suppose that, as a result of circumstances, a popular interest in aggressive resources had reached such dimensions that the threat of these resources to the various forms of human life was quite palpable. In such a case, the various responses of men to political experience would be overwhelmed by the pressure of this popular interest. Indeed, their conviction in the various forms of social and political life would be seriously weakened. As a result, men would lose their zest for a life that pressed upon them with its unrelenting necessity, and there would be no alternative but to take up the means at hand and respond mechanically to immediate threats. But this is not quite what happens. Men discover the possibility of a purely formal response to the pressures of a popular interest in aggressive resources. This response consists of a series of two-part statements whose fixed structure carries a certain authority. The legitimacy of this authority rests upon its *recognition and clarification* of the disturbing implications of a popular interest in aggressive resources.

As they work with such a form of expression, men feel they gain a certain power over their life situation, even though they accomplish nothing concrete, but merely elaborate in various ways the implications of a popular interest in aggressive resources. They sustain their zest for life. They even sustain an interest in aggressive resources which weaken their conviction in the various forms of social and political life. Bedouin poetry is a sign of how the human spirit prevails in adversity, and also of how, in prevailing, the human spirit links itself with adversity.

## 2

Inherent in the poems of raiding and warfare, there is a fascination with the use of aggressive resources. This fascination represents an interest in a means, the nature of which raises a question about how men make themselves a place in the world. The poet responds to this question by devising a formal statement which reveals the implication of this fascination. The form of his response (a two-part statement) and the dominance of this form (the restriction of responses to two-part statements) are evidence of the pressure of such a fascination upon artistic expression.[2]

The Rwala ceremonial poem of raiding and warfare is, in the final analysis, just like the Rwala ceremonial narrative - a reaction to the implications of the relationship of men and personal instruments of aggression. But it is a very different kind of reaction. Unlike the narrator, the poet does not seek to establish some basis for a hope that political anarchy might be controlled, moderated, or contained by a proper use of the very resources which provoke it. He is not committed to the belief that good men who use aggressive instruments for the defense of human values might surely prevail over bad men who use aggressive instruments instinctively and thoughtlessly. Instead, the poet addresses the relationship of men and personal instruments of aggression as a relationship which raises a question about human values. In doing so, he relies upon a purely formal power, the only decisive power which a literary expression has over a calculated response to experience. This is the formal power to reveal the uncertain value of any calculated response to experience.

As the possibility of a proper and effective response to political experience becomes questionable, but remains nonetheless necessary, a literary response proliferates. The form of this literary response, moreover, is marked by its value as recognition and clarification of the uncertain value of a calculated response. It consists of a series of two-part statements, which repeatedly juxtapose the shape of a response to experience with the unsettling implications of the nature of that experience.

In thus reacting to political experience, the poets never suggest that literature is a refuge from life. Such a suggestion would imply that a Bedouin interest in art might provide some release from an interest in politics. This would be a misunderstanding of the dilemma of these peoples. Their situation is one in which men are lured inexorably into a political interest. Their literature is not a refuge from this interest. It is an expression of this interest on a formal plane where men feel they have a certain mastery over it. As the poet expresses the implications of men's political passions, he proceeds to color these expressions with something of himself. The poet adds the music of his own voice. He accompanies this music with the music of an instrument. He plays with an implication of political experience by presenting it first one way and then another. By a lyrical manipulation of two-part statements, he identifies himself with a political interest in aggressive resources as he states that such an interest raises a question about the forms of social and political life in general.

With this understanding of the nature of poetry as a reaction to political experience, we can now see how the poets, like the narrators, are also drawn into the expression of a hope, but one that is very different from that of the narrators. The poets typically attempt to relate a victory of the Rwala with a Rwala recognition of the implications of popular interest in aggressive resources. Similarly, the poets typically attempt to relate the defeat of an enemy tribe with the failure of the latter to recognize these implications. Because the Rwala realize that a popular interest in aggressive resources is a threat to human life, the poets suggest, the Rwala are able to persist and to prevail in terms of such an interest.

By formulating such a hope, the poets are not deluded that their purely formal capabilities (a lyrical play upon the implications of popular interest in aggressive resources) might be the basis of a Rwala triumph over other tribes. No one could be more conscious of the difference between speech and action than these peoples. Rather, the formulation of such a hope illustrates how the poets are inclined to view their purely formal accomplishments as verifications of the legitimacy of an interest in aggressive resources, even though these formal accomplishments reveal that such an investment is a threat to human life in general. Formal literary expressions sustain a conviction in a way of life that is a threat to life. They do so simply because they constitute a response, even if it is only a formal response, to the dilemma which arises out of such a way of life. A literary accomplishment sustains an interest in the resources of power. A literary accomplishment even becomes the basis for an illusion of power in circumstances where everyone is threatened.

## 3

Popular artistic expressions among the North Arabian Bedouins were shaped in a remarkable way by the pressures of historical experience. Nowhere is this more evident than in the poverty of artistic forms in North Arabia. However, this poverty does not necessarily imply a poverty of conceptual or artistic capacities. It implies only that the idiom of these capacities was severely limited. We have already seen how the narrator's distinctive approach to political experience is revealed by subtle features of a factual account. In the remainder of this chapter we shall examine how different poets conceived of the implications of a popular interest in aggressive instruments in very different ways. And we shall also consider the degree to which this variety involved an art which focused upon the intricate details of verbal designs.

In the poem of raiding and warfare which follows, a popular investment in aggressive instruments is benignly construed as a form of social life like any other form of social life. This poem refers to a relatively minor raid against the Rwala which had no significant consequences beyond the embarrassment of one of the enemy raiders. It illustrates that, when the more disturbing aspects of heroic interests recede into the background, heroism can be conceived as a normative form of personal behavior by which men of firm intentions gain honor and men of weak intentions lose it. The most interesting feature of the poem, however, is the specific character of this normative vision of a life of heroism. It is delicately touched by the problem of an uncertainty that raises a question about whether intentions might be sufficient for the achievement of a good reputation.

Like the poems in sections 2 and 4 of the last chapter, this poem refers to the general conflict which Musil labeled "Wars between the Rwala and the Beni Wahab (1850–64)." He explains the specific incident which inspired the poem as follows:

> Muḥammad eben Smeyr, the head chief of the Weld 'Ali, became reconciled with the Rwala and promised not to allow the Fed'ân to cross his territory when bent on raiding the Rwala. It was then that he used the expression that he would hold both his people and the Fed'ân as if in a sack, *kîs,* from which nobody would crawl out against his will. But soon after the Fed'ân did cross, while many of Eben Smeyr's own men joined them and attacked the Rwala again. They were defeated and lost many of their own horses and camels, captured by the Rwala. In this raid the Fed'ân poet, Meḥda' al-Hebdâni, also took part; in some of his poems he had boasted of his bravery and threatened to humble the Rwala. During the attack Meḥda's mare stumbled . . . and threw him to the ground; fearing for his life, he crawled into the bushy perennials, where the Rwala youths found him.

Here is Musil's translation of the poem:

1. O ye who ride in the saddles of sterile, hardened she-camels
   Which are running through distant, multicolored hillocks!
2. These are the sterile she-camels at whose fast gait the loads flutter in the air
   So that their rider cannot hold his garment with his foot.
3. Show a stick with its bark peeled off to thoroughbred and eager she-camels,
   Whose steady though fast pace will cure a sick man when he awakens from sleep.
4. They keep to one course like one who has well surveyed a plain;
   An eight days' journey the riding camels make in one day.
5. On Tuesday morning – Oh, may both the ghost and devil vanish! –
   Ye will be in the allied country where ye must spend the night.
6. As soon as ye, exhausted, reach those who are ever roasting coffee,
   O sons! give them your wondrous news.
7. Thou wilt reach Muḥammad, that wall who protects the horse covered with sweat.
   May the breeze of good fortune blow upon thee, O thou tried bridle!
8. And as to thy people, they began to crawl from a sack,
   For ye must block the road against those who traverse the parallel hillocks.
9. They brought big spoons of greed but left empty-handed
   Because of the spear wounds dealt by those who ride the fiercest riding animals.

10. What! will fright throw the molting genius?
Nothing has befallen him, and yet he does not rise.
11. When our warriors reached him the old man belied his former words,
Crawling like an owl among the roots of perennials.
12. His fame, no matter by whom spread, proved a lie.
O daughter of mine! beware of one who acts like him on that day.
13. May the breeze blow good fortune towards you who seek a good reputation
With the help of our Lord steadfast in his decisions.

The meter of the Arabic is very likely the same form of *rajaz* that Landberg believed was typical of this kind of Arabian poetry:

– – ⏑ – | – – ⏑ – | – ⏑ – –

Here is the Arabic, which can be read in this meter without great difficulty:

1. Yâ râkebîn kwâr ḥîlen ʻarâmîs
yeṭwen mîd msâhamât al-ḥezûmi
2. ḥîlen tequbb ʻulûqahen ben-nisânîs
rakkâbahen mâ yistaḍaff al-hedûmi
3. hezzow al-manjûb al-ḥarâr al-melâhîs
yibri-l-ʻalîl nisâʻehen ʻoqob nowmi
4. yimshen brâʻi mukayyes al-qâʻ takyîs
mamsha thamânt ayyâm lel-hejen yowmi
5. ṣubḥ ath-thalâthe bgheyb al-jân wa-blîs
temsûn bediyâr ar-refâqa lezûmi
6. w-elya' lifeytu mutʻabîn al-maḥâmîs
yâ ʻeyâl hâtow min gharâyeb ʻelûmi
7. telfi mḥammad sûr kheylen marâwîs
habb al-hawa lak yâ ʻanân al-ʻezûmi
8. ʻan lâbetak qâmat tejadhdham ʻan al-kîs
teqaḍḍebû lemqaṭṭeʻîn al-ḥezûmi
9. maghâref al-aṭmâʻ râḥû mefâlîs
min ḍarb shilf mujarrebîn al-eqrûmi
10. keyf al-wahaq yarmi ʻarûd al-qerânîs
mâ beh khlâf w-ʻâjzen lâ yeqûmi
11. ḥâlow ʻaleyh w-nekkes al-ʻawd tenkîs
yelûq beqiyâʻ ash-shejar teqel bûmi
12. ṣârat ʻelûmeh kill abûha ḥamâlîs
yâ bint ʻan mithleh hâk al-yowm shûmi
13. habb al-hawa yâ dâyerîn an-nwâmîs
besʻûf nawlâna quwiyy al-ʻezûmi.

This poem about heroic conventions takes a highly conventional form. The meter is that typically associated with the poems of raiding and warfare. It is employed in such a way that the normal syllabic value of the spoken words is not distorted. The poem divides neatly into three blocks of four verses together with a concluding verse. Each block of verses represents one of the typical compositional elements of a poem of raiding and warfare. The first block (v. 1-4) presents the opening image of riders on mounts. The second block (v. 5-8) makes up the transition between the opening verses, which portray riders on mounts, and the closing verses, which portray specific events. The third block (v. 9-12) describes the intertribal conflict which inspired the poem.

A conventional view of a life of action is presented by a conventional style of poetic speech. As this poet addresses an intertribal conflict with no serious implications, he conceives of a life of heroism as if it assumed a normative design. And as he so conceives of a life of heroism, the normative features of poetic composition are enhanced and emphasized.

Instead of examining this poem verse by verse, we shall only consider the fashion in which the poet conceives of a heroic life as normative. To do so, the initial verses must be retranslated so that they are a more literal version of the Arabic:

1. Oh riders who are saddled on sterile she-camels which are durable,
   Who pass through distant multicolored hillocks.
2. Sterile she-camels which lift their loads with a fast gait,
   Their rider cannot hold with his knees his garments.
3. Shake the stick at the thoroughbreds of the eager mounts,
   The pace of which cures the sick man after his sleep.
4. They ride with the attentiveness of one who knows the well-surveyed
      plain,
   A ride of eight days with the mounts is a one day's journey.

The first verse evokes the relationship of riders and mounts as a distant image in the landscape, but there is no insistence here upon the separation of a domestic life in camp from a heroic life abroad. Rather, the relationship of rider and mount is more nearly conceived as an element within a *portrait* of a life abroad. By this initial gesture the poet indicates that he will more nearly describe the form of life abroad rather than uncover the disturbing implications of heroism for the forms of social and political life closer to home.

The next verse (v. 2) touches upon the relationship of rider and mount as the central element within the initial portrait. The verse divides into a characterization of beasts and a characterization of men. In the first hemistich, the spirited movement of the beasts is described as the cause of a slight separation between the beasts and their burdens. The energy of the beast ever so slightly unsettles the attachment of the man to the beast. In the second hemistich, the men are described as being unable to control their fluttering garments as a result of their movement. The important feature of these men is their concern for their formal appearance, their dress. The important feature of this concern is that they are nevertheless unable to control their formal appearance as a *result of beastly energies.* But let us examine these men once again. As they ride, they attempt to control their fluttering garments which are blown by the wind. They try to hold these garments fast to their mounts with their knees. A human intention implicitly takes the shape of a concern for formal appearances, which is indistinguishable from a determined attachment to beastly energies.

In the next verse, human intentions are described as the central element in the relationship of riders and mounts. In the first hemistich of verse 3, the intentional control of the riders over the mounts is described. As the riders shake their sticks, the mounts respond to their commands. Musil notes that the verb which he translates as "show" actually refers to the rhythmic movement of the riding stick (*manjûb*) by which riders urge on their mounts. In the second hemistich of the verse, the effect of the movement of the mount on the rider is described. It restores his body to health. It restores his mind to consciousness. This is a suggestion of the formation of a body and mind around the experience of riders on mounts. There is a human intention behind the heroic life (h. 3a), but it is nevertheless the intention of a man whose body and mind have been shaped by his attachment to a mount (h. 3b).

The next verse (v. 4) now elaborates this suggestion that a human intention is a central element in the relationship of riders and mounts. It does so by describing a form of heroic consciousness. In the first hemistich, the riders' purposeful awareness of space is described: "They ride with the attentiveness of one who knows the well-surveyed plain." In the second hemistich, their lack of awareness of time is described: "A ride of eight days with the mounts is a one day's journey." A heroic consciousness takes shape as a purposeful awareness on which the passage of time has little or no effect. This final hemistich of the opening block of verses also identifies the eight opening hemistichs of the poem itself with the unity of a form of heroic experience: "A ride of eight days . . . is a one day's journey."

The first two verses of the opening suggest that a heroic life abroad is one in which a concern for formal appearances is dependent upon but also unsettled by beastly energies. The two final verses suggest how, despite this uncertainty, a heroic consciousness takes shape within a life abroad as a purposeful awareness of space which is untouched by the passage of time. The two themes of a concern for form in a heroic life abroad which is touched by uncertainty (v. 1 and 2) and a form of heroic consciousness as a purposeful awareness that does not change (v. 3 and 4) reappear in the remainder of the poem.

In the transitional verses, the poet first identifies the riders on mounts as Rwala, and then describes their arrival in the territory of an ally (v. 5-6). In the second hemistich of the next verse (v. 7) he describes their greeting of Muḥammad: "May the breeze of good fortune blow upon thee, O thou tried bridle!" The opening image of riders who are tenuously connected with their mounts, but who cling to them with determination has here become the basis for a description of Muḥammad. He is a chief who is touched by the breezes of good and bad fortunes, and here we recall the garments of the riders blowing in the wind. He is a rider of firm intentions (O thou tried bridle), and here we recall the riders who attempt to hold in their garments as they cling to their mounts.

In the first hemistich of the next verse (v. 8), the poet offers his challenge to Muḥammad: "And as to thy people, they began to crawl from a sack (*al-kîs*)." This is an explicit allusion to the purposeful awareness of space on the part of the riders in verse 4 (*brâ'i mukayyes al-qâ' takyîs*). The two words which suggest the awareness of the plain by the riders and the noun which refers to the sack (*al-kîs*) are all derived from the same root. This verse thereby links the agreement of Muḥammad to contain the Fed'ân within their territory with the opening suggestion that heroes are men with a purposeful awareness of space.

The two themes of the opening verses surface again in the closing verses. These verses describe the Fed'ân poet Meḥda' al-Hebdâni, who fell from his horse during the raid and attempted to hide himself from the Rwala warriors. In the first hemistich of verse 11, the phrase which is translated as "the old man belied his former words (*w-nekkes al-'awd tenkîs*)" is a formal echo of the phrase in verse 4: "One who knows the well-surveyed plain (*mukayyes al-qâ' takyîs*)." Unlike the heroes who have a purposeful awareness, the poet's actions reveal that he does not mean what he says. The literal meaning of the phrase translated as "the old man belied his former words" suggests that the poet "inverted" or "lowered" himself. The phrase therefore literally refers to the "bad form" of his fall from a horse. In the second hemistich of verse 11, there is an explicit allusion to the quality of a life of heroism as a life of formal appearances (v. 1-2). Here the image of riders with fluttering garments - an image which suggests a resemblance between the hero and a bird - is the basis of an ironic characterization of the Fed'ân poet as a very different kind of bird: "Crawling like an owl among the roots of perennials." The Fed'ân poet, a man who appears to be a hero, but who behaves very unlike a hero, is described as a kind of bird which appears to be a bird, but behaves very unlike a bird.

With respect to the Rwala ally, the Weld 'Ali chief Muhammad eben Smeyr, the poet emphasizes the firmness of heroic intentions as he calls upon the chief to keep his agreements. At the same time he respectfully provides the chief with an excuse for his failure to keep his agreements, by observing how the best of intentions are touched by the breezes of good and bad fortunes. With regard to the Rwala enemy, the Fed'ân poet Meḥda' al-Hebdâni, the poet emphasizes the formal appearances of a life of heroism as he associates the Fed'ân poet's lack of resolve with his bad form in the raid. In this way the Rwala poet shades his conception of a heroic life as a normative form of life in accordance with the status of each of the two men whom he addresses. He ends his poem with a concluding verse, which alludes once again to the themes of heroic intentions and heroic forms:

> May the breeze blow good fortune towards you who seek a good reputation
> With the help of our Lord steadfast in his decisions.

Here again are the breezes of fortune, and men who are concerned about proper forms. Now, however, the uncertain relationship between men's fortunes and men's intentions is resolved by the invocation of a divine authority. The purposefulness of this divine authority who is "steadfast in his decisions (*quwiyy al-'ezûmi*)" lies on the side of men with good intentions, even though they are touched by good and bad fortunes.

A way of life that precipitates a question about the possibility of human life has here been transformed into a way of life that is touched by the gentle breezes of fortune. With this softening of the uncertain implications of men's fascination with aggressive instruments, the role of human intentions is amplified. Indeed, there is a final suggestion that a divine authority, which lies behind the sure design of human experience, is a support for all good men of firm intentions.

## 4

In the next poetic excerpt, we find that men are once again absorbed in the use of personal instruments of aggression. Here, however, the skillful use of these instruments assumes some prominence as a life of heroism is conceived as a performance. There are two curious features in this poetic excerpt. First, the poet turns to metaphors of a poetic performance in order to conceive of a heroic performance. Second, the poet settles upon a scene of men firing rifles, not men riding horses or wielding sabers, as the essence of a heroic performance.

The poetic excerpt is taken from the poem which was only briefly considered in section 3 of the last chapter. This poem referred to the "Wars between the Rwala and the Beni Wahab (1850–64)." On this particular occasion, the chief of the Weld 'Ali, Muḥammad eben Smeyr, was leading the Beni Wahab confederation. They were supported by contingents of Ottoman volunteers, composed of Druses, Turcomans, and Kurds, together with regular Ottoman cavalry. Let us recall that in this particular poem the setting of a general conflict was described in the first block of verses, a major battle that was part of the general conflict was described in the second block, and men firing rifles were described in the third block. By this progressive reduction in scope, the poet was isolating a Rwala heroic performance as the decisive feature of the intertribal conflict. The third block of verses, which refers to Jam'ân's sons firing their rifles, was the crucial presentation of this Rwala heroic performance. Musil's translation of these three verses is given below:

9. Thou wouldst say that Jam'ân's sons were Kurdish soldiers,
So have they besprinkled scorched stone heaps with blood
10. By their steel rifles, each shot of which reaches its goal;
If not some agha's head, then it is his stud horse.
11. When their rifles' load is once fired, it will not depart from its course.
For they first weigh each bit of powder.

Musil transcribed the Arabic as follows:

9. w-awlâd jam'ân teqel 'askar akrâd
min ad-damm bellaw yâbs al-murjumâni
10. bemqarrarât ramîhen ṣowb beṣmâd
brâs al-agha w-en akhṭateh bel-ḥṣâni
11. w-elya' qba' neqḏaha tesned asnâd
w-mzayyenîn melḥahen bel-wazâni.

My more literal translation of these verses is given below:

9. And the sons of Jam'ân, thou wouldst say, are Kurdish soldiers,
With blood, they sprinkled the heaps of stones.
10. By means of carbines their shot hits its target,
The head of an agha, and failing this, his horse.
11. When it fires its crack, it will not part from its course.
And the cut bits of their powder are well-measured.

In the first hemistich of verse 9, the sons of Jam'ân are vocally compared (thou wouldst say) with members of the enemy, who are on this occasion Kurdish soldiers. This puzzling simile, we shall find, suggests that a hostile relationship (between the sons of Jam'ân and the Kurdish soldiers) has a poetic aspect (the hostile relationship is associated with the vocalization of a metaphor). In the second hemistich, the violent actions of the sons of Jam'ân are described as having an artistic aspect. They add brilliant color to an otherwise barren landscape. This suggests that the poetic aspect of a hostile relationship surfaces as a feature of the actions by which men kill other men.

There is something poetic about a hostile relationship, and there is something artistic about an act of violence. In verse 10, a hostile relationship will be centered upon the use of aggressive instruments (rifles) which make a peculiar sound. In verse 11, the use of these aggressive instruments is conceived as an artistic performance in terms of its resemblance to a poetic performance. Thus, behind a hostile relationship there is the use of an instrument which makes a sound, and the use of this instrument involves an artistic capacity.

Let us examine the first hemistich of verse 9 once again. In doing so, we find that the theme of these three verses is implicitly suggested by its design. This hemistich describes a group of Rwala (the sons of Jam'ân) in terms of their resemblance to a group of the enemy (Kurdish soldiers). However, the vocalization of the name of the enemy (*'askar akrâd*) sounds like the reverberation of a rifle shot. By associating the sound of a rifle shot with the naming of the enemy (thou wouldst say), a connection has been established between a poetic performance (a vocalization) and the use of an aggressive instrument. The presentation of a hostile relationship in the form of a simile not only suggests that such a relationship has a poetic aspect, it also foreshadows the portrayal of the use of an aggressive instrument, which makes a sound, as the source of this poetic aspect.

In the next verse (v. 10), the use of an aggressive instrument is explicitly described as the central feature of the relationship between the Rwala heroes and their enemies. The first hemistich portrays the sons of Jam'ân shooting at targets with rifles. The second hemistich then describes the enemy as the targets: "The head of an agha, and failing this, his horse." Now let us examine the first hemistich in more detail. The initial phrase of verse 9 was an evocation of the name of the heroes, "the sons of Jam'ân." The initial phrase of verse 10 replaces the names of the heroes with an evocation of their use of aggressive instruments, "By means of carbines . . ." The first hemistich then concludes with a description of the heroes shooting their rifles, "their shot hits its target (*ṣowb beṣmâd*)." In this description, there is another phrase which resembles the sound of a rifle shot. The internal rhyme phrase in hemistich 9a, *'askar akrâd,* is followed by the internal rhyme phrase in 10a, *ṣowb beṣmâd.* This time, however, the sound of the rhyme phrase is more like the dull thud of a bullet striking its target. Again in this verse, the poet has suggested that there is something which is poetic about a hostile relationship. But now he portrays this relationship in terms of the use of an aggressive instrument, where this use has a poetic dimension (its sound).

In the next verse (v. 11), the use of an aggressive instrument is described once again. Here, however, such a use is no longer portrayed as the central element of a hostile relationship. Rather, the use of an aggressive instrument is described in such a way as to suggest a peculiar kind of capacity *behind* the use. The first hemistich begins by evoking the action of shooting a rifle as a sonorous event: "When it fires its crack . . ." The verb *qba',* which is translated as "fires," refers to the action of shooting in terms of the sound of exploding gunpowder. The noun *neqḍaha,* which is translated as "its crack," refers to the action of shooting in terms of the sound of the bullet. This description emphatically insists upon the sound value of the use of the aggressive instrument, as well as the sound value of the result of this use.[3] The first hemistich ends with a description of the trajectory of the bullet which suggests, however, a determined intention: "it will not part from its course." Again we hear the sound of the rifle shot as the poet describes the trajectory (*tesned asnâd*), but here the sound has a finer and more delicate quality. Now we can fully understand the design of this hemistich. The poet is suggesting that behind the sounds of a violent action, which have the value of a relationship (first a firing, then a cracking), there is a fine and delicate, but determined intention.

The second hemistich now clarifies the shape of this determined intention. It consists of an artistic capacity for a heroic performance: "And the cut bits of their powder are well-measured." The cut bits of the gunpowder are described by a word whose root is also used to refer to poetic revisions (*azyan*). The well-measured qualities of these cut bits are described by a word whose root also refers to poetic prosody (*bel-wazâni*). This description of gunpowder reveals an artistic intention behind its appearance and preparation. Here the poet is not exactly suggesting that the preparation of gunpowder is intrinsically related to poetry composition. Rather, his verses are designed to suggest that the articulation of a human skill is a fundamental dimension of political violence, and he has no more vivid concept of such an articulation than that of poetry composition.

Behind the general circumstances of a war described in block 1 of this poem, behind the major battle of riders on mounts described in block 2, there is a crucial heroic performance which is described in block 3 (v. 9–11). And behind this crucial heroic performance, which consists of men firing rifles, we now see the existence of a decisive human capacity for such a heroic performance. The poet follows verse 11, it will be recalled, with the general rout of the Beni Wahab, which is followed by the evaluation of a Rwala performance in verses 13 to 17. The poem concludes with a description of the rout of the Ottoman troops as the decisive result of this performance. A literary performance has very little to do with the actual conduct of Bedouin warfare. It arose as a reaction to the disturbing implications of men's fascination with aggressive instruments. Here, however, a literary performance has become the basis for conceiving of political violence as though it were an expression of a human capacity, instead of a problem which tended to polarize men's expressions around literary performances.

This excerpt underlines the absence of a romantic notion of heroism among the Rwala. They have no important conception of a heroic performance as a marvelous display of human capabilities in the midst of a dramatic clash of opposing armies. This is because it was neither personal skills nor personal courage which necessarily mattered above all else in North Arabia. In so far as men could believe in the possibility of a systematic response to political anarchy, they were committed to sober, pragmatic political procedures. This we have learned from the narratives.

But there were often doubts about the effectiveness of such a response, and these doubts arose precisely because of a popular investment in the use of aggressive instruments. That is to say, it was a popular investment in personal instruments of aggression which undermined any conviction that the exact way in which men used these instruments might really matter. This is why the Rwala poets insist upon a general tribal commitment to the unrestrained use of aggressive resources, instead of conceiving of personal skills and courage as a fundamental feature of political experience.

In the above excerpt, a poet does elaborate a notion of a heroic performance, but he conceives of it in terms of literary metaphors! In addition, the very occasion which is portrayed as a heroic performance defies our conventional, romantic ideas of heroism.[4] The poet does not portray an occasion of men riding mounts or wielding sabers, but an occasion of men firing rifles. A more *technical* aspect of Bedouin warfare is the basis of a conception of a heroic performance, because such an aspect approaches more closely the technical character of Bedouin poetry composition.

The excerpt confirms the interpretation given in sections 1 and 2 of this chapter. It illustrates how a mastery of verbal detail helped sustain an interest in a means of power that was largely destructive of human life. For the poet is able to conceive of the use of aggressive instruments as a display of a human skill only in so far as a poetic reaction to political violence conveys the illusion of being able to cope with political violence. But then it was men's zest for the use of aggressive instruments, a zest born out of the circumstances of their way of life, that tended to restrict the articulation of any intricate and delicate human skill to the domain of mastering verbal detail.

# 9. Shadows and echoes of the priority of the concrete

## 1

In the Rwala poems of raiding and warfare, we have found an insistence upon a principle that is usually associated with reactions to modern Western experience. This is the principle that a response to life must be based upon the properties of the material world. Among the more insightful of the North Arabian Bedouins, we also find what is usually considered to be a purely modern Western discovery. This is the realization that men's relationship with the material world sets limits on what kind of men they could be. The last Rwala poem to be considered is an example of such an insight. This poem is concerned with the relationship of formal expressions and political experience and, specifically, with the relationship between poetry and heroism.

The poem is associated with the general intertribal conflict, which Musil described as the "War between the Western Tribes and the Rwala (1902)." A narrative which is also associated with this conflict was analyzed in Chapter 5. The poem refers to a Rwala response to a raid by the Beni Ṣakhr. Musil describes this incident as follows:

> Of the Beni Ṣakhr tribe 280 warriors commanded by Shlâsh eben Fâyez assailed the herds of the Zeyd kin near the watering place of Mayqû' and, capturing them, fled in the direction of the al-Jerâwi wells . . . Overtaking the latter at al-Jerâwi, they [the Rwala] recovered the booty, killed thirty riders, and also captured seventy mares and over one hundred camels.

The Rwala hero who is described in the following poem is Khalaf âl Idhen. This is the same man who appeared in the stories concerning the death of Turki and who composed one of the poems in Chapter 7. The Âl Jenk, mentioned in verse 5, were a group of Druses among the Beni Ṣakhr raiding party. Rmeyḥ, who is mentioned in verses 9 and 11, was a relative of Shlâsh, the commander of the raiding party. Here is Musil's translation of the poem:

1. Tidings reached us by camels with muscular shoulders,  
   War tidings piercing our entrails.

2. "Sisters of Ref'a!" [they shouted], and all obeyed at once,
To take vengeance on the leader for their wounded
3. With the spear blade that cuts through flanks and ribs
And carries three parts of the shaft after it.
4. The wolf from Mayqû' gladdened with a supper
Has invited eighty jackals to its remains.
5. The Âl Jenk fled on mares of paces a fathom long,
And Shlâsh alone of the whole reserve remained.
6. He who protects a lone wolf from hunger rode at him in a gallop
And with her hoofs made his steed stamp on him.
7. For the clash made both Shlâsh and his mare fall to earth;
Thus a rich supper fell to the negro and servant.
8. Ah, how many men were thrown from the saddle by the fringe-adorned spear blade,
Whose heads then the hyena left lying near al-Jerâwi!
9. While Shlâsh was trampled by mares, Rmeyḥ yielded himself
Because of the burning wounds [he received] from those who dealt death all around.
10. Khalaf, he who splits the enemy's troops,
Fights all the more boldly the more numerous his opponents.
11. When Shlâsh by Rmeyḥ was deserted, his head was cut off,
And a few Rwala sang over him with loud voice.

The meter of the poem cannot be determined from Musil's transcription, but an indication of how it is sung arises from an analysis of the poem. Here is the Arabic:

1. Al-'elem jâna fowq maslûb al-kow'
'elmen yisaqqi leḍ-ḍamâyer neqâwi
2. ekhwât ref'a kill abûhom 'ala ṭow'
w-'ala-l-'aqîd yi'âqebûn al-ahâwi
3. bshilfen yiqeṣṣ al-jeneb wiyyet aḍ-ḍlow'
w-yiheff thalâth ek'ûb bḥadd ar-reshâwi
4. alli bakhît bel-'asha' dhîb mayqow'
'azam 'ala-l-faḍla thamânîn wâwi
5. âl jenk qowṭar fowq ṭawîlet al-bow'
wa-shlâsh kanneh min kemîneh khalâwi
6. rakaḍ 'aleyh rîf al-khalâwi 'an al-jow'
w-khalla' jwâdeh tedhekeh bel-ḥadhâwi[1]
7. hw. w-al-faras behwâh ṭâḥaw 'ala kow'
w-ṭâḥ al-'asha' lel-'abd w-al-fedâwi
8. wa' kam wâḥeden bedhwâbet ar-rumḥ mashlow'
'arashet râseh ḍaba'aten bel-jerâwi
9. shlâsh waṭaneh wa-rmeyḥ mamnow'
min ḥarr ḍarben mu'aṭṭebîn al-ahâwi
10. khalaf alli 'ala-l-qowm qâṭow'
yizûd elya' kathrat 'aleyh hal-balâwi
11. rmeyḥ khalla shlâsh w-ar-râs maqṭow'
'aleyh rweylâten yiziqqûn al-ghanâwi.

This is the most difficult of all the poems of raiding and warfare recorded by Musil. Unfortunately, it is also translated with less care than the other poems. However, if we proceed with a verse-by-verse analysis of its composition, the poem can be understood with precision. Like all the discussions of the narratives and poems in this book, the validity of this interpretation rests upon discovering a consistent pattern in the design of specific details.

## 2

In the initial verse of the poem, there is a theme of a *form of signification* and its relationship with men and beasts. Musil probably mistranslates two words in the verse. These errors are corrected in the following more literal version:

> The news of events reached us upon muscular shoulders,
> News of war (*'elmen neqâwi*) which gives to drink (*yisaqqi*) the lean and lank (*leḍ-ḍamâyer*).

The verse begins with a form of signification which refers to specific, concrete events abroad, "the news (*al-'elem*)." This form is then associated with a general feature of life abroad, "muscular shoulders (*maslûb al-kow'*)." The description of the news arriving "upon (*fowq*)" this beastly energy suggests that the concreteness of this form is based upon the concreteness of this general feature of a life abroad. In the second hemistich, the news of events is characterized as a general form of signification, "news of war." This general form is then described as having a specific, concrete property. It nourishes men's bodily natures: "which gives to drink the lean and lank."[2] Like the more conventional openings of a poem, these lines touch upon the relationship of men and beasts in connection with a heroic life abroad. But unlike the more conventional openings, there is an insistence upon the role of a form of signification (news) which mediates this relationship. This insistence foreshadows a concern with the place of formal expressions in a life that is based upon concrete actions with instruments of aggression.[3]

The second verse describes an active response as it takes shape among the Rwala. A more literal translation of this verse brings out certain features of the Arabic which Musil's translation obscures:

> "Sisters of Ref'a!" which brings (literally: causes) all to obedience,
> And on the leader they are seeking vengeance for (literally: following up) the wounds.

The first verse began with the news of specific events, a form of signification which arrived from abroad upon beastly energies. The second verse now begins with a war cry, another form of signification which represents a response to the news of events abroad.

Let us examine the construction of the first hemistich. The war cry refers to a herd of riding camels belonging to the Rwala in question and suggests their devotion to these camels. As an energetic, personal response, the war cry signifies that men are turning their attention to their beasts, which will carry them abroad. The following phrase (*kill abûhom*) describes the initial vocalization as a cause which acts on all men. The final phrase (*'ala ṭow'*) describes the men's active command of their mounts as the result of this cause. The first hemistich, in other words, describes a response which consists of a causal movement from a more formal energy (a vocal response of men addressing beasts) to a more concrete energy (an active response of men who control beasts.)

In the second hemistich, an assault upon the enemy leader ensues from the response that took shape in the first hemistich. This Rwala assault upon the enemy is itself described as a response (seeking vengeance, *yi'â-qebûn*) to the enemy assault upon the Rwala (for the wounds, *al-ahâwi*). This is the climax of a movement which began in the first verse. If we now consider the character of this movement, we can begin to understand the intent of the poet. In h. 1a, a form of expression (the news), which is directly derived from concrete events abroad (muscular shoulders), comes to the Rwala. In h. 1b, this form of expression (news of war) is described as having the property of nourishing men physically (gives to drink the lean and lank). In h. 2a, a relatively formal kind of physical response (the war cry) is described as having the property of causing a relatively concrete kind of physical response (all to obedience). From this response there ensues, in h. 2a, a concrete assault upon the enemy, which is described as a response to the physical wounds which were inflicted by the enemy.

Unlike the hemistichs of any poem that we have considered, these four hemistichs are designed as a series of events. By such a design, the poet suggests that a Rwala response to a threat from abroad takes shape as a movement from a formal expression to a concrete action. This movement is described, moreover, as though it consisted of a sequence of causes and effects or even of a flow of physical forces.

With the completion of verse 2, we might expect the poet to begin a description of the specific Rwala attack upon the enemy. The Rwala response to political events has taken shape, there is nothing left to do but to describe the Rwala heroic performance. However, there are two more verses of the opening. These two verses are designed as a continuation of the natural flow of causes and effects which began with the first two verses, but they are not specific descriptions of a Rwala attack. Verse 3 describes how "the form" of a heroic action follows upon the Rwala response which took shape in verse 2. Verse 4 then describes how "the form" of a poetic expression follows upon the conclusion of this heroic action. In this way, the opening verses will suggest how the problem of the relationship of formal expressions and concrete actions with aggressive instruments surfaces and takes a certain shape as a necessary result of Bedouin political experience.

Let us now consider the second pair of opening verses in detail. Following upon the active response which has taken shape in verse 2, we find a description of the form of heroic action in verse 3. This verse can be more literally translated as follows:

> By means of a spear which cuts through flanks and ribs,
> And which whizzes (hisses) three parts by means of the iron-ringed blade.

The first hemistich describes the means of heroic actions (by means of a spear, *bshilfen*) and the use of this means (which cuts, *yiqeṣṣ*). The second hemistich is a more stylized description. Musil notes that the first phrase (which whizzes three parts, *w-yiheff thalâth ek'ûb*) implies that the spears were used so forcefully that they carried three parts of their bamboo shafts into the body of their victim. The second phrase (by means of the iron-ringed blade, *bḥadd ar-reshâwi*) describes once again the means of this action. This analysis clarifies that both hemistichs describe the same means of an action and the use of this means, but from a different perspective and in reverse order. The first hemistich begins with the means and ends with the use of the means. This design is consistent with a description of a cause which is followed by its effect. The second hemistich, however, begins with the use of the means and ends with the means. This is a clear sign of a *reversal.*

If we examine the stylization of the second hemistich in detail, the implications of this reversal become clearer. First, let us examine the use of the means: "And which whizzes three parts . . ." The spear moves so quickly that it whizzes or hisses in the air, and the spear is used so energetically that it sinks deeply into the body of its victim. This description is designed in such a way as to suggest an energetic capacity, which is displayed by the use of a means. Now let us examine more closely the means: "By means of the iron-ringed blade." This description is designed in such a way as to direct our attention to the point at which the blade of the spear is attached to its bamboo shaft with an iron ring. It suggests, ever so slightly, something which lies behind the blade. The presence of the hero (as a kind of man) is displayed by the use of an aggressive instrument. The heroic identity consists of an energetic capacity behind an aggressive instrument.

This stylization of a heroic identity as an energetic capacity which lies behind the use of a weapon recalls the beastly energies in the initial verse (h. 1a). Now however, the energies in question are a feature of a man whose heroic actions are a response to the beastly energies upon which a life abroad is based. This recalls the nourishment of the bodily features of men in the initial verse (h. 1b). As a man has responded to a life abroad, which is based upon the physical energies of beasts, his responses have taken shape as a purely physical energy. More specifically, an energetic capacity for heroic actions has been evoked in connection with the sound of a weapon. The spear whizzes as it moves through the air. This sound recalls the energetic vocalization (the war cry) which initiated a heroic response to events abroad (h. 2a). The hero is a man whose voice has taken the concrete form of the sound of an energetic use of a weapon. And finally, the physical wound that results from this heroic action recalls the active response which resulted from a physical wound (h. 2b). A wound is the reply of the "physical" voice of the hero to the wounds inflicted by the enemy.

But the second hemistich of the third verse is not only a crystallization of the themes found in the four hemistichs of the first two verses. It also includes a reference to the concatenation of causes and effects which is suggested by the serial design of these hemistichs. The use of the weapon in the second hemistich of verse 3 refers to the three sections of the bamboo shaft that followed the blade into the victim. These "three sections" of the shaft are a reference to the three opening verses which have concluded at this point. Or more precisely, they are a reference to what this series of verses represents. The three-part structure of the bamboo shaft, unlike the three-part structure of the poem, is a material entity, which translates the force of an actor via the means of his action into the body of his victim. That is to say, the reference to "three sections" is a figure of the necessary chain of causes and effects described in the three opening verses, which here concludes with the precipitation of a purely physical human energy. The arrival of the news of concrete events (*al-'elem*) nourishes a bodily nature (v. 1); an energetic formal expression (*ekhwât ref'a*) causally moves toward concrete actions (v. 2); and finally, the results of the use of a weapon (h. 3a) display the presence of a heroic identity as an energetic capacity (h. 3b).

With this complete understanding of the stylization of the second hemistich of verse 3, we can now examine the implications of this verse as a reversal. The first hemistich of verse 3 describes the concrete action with aggressive instruments, which crystallizes as men respond to political experience. The first hemistich is then followed by a figuring of the form of a heroic identity, which lies behind such a concrete action. The crucial aspect of this figuring is that it turns upon contrasting the form of a heroic identity with the form of a poetic identity. As the sound of the energetic use of a weapon (which whizzes) takes the place of an energetic voice (v. 2), we discover a form of response which consists purely of a physical energy which, unlike a voice, has no formal dimension. As this use of a weapon refers to a chain of causes and effects (three sections), we discover a form of response which consists of a natural flow of physical forces and which, unlike a poem, does not really separate into a series of formal parts. This hemistich figures an energetic use of a weapon as a form of heroic expression, which is wholly unlike the form of a poetic expression.

Now we can see the implications of a heroic response that moves from formal energy to concrete energy. This is a response which concludes by precipitating the question of the relationship of formal expressions to concrete actions. And now we can also see that this question is implicitly the central problem of all of the verses we have read so far, all of which deal in some way with a contrast between the formal and concrete aspects of a response to political experience. This is the question which is implicitly behind the initial concern with the role of forms within a life abroad (v. 1). This is the question which is implicitly behind the description of a heroic response as a causal movement from formal energy to concrete energy (v. 2). And this is the question which surfaces in verse 3. The design of verse 3 suggests that a heroic response, which concludes in concrete actions with aggressive instruments, is followed by a figuring of this result, which reveals a question about the place of formal expression in a life based upon concrete actions with aggressive instruments. The reversal which is indicated by the design of this verse is a sign of this shift - from a concern with the form of actions to a concern with the formal implications of these actions.

In the last verse of the opening (v. 4), we find a figure of such a formal response. This verse describes how a questionable kind of formal expression is a "natural" result of heroic actions. Where the character of experience demands responses that raise a question about the place of formal expressions in experience, the result is a kind of formal life which is of questionable value. This verse can be more literally translated as follows:

> He who is happy with the supper, the wolf of Mayqû'
> Has invited to the excess (remains) eighty jackals (howlers).

In the first hemistich, there is a figure of the poet of raiding and warfare, which suggests his relationship to the hero. Here the cutting of flanks and ribs in hemistich 3a is conceived as a preparation of a supper, and the poet is conceived as a carrion-eating wolf with a ravenous appetite for death. The second hemistich then describes this beast as the author of a formality. He invites his fellow predators to feast upon the dead who are the remains of heroic actions. And now note that this last verse of the opening concludes with a specific figure of poetic form itself. The eighty jackals represent the eighty beats of the eight opening hemistichs, which consist of ten beats each. The literal name for the jackals, "howlers (*wâwi*)," figures the sound elements of this formal poetic expression as the raucous cry of an animal which preys upon the dead. Unlike the three sections of the bamboo shaft in verse 3, this reference to eighty howlers is an explicit figure of poetic form.

We shall have to examine the verses which follow to understand exactly what the poet is suggesting by these metaphors of a poet and his poetic expressions. Nevertheless, the general implications of the opening verses are clear. In the first two verses the poet reveals that concrete actions with aggressive instruments are the result of a natural flow of causes and effects. In doing so, he suggests that heroic actions are right because they are a necessity. But then in verse 3, he reveals that a heroic response to political experience provokes a problem about the place of forms in political experience. And now, in verse 4, the poet suggests that heroic actions are inevitably followed by a questionable kind of formal life. This is a formal life which only begins when heroic actions have concluded and which then flourishes upon the results of heroic actions. This is a formal life which takes shape as a celebration of death, resembling the howling of beasts. Like the predators that come quite "naturally" to feed upon the dead after a battle, this beastly kind of formal life follows quite "naturally" upon heroic actions. Heroic actions may be a necessary response to political experience in the desert and steppe, and in that sense a legitimate response. However, heroic actions are relentlessly accompanied by a kind of formal life which is beastly and therefore grotesque and senseless.

With this understanding of the general implications of the opening verses, we can consider aspects of their composition which we have until now entirely overlooked. These verses, which describe a heroic action as a necessary and therefore a natural response to political experience, have certain strange shadings and resonances. Throughout these verses there are the shadows and echoes of a wolf and his wolfish activities. The initial verse of the poem was first read as a suggestion that the concreteness of a form of signification, "news (*al-'elem*)," was derived from the concreteness of beastly energies, "muscular shoulders (*maslûb al-kow'*)." Now let us note that these beastly energies take a wolfish form. For the word *maslûb,* which describes the powerful shoulders of a mount, is conventionally employed by the Rwala to describe the shape of a wolf: broad in the front and narrow in the back.[4] And so we see that a formal feature of the concrete basis of a life abroad casts the shadow of a wolf. We first read the final hemistich of this same verse as a suggestion that a general form of signification, "news of war (*'elmen neqâwi*)," had a specific concrete property: it nourished the bodily nature of men. However, this hemistich was curiously constructed. While the noun, *'elmen,* was the first word in the hemistich, the qualifier of the noun, *neqâwi,* was the last word in the hemistich. As the terminal rhyme phrase of the verse, the qualifier contrasted emphatically with the internal rhyme phrase of the verse "muscular (wolfish) shoulders." The literal meaning of the qualifier, *neqâwi*, is "pure," but it is derived from a verbal root whose primary meaning is "to suck the marrow from a bone." And so we see that a formal feature of a concrete form of signification echoes the satisfaction of a wolfish desire.

And consider also the musical design of each verse. As we hear the glottal stop of the internal rhyme of each verse, there is an echo of the cutting action of the hero's spear in verse 3 (*yiqeṣṣ al-jeneb wiyyet aḍ-ḍlow'*). As we hear the liquid vocalization of the terminal rhyme, a rhyme generally repeated by the audience in unison, we hear the poet's howls in verse 4 (*'azam 'ala-l-faḍla thamânîn wâwi*), which follow upon and conclude heroic actions. The poet suggests that heroic actions, although necessary and therefore natural, are in the company of and inseparable from the shadows and echoes of a questionable kind of formal life.

## 3

The first four verses complete the opening of the poem. The next four verses (v. 5–8) describe a series of specific events during the battle between the Rwala and the enemy. We are moving from the more formal part of the poem, where its central themes are developed, to the more concrete part of the poem, which refers to specific events. As we do so, the design of these next four verses will parallel the design of the first four verses. While the first pair of verses (v. 1–2) suggested that a heroic response takes shape as a movement from a formal energy to a concrete energy, verses 5 and 6 will derive the priority of concrete actions over formal expressions from the specific events of this battle. And while the second pair of verses (v. 3–4) suggested a relationship between heroism and poetry, verses 7 and 8 will clarify the character of this relationship in connection with the specific battle results.

The first of these verses (v. 5) begins with a portrayal of the enemy as they are confronted with the Rwala onslaught. A more literal translation of this verse follows:

> The Âl Jenk fled upon a full measure of the span (figuratively: an abundance),
> And Shlâsh he was of their reserve the lone-one.

The first hemistich describes an action of flight and ends with a figure of this action as a use of beastly energies. The phrase which figures the use of beastly energies, "a full measure of the span," literally refers to the length of the mounts' paces, but this same phrase is also a conventional figure of abundance. The phrase suggests, therefore, an abundance of lengthy paces. But let us examine the place of the phrase in the hemistich more precisely. As a description of the use of beasts, it insists upon a formal quality of such a use (the span of the beasts' paces) by a phrase which suggests an abundance. And so the description suggests not only an abundance of lengthy paces, but more ironically an abundant formal use of beastly energies. Once we have noted this feature of the description, we can also see that a quality of the flight of the Âl Jenk is reflected in a formal quality of the way in which they use their beasts. The flight leads to an opening between the Âl Jenk and the Rwala, and we see the paces of the mounts of the Âl Jenk "opening widely" as they flee from the Rwala.

The second hemistich describes the results of the action of the Âl Jenk. Shlâsh was deserted by his allies on the field of battle where he had to face the Rwala all alone. The description of Shlâsh characterizes him as the last remaining member of a reserve force of men and beasts. The result of the flight of the enemy in the face of the Rwala is a depletion of the men and beasts which are conventionally held in reserve, to be deployed at the crucial moment of battle. This enables us to understand the design of the verse as a whole. The result of an action, which takes shape as an abundant formal use of beastly energies, is the depletion of resources for effective actions with aggressive instruments.

The second of the four verses describes a Rwala hero, the notorious Khalaf, as he confronts Shlâsh on the field of battle. A more literal translation of this verse (v. 6) follows:

> He galloped upon him, the pasture of the wolf (literally: the lone one) who is protected from hunger,
> And pierced him, his steed crushing him with its hoofs.

The form of this verse parallels the form of the preceding verse. The first hemistich begins with a description of an action and ends with a description of the formal implications of that action. The second hemistich then describes the result of this action. Now, however, all these elements are inversions of the elements in the preceding verse, just as the structure of the verse itself is an inversion of the preceding verse. In the first hemistich, for example, the action of the hero is an inversion of the action of the Âl Jenk. The latter used their beasts to put some distance between themselves and their opponents. The hero now uses his beast to close in on his opponents: "He galloped upon him . . ." The phrase which follows does not describe the formal quality of the use of a beastly energy by Khalaf. Instead, the phrase suggests that the action is an abundant resource for a man of formal expressions: "the pasture of the wolf who is protected from hunger." Heroic actions do not appear as a certain form of action; instead, they cast the grotesque shadow of the poet of raiding and warfare. Moreover, the phrase that alludes to the poet who follows in the wake of heroic actions is an inversion of the result of the actions of the Âl Jenk in the second hemistich of the preceding verse. There, an opening action resulted in a depletion of resources for concrete actions. Here, a closing action has the quality of an abundant resource for formal expressions. The poet, moreover, insists upon this inversion. There is a *formal* identification of Shlâsh, who is all alone (*khalâwi*), and the man of formal expressions, who is the lone-one (*al-khalâwi*), a conventional designation of a wolf. There is something similar about Shlâsh, who tries to respond to the hero, but does not have the resources to do so, and a man of formal expression, who feeds upon heroic action. Both lack the capacity for effective concrete actions.

In the second hemistich of the verse, the result of the closing action of the hero is described. This result is an inversion of the quality of the Âl Jenk's use of beastly energies in the first hemistich of the preceding verse. In the place of an ineffective opening action, which had the quality of a formal use of beastly energies, we find a closing action which results in an effective use of beastly energies: "And pierced him, his steed crushing him with its hoofs." The result of an action, which takes shape as an abundant resource for a man of questionable formal expressions, is the effective use of beastly energies as an aggressive instrument.

The first two verses have illustrated how the priority of concrete actions over formal expressions arises out of the course of specific events. Men whose use of beasts has a formal quality (the Âl Jenk) are men who become incapable of effective concrete actions (Shlâsh). Men whose use of beasts provokes a questionable kind of formal expression (Khalaf who feeds the wolf) are men who triumph by effective concrete actions (the death of Shlâsh). The next two verses will now illustrate how grotesque and senseless formal expressions arise out of the course of specific events. A more literal translation of verse 7 follows:

> He and the horse, with the blow, fell to their shoulders,
> And fell the supper to the negro and the servant.

Again the verse is designed to suggest a natural flow of causes and effects. In the first hemistich, the enemy, who is the "inversion" of the hero, is literally inverted as Shlâsh and his horse fall to their shoulders. The description of this inversion suggests a conclusion of heroic actions. As man and beast fall to their shoulders, there is an echo of the beastly shoulders in verse 1. There, events abroad began as men put into play beastly energies. Here, events abroad conclude as the beastly energies, which these men use, are taken out of play. This has come about as a result of a blow (wound) struck by the hero. Here there is an echo of the wounds (blows) in verse 2. Events which began with wounds (*al-ahâwi*), which precipitated an assault, have now come to a conclusion once again with a blow (*behwâh*).

In the second hemistich, this conclusion of a heroic action is followed upon by the actions of the retinue of the hero, who rush in to seize the spoils of war. These men, Musil notes, are not normally known for their valor. As a man with aggressive instruments becomes helpless, lesser men appear upon the scene and take advantage of his vulnerable condition. Where priority is placed upon concrete actions with aggressive instruments, cowardly men are naturally going to seek umbrage from such circumstances by letting themselves be dominated by heroic men. And these same men of defective character are naturally going to exploit the results of heroic actions in a self-serving way. The plunder of Shlâsh is described as a result that inevitably follows the conclusions of heroic action, where such actions are a dominating feature of life. But now let us note that this plunder also has a formal dimension. As Shlâsh and his horse fall (*ṭâḥaw*) to the ground, a feast metaphorically falls (*ṭâḥ*) to the retinue of the hero. The heroic actions of Khalaf have a formal value. They are the means of a celebration. The plunder of the belongings of Shlâsh has a formal value. It takes shape as a kind of celebration. And so the scene about a plunder of a dead man's goods by cowardly men suggests how a certain kind of formal life is inevitably nourished by the circumstances of life in the desert and steppe.

The next verse is the last of the four verses that describe the course of specific events. In verse 8, the specific conclusion of heroic actions (h. 7a) and the specific results which follow this conclusion (h. 7b) are generalized as a form of life which is based upon concrete actions with aggressive instruments. A more literal translation of verse 8 follows:

> How many a one by means of the unhorsing of the fringe-adorned spear,
> Did he grind his head, the hyena of al-Jerâwi.[5]

This verse describes the very same events as the preceding verse. Again the fall from a mount is described, and again a feast upon the victims follows, but now these events have been stylized in a very different way. In the first hemistich the poet stylizes Shlâsh's fall as a generalization of the form of the events of the day. Here we see the features of a life that is based upon concrete actions with aggressive instruments. There are, on the one hand, lonely victims (how many a one) who are deprived of energetic resources (the unhorsing), and there are, on the other hand, heroes who appear as no more than an ornament of an aggressive instrument (the fringe-adorned spear). And this is a life which is inseparable from certain shadows and echoes. As we hear the word that announces the unhorsing (*bedhwâbet*) of the enemy, we glimpse a wolfish form as we hear the echo of a wolfish name (*dhîb*). Then, following upon this general form of events, such a beast appears quite vividly upon the scene. In the second hemistich, a cowardly, howling beast (the hyena) uses his teeth to gnaw upon the head of a man who has fallen in battle. Now we can see that the formal life suggested by the scene of plunder in verse 7 foreshadows this figure of the poet, a man of purely formal expressions. Like the retinue of the hero, the poet of warfare is a man of defective character who appears, in a cowardly fashion, only when heroic actions have been concluded. But worse than the retinue of the hero, who only metaphorically feast on the possessions of a man fallen in battle, the poet of warfare, in a more genuinely beastly fashion, uses his teeth to satisfy a ghoulish appetite. Grotesquely and senselessly, he mauls the character (grind his head) of a dead man for personal amusement.

And now let us note that the relationship of the hemistichs of verse 8 is different from the relationship of the hemistichs of verse 7. In the preceding verse, the unhorsing of Shlâsh (h. 7a) was a conclusion of heroic actions which caused a result, the plunder of Shlâsh's personal possessions (h. 7b). Now the description of an unhorsing as a general feature of life, in h. 8a, has become not the cause, but the means of what follows in h. 8b: "By means of the unhorsing of the fringe-adorned spear // Did he (the hyena) grind his (Shlâsh's) head . . ." As the poet moves from a description of the course of events to a characterization of the form of life, which is based upon those events, heroic actions lose their status as a response to concrete events and appear as the means of a certain kind of grotesque and senseless formal life. Heroism is necessary, and therefore heroism is a natural response to political experience, but then heroism is the basis of a disgusting kind of formal life. This formal life flourishes upon misfortunes, which are the inevitable result of the priority of concrete actions with aggressive instruments.

In the concluding three verses, the poet summarizes the principal implications of the events he has described, by citing their specific concrete results. The first of these verses insists that the fate of men is decisively determined by the *energetic use* of aggressive instruments. A more literal translation of verse 9 is:

> Shlâsh was trampled and Rmeyḥ has surrendered,
> Because of the burning blows of those who inflicted wounds.

As the result of the use of aggressive resources (h. 9b), one man has been physically crushed, and another man no longer has the will to act (h. 9a). The second of these verses then insists that because the fate of men is so determined, men can prevail only by *responding* to the priority of the energetic use of aggressive instruments. Verse 10 can be more literally translated as follows:

> Khalaf he who has cut the enemy,
> Redoubles himself when the opposition grows.

Khalaf, the man who has prevailed, is a man who has used an instrument to kill men (h. 10a). And in doing so, Khalaf has responded to the priority of concrete actions. His personal physical energy always matches the energy of the men who threaten him (h. 10b). The third of these verses then concludes the poem, insisting that a kind of *formal response* follows upon a failure to respond to the energetic use of aggressive resources. Verse 11 can be more literally translated as follows:

> Rmeyḥ deserted Shlâsh and his head is cut off,
> Over him these Rwala shout the war song.

In the face of men who use aggressive resources, one man flees for his life in a cowardly way, leaving another man to meet his death by an instrument of violence. This is a life in which some men inevitably fail to respond, and because of this, braver men meet their death. Following upon this ruthless necessity which has resulted in misfortune, there is an occasion for triumph. We see the shadows of the Rwala poised wolfishly over a corpse, and we hear the echoes of their strange cries in the Arabian wastes.

Sometimes the North Arabian Bedouins were convinced that they could make a place for themselves in the world by means of a measured, pragmatic use of aggressive resources. The narrative tradition of these peoples consists of troubled compositions that examine how the course of events might confirm such a possibility. At a very early date, however, their hope to make a place for themselves in the world by such a means raised a question about whether any form of life was possible that limited the readiness of men to abandon themselves to the use of deadly instruments. The poetic tradition of these peoples reveals the pressure which such an extreme situation exerted upon them, but then it also reveals just how over the course of many, many centuries, they developed an eloquent response to these pressures.

# Part IV
# Segmentary politics and the cult of saints in North Africa

We came from the south and fought our way through the mountains with guns, and we took this land with the gun. We kept it with our guns and later we were driven off it only with the cannon.

A quote from the Beni Mtir tribe of Morocco by Rassam (Vinogradov) in Gellner and Micaud, *Arabs and Berbers* (1973), p. 69.

# 10. The forms of segmentary politics and their relative absence among the North Arabian Bedouins

## 1

An analysis of Rwala ceremonial narratives and poems of raiding and warfare has revealed how a pattern of motivations and circumstances dominated the historical experience of the North Arabian Bedouins. Such a pattern was a more or less important aspect of all the pastoral societies throughout the arid zone, stretching from western North Africa into eastern Central Asia. Among the North Arabian Bedouins, however, the forces of Near Eastern pastoral nomadism were not only at work from very early times, these forces eventually pressed upon them to an extreme degree as a result of their way of life. Among these herders and riders of camels, a popular investment in aggressive instruments was relatively untempered by any deep involvement in a life of patient and diligent labor.

In this part, we shall examine the shape of Near Eastern institutions where a popular interest in aggressive resources was tempered by a popular involvement in patient and diligent labor. Such a tempering becomes increasingly important as one turns from the motivations which were most intensely (but not solely) at work among Near Eastern nomadic peoples to the motivations which were most intensely (but again not solely) at work among Near Eastern sedentary peoples. To pursue this issue, we could develop the argument set forth in the last part of Chapter 5 where the Arabian pastoralists were briefly compared with the Arabian settlers. By means of this comparison, we saw how the circumstances which increasingly favored a settled life resulted in an increasingly different conception of social morality, whose form indicated, nevertheless, the pressures of a popular investment in aggressive resources. In this way we glimpsed how a problem that originated among the Arabian pastoral nomads shaped the traditions of all Arabian peoples. It will be more interesting however to turn to certain areas of North Africa. Here the environment favored the involvement of the pastoralists themselves in peaceful productive activities. It will be possible for us to understand how such an involvement led to very different kinds of tribal political institutions. This will enable us to see how the differing rhythms of Arabian and North African political history are in part a result of the different prevailing pattern of motivations and circumstances among the peoples of each region.

The comparison of the North Arabian pastoralists with groups of North African pastoralists will raise two familiar issues in Near Eastern anthropology – segmentary politics and the cult of saints. These issues have been of special interest for the ethnographers of North Africa. By and large, these ethnographers have argued that segmentary politics and the cult of saints are unusually important features of tribal societies in this part of the world. Indeed, the standard anthropological interpretations of segmentary politics and the cult of saints are thought to be most perfectly demonstrated by the institutions of a North African peoples, the Cyrenaican Bedouins.

In Cyrenaica, anthropologists seem to have found an example of the precise circumstances that had resulted in an ideal type of segmentary political system. The Cyrenaican Bedouins were divided into a large number of independent groups, which were competing for the same resources, but which lacked any elaborate governmental devices to control their competition. Among these Bedouins, anthropologists were able to record an elaborate tribal genealogy, which described a system of political alliances. By means of this system of alliances, groups of more or less equal size were consistently pitted against one another (see Figure 1). This confirmed a standard anthropological interpretation of segmentary political systems. Such systems were said to result from the unsettled political conditions among peoples without developed political institutions. A politically segmenting genealogy, which consistently balanced groups of equal sizes, was a kind of primitive solution to this problem.

The Cyrenaicans were also devoted to the cult of saints, and so they also provided a confirmation of a standard anthropological interpretation of such a religious institution. Cults of saints were characteristic of many tribal peoples all over the Near East. Such cults, it was argued, arose in connection with the need for mediators between two political groupings on the occasion of a political conflict. As the groupings assembled with the purpose of contesting one another, a representative of the cult of saints attempted to conciliate them. He showed them the senselessness and futility of a balanced political struggle in which there was more to lose than to gain. He provided them with the possibility of backing away from their threats and reaching a peaceful settlement without losing face. He invoked the moral value of peace to which all groups were equally committed. Various features of the cult of saints among the Cyrenaican Bedouins confirmed such an interpretation. In this way, the ethnography of the Cyrenaican Bedouins led to the conclusion that segmentary political systems and the cult of saints were closely associated in the Near East, because both institutions were the result of the political conditions characteristic of tribal Near Eastern peoples.

The ethnography of the North Arabian Bedouins contradicts these principal conclusions of several decades of anthropological discussion. The political circumstances of the North Arabian Bedouins, a group of "pure" mounted pastoral nomads, conform unusually well with the conditions which are thought to give rise to segmentary politics and the cult of saints. Indeed, the political circumstances of these Bedouins conform with such conditions far better than the circumstances of the Cyrenaican Bedouins, among whom one finds a good deal of agricultural activity. However, among the North Arabian Bedouins we do not find a remarkable example of a tribal genealogy that describes a system of political alliances among little groups. And as for the cult of saints, the North Arabian Bedouins, who were well aware of the existence of such a cult, ridiculed and scorned its beliefs and rituals.

We might conclude that the entire discussion of segmentary politics and the cult of saints is misconceived, but such a conclusion would leave us with the more difficult problem of explaining how so many gifted ethnographers could have been misled. Also, such a conclusion would undercut much of the ethnography of tribal North Africa, which has enabled us to understand these societies in terms of the close coordination of these peculiar institutions. Instead, it would be more reasonable to assume that the pattern of popular interests, which underlies segmentary politics and the cult of saints, has been partly, but not completely, understood.

Let us begin with the problem of segmentary politics. Drawing upon what we have learned from Rwala political literature, we can examine an element of a politically segmenting genealogy as a kind of theoretical construction which is fashioned as a response to a political problem. This will reveal how such constructions are inspired by a contradiction, which is typical of a tribal approach to political experience in the Near East. We shall then consider how certain segmentary constructions among the North Arabian Bedouins reflect such a contradiction. After this, we shall consider, in Chapter 11, how this contradiction, which more or less affected the life of all pastoral nomads in the Near East, became a central feature of political experience among the Cyrenaican Bedouins. In this way, we shall be able to understand why the Cyrenaican Bedouins elaborated a "classical" example of a politically segmenting genealogy.

## 2

Among various traditional peoples all over the world, genealogies frequently have political dimensions. But unlike all other parts of the world, genealogies in the Near East, and especially those in the tribal Near East, tend to have a solely political dimension. At all levels of traditional Near Eastern society, but especially among tribal peoples, a political group is typically conceived as consisting of all the male descendants of a paternal ancestor. Such groups commonly designate themselves as the descendants of this ancestor. The members of such a group are said to be obligated to support one another. However, this obligation typically takes a relatively narrow form, especially among tribal peoples. The members of such a group should support one another, not necessarily with respect to all the affairs of life, but more particularly with respect to threats from other similar groups. This curious and almost universal form of representing political groups in the Near East is closely associated with a historical problem in this part of the world: the threatening uncertainty of political relationships. If we examine this form of representing political groups in detail, we can learn something about the character of the historical problem to which it was a response.

The pastoral nomads were faced with the threatening uncertainty of political relationships. As a result, they were obsessed with those features of human experience that suggested how men were naturally and concretely related with one another. Such features promised a natural and concrete protection from a situation in which certain forces persistently drove men apart and set them against one another. This obsession settled upon a familial idiom of political relationships, partly because other forms of relationships beyond the family were in question, and partly because the family presented them with just such a natural and concrete dimension of human relationships. Political relationships were conceived in terms of an idiom of familial relationships, and this idiom stressed the status of familial relationships as natural and concrete biological facts. But the biological facts of family life were, to be sure, "interpreted" in a specific way. Some important facts were ignored, while other less important ones were lent an overriding significance.[1]

The threatening uncertainty of political relationships was a result of men being drawn into a political struggle in which an individual with weapons came together with others to resist still others. In this situation, one had to begin with the individual actor in conceiving of a response to the problems of political experience. That is to say, the life of the pastoral nomads took shape as one in which individuals were actively and energetically engaged in political experience. Therefore, the familial idiom of political relationships largely ignored the role of women, even though motherhood is the most central biological feature of familial relationships. Instead, this familial idiom highlighted a necessary, but almost insignificant biological feature of familial relationships: the father as a progenitor.[2] The father, as a progenitor, was a natural and concrete maker of relationships. He was a metaphor of the political actor in the biological idiom of familial relationships. Therefore, the father as a progenitor seemed to represent a natural and concrete dimension of human experience, which promised some protection from a situation in which certain forces continually drove men apart and set them against one another.

Political relationships were too uncertain for political groups to be institutionally articulated. And yet there was intense pressure to conceive of political groups in some way, because the uncertainty of political relationships was threatening. The result of this dilemma was a "collapsed" concept of political groups as the progeny of a progenitor. There was no active political authority who articulated the strategies of the group's political responses. There was only the name of a dead, and therefore absent, paternal authority. There was no organization by which the group articulated its political responses. Instead, the significance of the name of the paternal ancestor was restricted to an obligation to unite when the group was actually threatened by some other similar group. This idiom unites a natural and concrete conception of the basis of political relationships (the progeny of a progenitor) with a severely limited conception of political experience (the obligation to unite only where there is a threat from other groups). The form of this idiom reveals an obsession with discovering some natural and concrete basis for political relationships, the connection of this obsession with a threatening uncertainty of political relationships, and the undermining of the institutionalization of communities and authorities as a result of this uncertainty. Men are convinced they are really related to one another in a definite way, even though they are engaged in a constant struggle with one another and are unable to develop any political institutions. Indeed, their desperate conviction that they are really related to one another is strengthened just because they are engaged in a struggle which prevents the development of political institutions.[3]

With this understanding of how a familial idiom of political relationships is the germ for a political response in the Near East, we can now understand how a conception of groups in terms of a politically segmenting genealogy is one specific form of such an idiom. Consider the most elementary unit of a politically segmenting genealogy in Figure 2. The name of a man, *P*, represents the common paternal ancestor of two groups. This representation of the political unity of the two groups is associated with an obligation to support one another in the face of a threat. Each of the two groups also represents itself in terms of a name of a more immediate paternal ancestor, *A* and *B*, respectively. These representations of the political unity of each subgroup, moreover, are specifically associated with an obligation of the members of each subgroup to support one another in the face of the threat of the other subgroup. The elementary form of a politically segmenting genealogy defines a point of political

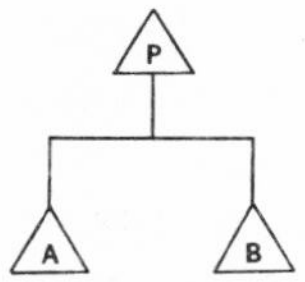


Figure 2. An elementary unit of a politically segmenting genealogy

fusion, which is also a point of political fission. There is something faulty about the supergroup, which is formed from two groups as a response to other hostile groups, but which also tends to break apart into two hostile groups. What is the source of this faulty concept of a union, which is also a disunion? If we recall men's interest in political adventurism, the source of the threatening uncertainty of political relationships among these peoples, we can provisionally understand why this elementary form of a politically segmenting genealogy became so common a feature of Near Eastern tribal political institutions.

There are two contradictory motivations at work in the elementary form of a politically segmenting genealogy. There is a threat from abroad, which provokes an attempt to construct a political relationship as a source of protection from that threat. However, there is also an interest in preserving one's political freedom from such a relationship, which otherwise restricts an interest in political adventurism. This means that political relationships take a "segmentary form" at every level where the threat from abroad (which brings men together) is indecisively balanced against a reluctance to relinquish an interest in political adventurism (which drives men apart).

There would always be a tendency for such a political relationship to be represented genealogically. This follows from the history of political experience in the Near East. It is derived from a popular investment in personal instruments of aggression, which provokes the general uncertainty of relationships and drives men to resort to a concrete idiom of progenitors and their progenies. With this interpretation in mind, let us turn to examine the representation of political relationships among the little herding groups of the North Arabian Bedouins.

## 3

The ethnographic accounts of the North Arabian Bedouins clearly reveal that, rightly or wrongly, these peoples can at least be construed as an example of a segmentary society. The 'Aneze tribal confederation of North Arabia segmented into two major tribal groupings, consisting of the Bishr and the Ḍana Muslims. The Bishr segmented in turn into the

'Obeyd and the 'Ammâr, and the Ḍana Muslims segmented in turn into the Beni Wahab and the Âl Jlâs. These latter groupings segmented into tribal entities, among which one finds most of the tribes mentioned in this study, for example, the Sba'a, the Fed'ân, the Weld 'Ali, the Swâlme, the 'Abdelle, and the Rwala.[4] Each of these tribes divided into sets of little herding groups, each with its own distinctive name. And finally, these sets divided into the little herding groups of a tribe, which also had their own distinctive names.

There are various ways, however, in which this pattern of political segmentation among the North Arabian Bedouins failed to conform to the "classical" notion of a segmentary political system, such as it was developed by E. E. Evans-Pritchard and others. For example, the political relationships of these groupings were not represented in terms of a politically segmenting genealogy. Instead, one level of political grouping, the tribe, stood out as a clear-cut political community with clear-cut political authority. This is the level which is designated by the names Sba'a, Fed'ân, Weld 'Ali, Swâlme, 'Abdelle, and Rwala. The very names of these tribes did not usually refer to the descendants of a paternal ancestor (although some did, such as Weld 'Ali); instead, these names are best glossed as designations of "a people." Moreover, the Bedouin discussion of the relationships of these tribes with one another, or the relationships of the subgroups of the tribe, did not normally involve a genealogical idiom of patrilineal descent. It is true that the North Arabian Bedouins had traditions about the names of the paternal ancestors of almost all their political groupings, just as they had traditions about the genealogical relationships of almost all political groupings. But there was certainly no great genealogical tradition among these peoples, which analyzed the structure of their tribal confederations at its upper levels, and analyzed the patrilineal descent of each individual male tribesman at its lower levels. It might very well have been theoretically possible for an ethnographer to have constructed such a genealogy, but the North Arabian Bedouins, unlike some other Near Eastern tribal peoples, did not present their ethnographers with such a genealogy as a political fact. Musil even asserts that ordinary Bedouin tribesmen were remarkably uninterested in genealogies. Few men, he notes, could trace more than three ascending generations of male ancestors.[5]

These features of the designation of political groupings among the North Arabian Bedouins suggest that these people had a more definite concept of community and authority than might have been the case among Near Eastern tribal peoples who were more concerned with tribal genealogies. In North Arabia there were great dynasties of tribal chiefs, such as the Eben Sha'lân, as well as particular chiefs who were well known all over North Arabia, such as Saṭṭâm and an-Nûri. There were impressive tribal entities, such as the Rwala, who were clearly dominant over other tribes. The dominant tribes, such as the Rwala, sometimes had a system of dual chiefs. A political chief, *sheykh al-bâb*, conducted peaceful negotiations with other tribes. A military chief, *sheykh ash-shdâd*, led the tribe in wars against other tribes.[6] The dominant tribes also had tribal symbols, like the Abu-d-Duhûr camel litter of the Rwala and the ʻAlya herd of white riding camels. And certainly, not least of all, these tribes had their own oral traditions, such as the ceremonial narratives and poems of raiding and warfare which we have considered in Chapters 4 through 9.

This unusual North Arabian elaboration of the tribal association as a distinctive political grouping, which was different from every other political grouping (either beyond it or within it), is one of the two keys necessary for a proper understanding of the North Arabian tribal regime. The other is the narrow restriction of tribal institutions to the problem of a threat from abroad. The chiefs represented the interests of the tribe primarily in connection with its conflicts with other tribes. The tribal camel litter was a symbol of political unity in times of warfare. It led the tribal columns into battle and served as a rallying point during the battle. The tribal herd of riding camels was a symbol of tribal power which rested primarily upon such beastly energies. Quite clearly, the tribe was a political community that was founded upon a response to a threat from abroad. This means that there was a decisive difference between the quality of intertribal as opposed to intratribal political relationships.

In the world beyond the tribe, the political relationships of the tribes were uncertainly balanced between a threat from abroad and an interest in political adventurism. Musil's introduction to his chapter entitled "War and Peace" suggests how this is so:

> The Rwala are ever at war with one tribe or another. Without war a Rweyli could not live. War gives him an opportunity of displaying his cunning, endurance, and courage. He neither loves the shedding of blood, nor craves booty, but is allured by danger and delights in the predatory art. The booty itself he will give away without thinking much about it – even to the wife of the very man he has just robbed. Some tribes, not always entire strangers, hate each other cordially. Between them peace is never of long duration. Despite the greatest efforts of the chiefs to prevent war, their people continue to attack and destroy one another.[7]

The tribal chiefs like Saṭṭâm and an-Nûri attempted to secure the tribe against attacks by working out alliances with other tribes. But ordinary tribesmen could never be completely prevented from raiding other tribes, and so these alliances were always tenuous. We have seen evidence of this in the Rwala narratives and poems. On two occasions we found that the Rwala and the Beni Wahab were bitter enemies. On a third occasion we found that they were friendly allies against the Fedʻân, but that this alliance was troubled by groups of the Beni Wahab who were joining Fed'ân expeditions against the Rwala.[8] It is this world of intertribal relationships which very nearly takes the "classical" form of a politically segmenting genealogy among the North Arabian Bedouins.

Since the relationships of all tribes were more or less uncertain, conventional pairings of tribes formed in reaction to the threat of the conventional pairings of other tribes. However, the precise form of these relationships was not exactly like the classical form of a politically segmenting genealogy. Intertribal relationships were not normally represented in genealogical terms. In addition, the Bedouins were aware that the intertribal relationships tended to shift. Musil never even attempted to describe these relationships systematically. The account of the architecture of the 'Aneze confederacy in the first paragraph of this section is drawn from von Oppenheim, who was determined to describe the relationship of all the Bedouin tribes of Arabia in a systematic way. The Bedouins were always willing to entertain his interest in such a fanciful project.

In the world within the tribe, the political relationships of groups had a very different value. The only common interest of the groups within the political community was the threat of other tribes. This is reflected by the more or less exclusive concern of tribal institutions with a threat from abroad. At the same time, there were no serious conflicts of interest between the groups which constituted the tribe. As a result, the political community was clearly defined as a unity only vis-à-vis conflicts with other tribes. It was not a political community which had a clearly defined *internal* structure. Let us examine more closely the pattern of intratribal relationships in order to see more clearly this feature of the tribal political community.

In an article on the North Arabian Bedouins, R. Montagne provides an account of the tribal polity of the Shammar, Bedouin neighbors of the Rwala. Montagne at this time had already developed a view of North African tribal political relationships which emphasized their segmentary structure. By insisting upon the segmentary character of the relationships of the little herding groups of the Shammar, he could have easily suggested that the North Arabian Bedouins provided confirmation of his work in North Africa. This, however, he did not do. Instead, he describes the vagueness of all intertribal and intratribal relationships within the North Arabian tribal confederation, while insisting on the role of tribal chiefs as political architects. He writes:

> It is usually not possible to establish a complete and definitive picture of the structure of a Bedouin confederation . . . In fact, all the Shammar do not represent the internal architecture of their confederation in the same way. Each man is only familiar with his own group and its relationship with neighboring

> groups. The chiefs, who have a broader political perspective, deform the social structure in accordance with their rivalries. They jumble their recollections of historical events, on which are founded the great internal divisions, with conflicts in the present.[9]

Only the structure of low-level relationships was clear to an ordinary tribesman. He had some idea about the relationship of groups in his own vicinity, but not much more than this. This means that the tribe had no precise structure as a political community. The tribal chiefs appear as the only men who had views about the architecture of the tribal confederation. This means that the confederation also had no precise structure. Rather, the tribal chiefs, as political architects, represented the confederacy in accordance with the intertribal conflicts of the moment.

The North Arabian tribe was a clearly defined political community which was led by a clearly defined political authority, but only on the occasion of intertribal conflicts. Within the tribe, the relationship of specific political groupings was not altogether clear, because there was no systematic common interest among these groupings, but only a contingent one (the threat of other tribes), and there was no important conflict of interest among these groupings. Beyond the tribe, the relationships of tribes were not altogether clear, because a popular interest in political adventurism unsettled chiefly attempts to systematize intertribal alliances.

But we have already seen a far more elegant demonstration of this curious character of the North Arabian tribe. The ceremonial narrative of raiding and warfare conceives of the tribe in connection with the leadership of a chief on the very occasion of an intertribal conflict. These narratives do not suggest any developed concept of the structure of an intertribal world, nor of an intratribal world. They do involve a highly developed concept of a tribal political authority as an architect of tribal political responses, where the domain of these responses is narrowly restricted to the occasion of intertribal raids and wars.

The North Arabian camel-herding tribes, like the Rwala, were not "structured" communities, and the political relationships of these camel-herding tribes were not structured. In particular, we find that it is not possible to describe the political relationships of the North Arabian Bedouins as a fixed pattern of segmenting political alliances. Within the tribe, there was no systematic representation of the tribe as a politically segmenting structure. Beyond the tribe, intertribal relationships were represented in a segmentary form, but these representations did not take the shape of a politically segmenting genealogy, since the intertribal alliances were not quite stable enough to be conceived in a genealogical idiom. By understanding the degree to which we do or do not find segmentary representations of political relationships among the North Arabian Bedouins, we are now prepared to consider just why such representations were so important among the Cyrenaican Bedouins.

# 11. Political wildness and religious domesticity among the Cyrenaican Bedouins

## 1

The Cyrenaican Bedouins in North Africa can be closely compared with the North Arabian Bedouins. The Cyrenaicans, like the North Arabians, spoke a dialect of Arabic. The pastoral traditions of the Cyrenaicans originally took shape in the Nejd region of Arabia, from whence their forebears came sometime after the middle of the eleventh century A.D.[1] Indeed, more than a few of the Cyrenaicans pursued the same kind of camel-herding nomadism that was typical of the dominant tribes in North Arabia. If, however, we examine these Bedouins of the North African littoral more closely, we see certain crucial differences between their way of life and that of the camel-herding Bedouins of North Arabia.

The Cyrenaican Bedouins, even the dominant tribes among them, were more or less involved in sheep-, goat-, and cattle-herding, as well as camel-herding. Many of the Cyrenaicans, even the dominant tribes among them, were more or less involved in agricultural activities. Sheep, goats, and cattle bring pastoralists into a closer relationship with the land. They are less mobile animals than camels, and they depend more nearly upon specific plots of pasture and specific sources of water. Agricultural activities not only tie pastoralists firmly to the land, such activities involve them in a routine of patient and diligent labor, which is not at all characteristic of a mounted camel-herding way of life.

Just why the Bedouins who came to Cyrenaica altered their Arabian form of life is not altogether clear. Perhaps the character of the Cyrenaican environment demanded such an adaptation. Perhaps the less arid Cyrenaican environment simply made such an adaptation so tempting that it was irresistible. Or perhaps these Bedouins first dominated and then absorbed a more sedentary indigenous North African population. Whatever the reasons, the Cyrenaican Bedouins were more closely tied to the land and more deeply involved in peaceful, productive activities than the North Arabian Bedouins.

The importance of a productive relationship with the land among the Cyrenaican Bedouins is clearly reflected by the status of their dominant tribes. These tribes, the so-called noble or free (*ḥûrr*) tribes, were recognized as the possessors of the land. The other tribes, the so-called dependent (*al-laff*) tribes, used the land only with the permission of the former.[2] In contrast, the noble or free tribes in North Arabia were simply those tribes that herded camels (and were therefore powerful), while the other tribes were simply those that herded sheep and goats (and were therefore weak). A relationship with the land was more nearly the central basis of a dominant political status in Cyrenaica, whereas a relationship with animals was more nearly the central basis of such a status in North Arabia.

At some time in the distant past then, Arabian Bedouins came to Cyrenaica and over a long period became increasingly involved in a productive relationship with the land. One might assume at first that the tribes of these camel-herding Bedouins would have become firmer political communities as these peoples became gradually more interested in specific plots of land. A more routinized and systematic way of life should have permitted the development of a more routinized and systematic organization of the political community. Such a political organization could have provided more effective protection than a purely contingent political association. Such a political organization might even have evolved to the point that it would have facilitated the pursuit of peaceful, productive activities. In Cyrenaica, the Arabian tribe should have become more like a state of public authorities, political associations, and private interests. But this is not at all what happened. Instead we find that the Bedouin tribe after its arrival in Cyrenaica was weakened, not strengthened. It became even more completely a contingent political association, which took shape only in connection with an even more narrowly defined political situation. To understand this development, we must consider the implications of an involvement in peaceful, productive activities among a people whose traditions have first been shaped by an extreme kind of pastoral experience.

In Arabia, the forces of Near Eastern pastoral nomadism were at work with an unusual intensity from very early times. As a result, Bedouin political life was polarized around the use of personal instruments of aggression. Cooperation involved the assemblage of a group of men with mounts and weapons for the purpose of a political struggle. Leadership involved the design of political strategies in a contest among groups of men with mounts and weapons. This polarization of political life around the use of personal instruments of aggression drove men to commit themselves to tribal associations and to submit themselves to tribal chiefs. But in Cyrenaica where such peoples were drawn into a productive relationship with the land, they became all the more vulnerable to a threat from abroad. This brings us back to the hypothesis with which we began. The solution to this problem would have been the institutionalization of a tribal armed force and the institutionalization of a tribal authority as its commander. That is to say, as the Cyrenaicans were drawn into peaceful, productive activities, there was a distinct pressure to routinize and to systematize those very features of the Bedouin tribe which had taken shape in Arabia. But, in spite of this pressure, this routinization and systematization did not take place. Why was this so?

When the North Arabian Bedouins committed themselves to their tribal associations and submitted themselves to their tribal chiefs, they had nothing to fear from their involvement in such a political community. As mounted camel-herding nomads, they lived in mobile little groups, each of which was entirely self-supporting. No one could unite or lead these little groups, unless they wanted to be united or led, and there was no occasion on which they wanted to be united or led except when they were threatened by other groups of camel-herders. In Cyrenaica, however, the Bedouins were more involved in the production and consumption of private resources by means of specific day-to-day activities, which tended to tie them down to specific places. As such a people, they could have been more easily dominated and exploited by any organized political force. Let us also recall that these were men who had an impressive background in the organization of armed political forces for aggressive purposes. Thus a new kind of opportunity presented itself to these men who had the means and skills of political adventurists. This was the possibility of dominating and exploiting other men who lived by specific day-to-day activities and were tied down to specific places. But this was not an opportunity which carried men abroad into alien lands and among alien groups. This was an opportunity which arose within the tribe itself. And just as men clearly perceived this opportunity for themselves, they saw that that same opportunity presented itself to the men with whom they were associated. As a result, the tribe was weakened as factions took shape within the tribe in response to this growing internal threat. And then each of these factions was weakened, as subfactions took shape in response to this same threat. All political associations were a potential threat to private needs, private activities, and private resources. No political association, therefore, could come to play any legitimate role in connection with the facilitation of these needs, activities, and resources. Peaceful, productive activities were purely personal and familial concerns. A life of patient and diligent labor was conceived as a purely domestic kind of life. The increasing involvement of the Cyrenaicans in a relationship with the land took shape as an increasing concern with private and domestic interests. The result was a dilemma. Some form of political association was necessary as a response to a threat from abroad, but any form of political association was also a potential threat to domestic interests.

## 2

A popular interest in the use of personal instruments of aggression creates a need for political organization, and a domestic interest in a life of peaceful, productive labor is threatened by any such political organization. This contradiction is at the root of a kind of politics that anthropologists have attempted to describe as segmentary politics. We shall see how this is so by examining just how Near Eastern tribal peoples responded to this contradiction by constructing "classical" segmentary representations of their political relationships.

Let us consider an ideal case of a set of little groups of transhumant peoples who work the land during part of the year and move with their herds during part of the year. Previous to their adoption of such a life, the political traditions of these groups have been shaped by their experiences as Near Eastern pastoral nomads. There is therefore a problem of political adventurism among them which takes the form of a threat from abroad. Since these little groups live a sedentary life during part of the year, their neighbors are natural allies against a threat from abroad, especially since the little groups are most vulnerable when they are sedentary. The little groups therefore respond to a threat from abroad by institutionalizing political associations with their neighbors. Now, however, the other little groups in these political associations present a potential threat to domestic interests. And so the little groups seek alliances among their closest neighbors within the political association as a means of protecting themselves from their involvement in the political association itself. But these political alliances are also a potential threat to domestic interests. There is a pressing need for political relationships because of a threat from abroad, but all political relationships are themselves dangerous because of a threat from within. There is therefore an attempt to conceive of political alliances as concrete, natural relationships at the same time as there is a refusal to elaborate these relationships beyond an obligation to respond to the threat of other similar political alliances. Men insist that they are absolutely obligated to join with other men in response to a political threat, but they refuse to do so unless they are actually faced with a political threat which forces them to join other men. The result is a "collapsed" conception of political groups in terms of the familial idiom of political relationships that was discussed in the second section of Chapter 10. Associations of little groups are conceived as the progeny of a progenitor, and the mutual obligations (of the members) of such a progeny are narrowly restricted to a response to the threat of other similar progenies.

With this idiom of political relationships in mind, let us consider how the elaboration of these alliances among the little groups might have proceeded. Imagine, for example, a set of eight little residential groups which are faced with a threat from abroad. As they represent themselves as a protective political association, they choose the name of a paternal ancestor, *X*, for such a representation (see Figure 3).

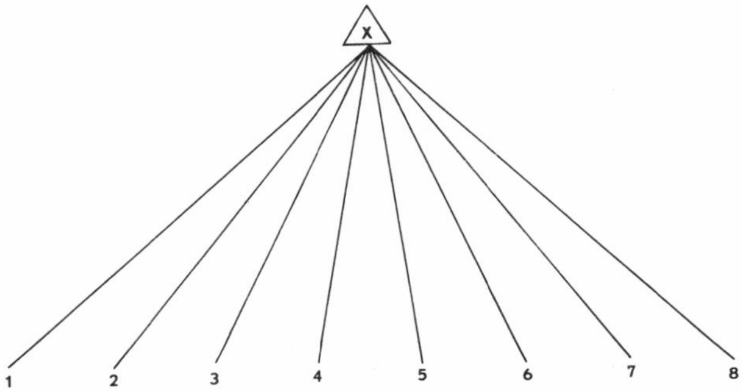


Figure 3. The representation of the political association of eight little groups

Despite this representation of a protective political association, the little groups have private domestic interests, which are threatened by the protective political association. The political association is therefore qualified by a representation of these interests. Each little group represents itself by the name of a more immediate paternal ancestor; *A, B, C, D, E, F, G,* and *H*, as shown in Figure 4. The protective political association has now shattered into little groups. Political uncertainty has erupted within the association, yet almost no institutional elaboration of the political association has been accomplished. Or more exactly, the only articulation of the political community which has taken place is an insistence by each little group of its independent status as a political entity within the protective political association. The little groups therefore respond to the threat of this uncertainty within the political association itself by seeking alliances with their closest neighbors. There are two possible responses to this move. Each little group might ally with some other little group in the immediate vicinity, as shown in Figure 5. Or the political association of the eight little groups might be split into smaller political associations of neighboring groups, as shown in Figure 6.

The first response reveals the possibility that pairs of groups can form alliances, and so the very danger of this possibility encourages other pairs of groups to respond by forming such alliances. The second response leads to smaller, more localized subassociations. However, these subassociations are also troubled by the problem of a contradiction between their political and domestic interests. And so the little groups respond to this problem by making alliances within the subcommunity itself. Whatever

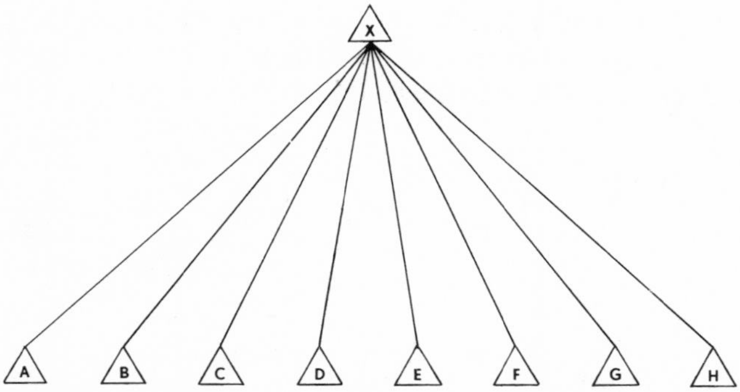

Figure 4. The representation of the domestic interests of each little group

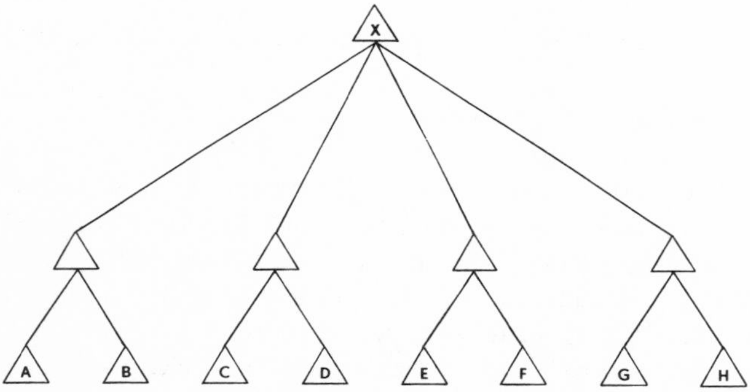

Figure 5. The formation of paired alliances within the political association

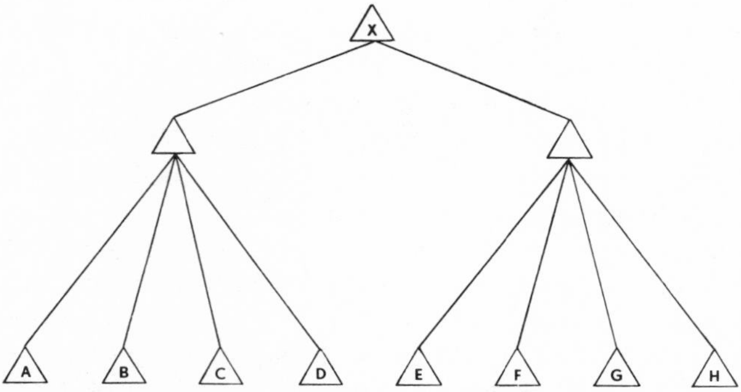

Figure 6. The formation of little political associations within larger political associations

the number of groups, these attempts to deal with threats from abroad and threats from within come to rest only when there is everywhere a pairing of the names of more immediate paternal ancestors under the names of a less immediate paternal ancestor. The result is a "classical" politically segmenting genealogy (see Figure 7). A response to a threat from abroad has resulted in a paradigm of political alliances, but the form of the paradigm itself illustrates the ineffectiveness of the alliances which it describes. Every level of political relationships fragments into a pair of opposed groups. Every level of political relationships among the groups is therefore unstable.

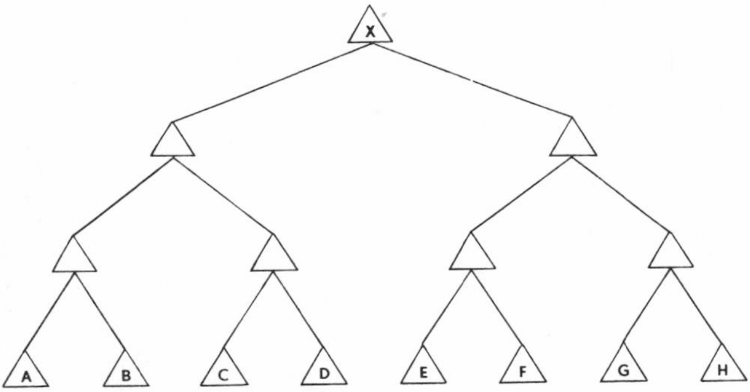


Figure 7. The classical form of a politically segmenting genealogy

The only form of political community is the little residential group itself.[3] It should not be a surprise that where we find such a tribal genealogy, it does not resolve the problem of a threat from abroad and a threat from within, even though it maps the political relationships of all the little groups. Nor should it be a surprise that where we find such a tribal genealogy, the actual alliances of groups during political conflicts do not conform in any exact way with the implications of the tribal genealogy. Such a tribal genealogy is an anxious, "theoretical" response to a dilemma. The form of this response reveals the dimensions of the dilemma itself, but it does not resolve it. Men would like to find protection from the threat of a popular investment in aggressive resources, and so they dream of political alliances. They cannot, however, commit themselves to these dreams of political alliances because, as commitments, these dreams would be a threat to their domestic interests.

Wherever we find such a classical form of a politically segmenting genealogy, we may conclude that the political alliances which it describes are practically ineffective. A perfectly segmentary political system is therefore, above all, an ineffective system. And where we find that a tribal genealogy marginally deviates from such a classical form, we may surmise that the political alliances it describes are only marginally effective.

## 3

We have seen how a classical politically segmenting genealogy might have arisen among a set of little groups in connection with a pattern of contradictory political and domestic interests. Now we can consider the extent to which the genealogy of the dominant tribes of the Cyrenaican Bedouins corresponded with this ideal type. Emrys Peters has described the genealogy of these tribes in detail.[4] He has explained how the genealogy, which charted the patrilineal relationships of tens of thousands of tribesmen, was interpreted by the Bedouins as a paradigm of political alliances. He has also demonstrated how the genealogy was a living political fiction, even though the Bedouins assumed it to be a factual account of their patrilineal descent. For example, he has shown how the genealogy was adjusted in accordance with changing demographical and ecological constraints. And he has shown how the lengthening of lines of descent within each new generation of Cyrenaicans was suppressed by adjustments between the political fictions of the tribal genealogy and the more or less factual accounts of patrilineal kinship among the men of each little group.

An adaptation of one of Peters's diagrams of a portion of the tribal genealogy appears in Figure 8. The groups at level 1 represent the little groups. Peters significantly refers to these as "residential groups," a term which would not be appropriate among the more mobile camel-herding pastoralists of North Arabia. The groups at level 2 are the primary alliances of these groups. The groups at level 3 are the secondary alliances of these groups. The next level is designated as the tribal association by Peters.

Peters provides the following explanation of his diagram of the tribal genealogy: "The names given in this genealogy are the tribal names in use. All are derivatives of personal names of ancestors, like all tribal names, except for some nicknames (e.g. Baraghith means 'the fleas') and a few which refer to a general location (e.g. the Magharba means the 'Westerners')." The names of the political groups are primarily derivatives of the names of ancestors and only secondarily names which would have the value of designations of a people. This is the reverse of the names of tribal groupings in North Arabia.[5] There is a tendency for political groupings to split into pairs of subgroupings only at the upper levels of the genealogy. In this respect, the upper levels of the genealogy

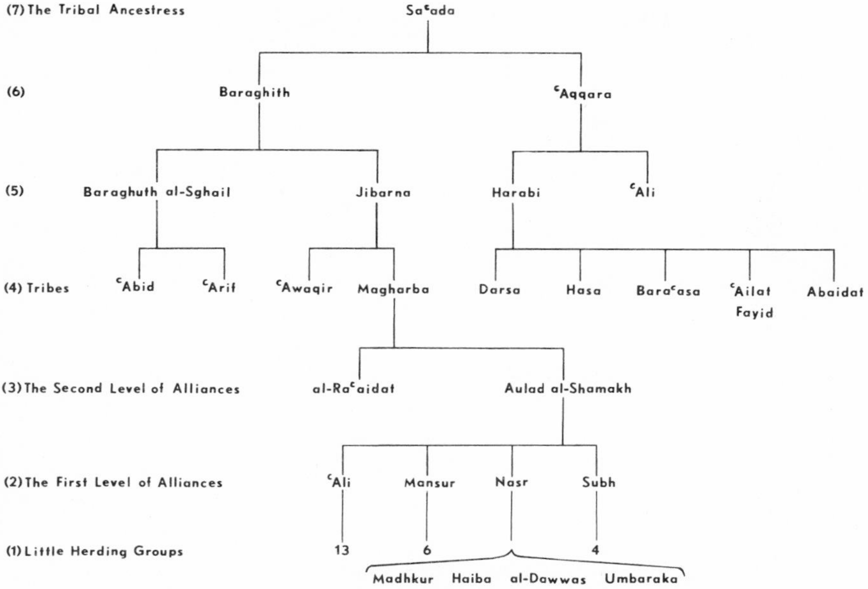


Figure 8. A portion of the tribal genealogy of the Cyrenaican Bedouins (after Peters)

resemble the traditional intertribal alliances of the North Arabian Bedouins. So it is the largest political groupings that tend to take a purely classical segmentary form in both Cyrenaica and North Arabia. However, the classical splitting of the large political groupings in Cyrenaica is represented by a genealogical idiom. The design of the Cyrenaican genealogy at its upper levels probably had remained unchanged for many, many decades, if not for centuries, but then this design was so unchanging precisely because it had only a "theoretical" significance.[6] At the lower levels of the genealogy, the attempt to construct alliances beyond a pair of groups was favored to a degree over the instability of the resulting political alliances, and so we find groupings of three, four, and five subgroups. This deviation from the classical segmentary form suggests that the political alliances at the lower levels were not altogether ineffective.

We find then that the Cyrenaican Bedouins primarily understood their political relationships in terms of a detailed genealogical paradigm, while the North Arabian Bedouins did not develop such a genealogical idiom of political relationships. The greater importance of a genealogy as a representation of Cyrenaican political relationships also implies the weakening of the Cyrenaican tribe as a distinctive political community with a distinctive political authority. There were no chiefly lineages, such as the

Eben Sha'lân. There were no renowned chiefs, such as Saṭṭâm and an-Nûri. The Arabian tribal chief, the architect of tribal policy, was no longer on the scene. Peters writes: "Tribes, further, lack the leadership to make war. I repeat that leadership does exist, but not even the greatest leaders, past or present, can rightly be described as leaders of their tribes, using the term in its structural connotation."[7] And indeed, the very concept of the tribe is suspect, for there is even a question about which level of the genealogy might have represented the tribal association. Evans-Pritchard writes: "Use of the term 'tribe' in Cyrenaica, even if it be restricted to the big free tribes, is always to some extent arbitrary for the political structure is highly segmentary."[8] The Arabian tribe is in the process of degenerating in Cyrenaica. As these Bedouins have been drawn into peaceful, productive activities, they have reacted to the danger of their involvement in a tribal community by qualifying their involvement with a commitment to subtribes and subchiefs. Let us read the celebrated passage in which Evans-Pritchard ingeniously, but erroneously, attempts to synthesize this degeneration of the tribe as a kind of practical political system:

> Each section of a tribe, from the smallest to the largest, has its Shaikh or Shaikhs. The tribal system, typical of segmentary structures everywhere, is a system of balanced opposition between tribes and tribal sections from the largest to the smallest divisions, and there cannot therefore be any single authority in a tribe. Authority is distributed at every point of the tribal structure and political leadership is limited to situations in which a tribe or a segment of it acts corporately.[9]

This description is sometimes criticized for its excessive formalization of an actual situation that was certainly not so neatly defined. More importantly, it is mistaken in principle. It suggests that the nesting of tribes and chiefs within tribes and chiefs was the basis of a practical political system, instead of a sign of the very degeneration of political relationships as their value became increasingly ambiguous. Nevertheless, the passage, especially its excessive formality, clearly reveals how the Bedouins who settled in Cyrenaica responded to the increasing threat of their tribal political association and their tribal chiefs by attempting to devise secondary tribes within tribes and then tertiary tribes within secondary tribes. The Arabian concept of a tribal political association led by a tribal political architect persists as a dream in Cyrenaica, but not as a reality.

The contradiction between political and domestic interests, which lies behind the Cyrenaican genealogical representation of political groupings, is also indicated by the territorial demarcation of the groups described by the genealogy. To see how this is so, we must briefly consider the ecology of Cyrenaica.[10] The lands of the Cyrenaican Bedouins were divided into pastoral zones (see Map 2). The well-watered Cyrenaican highlands lie

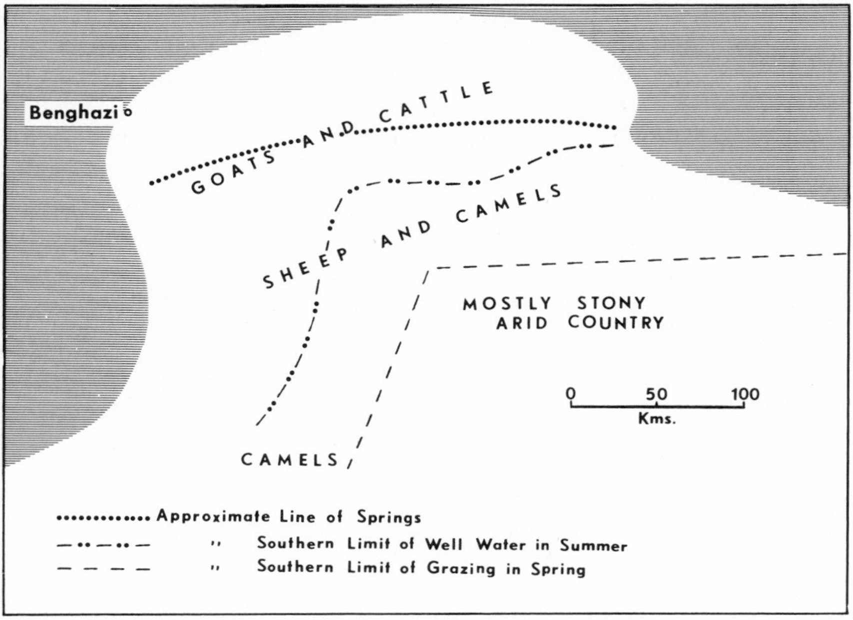


Map 2. Pastoral zones in Cyrenaica (after Evans-Pritchard)

along the coast. As one moves into the interior, the land drops in altitude, and the amount of yearly rainfall progressively declines. During the dry season (summer), little residential groups of Bedouins settled in the highlands near the coast where water for their herds was available all year round. Here they also engaged in agricultural activities and herded cattle and goats. During the wet season (winter), groups of sheep- and camel-herders moved inland to take advantage of the fresh pastures produced by the rains. Those who herded sheep were not able to move far from the wells in the interior, as these animals are dependent upon a ready source of water. Those who herded only camels, however, were able to move farther into the interior.

Now let us examine how the territorial demarcation of the various Bedouin political groupings indicates a certain pattern of land use. Evans-Pritchard provides a map of the subdivisions of the Hasa tribe (see Map 3).[11] In this map, the "fourth subdivision" refers to the little residential groups, the "third subdivision" refers to the first level of alliances of these groups, and so on. The very possibility of drawing such a map illustrates just how much more closely the Cyrenaican Bedouins were tied to the land than the North Arabian Bedouins. Montagne, who attempted to make such a map among the Shammar in North Arabia, found that the little groups were so unsystematically related to the land that no reliable mapping of the tribe was possible.[12] But note the specific shape of the territory of each subdivision of the Hasa tribe. There is a clear tendency for each territory to take the shape of a narrow strip of land extending from the coast to the interior. This suggests that the little groups were all striving to secure access to scarce agricultural land near the coast, while

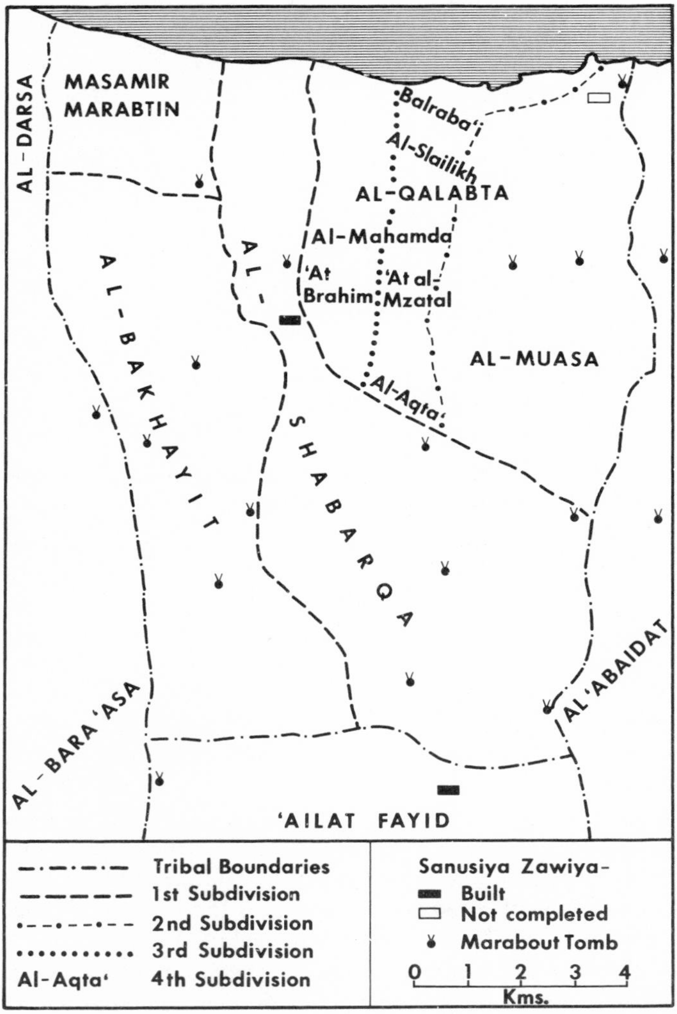


Map 3. The divisions of the Hasa tribe in Cyrenaica (reproduced from Evans-Pritchard)

preserving access to pasture in the interior. They could not resist the promises of agricultural life, but as they took up such a life, they did not surrender their interest in a pastoral life.

Inevitably, some of the Cyrenaican tribes had remained more thoroughly involved in a camel-herding way of life. These tribes tended to have, Evans-Pritchard has implied, somewhat more clear-cut tribal associations. The boundaries between these camel-herding tribes in the Cyrenaican interior, he has also noted, were indistinct.[13] That is to say, those Cyrenaican tribes whose way of life was most like that of the North Arabian Bedouins had tribal associations and a relationship with the land which were more nearly like those of the North Arabian Bedouins. The effects of an increasing involvement of an Arabian camel-herding peoples in a North African life of peaceful, productive labor could be observed by surveying the spectrum of life in Cyrenaica, which extended from agriculture at one end to camel-herding at the other.

We have seen how the Cyrenaican tribal genealogy is closely associated with a certain pattern of political and domestic interests. Now we can consider just how this way of representing political relationships indicates that a Cyrenaican political experience had a quality that was completely different from that of a North Arabian political experience. The tribal genealogy, as we have seen, is a symptom of the weakness of the institutions of political community and political authority in a situation where there is a pressing need for such institutions. This feature of Cyrenaican political experience is most vividly apparent on those occasions when the Cyrenaican Bedouins looked upon their genealogy not as a paradigm of contingent political alliances, but instead as a paradigm of persistent political anarchy.

In one of Peters's articles on the Cyrenaican Bedouins, he presents a diagram that tabulates a Cyrenaican interpretation of the various alliances as described by their tribal genealogy.[14] In Figure 9, this diagram has been adapted to the present discussion. In the diagram, only the little residential group is interpreted as a moral association. Within its boundaries, violence is regarded with shock and disgust, so much so, that any man who is guilty of such an offense is punished by expulsion rather than by any equivalent act of violence. Every political relationship beyond the little group, however, is conceived as a hostile relationship, which is specifically characterized by some form of violence. This diagram does not insist upon the way in which groups come together to deal with a threat from abroad. It insists upon the varying forms of political violence that color a pervasive struggle among all the little groups, and it suggests that the more distant the relationship of little groups, the more violent this struggle tends to be.

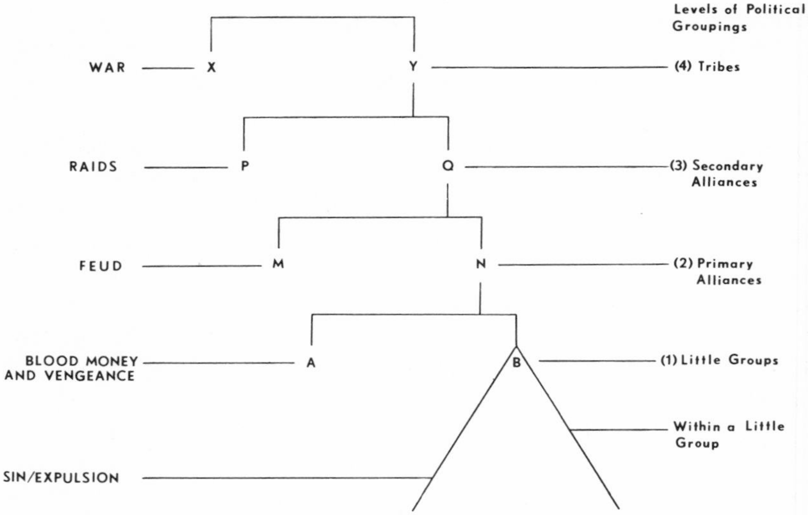


Figure 9. A Cyrenaican Bedouin interpretation of the alliances described by their tribal genealogy (after Peters)

Let us examine the implications of this escalating political violence. The relationship of two neighboring little groups at level 1 is conceived in connection with vengeance and blood money. If one man kills another man, then all the members of the group of the murdered man are obliged to seek vengeance, and all the members of the group of the murderer become potential targets. The problem of homicide is conceived as a basic political experience. As a problem, it defines the character of political groups and the character of their political relationships. There is no political dialogue of the following kind: "If you help me, I shall help you." There is no social contract based upon mutual cooperation, which is in the interest of each party. There is instead a dialogue which takes the following form: "If you kill one of us, we shall kill one of you." This is not a primitive form of political relationship. This is a specific kind of political relationship in which groups are conceived in connection with their capacities for a political struggle with deadly instruments. And yet the curious feature of this political relationship, which rests upon a capacity to kill, is that it has a legal aspect. In the place of the dialogue, "If you kill me, I shall kill you," we have the dialogue, "If you kill one of us, we should like to settle the affair by killing only one of you," and even the dialogue, "If you kill one of us, we should like to settle the affair by accepting a customary payment in lieu of killing one of you."

There is indeed a social contract here. It is a contract based upon the assumption that group relationships consist of a struggle with deadly instruments. It is a contract that takes the form of establishing procedures for keeping this struggle in bounds. But why have neighboring little groups agreed to place a limit upon their hostility by exercising it in accordance with established procedures? The two groups do not seem to have any common interests; otherwise they would not conceive of their relationship in hostile terms. And if men think of themselves as engaged in a violent struggle with one another, why should there be limits placed upon this struggle? If we observe the diagram once again, we discover the reason for such limits. There is a social contract between the neighboring little groups at level 1 because of the greater threat of more distant groups at level 2. But now we find that the hostile relationship at level 2 is also limited, even if less so. It is restricted to responses to homicides. At level 2 there is no possibility of an agreement to reckon homicide for homicide, or to accept a sum of money in lieu of seeking vengeance. Instead, the two political groupings are always at feud. But then this is a strict limitation of hostility. The political groupings at level 2 do not consider themselves free to assault one another at will. They limit their attacks upon one another to the serious business of responding to homicides. Political violence at this level is also circumscribed, but less so than at level 1. Again, there is a social contract. But why should the hostility of these political groupings at level 2 be limited to the feud? If we observe the diagram once again, we discover a still greater threat from more distant groups at level 3. But then we again find that this hostile relationship is also limited, although even less so than at level 2. It is *restricted* to an unrestricted engagement in raids upon one another, whether or not they have been provoked by a recent homicide. Political relationships are yet a little wilder, but they are still not as wild as they could be. When we look abroad yet again, we find the threat of war beyond the tribe at level 4, the threat of indiscriminate murder and pillage. By implication, the groups at level 3 do not murder and pillage one another, only because they seek some protection from this intertribal murder and pillage at level 4.

This explication of the tribal genealogy should not be seen as an indication of the level of political violence in the course of everyday life for the Cyrenaican Bedouins. Judging from the accounts of Peters, one would guess that tribal warfare was much less frequent among the Cyrenaican Bedouins than it was among the North Arabian Bedouins. At the same time, the problem of intentional homicides among neighboring groups was probably a great deal more frequent than it was in North Arabia. The significance of this explication of the genealogy is not that the level of political violence was worse in Cyrenaica than in North Arabia. Rather, the significance is that the Cyrenaican Bedouins often perceived the entire domain of political experience as a wild world of brutality and savagery. Such an elegant academic phrase as "ordered anarchy" cannot conceal this dimension of Cyrenaican political experience. And even though it might be argued that the Cyrenaican interpretation of the tribal genealogy itself suggests a kind of ordered anarchy, one would have to admit that it does so with a cruel irony that never appears in the writings of Evans-Pritchard.

The standard anthropological interpretation of the Cyrenaican genealogy as a specific kind of political system is therefore only partly correct. Such an interpretation more or less rightly conceives of the genealogy as the basis for a response to a threat from abroad. However, it fails to analyze the origins of this threat, as well as its character or its intensity. Because of this failure, the standard anthropological interpretation of the Cyrenaican genealogy overlooks the contradiction between political and domestic interests, which leads to a classical segmentary representation of political relationships. As a result, the Cyrenaican tribal genealogy is misconstrued as a "primitive" kind of political system. Although the Cyrenaican tribal genealogy was an undeveloped political system, this was not because the Cyrenaican Bedouins were somehow at an early stage of human political history. The biological idiom of their political relationships was a direct product of a way of life, which inspired in them a wish for a protective political association, but undermined any attempt to develop the institutions of such an association. In this respect, the Cyrenaican tribal genealogy, in so far as it took a classical segmentary form, was not really the basis of a political system, nor even a system of ordered anarchy.

The Cyrenaican tribal genealogy was instead a sign of the incipient degeneration of Arabian tribal institutions. It was the sign of a growing problem about dealing with political experience in an effective way. There was less certainty than in North Arabia about just where a political threat might arise since it could potentially arise anywhere beyond the little group. There was less certainty than in North Arabia about the possibility of cooperation and leadership since all potential groups and potential leaders were qualified by a commitment to subgroups and subleaders. This does not mean that political experience consisted of an unrestrained indulgence in political violence among the Cyrenaicans; but it does mean that they must have been far less convinced of being able to deal with the problems of their political experiences.

## 4

The Cyrenaican tribal genealogy can be conceived as an Arabian tribal ideology, which has been transformed by a contradiction between political and domestic interests. This contradiction was of no great importance among the North Arabian Bedouins because they were not so involved in a productive relationship with the land. If such an interpretation is correct, we might expect to find among the Cyrenaicans some more direct expression of their involvement in such productive activities. This would be a kind of expression that was more or less absent among the North Arabian Bedouins. And it might also be a kind of expression which revealed the vulnerability of such a way of life where men were absorbed in the use of deadly instruments. This brings us to the cult of saints.

Throughout the lands of the Cyrenaican Bedouins, there were scattered a goodly number of religious shrines.[15] Each of these shrines was viewed by the Bedouins as the tomb of a holy man or saint. Most of these shrines were simple little monuments consisting of not more than a wall of stones. One could reasonably doubt whether anyone at all was buried beneath many of these little monuments, let alone whether they might in fact be the tomb of a man who, in his lifetime, was reputed to be a saint. These shrines were embryonic cult centers. The Bedouins made annual pilgrimages to a particular shrine, where they performed very simple rituals. In this way, various little residential groups would be linked to the same cult center. Some of the more well-known shrines, in recent times at least, were recognized as pilgrimage centers for virtually all of the Cyrenaican Bedouins.

The area around a saint's tomb was considered to be a sacred district, where political strife of any kind was forbidden. In the vicinity of a shrine, groups who had been engaged in hostilities sometimes met to settle their differences, and fugitives were supposed to be beyond the reach of their pursuers. Market places were usually located near a tomb. This suggests that the tomb as a traditional sacred district permitted the development of a market place, or perhaps that a traditional market place was characteristically sanctified with a tomb. Some shrines had even become the focus of little settlements. Typically, the inhabitants of these settlements claimed to be descendants of a saint.

Peters and Evans-Pritchard have shown how the location of the tombs are related in various ways with the political organization of the tribes. Peters, for example, observes that the number of tombs in any area is correlated with the way of life of the inhabitants of the area in question. He writes:

> The number of saints' tombs varies from tribe to tribe, there being fewer among the camel herders of the semi-desert than among the cow-herding, almost sedentary folk of the plateau area. Whatever the number, the members of the group that venerates a particular saint make an annual pilgrimage to his tomb, and sometimes more frequent pilgrimages are made.[16]

Just as there were no saints' tombs among the camel-herding Bedouins of North Arabia, so there were fewer tombs of saints among those Bedouins in Cyrenaica who were camel-herders. There was then a proliferation of religious shrines among those men with greater domestic interests. This suggests a provisional interpretation of the cult of saints. The veneration of the saints' tombs was an anxious religious response on the part of men who had vulnerable domestic interests, but who were unable to devise an effective political response to the problem of their vulnerability.

Evans-Pritchard has observed that the tombs tended to be located along the borders of political groupings where there was a greater potential for conflict. He illustrates this in Map 3, which indicates the location of the saints' tombs in the territories of the Hasa tribe. This tends to confirm the above provisional interpretation of the cult of saints. The veneration of their tombs was not only more developed among men with vulnerable domestic interests; such a religious devotion found its expression at strategic points in the political geography of the tribes. A religious response, which was provoked by the lack of any effective political response to the problem of vulnerability, attempts to substitute for such a lack.

Here we have parted from the standard anthropological interpretation of the cult of saints, while preserving the value of this interpretation. The standard interpretation of the cult of saints suggests that it was like grease in the wheels of the segmentary political system. It was supposed to provide a mechanism for balanced and opposed groups to settle their differences. Such an interpretation fails to recognize that the cult was an anxious response to the very ineffectiveness of a so-called segmentary political system. However, the standard interpretation does recognize that the cult of saints was closely associated with a political problem and attempted in some way to alleviate that problem. Men were devoted to the cult of saints only in so far as they lacked any effective political organization for dealing with a political problem. They lacked any effective political organization, moreover, because they could not afford to recognize the legitimacy of any groups or leaders, which would themselves pose a threat to their peaceful, productive activities. As they were drawn into such activities, a moral commitment to pragmatic political action in the interests of peace was undermined and a more anxious devotion to a cult of saints, with a more problematic political value, took its place.

Now let us examine more closely the form of this religious response to see if we might confirm this provisional interpretation. Each of the religious shrines of the Cyrenaican Bedouins was reputed to be the tomb of a man. The man in question was thought to have been an exemplary person, even though very little, if anything, was actually known about him. We may conclude then that the really important thing about the man reputed to be in the tomb is that he is a symbol of something. But in so far as he is a symbol of something, it is only the mark of his tomb on the landscape that is important. That is to say, the principal religious symbol among the Cyrenaican Bedouins is a sign of personal mortality, which takes the shape of a monument, a wall of stones or a little cupola which houses a grave. Noting this crucial feature of the Cyrenaican cult centers, we may now link the cult of saints directly with the problem of vulnerable domestic interests that involve a productive relationship with the land. As a form, the tomb of the saint represents a fixed link between a man and the land. In doing so, the condition of being in a fixed place is linked with the condition of personal mortality.

The tomb of the saint is a metaphor of a vulnerable domestic relationship with the land. The expression of this metaphor marks the landscape with monuments among a people who are halfway between a shifting life of camel-herding pastoralism and a fixed life of agriculture. Such a monument imposed itself upon the Bedouins as an awesome sign of their predicament. They perceived its location as an enchanted district, where political conflict of any kind was mysteriously forbidden. Such monuments, therefore, had a limited value as the basis of a response to political anarchy. They marked a place where the vulnerability of all men to the organized use of arms was plainly stated, and this was a place where the marginal basis of peace among persistently hostile groups was clearly evident.

In so far as the Cyrenaicans were drawn into a life of vulnerable domestic interests, the effectiveness of their political responses to a threat from abroad was undermined. In so far as they were drawn into such a life, they devoted themselves to a politico-religious cult, and in the course of such a devotion, religious monuments accumulated across the landscape. In time, the existence of these monuments was perceived as evidence that men with vulnerable domestic interests could nevertheless persist. There was still a problem of popular political anarchy, which made men feel anxious and insecure, but there was also some confidence that such feelings had an exalted place in human experience. There was even a belief that the accoutrements of a cult which expressed those feelings had a mystical power that could bring to ruin those men who failed to respect them. Since the Bedouins could be awed by more or less articulate statements of their helplessness, an articulation of the cult of saints had the power to make men hesitate before resorting to aggressive actions. This brings us to the representatives of the cult of saints in Cyrenaica.

The tomb of a saint was the principal artifact of the cult of saints in Cyrenaica. However, there were also more or less active representatives of the cult of saints. Certain little lineages were termed "clients with grace (*marabṭîn bi'l baraka*)." These lineages were not included in the genealogy of the dominant tribes, and they did not possess any tribal lands. Instead, they were seen as the descendants of a saint, and in this respect they were usually closely associated with a particular tomb. The ethnography of these little lineages is exceedingly scant. This suggests that the role which they played in tribal affairs was minor. No living man among these little lineages seems to have been considered a saint. Perhaps most often these lineages were little more than the caretakers of a tomb. However, Peters does mention some of their activities that were not so closely linked with the tombs themselves: "They succour the sick, they write amulets for a number of purposes, they circumcise the young boys, and they are always present at peace-meetings. These clients of the goodness are found in small numbers dispersed among the tribal sections."[17] This brief description suggests that the clients with grace were embryonic ritual specialists. We are not told much about the character of the rituals in question, but we may at least note that they are personal rituals (amulets) and familial rituals (circumcision). Moreover, these rituals are linked with conditions of personal debility or weakness (disease), or consist of the symbolic infliction of violence on features of the person which are associated with the generation of concrete and natural human relationships (circumcision). This is a ritual life proliferating around the problem of human vulnerability in a context that demands energetic personal responses and organized political responses.

Peters also mentions the presence of clients with grace at peace meetings. It was this sort of activity on the part of these ritual specialists, which led to the standard anthropological interpretation of the cult of saints as the grease in the wheels of a segmentary political system. We may, however, revise this interpretation in the following way. These men were the representatives of a cult that had marginal power in the domain of political experience, since men were in awe of it. There was also the belief that the representatives of this cult had a role to play in politics, especially in the resolution of political conflict. Mediation, however, was only one activity in which these men were sometimes engaged. More routinely, they were little more than modest ritual specialists and caretakers of shrines. However, on some exceptional occasions they were the representatives of devotional energies in the domain of political experience. As such, they could potentially become the central figures of more or less ecstatic politico-religious movements, which united a people who were normally divided by political anarchy. Many examples of such movements have been recorded among tribal Near Eastern peoples, especially in North Africa. The recent history of the Cyrenaican Bedouins themselves provides an especially striking case.

In the course of the nineteenth century, a religious brotherhood of Islamic scholars settled among the Cyrenaican Bedouins. Evans-Pritchard has described how these scholars made a place for themselves among the tribal peoples by serving their domestic interests, a possibility that would not have been open to them had they settled among the North Arabian Bedouins. Here is his description of the various services which the lodges (*zâwiya*) of this religious brotherhood performed for the Cyrenaican Bedouins:

They were schools, caravanserai, commercial centres, social centres, forts, courts of law, banks, store houses, poor houses, sanctuary, and burial grounds, besides being channels through which ran a generous stream of God's blessing [*baraka*]. They were centres of culture and security in a wild country and amid a fierce people, and they were stable points in a country where all else was constantly on the move. A Bedouin camp might be anywhere. A zawiya was fixed to the earth and its community with it.[18]

Evans-Pritchard goes on to describe how the head of this religious brotherhood became the principal leader of the Bedouin resistance to the Italian occupation of Cyrenaica, (1911–23), and how its lodges, as the only centralized organization among the Bedouins, coordinated the Bedouin resistance. His documentation of the protracted struggle of the Bedouins against foreign domination illustrates how religious institutions among tribal peoples were not simply a means for political mediation. Where there was a general feeling among such peoples that their very way of life was at stake, religious institutions became the vehicles of politico-religious movements, even though these institutions were not developed in the idiom of an organized political community commanded by political authorities.

Before the arrival of this religious brotherhood of Islamic scholars, the cult of saints in Cyrenaica was only embryonic. If we now shift our attention further west to Morocco at the turn of the century, we find there a luxuriant development of the cult of saints. With the Moroccan materials we can confirm the provisional interpretation of such a cult, and go on to see how it was a distinctive aspect of North African political history.

# 12. Narratives of the mystical power of saints in Morocco

## 1

The case of the Cyrenaican Bedouins illustrates a historical process which was of some importance at various times and in various places throughout the arid zone which stretches across North Africa, through the central Near East, and into Central Asia. However, this particular historical process seems to have been a dominant feature of popular experience in certain parts of the Maghreb region of North Africa. The deserts and steppes of North Africa, like those of Arabia, were a cradle of an extreme kind of Near Eastern pastoral nomadism even before the arrival of the Arabian Bedouins. But much of the Maghreb region of North Africa, unlike Arabia, is a marginal agricultural region penetrated and bordered by deserts and steppes. In these parts of the Maghreb, pastoralists were constantly being pressed out of the deserts and steppes by other pastoralists. Upon entering these agricultural areas, these peoples were lured into agricultural activities, even though they remained under the pressure of other pastoralists who were following in their footsteps.

One other decisive feature about the history of this part of the arid zone should be added. The centers of civilization in the Maghreb have been especially vulnerable, from very early times, to destabilization by foreign powers. This means that in many parts of the Maghreb no state was able to provide an extended period of security during which the pressures by pastoralists on partially settled peoples was controlled or moderated. The marginal agricultural regions of the Maghreb were therefore populated not by peasants, but by peoples with the political experiences of the most extreme kind of Near Eastern pastoralists, even though they were sometimes partially and sometimes completely settled on the land. We have seen in Cyrenaica how this situation undermines the basis for any routinized and systematic form of legitimate political organization. That is to say, a history of the weakness of indigenous states in these regions contributed to the generation of popular traditions in which the very concept of a state as a routinized and systematic form of political organization would have been illegitimate. And so a history of state weakness during an epoch of Near Eastern pastoralism led to a situation in which the development of the state as an instrument of public administration was popularly resisted. The result was a political stalemate, which fostered popular traditions that were dominated by segmentary politics and the cult of saints to a degree without parallel anywhere else in the arid zone.

This sketch of a general historical process is only more or less applicable to various parts of the Maghreb. However, it seems especially appropriate as the basis for understanding the history of popular experience in Morocco. Like many parts of the Maghreb, much of Morocco is a marginal agricultural region bordered or penetrated by desert and steppe (see Map 4). Ross E. Dunn, a historian, has been particularly interested in the southern slopes of the Atlas, the "pre-Saharan" region of Morocco. He writes:

> The migratory movement of pastoral populations has been a continuous theme in the history of Morocco and the western Sahara for almost a thousand years. Beginning with the Almoravid explosion out of the Mauritanian desert in the eleventh century, the major thrust of these movements has been from the fringes of the Sahara northward into the Atlas and beyond to the fertile Atlantic coastal plains.[1]

Here is evidence of a constant pastoral penetration of an agricultural area. Much of Morocco, however, was not exactly like many other marginal agricultural regions of the Maghreb. It was not altogether exposed to pastoral peoples like Cyrenaica. The Atlas Mountains presented a kind of barrier, or more exactly, a kind of damper. Saharan pastoralists were lured and pressed into the broken terrain of the Atlas. Here they found enough of a refuge to permit their settlement on the land, but not enough of a refuge to protect them from the constant pressure of other pastoralists who were following in the footsteps of their pastoral ancestors. Dunn also describes just such a process:

> The movements generated on the margins of the desert, if involving large numbers, eventually produced population congestion in the High Atlas pastures. As a result, mountain tribes, themselves grandsons of desert-dwellers, were forced to advance still further. The effect over the centuries was a kind of recurring bumping action with both Arabic- and Berber-speaking tribes pushing one another ever closer to the northwestern coast. The Berber collectivity known as the Zummur (Zemmour), for example, left the pre-Sahara by the sixteenth century, finally settling in their present location in the hinterland of Rabat-Salé only at the end of the nineteenth.

For a very long period much of Morocco was a kind of cauldron in which peoples, whose traditions had first taken shape in a pastoral setting, were being settled and desettled. In so far as this was the case, this feature of popular experience must have had some important effect upon

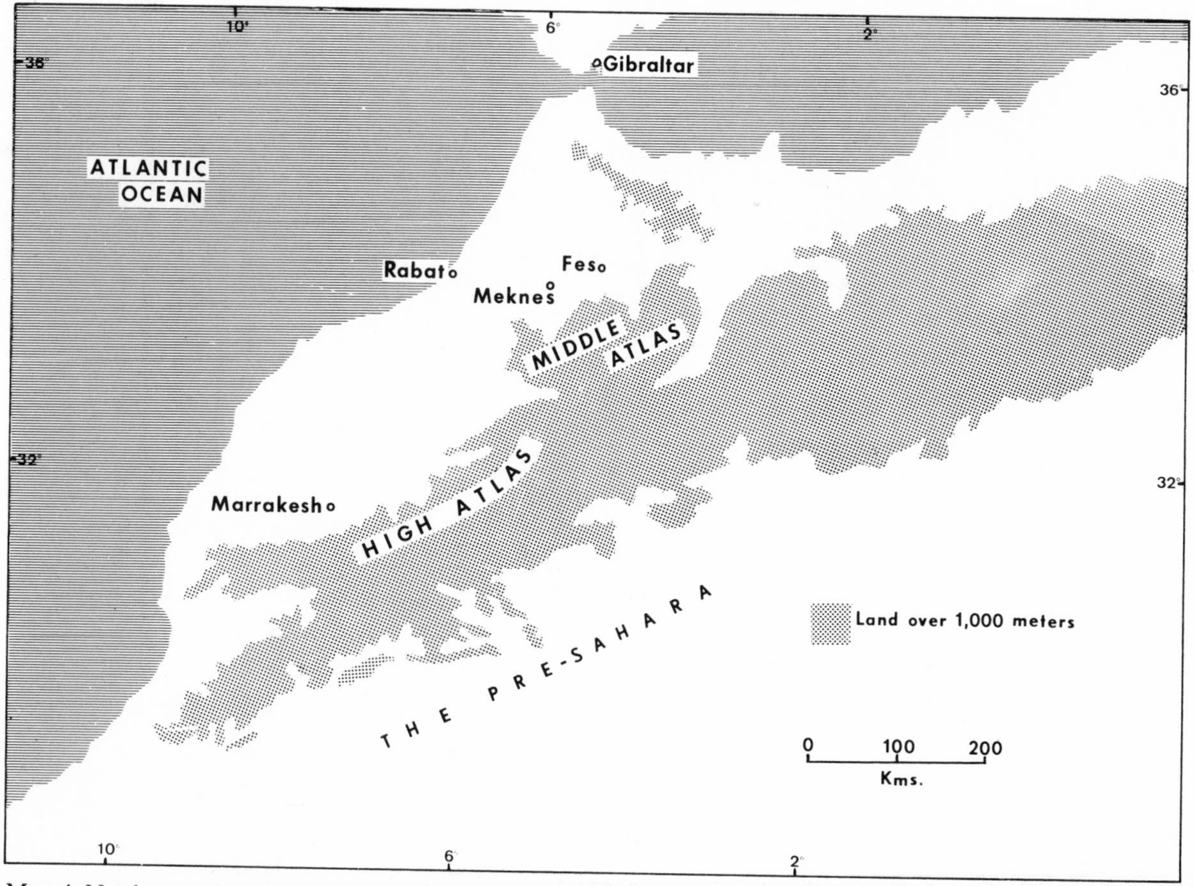


Map 4. Northwest Africa

the shape of Moroccan society. Again, Dunn has insisted that the effects were not only important, but fundamental:

> The stages of tribal migrations were accomplished in a variety of ways, sometimes by aggressive expansion, sometimes by gradual infiltration and nomadic drift, sometimes even at the invitation of the Moroccan Sultan, who used the services of one predatory tribe to halt the expansion of another. In any case these sporadic but persistent movements help account for the continually changing territorial pattern of Morocco's tribes, some expanding, some contracting or even disappearing, but none remaining static. And it was of course in the process of interaction between pastoral groups or between them and the sedentary and urban populations that Morocco's unique institutions for regulating social and political relations were hammered out.

Here we glimpse the other crucial feature of the settlement and desettlement of pastoral peoples in this part of the Maghreb. The Sultan of Morocco was recognized all over northwest Africa as the representative of an Islamic civilization that was based upon the imperial cities of the western plains region of Morocco. In spite of this, the political authority of the Sultan, in contrast to his religious authority as a representative of Islam, was largely polarized around the problem of intimidating and manipulating a turbulent populace, among whom the very legitimacy of any political authority whatsoever was in question. A situation in which the state was historically weak resulted in a kind of state that was religiously legitimate and politically illegitimate.

In the last chapter we have understood the pattern of popular interests that tends to develop as a vigorous pastoral people are drawn into peaceful, productive activities. This means that we have the possibility of examining with some precision an aspect of the problem which Dunn describes above. We can reach some understanding of just how a certain kind of historical experience, which generated a certain pattern of popular interests, lay behind traditional Morocco's "unique institutions." In particular, we might be able to achieve some understanding of the curious character of the Sultanate of Morocco.

## 2

Most Moroccan peoples were deeply involved in a productive relationship with the land, more so, by and large, than the Cyrenaican Bedouins. This had come about simply because most Moroccans lived in marginal (and sometimes not so marginal) agricultural areas rather than in deserts and steppes.[2] Because of their greater involvement in peaceful, productive activities, the Moroccans were therefore that much more vulnerable to the threat of the organized use of instruments of aggression, which persisted among them despite their settlement upon the land. In comparison with the Cyrenaicans, most Moroccan peoples were under an even greater pressure to institutionalize some form of political organization, while the threat that such an institution would become the vehicle for tyrannical domination and exploitation was also just that much greater. As a result, the incipient crisis of political organization, which we discovered among the Cyrenaicans, was a full-fledged crisis in Morocco.

By a kind of reversal, the Arabian problem of a threat from abroad became in Morocco the problem of a threat close to home. Just as the Arabians were constantly enticed by the possibility of raiding, simply because of their circumstances (aggressive resources and vulnerable wealth), so the Moroccans were enticed by the possibility of domination and exploitation, simply because of their circumstances (aggressive resources and men vulnerable to domination and exploitation). As a result, a political authority close to home, the very center of an Arabian hope for the control of anarchy in the world abroad, became the very origins of a Moroccan problem of tyranny close to home.[3]

Tyranny was a common feature of popular experience in Morocco. There was always a strong man with armed followers somewhere just over the horizon. Indeed, potential strong men with armed followers were familiar figures in everyday political experience.[4] Given these circumstances, the slightest routinization or systematization of political authority in tribal Morocco was also the potential basis for the emergence of tyrannical domination and exploitation. As a result, we find a popular tradition in Morocco that lacked any legitimate conception of a routinized or systematic form of political authority and, conversely, a popular tradition in which any routinized and systematic form of political authority was conceived as illegitimate. Here it becomes clear that the crisis of political organization, which develops as pastoralists settle on the land, is above all a crisis of political authority.

There was a need for political communities and political authorities in Morocco, a greater need indeed than in Cyrenaica. The dilemma of contradictory political and domestic interests was a still more incisive kind of dilemma. In response to this not altogether resolvable problem, various peculiar institutions were developed by the Moroccan tribesmen. While the ethnographers of Morocco have often insisted upon the impressive variety of these institutions in a land where political circumstances were as varied in their details as the landscape itself, these institutions, taken as a whole, contrast with Arabian tribal institutions in a remarkably consistent way.[5]

As in Cyrenaica, the basic framework of any legitimate political association was understood in terms of a segmentary representation (see Figure 10),[6] but in a far more uncompromising way. Every potential political grouping was qualified by a commitment to a subgrouping. Now, how-

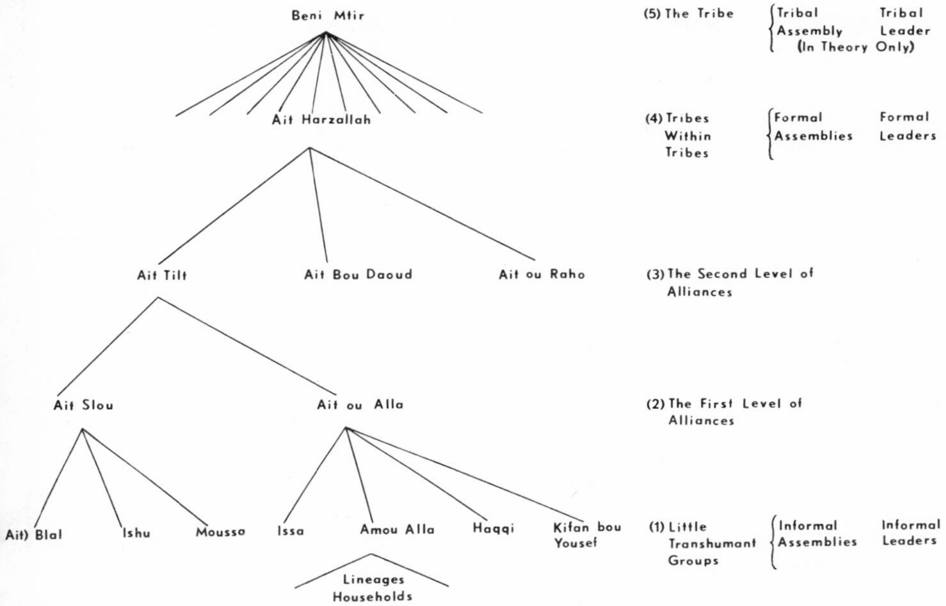


Figure 10. A segmentary representation of tribal political organization in Morocco (after Vinogradov)

ever, there was no permanent status of leadership for any political grouping beyond a domestic unit. Instead, political decisions were taken by consensus. To achieve such a consensus, an assembly of elders was associated with each potential political grouping. This assembly, not a chief, was the vehicle of political decisions. That is to say, the assembly was a device for political leadership that avoided the necessity of a leader. As the potential political grouping increased in size, the formal mechanisms for constituting the assembly were increasingly elaborated. Among some Moroccan tribes, the members of the assembly were even chosen by election. The development of such formal procedures reveals to what lengths the tribesmen would go to avoid the dangerous alternative of submitting themselves to a leader. They devised institutions of policy making by consensus in a situation where policy making by leadership would have been far more efficient.[7]

But policy making by consensus was so inefficient that the Moroccan tribesmen were often forced to recognize a leader. In this respect, they chose purely provisional leaders to represent some specific level of political grouping. That is to say, the authority of such a leader was strictly limited to a response to specific circumstances for the specific duration of those circumstances. Only in the case of the more nomadic tribes of the pre-Sahara, which more closely resembled the North Arabian tribes, do we find a systematic and routinized form of tribal political authority. But even with these tribes, the tribal chief was not chosen for life from among the members of a chiefly lineage; he was chosen to serve for only one year from among five sections of the tribe. The office of tribal chief rotated between these five sections, and the section from which the chief was chosen did not participate in his election.

Everywhere the tribal Moroccans went to extravagant lengths to qualify their commitment to communities and authorities. They devised segmentary political representations of their tribes, which were elegantly conceived as a hierarchy of altogether contingent coalitions of atomistic units. They devised inefficient institutions of policy making as a substitute for the efficiency of a permanent leader as a policy maker. And they conceived of these strictly qualified and exceedingly clumsy forms of communities and authorities in a situation in which there was a pressing need for communities and authorities.

As in the case of Cyrenaica, the ethnographers of Morocco have sometimes distorted the character of the political experience in tribal Morocco by insisting that these tribal institutions were the workable basis of a practical political system, which was a reasonable way of conducting political affairs given the incidental absence of governmental institutions.[8] In doing so, they have rightly insisted that the problem of political experience in tribal Morocco often demanded a pragmatic approach to persistent conflict between groups. But at the same time, they have also suggested, quite wrongly, that political life in tribal Morocco, although turbulent, was a highly predictable, structured kind of life. That is to say, they have interpreted the sheer elaborateness of tribal institutions as a sign of a coherent political system, rather than as a sign of tensions which undermined the basis of any routine or systematic response to political experience.

There is perhaps a lesson here that demonstrates a serious fault of the ethnographic tradition. In comparison with the Moroccan tribe, the North Arabian tribe seems to be a formless and disorderly mass. In North Arabia there were no elaborate paradigms of political alliances within the tribe, no mechanism for electing ad hoc and pro tempore assemblies and leaders at various levels of political alliances, and no intricate mechanisms for electing tribal assemblies and tribal leaders. Political life in North Arabia would seem to be unstructured whereas political life in tribal Morocco would seem to be structured. Such a conclusion demonstrates the common failing of the ethnographer who identifies the possibility of precisely defining the structure of legitimate political groups as a sign of order, even if it is only an ordered anarchy.

Let us set aside the concept, or rather the ideology, of "structure" and examine instead how certain kinds of articulations are generated as responses to certain kinds of political situations. In North Arabia, the explosive problem of political experience arose in the domain of intertribal relationships. There was a distinct possibility, even if only a possibility, that a legitimate articulation of tribal policy by a chief might control this problem. And yet, because the tribe itself was not internally articulated as a political organization, there was always a question about the effectiveness of any chiefly policy. But even when the chief failed to lead the tribe in peace or in war, there was the possibility of the tribe (which although unorganized was also undivided by conflict) coalescing in response to the threat from other tribes.

In tribal Morocco, the explosive problem of political experience potentially arose as much from within as from without the body politic. In response to this crisis of political organization, the Moroccan tribesmen did what they could, which was indeed a great deal. They had a remarkable capacity for conceiving of legitimate forms of ad hoc and pro tempore cooperation and leadership. In this way they anticipated the necessity of a political response to both a threat from without and a threat from within. Nevertheless, the segmentary design of their institutions - the nesting of subgroups under supergroups, subassemblies under superassemblies, and subleaders under superleaders - reveals that the Moroccans, unlike the North Arabians, could not really locate a precise political boundary at which a threat might arise.

While Moroccan conceptions of the relationship of groups within the tribe were far more elaborately structured than in North Arabia, these conceptions took the shape of a political structure, which responded to the dangers of a political structure. This was a structure that aimed at subverting structure. This means that there was a serious question about the very possibility of a conception of a legitimate political community or a legitimate political authority. There was a serious question in Morocco about whether the organized use of instruments of aggression had any connection with human welfare. Given this feature of popular experience, it is clear that there was far less of a basis in Morocco for a belief that cautious and sensible men who had an interest in human welfare could organize a moral struggle against anarchy. That is to say, the character of popular experience in Morocco subverted the possibility of an "Arabian" response to political experience.

It is, however, in the domain of the cult of saints that the character of political experience in Morocco becomes most vividly apparent; for in the precise way in which the cult of saints takes shape, we see the clear signs of a crisis of political community and political authority. In Morocco, a long history of a vulnerable productive relationship with the land amid political uncertainty had not only led to an impressive elaboration of religious monuments and rituals on a much grander scale than in Cyrenaica. There was also a conviction that living saints played an active role in political experience.

The living saint was seen as the representative of a religious authority which presided over all human experience. As such a representative, he was attributed a formidable mystical power (*baraka*), which flowed from this religious authority.[9] This aspect of the living saint reveals his status as a metaphor of political authority. The living saint appears in circumstances which required an effective moral authority with an effective moral power, but which also disallowed their practical realization. These living saints were a fulfillment, in the form of an ideal, of what could not be realized in fact. An intense wish for an authority with a power, which would represent the vulnerable features of human experience, attached itself like a contagion to certain persons who were unassociated with the organized use of instruments of aggression.

While this explains why the Moroccans dreamed of living saints, it does not explain why Moroccan political history was overrun with living saints, why the Moroccan landscape is cluttered with the accoutrements of the cult of saints, and why the Moroccans were devoted to the myths and rituals of this cult. In some way, living saints did articulate a wish for authority, which could not be practically articulated. In some way, they were the representatives of a power, even though they did not command armed groups. Otherwise the cult of saints would have never become more than a fantasy inspired by a hopeless predicament. If we consider the character of the role played by living saints in the domain of Moroccan political experience, we can see how this might have been so.

The living saint was the representative of vulnerable features of human experience which could not be practically represented. Nevertheless, these features of human experience, such as a life of patient and diligent labor and a productive relationship with the land, were substantial matters of considerable interest to all men. The living saint represented these general features of human experience simply by articulating their existence. The words and deeds of the saint, and indeed his very physical person, assumed the status of "signs" of the vulnerability of a peaceful productive life at home. In so far as men were involved in such a way of life, they stood in awe of these signs. And in so far as they stood in awe of these signs, the representations of the living saint did indeed play a role in the enhancement of this domain of human experience. So when the Moroccans insisted that their society had taken a shape through the active representations of living saints, they were not mistaken. And although it might be said that the real force behind the vulnerable features of human experience lay in the universal allure of a peaceful way of life or a productive way of life for any men of any place and any time, living saints were nevertheless the vehicles of such a universal allure in Moroccan political history.

This suggests a series of parallels. In North Arabia, a wish for authority attached itself to a tribal chief who led armed men in a cautious and sensible struggle against anarchy. In Morocco, this wish was displaced onto a living saint, precisely because of the threat of any form of political association. In North Arabia, a wish for authority was marginally fulfilled by means of chiefly strategic policies, which turned upon the measured use of aggressive resources. In Morocco, a wish for authority was marginally fulfilled by means of saintly representations of the very dilemma of political experience whose awesomeness made men hesitate. Curiously, these parallels extend into the domain of popular traditions. In North Arabia, we found ceremonial narratives of raiding and warfare, which addressed the events of a tribal conflict in an attempt to lend some substance to a concept of a political authority who was on the side of peace. In Morocco, we find narratives of the lives of saints with the power of *baraka,* which addressed the events of Moroccan political history in an attempt to lend some substance to a concept of a religious authority who was on the side of human welfare. Let us consider two such narratives, not only to confirm the above interpretation of a crisis in Moroccan political experience, but also to examine the intimate details of how a response to this crisis turned upon a devotion to living saints.

## 3

The first narrative to be considered was collected by Dale F. Eickelman and Bouzekri Draioui among the Arabized peoples of the western plains region of Morocco (see Map 4). Since the tale was told in Arabic among peoples who identified themselves as Arabs, we can compare it quite closely with the Arabian materials, which we have considered already in Parts I, II, and III.[10] The narrative concerns a saint named Sidi Mḥammed Sherqi and the role he played in the settlement of the region where the tale was collected. Sidi Mḥammed Sherqi, who died in 1601 A.D., was a saint during his own lifetime. He lived in a period of turmoil known as the Maraboutic Crisis which lasted from the fifteenth through the seventeenth century.[11] During this period the Sultan of Morocco was weak and there was a general settlement and desettlement of peoples in many parts of Morocco. The tale is somewhat like the Rwala ceremonial narratives in that it refers to a real man and his role during the course of real political events. However, the tale is more exactly a displacement of such a factual account. It does not demonstrate the moral value of a strategic practical response to experience; rather it explicates ritual mysteries which originated as a religious response to experience.

The tomb of Sidi Mḥammed Sherqi, along with the Sherqawi *zawya* which he founded, is located in the town of Boujad.[12] Today the town is still a pilgrimage center of considerable importance, which lies at the foot of the Atlas Mountains in the central section of the western plains of Morocco. Numerous other shrines, many of them associated with the tombs of Sidi Mḥammed Sherqi's descendants, are also located in the town. At the end of the nineteenth century, the town had a population of about 2000 people. In 1970, about one in three of the townsmen considered themselves descendants of Sidi Mḥammed Sherqi. The proportion must have been much higher before 1900. Eickelman, who has published an ethnography of Boujad, describes the relationship of the town with its immediate surroundings as follows:

> Boujad emerged as a mediating point for trade and political negotiation with the Berber highlands to its immediate east and as a local market center. Nevertheless, the most important ties between the Sherqawa and their tribal clientele for at least the last 150 years have been with the Arabic-speaking tribes of the western plains, Shawya, Tadla, and Dukkala. These ties continue to the present.
>
> The town is located near, but significantly not at, points of former strategic importance. In the frequent campaigns of reconquest characteristic of the more ambitious sultans in precolonial Morocco, the main route of penetration of the western plains and the Middle Atlas Mountains was along the Umm er-Rbi' River. A religious lodge located along this route would have been more vulnerable to the vicissitudes of Makhzen [the central government of the Sultan] politics. Similarly, settlement closer to the Middle Atlas Mountains would have left the town more open to attacks from the Berber highlands. Such threats remained significant several years after the French established a military post in Boujad in 1913. The town of Bni Mellal to the south, located directly at the base of the mountains, was still subject to the incursions of "dissident" tribesmen in the early 1930's.[13]

Eickelman and Draioui have published three of about sixty stories of saints, which they collected in and around the town of Boujad. Each of the three published stories was recited by the wife of the custodian of one of the major shrines in Boujad. This woman, like others who are connected with such shrines, recites these kinds of tales to the devotees of the shrine. All three of the stories have a similar form. They are biographical sketches of the life of some particular saint, but they do not purport to describe the entire life of the saint. They are presented instead as one incident among many others. Each of the three tales divides into two sections. The first section of each tale begins with a life crisis of a saint: the death of a son, the occasion of a saint choosing a bride, or a dispute between a saintly father and a saintly son. The second section of the tale then connects this life crisis with the occurrence of a decisive political event. In this way, the crisis in the life of the saint seems to lend shape to political experience. Similarly, there is a suggestion that one can read the crisis in the life of the saint in the design of a political geography. Here is one of these stories, which divides into seven separate episodes:[14]

How Sidi Mḥammed Sherqi
came to Boujad and
filled the land with people

1. Why did Sidi Mḥammed Sherqi settle there? It was because of that boy, Sidi l-Ḥajj l-Meknasi. He used to go on pilgrimages to Mecca. He made seven pilgrimages and on the seventh he died atop Mount ʻArafa. That camel which carried him living (to Mecca), by Sidi Mḥammed Sherqi's covenant with it, returned him dead.
2. When the camel returned his son dead, Shaykh Sidi Mḥammed Sherqi went in to his wife('s room) and said to her: "O Khelfiya!" She replied: "Yes?" He asked her: "Wasn't there something of value given to us? Today shall we give it back or not?" She answered: "By God, Sidi Mḥammed Sherqi, we'll return it in the same condition it was given to us." He said to her: "Whoever is like me can find strength in destiny. Death is hot, acrid. She gave me a cup of bitterness. Go on, O Ḥajj l-Meknasi, O my son, we meet in the next world."[15]
3. His wife did not restrain herself, fell to the ground and rolled in convulsions in front of Shaykh Sidi Mḥammed Sherqi. He asked her: "Why don't you forbear over (the loss of Sidi l-Ḥajj l-Meknasi), who belongs to God? Look at what we have done because of that loss. What will happen when the next comes? Go on! Khelfiya will never again bear one who gave her joy like Sidi l-Ḥajj l-Meknasi."[16]
4. When Shaykh Sidi Mḥammed Sherqi's wife did not contain her grief at that place where they were (living), he said to her: "I'm not going to stay in this land which disturbs my praising of God. I'm going to settle in that place which is free (of the thought) of Sidi l-Ḥajj l-Meknasi." Shaykh Sidi Mḥammed Sherqi went down there, lived in that land and began looking for water. He came to ʻAyn Shaykh. He struck his walking-stick against the spring, water gushed forth by the will of God and he said: "There will be a settlement here."
5. When Shaykh Sidi Mḥammed Sherqi settled, he needed people to fill the land with him. He called for seven from Bni Zemmur, seven from Bni Shegdal and seven from Smaʻla. He said to them: "Who wants to sacrifice?" He picked up the knife, went into trance and the knife dripped with blood. He said to the tribesmen: "Who wants to sacrifice?" They replied: "We will sacrifice." The marabout said: "Come! I'll take your sacrifices in turn: (first) a Semʻli, (then) a Shegdali." When he went out,[17] he called: "Bring your necks for the sacrifice." The Semʻli came forward but the Shegdali fell back, until all seven (of the Smaʻla) had sacrificed. (When the marabout came out of trance) he asked: "Who entered and who remained (outside)?" Someone replied: "O Sidi, the Smaʻla went in and the Bni Shegdal remained outside." (Then) the marabout said: "The

Sma'la will be watered (with *baraka*) but Bni Shedgal will remain without."

6. The 'Umariya whom Shaykh Mḥammed Sherqi had married[18] said to him: "Here is my neck, O Sidi Mḥammed Sherqi, on behalf of Bni Shegdal." Then Shaykh Sidi Mḥammed Sherqi said to the Bni Shegdal: "Since the woman offered her neck on your behalf, you are now milk brothers of the Sma'la." She gave her two breasts: that for the Sma'la overflowed with milk; that for the Bni Shegdal overflowed with water. The marabout said to them: "Go, O Sma'la! Whatever I break, you can mend; but that which you break, no one can mend."
7. Those are the people who filled the land with Shaykh Sidi Mḥammed Sherqi and who remain in it to this day.

The central motifs of the tale all appear in the first episode. This episode begins with a question to which the tale itself will provide an answer: "Why did Sidi Mḥammed Sherqi settle there?" This is a question about the relationship of the life of the saint and a particular place. The question itself suggests the character of the answer to be given. The man and the place will be linked in terms of a settlement.

Following the question, there is a statement of the cause behind the saint's settlement: "It was because of that boy, Sidi l-Ḥajj l-Meknasi." The cause is traced to a son of the saint. Behind the eventual settlement of a land there is a domestic matter. At the same time, there is just a hint of the innocence and vulnerability of this domestic matter; the son is only a boy.

There follows the theme of a religious movement: "He used to go on pilgrimages to Mecca." Here is a link with an Arabian past. At first, this link seems to be conceived in orthodox Islamic terms. The performance of the pilgrimage to Mecca, like the performance of the five daily prayers in the direction of Mecca, suggests that an Arabian shrine is a sacred center of the world at large where a religious authority has become manifest. The life of the son consists of movements toward this center, followed by returns to his home. As such, his life signifies a recognition of the religious authority which is manifest in the world at large and which transcends a life at home.

In the next line, however, we discover something about the pilgrimage to Mecca which is less than orthodox. The son makes not just one – the orthodox requirement – but a number of pilgrimages to Mecca: "He made seven pilgrimages and on the seventh he died atop Mount 'Arafa." The number seven features in many traditional Moroccan beliefs. Here it suggests a *mystical* ideal of completeness and wholeness. It serves to do so precisely because, as an odd number, its constitution is a mystery. But there is also another more important deviation from orthodox Islam. The son not only moves repeatedly toward Mecca, he also ascends Mount 'Arafa. Such an act is forbidden by orthodox Islam.[19] However, the son does not die because he breaks an orthodox religious rule. The death of the son atop Mount 'Arafa attributes a Moroccan, rather than an orthodox, significance to the pilgrimage. The pilgrimages of the son constitute an approach to God. The climax of such an approach is suggested both by the completion of the seventh pilgrimage and by the ascent, during this pilgrimage, of Mount 'Arafa. With the climax of his approach to God, the son dies. And so there is a mysterious association of the death of the innocent and vulnerable son with his very approach to a religious authority. The significance of this mystery will be revealed in the first half of the tale. The father's response to the son's death will constitute a confirmation of the existence of a religious authority.

The first episode ends by linking the death of the saintly son with the saintly father: "That camel which carried him living (to Mecca), by Sidi Mḥammed Sherqi's covenant with it, returned him dead." Here the attribution of a Moroccan significance to an orthodox pilgrimage is colored by a popular Arabian idiom. The camel is the vehicle of a performance. The performance in question is one marked by death. But it is no longer a heroic performance; it is a religious performance that is in question. The camel carries the son abroad alive, and then the camel returns the son home dead. An approach to a religious authority in the world abroad by the son results in death coming home to the father. There is a discontinuity between the religious fulfillment of the son and the domestic loss of the father, but not quite. The saintly father has made a covenant (*'ăhd*), an intimate, personal agreement with the camel, the vehicle of a religious performance. It is this covenant that causes the camel to bring the body of the dead son home. And so the very form by which the death of the son appears as a domestic loss also signifies a mysterious link, by means of an instrument of a ritual life (the camel), between the person of the father at home and the existence of a religious authority that shapes the world at large. The significance of this mystery will be revealed in the second half of the tale. The father's capacity to respond to the death of the son will become a power to represent, by means of ritual instruments, such a religious authority in the world at large.

In the second episode, the death of the son impinges upon the domestic scene. The saint goes into his wife's room. Here we are in the domestic interior where an exchange takes place between the husband and wife. This exchange involves the conception of an ideal form of exchange. Let us listen to the voices of the domestic interior:

> "O Khelfiya!" She replied: "Yes?" He asked her: "Wasn't there something of value given to us? Today shall we give it back or not?" She answered: "By God, Sidi Mḥammed Sherqi, we'll return it in the same condition it was given to us." He said to her . . .

Something has been given; now it will be returned in the same condition. By conceiving of the life and death of the son as an exchange, the death of the son is represented not as a loss, but as a return of an article whose value remains undiminished. A death is not conceived as a loss, but a reminder of a life that was given and is now taken back. A death is not conceived as the end of a life, but as a persistence of life in another world. Here we see how a devotion to the value of life in the face of a loss of life is expressed by figuring a loss of life in this world (death) as a sign of the presence of life in another world.

A dialogue in the domestic interior has taken shape around the expression of devotion to the persistence of life at a moment when there is a death. A domestic response to the death of the son seems to have been achieved, but then in the announcement of this achievement there is a painful hesitation. The saint himself is all too human: "He said to her: "Whoever is like me can find strength in [can forbear with] destiny. Death is hot, acrid, *merrara.* She gave me a cup of bitterness, *al-mrar.*" The saintly father first announces his ability to forbear in spite of a loss. But then there is a further penetration of the experience of the loss of the son. Having touched the domestic interior, it now touches the personal interior of the saint himself as it is conceived as a painful sensation: "Death is hot, acrid." An articulated response to an experience collapses, as the father merely senses the pain of the experience. And at this moment, as the wife ceases to participate in the dialogue, death itself is conceived as a domestic companion: "She gave me a cup of bitterness." But then immediately the saint articulates a response to this further penetration of the loss of the son as the second episode comes to a conclusion.[20] This response takes the shape of a call for the continuity of a movement despite the discontinuity of experience: "Go on, O Ḥajj l-Meknasi." The concept of another world beyond this is also explicitly stated: "O my son, we meet in the next world." A domestic loss in this world is conceived as a reminder of an eventual fulfillment in another world.

By means of a call for continuity of movement (Go on) in spite of the discontinuity of experience, the saint has not only endured, but responded to his personal loss. In the third episode, we find that the wife of the saint cannot even endure her personal loss: "His wife did not restrain herself, fell to the ground and rolled in convulsions in front of Shaykh Sidi Mḥammed Sherqi." The loss of the son not only disorders the wife's thoughts and feelings, it disrupts the very physical processes of her body as she literally collapses and is seized by convulsions. The question of a response to death is not only a question of the control of human thoughts and feelings, it is a question at the very basis of a human physical constitution. It is *the* question, which lies at the core of a human existence.

The saint attempts to resume the dialogue in the domestic interior by urging his wife to follow his example: "He asked her: 'Why don't you forbear over (the loss of Sidi l-Ḥajj l-Meknasi), who belongs to God?'" But it is no use, the wife does not respond. The saint then remonstrates his wife: "Look at what we have done because of that loss. What will happen when the next comes?" One must learn to deal with a present loss, for there are more in the future. One must deal with the discontinuity of experience for that is the very essence of experience. Life must take shape around this very problem. Again it is no use, the wife does not respond. The saint calls out once again: "Go on!" But his following statement is spoken as though the wife is no longer present. It is the announcement of a decisive acceptance of the end of an episode of domestic life: "Khelfiya will never again bear one who gave her joy like Sidi l-Ḥajj l-Meknasi." Joy has been given, but it is now a matter of the past. One must look to the future. One must go on.

The first three episodes have described a crisis in the personal and familial life of the saint, as well as a saintly response to this crisis. The last three episodes will describe how the capacity of the saint to respond to this crisis in his personal and familial life becomes the basis for his founding of a religious community. The next episode begins with the anticipation of such a founding:

> When Shaykh Sidi Mḥammed Sherqi's wife did not contain her grief at that place where they were (living), he said to her: "I'm not going to stay in this land which disturbs my praising of God. I'm going to settle in that place which is free (of the thought) of Sidi l-Ḥajj l-Meknasi."

A domestic life in a particular place has been disrupted by a loss. The result is the disturbance of the saint's personal response to experience, which is conceived, like the pilgrimages of the son, as a ritual recognition of a religious authority.[21] The saint therefore determines to settle in another land where his ritual recognition of a religious authority will not be disturbed. As the episode continues, the saint, whose response to the discontinuity of experience has been a call for a continuity of movement, begins to become more active as he literally begins to move. He goes to another land where he looks for water, the essential resource for a settlement. Discovering a spring ('Ayn Shaykh), he strikes it forcefully with his walking stick and the spring gushes forth. The episode concludes with the saint's announcement of the significance of the miracle that has been worked: "There will be a settlement here."

Let us consider this crucial manifestation of the power of *baraka,* which this episode describes. The saint performs a gesture. It consists of making a contact between two objects, his walking stick and the spring. The first of these objects, the walking stick, is a means of the saint's personal movement. As a form of response, this movement is a way of life which is itself scarred by discontinuity. A continuous movement is a shifting from one place and then to another. We can conclude that the walking stick is a symbol of an instrumental means of a response to the discontinuity of experience. The second of the two objects (the spring) is a feature of the world at large, which has the value of a domestic resource. We can conclude that the spring is a feature of the world at large upon which a domestic form of a response to the discontinuity of experience might thrive.

The saint then makes a contact between an instrumental means of a response to the discontinuity of experience, and a natural resource in the world at large upon which a domestic form of such a response might thrive. But now let us examine first the form of this contact and then its result. The saint takes the stick and uses it, not simply to touch the spring, but to strike it with a blow (*ḍrab*). Both the form of the symbol (it is an instrument) and the form of the symbolic act (it is a forceful gesture) emphasize that the saint is an active representative of the possibility of a response to the discontinuity of experience. The incident suggests, then, that the basis for the settlement of a land consists of a combination of the role of a saint and a specific feature of the world abroad. As there is an addition of an active saint to a domestic resource in the world abroad, a miracle takes place: the spring gushes forth. The basis for a settlement of the land has been enhanced.

In describing the miracle as a fact of history, the story hinges upon a deception. Striking a spring with a walking stick does not make a spring gush forth. However, the miracle is nevertheless an articulate metaphor of the role that living saints did play in Moroccan political history. It suggests that a saint might, by a purely formal gesture, act on behalf of a certain way of life, that a formal gesture might have concrete power. The episode which follows demonstrates just how saints might indeed have exercised such a power to enhance the settlement of the land in so far as men were in awe of their formal gestures.

As the fifth episode begins, the saint calls for seven members from each of three political groups "to fill the land with him." The "odd" number seven will now figure a completeness and wholeness of a religious community (not a political community) whose structure hinges upon a mystery. The saint then asks who among all these men would like to perform a sacrifice. Let us note carefully the line which follows this query: "He picked up the knife, went into trance and the knife dripped with blood." The saint's active representation of a response to the discontinuity of experience takes the shape of a ritual in a political environment (the calling of the three tribes). The character of this ritual translates the problem of a response to the discontinuity of experience from the domain of personal and familial life to the domain of political life. The knife is a personal instrument of aggression. As the saint picks up the knife, he goes into a trance. He passes from this world into another world. The knife then drips with blood.

The suggestion that the saint has entered another world (the saint passing into a trance) is associated with the political vulnerability of life in this world (the visible presence of the bloody knife as a sign). This ritual of personal sacrifice will constitute a test of faith. It is a sign of the transcendental ideal of human life in circumstances where human life is threatened by political violence. In what follows, a religious community will take shape around the degrees to which each political group accepts this ritual. That is to say, the differentiation of a religious community will turn upon the varying intensity of men's devotion to the transcendental value of human life where human life is concretely threatened. In so far as men cling to a ritual that arises as a reaction to a problem of political anarchy, a religious community will take shape.

While the saint is still in a trance, he calls out again to the tribesmen: "Who wants to sacrifice?" They respond: "We will sacrifice." He then instructs them: "Come! I'll take your sacrifices in turn: (first) a Sem'li, (then) a Shegdali." The instructions suggest a merging of the two tribes by alternating the sacrifice of a Sem'li with a Shegdali. According to the intent of the saint, there will be no differentiation of these two tribes. But note that, at this point, the third tribe, the Bni Zemmur, has been left out. It will not be mentioned again in the story, and so a differentiation has taken place. The Bni Zemmur has been recognized as a tribe that has been called to settle the land, but they are not accorded any special relations with the founding ritual.

Following the instructions of the saint, there is another differentiation with respect to the founding ritual. The saint calls out: "Bring your necks for the sacrifice." But now one tribe hesitates to respond to this call, which seems to demand the sacrifice of their very lives: "The Sem'li came forward but the Shegdali fell back, until all seven (of the Sma'la) had sacrificed." The Shegdali fail to accept the ideal of a life in another world as they fall back in fear of their lives in this world. Such a resort to self-protection in the face of a threat to life is the very origin of a problem of political violence. When the saint comes out of his trance and learns who has and who has not responded to his call, he announces a differentiation: "The Sma'la will be watered (with *baraka*)" because they "went in," but the "Bni Shegdal will remain without," because they "remained outside." This differentiation takes the shape of a domestic inclusion and exclusion. In a domestic interior, the Sma'la acquire a mystical power (*baraka*), which is identified with a domestic resource in the world at large (water).

The sixth episode continues the differentiation of the three tribes "on the outside." A new wife who represents the new domestic life of the saint, which has taken shape in this new land, comes forward: "Here is my neck, O Sidi Mḥammed Sherqi, on behalf of Bni Shegdal." The saint accepts the offer of his wife as he announces the shape of a ritual relationship between the Bni Shegdal and the Sma'la: "Since the woman offered her neck on your behalf, you are now milk brothers of the Sma'la." A ritual relationship with the family of the saint results in ritual relationships between two political groups. The wife of the saint then offers her two breasts to the two tribes: "That for the Sma'la overflowed with milk; that for the Bni Shegdal overflowed with water." The Sma'la retain their precedence over the Bni Shegdal, since milk is a domestic resource of the inside and water is a domestic resource of the outside. Following the establishment of a religious community by a founding ritual, the development of a ritual idiom is leading to the elaboration of a religious community around the performance of rituals by political groups. Like an undercurrent, a vulnerable domestic life, which inspires a wish for a community, is leading inexorably to the determination of the relationships of political groups in connection with the proliferation of a ritual idiom. Furthermore, the character of this ritual proliferation implies a religious hierarchy of political groups. Like an undercurrent, a vulnerable domestic life, which inspires a wish for authority, is leading inexorably to a distinction among groups in terms of their religious authority.[22]

The sixth episode concludes with a conundrum that distinguishes between the saint himself and the tribe which has acquired the power of *baraka*, the Sma'la. First the saint calls out once again for a continuity of movement in the face of the discontinuity of experience: "Go [on], O Sma'la!" This is a suggestion of a movement that will continue beyond the life of the saint himself. In the course of the movement, the Sma'la, who have been delegated the power of *baraka*, will be the representatives of the saint. It is followed by another statement which seems to differentiate the time of the saint's life and the time which follows his life: "Whatever I break, you can mend; but that which you break, no one can mend." The time of the saint was a time when a religious community took shape around a ritual that revealed the vulnerability of life in the face of political experience. The time that follows the life of the saint is a time when the political world can be given a shape in terms of the rituals of this religious community, even though that shape will recall the discontinuities of the founding. The Sma'la are here assigned this task as representatives of the saint: "Whatever I break, you can mend . . ." But the time that follows the life of the saint is also a time when the religious community is still dangerously threatened. In so far as the Sma'la fail to fulfill the task which has been assigned to them, the community cannot be given a shape: ". . . but that which you break, no one can mend."

Eickelman and Draioui add an explanatory footnote to their translation at this point. In the ethnographic present we find that the Sma'la are indeed the representatives of the saint's founding ritual which has been described in the story:

On the Tadla plain the Sma'la are regarded as themselves possessing maraboutic qualities. Some [of these] tribesmen go into trance during the fall festival . . . of Sidi Mḥammed Sherqi and while in this state drink the blood of sacrifices and smear it on their clothing. Sma'la also claim that while in trance they can see water gushing forth from the cenotaph of Sidi Mḥammed Sherqi.[23]

Here is a dramatic enactment of a conception of a life in another world (the trance), an association of this conception with violence (the sacrificial blood smeared over the clothing), and the promise of a domestic resource in the world abroad (the spring gushing forth from the cenotaph of the saint).

A seventh episode, which is really no more than a concluding statement, follows: "Those are the people who filled the land with Shaykh Sidi Mḥammed Sherqi and who remain in it to this day."

The tale begins with a personal accomplishment of the saint. He responds to a death by insisting upon the value of human life. Next, the combination of the saint's representation of such a response and a domestic resource in the world at large lays the basis for the possibility of a settlement. And finally, the ritual of personal sacrifice, which fuses an insistence upon the value of life with a sign of death by an instrument, becomes the founding ritual of a religious community. The problems of a lack of political community and political authority have not been resolved. Nevertheless, an awe of rituals, which state the vulnerability of personal and familial life, is a potential basis for a form of community and authority. In the domain of the performance of rituals, relationships of political groups are determined in a hierarchical fashion. In so far as these groups retain their awe of these rituals, a community and an authority exist.

So the living saint who did no more than represent a peaceful and productive way of life by formal gestures did perhaps play a crucial role in Moroccan political history. But then, of course, there was another side to this accomplishment. With the accumulation of monuments and the proliferation of rituals, the possibility of effective responses to political experience was ever more decisively undermined in Morocco. For by turning to such mystical substitutes, the Moroccans sealed themselves off from routinized, systematic forms of community and authority, and thereby remained potentially vulnerable to more practical men in other lands.

## 4

In the first section, a curious feature of the Moroccan Islamic empire was mentioned. While the Sultan of Morocco was seen as a representative of an Islamic civilization over a wide region of northwest Africa, the legitimacy of his political authority was in question just beyond the imperial cities of the Atlantic coastal plains. The tenuous character of the Sultan's political authority is usually discussed in connection with a much abused model of the Moroccan state. Among the French historians and ethnographers of the colonial period, traditional Morocco came to be conventionally described as two separate political entities.[24] "The land of the central government (*blad l-makhzen*)" was associated with the western plains areas in which the imperial cities were located. Bordering and penetrating this domain lay "the land of dissidence (*blad es-siba*)," which was populated by tribal peoples who openly resisted the central government. This feature of traditional Morocco was usually said to be a result of "tribalism." The peoples of Morocco, simply because they were tribesmen, were devoted to preserving their independence from the state. In the land of the central government, they were overcome by the state. In the land of dissidence, the central government was too weak to overcome them. However, this view of traditional Morocco raises the problem of explaining why the tribes of Morocco, if they were so fiercely autonomous, should have accepted the Sultan as the representative of an Islamic civilization.

Another view of the bipartite status of traditional Morocco is revealing. The division of Morocco into two parts, it is sometimes suggested, should be linked with the problem of state tax collections.[25] The tribal peoples in the land of the central government paid their taxes, but only because they were forced to do so. The tribal peoples in the land of dissidence did not pay their taxes because they could not be forced to do so. Here we have the clear sign that the state, as a form of public administration, had only a marginal legitimacy. The "state" was reduced to a tax-collecting mechanism, and the collection of taxes was illegitimate in the eyes of its "citizens." Would this not be the character of the state among peoples whose political experience had undermined their belief in the legitimacy of any routinized, systematic form of political authority? Now if we recall the problems of peoples who cannot accept any routinized and systematic form of political authority, we can readily understand why the Sultan of Morocco was nevertheless accepted as the representative of an Islamic civilization. While the Moroccan tribes could not accept the state as a form of public administration, they were in dire need of a moral authority who might moderate the problem of popular political anarchy.

From the beginnings of the state in Morocco, the way was open to any religious claims the Sultan might make. From the beginnings, the way was closed to any legitimate development of a public administration. This explains why the Sultan of Morocco went to such extravagant lengths to claim that he was both a Descendant of the Prophet and the Caliph of

Islam, as well as why these claims were enthusiastically accepted all over northwest Africa. The division of traditional Morocco into two parts was therefore only one reflection of the problem of a distinctive popular culture where there was a devotion to religious authority because there was an absence of legitimate political authority.

But the Sultan of Morocco could not remain content with his status as a representative of an Islamic civilization, for he had to be able to defend the cities, on which this civilization was based, from a turbulent populace which was experienced in the organized use of aggressive instruments. The Sultan of Morocco, as a result, was constantly moving through his realm accompanied by his court and army.[26] These royal expeditions had an ambiguous quality. In part the Sultan was engaged in the constant renewal of intimate personal agreements with the various leaders (legitimate and illegitimate) of local groups. As we have seen in the case of ad hoc and pro tempore tribal leaders, this was the only means of exercising authority, since there was no routine and systematic basis for political authority. In part, however, the Sultan was also engaged in a military expedition by which he put down open rebellions to his authority, coerced dissident groups into the payment of taxes, and terrorized unruly tribes with a display of power. But the most astonishing feature of these military expeditions was that they were seen by some as a display of the *baraka* of the Sultan. The display of military power on the part of a distant state authority was seen as confirmation of an awesome moral power to act in the general interest of a populace that was afflicted by its own involvement with aggressive means and actions.

Let us now turn to another narrative, which raises the question of the relationship of a saint and a sultan. This story will reveal how the conflict between political and domestic interests, which was rooted in Moroccan popular experience, left its mark upon the Moroccan Islamic empire. As we understand how this came about, we can glimpse how the differing rhythms of Arabian and Maghrebian history, during the epoch of Near Eastern pastoral nomadism, were shaped by differing patterns of popular interests in these two regions.

In his book, *Islam Observed,* Clifford Geertz has compared popular traditions of Islam in Indonesia and Morocco. In the case of Morocco, he draws in large part upon a story of a saint who is colloquially known in Morocco as Lyusi.[27] The story is still current in the town of Sefrou, which is located about fifteeen miles from the city of Fes. Like Sidi Mḥammed Sherqi, Lyusi (1631–91) also lived during the period known as the Maraboutic Crisis. Similarly, the narrative of his life has some vague relationship with the actual events of this period. Again, however, the tale is not properly viewed as a factual account. It is aimed at revealing the importance of certain kinds of religious and political figures in popular experience. In doing so, it provides us with an authentic popular perception of Moroccan history, but no accurate information about this history.

We shall consider only the two most important episodes in the narrative. These two episodes concern Lyusi's acquisition and exercise of the power of *baraka* in the arena of imperial political experience. The first episode describes how Lyusi acquired the power of *baraka* from another Moroccan saint of the pre-Sahara who is colloquially known as ben Nasir. The latter is also a well-known historical figure, having founded a religious order which played an important role in Moroccan history. As we read the episode, we find that the power of *baraka* is not associated with the rituals and beliefs of this religious order, with its institutions as an organization, or with its potential role as a vehicle of power or influence in Moroccan society. Instead, the power of *baraka* is specifically dissociated from these aspects of the religious order. The legitimacy of *baraka* depends upon its freedom from any kind of routinization and systematization. Each episode will be examined and analyzed line by line as it is translated by Geertz. The scene of the first episode is the pre-Saharan oasis of Tamgrut, where the ageing saint ben Nasir is surrounded by his students.

Ben Nasir was "critically ill with a loathsome disease," which resembled smallpox. This apparent personal affliction is in fact a sign of ben Nasir's *baraka.* The power of the afflicted is represented by a man who seems to be afflicted, but is really powerful. The affliction in question is physical; it involves running sores. There is something inside ben Nasir's body which is coming outside. This mechanical eruption foreshadows the coming event of the transference of *baraka.*

> The sheikh called his students to him, one by one, and asked them to wash his nightshirt. But each was so repelled by the sickness, so disgusted by his and the nightshirt's appearance, as well as afraid for his own health, that he refused to do it, or indeed to come anymore into the sheikh's presence.

The students of the saint are implicitly members of his religious order. They are related to him in orthodox Islamic fashion, since they are engaged in the mastery of religious sciences by his instruction. He requests them to perform a domestic task as a personal service. However, his students are men of literal perceptions. They take the disease for what it appears to be. They fear for their own lives and refuse to approach the saint. The transference of *baraka* is specifically deflected outside the context of the religious order and orthodox Islam.

> Lyusi had just arrived and was unknown to the sheikh, and everyone else, and so was not called. But he approached ben Nasir unbidden and said, "My teacher,[28] I will wash your clothes." Given the shirt, he took it to a spring where he rinsed it and, wringing it out, drank the foul water thus produced. He returned to the sheikh, his eyes aflame, not with illness for he did not fall sick, but as though he had drunk a powerful wine.

The appearance of Lyusi in Tamgrut is described as a mystery. Unlike the students of the saint, he was not called. The students are routinely and systematically related to ben Nasir, while Lyusi is inexplicably related to him. By performing a domestic task for ben Nasir as a personal service, Lyusi acquires the *baraka* of ben Nasir. In this way, he becomes the representative of a simple humanity, which is identified with simple domestic ways of life.[29] In the course of this performance, Lyusi mechanically ingests the fluids which have come from the running sores of ben Nasir. After this ingestion, the physical appearance of Lyusi is transformed. His flaming eyes are a sign of a newly gained potency, just as the running sores of ben Nasir were a sign of imminent loss of potency. Here the first episode ends.

This episode describes a succession. The mystical power of *baraka* passes from an older saint to a younger saint. With this passage, Lyusi takes the place of ben Nasir. The key to this succession is its clarification that the mystical power of *baraka* is an entity in itself, which exists and persists apart from the lives and deaths of the particular men who possess it. Let us turn to a more concrete analogy to see how this is so. On the occasion of a succession, it becomes especially clear that the power of the state is an entity in itself, which is separable from the person or character of any particular man since one man, who was formerly powerful, loses it and another, who was formerly powerless, gains it. The analogy is far more appropriate than it might seem to be at this point in the story. In the next episode, a confrontation between a saint and a sultan will clarify the difference between the mystical power of *baraka* and the political power of the state.

Let us consider more closely the form of the succession that is described in the first episode. Ben Nasir's possession of the mystical power of *baraka* is revealed by nothing more than his physical appearance. More precisely, it is revealed by nothing more than a sign upon his body. He has running sores. The running sores of ben Nasir do not indicate that he himself suffers from an affliction. Quite the contrary, they indicate that he is a representative of a humanity which is afflicted. And while a humanity which is afflicted is not powerful, the man who bears a sign of a general human condition, we shall find, has a certain kind of power, since he is representative of all humanity. But just why is it that only the very body of ben Nasir stands for the condition of all humanity? Why do we not see ben Nasir's capacity to speak for humanity? Why do we not see his capacity to act for humanity?

Let us recall that a central problem of popular political experience in traditional Morocco was the threat of an effective form of personal authority as a potential vehicle of domination and exploitation. Ben Nasir, the saint, does not appear in the story as the influential founder of a religious organization that represented the moral ideals of a Moroccan Islamic society. Ben Nasir, the saint, does not appear in the story as an accomplished student and teacher of those moral sciences which constituted the basis of a Moroccan Islamic polity. As the representative of the general condition of humanity, ben Nasir, the saint, is specifically dissociated from any practical representation of a moral ideal or even from any theoretical foundation for such a practical representation of a moral ideal. Instead, he is a man who only reveals the general condition of humanity by becoming in an awesome way the very embodiment of that condition. His physical person is a "sign" of the general condition of humanity. This is why the passage of *baraka* from saint to saint must take shape as a mechanical transmission of a personal physical state.

The running sores of ben Nasir, besides being a sign of his possession of a power to represent an afflicted humanity, are also a sign of his impending loss of this power, which is identified with his body. *Baraka* is erupting and effusing through the very surfaces of his body, as though it were a physical entity which was both within and of his very body. To acquire this *baraka,* Lyusi takes the soiled clothes of ben Nasir and performs an action by washing them. Here Lyusi's performance does not reveal a pragmatic capacity for acting on behalf of the afflicted. Rather, as a performance which has a purely formal, instead of a pragmatic value, Lyusi's washing of the clothes signifies only a formal capacity to represent an afflicted humanity which lives a simple, domestic way of life. After washing the soiled clothes, Lyusi ingests the filth from the body of ben Nasir. The substance of *baraka,* which exuded from the body of one saint, enters the body of the other saint. The succession to saintly power is complete. The very physical appearance of Lyusi changes. His eyes are aflame. Now Lyusi's physical condition, unlike ben Nasir's physical condition, does not suggest exactly what he has the capacity to represent, it only suggests that there is a sign of power upon his personal physical state. The general condition of a simple humanity when it is afflicted by the exercise of power is one of weakness and vulnerability, but when a simple humanity is represented, then the powerful must stand in awe of this representation. Just how this is so will be revealed in the following episode.

The second episode describes a contest of power between Lyusi and the Sultan of Morocco during his lifetime, Mulay Isma'il. Again the latter is a well-known historical figure. During his reign (1672–1727), Sultan Mulay Isma'il consolidated the 'Alawi dynasty of the Moroccan Islamic empire, bringing to an end the Maraboutic Crisis. This dynasty still rules Morocco today. As the episode begins, there is no apparent conflict between the saint and the sultan.

Thirty years after his acquisition of *baraka,* Lyusi goes to Meknes, the new imperial city of the Sultan Mulay Isma'il. "Mulay Ismail received him as an honored guest, fed him and housed him, and brought him into his court as his spiritual advisor." The saint is given a place within the domestic interior of the sultan's court. He is identified with a feature of the state, which is compatible with what he represents. As a spiritual advisor, his role consists of an articulation of an Islamic moral tradition as a necessary dimension of state policy. Such a role is thoroughly compatible with an orthodox Islamic conception of the state.

> The Sultan was at that time building a large wall around the city, and the people working on it, slaves and others, were being treated cruelly. One day a man fell ill while working and was sealed into the wall where he fell. Some of the workers came secretly to Lyusi to tell him of this and to complain of their treatment generally.

The sultan's new capital is a display of the grandeur of his political regime. The wall around the city is therefore aimed at preserving the power of the sultan by protecting his capital, rather than serving the interests of a political community. Indeed, the very construction of the wall involves a cruel exercise of power over simple humanity, which lives by patient and diligent labor. Oppressed by a sultan, the people turn to a saint for help. In the lines which follow, Lyusi will represent a vulnerable humanity, which is afflicted by a man of political power.

"Lyusi said nothing to Mulay Ismail, but when his supper was brought to his chambers, he proceeded to break all the dishes, one by one, and he continued to do this, night after night, until all the dishes in the palace had been destroyed." Outside the palace, the sultan exercises his authority in a fashion that is cruel to a simple humanity. Inside the palace, the saint breaks domestic articles. The political cruelty of the sultan on the outside is mirrored by the domestic improprieties of the saint on the inside.

"When the Sultan asked what had happened to all his dishes, the palace slave said, 'That man who is our guest breaks them when we bring his food.' The Sultan ordered Lyusi to be brought to him . . . 'My Lord we have been treating you like the guest of God, and you have been breaking all our dishes.'" Lyusi replied to him: "'Well, which is better – the pottery of Allah or the pottery of clay?' and he proceeded to upbraid Mulay Ismail for his treatment of the workers who were building the wall." The saint explicitly compares the sultan's political cruelties with his own domestic improprieties. The phrase, "the pottery of Allah," both figures a simple humanity as a fragile domestic product and it associates this very feature of humanity with the existence of a religious authority. The saint's remark also illustrates the relationship between a feature of humanity and the saint. The latter has spoken for a humanity that is involved in a vulnerable life of patient and diligent labor. He takes a stand for such a humanity, but merely by articulating its existence.

> The Sultan was unimpressed and said to Lyusi, "All I know is that I took you in, gave you hospitality, . . . and you have caused all this trouble. You must

leave my city." Lyusi left the palace and pitched his tent in the graveyard just outside the city near where the wall was being built. When the Sultan heard of this he sent a messenger to the saint to ask why, since he had been told to leave his, the Sultan's city, he had not in fact done so. "Tell him," Lyusi said, "I have left your city and I have entered God's."

When the sultan expells the saint, he breaks with the man who represents a religious authority. At this point it begins to be clear that a sultan whose political authority is based upon power is illegitimate, and that a saint who represents a religious authority is threatened by power. Upon his expulsion from the sultan's household, the saint sets up his new household outside the city walls. In the shadow of the terrible wall, which surrounds the sultan's new city, we now see a simple domestic structure which is identified with the dead. By means of a formal gesture, the saint has revealed a contrast between the domain of a political authority and the domain of a religious authority. The saint then challenges the sultan with his clarification of the separation of a political domain from a religious domain: "Tell him I have left your city and I have entered God's."

Hearing this, the Sultan was enraged and came riding out himself on his horse to the graveyard where he found the saint praying. Interrupting him, . . . , he called out to him, "Why have you not left my city as I ordered?" And Lyusi replied, "I went out of your city and am in the city of God, the Great and the Holy." Now wild with fury, the Sultan advanced to attack the saint and kill him.

The sultan is angered by the suggestion that his political authority is illegitimate, but his reactions merely confirm that he is a man who only believes in power and is only concerned with power. He rides out upon his horse to confront the saint. He interrupts the prayers of the saint. He demands an explanation for the disobedience of his commands. When he is challenged once again by Lyusi's reply, he completely loses control of himself as he resorts to the instruments of power, a horse and a weapon.

But Lyusi took his lance [his own lance or the lance of the sultan riding upon him?] and drew a line on the ground, and when the Sultan rode across it the legs of his horse began to sink slowly into the earth. Frightened, Mulay Ismail began to plead to God, and he said to Lyusi, "God has reformed me! God has reformed me! I am sorry! Give me pardon!" The saint then said, "I don't ask for wealth or office, I only ask that you give me a royal decree acknowledging the fact that I am a sherif, that I am a descendant of the Prophet and entitled to the appropriate honors, privileges, and respect." The Sultan did this and Lyusi left, still in fear for his safety, fleeing to the Middle Atlas forests, where he preached to the Berbers (and against the king) . . .

The saint is faced with an armed man on a horse. He himself takes a lance, but he only uses this weapon to mark the landscape. Where there are instruments of aggression, this gesture suggests, there one also finds a separation of the world into two domains, one of a legitimate religious authority and the other of an illegitimate political authority. As the sultan crosses this mark upon the ground, there is a manifestation of the *baraka* of the saint. The legs of the sultan's horse miraculously sink into the earth. In the domain which is represented by the saint, the instruments of power mysteriously lose their effectiveness. As he realizes that this is so, the sultan becomes terrified. He renounces his former reliance upon power, as he asks that the saint forgive him. Note the requirement which the saint sets for his pardon. He asks only that his religious status be recognized by the sultan. Lyusi, who only has the power to reveal the existence of a religious authority, is only able to coerce the sultan into a recognition of the existence of a religious authority. There is no resolution of the tragic involvement of the head of state in the illegitimate exercise of power. Fearing for his life, the saint flees the sultan with his royal decree in hand. A man who represents the power of the state has been forced to recognize a religious domain which is separate from the political domain; nevertheless, the man who represents this religious domain remains threatened by the power of the state.[30]

The miracle of course never occurred, and so this story, like the preceding one, deceives in so far as it suggests that the saint could have defended himself against a man on a horse with a weapon by marking the ground with a lance. Nevertheless, as a mystery which conceals a truth, the miracle is an articulate metaphor for a fact in Moroccan political history. Living saints who represented the vulnerable interests of simple humanity could indeed from time to time shake the very foundations of the state, merely by revealing the illegitimacy of political power, even though in the end these living saints remained themselves threatened by men of power.

## 5

Now we can examine just how the traditional Arabian state was different from the traditional Moroccan state and how this difference was derived from the character of popular interests in these two regions of the arid zone.[31] In Arabia, the camel-herding Bedouins were not attracted by the cult of saints even though there was a great deal of political turmoil among them. Instead, the Arabian Bedouins recognized the strategic leadership of tribal chiefs who were on the side of peace, rather than the mystical power of saints. In the settlements of Arabia, however, the cult of saints more or less flourished for the same reasons as it flourished in Morocco. The settled way of life was especially vulnerable to a threat from abroad, and so there was a need for the organized use of weapons. There was nevertheless an absence of any legitimate local leaders, since such leaders themselves posed a threat. In other respects, however, many of the settlers of Arabia were not like the rural peoples of Morocco. They were townsmen rather than rural peoples and they were often as much involved in trade as in agriculture. These were crucial differences, which laid the basis for a religious conception that challenged the myths and rituals of the cult of saints.

In so far as the Arabian settlers were townsmen with a stake in the market place, they had a deep interest in the social norms of a communal way of life. As we have seen in Chapter 5, such social norms were elaborated as a code of personal and familial morality, which spelled out in detail how the family was separated, protected, and concealed from a disorderly exterior. Although these social norms stated that the most intimate features of individual experience were set apart from public life, they were nonetheless the basis of interpersonal relationships in the community. Conformity with such a moral code was directly linked with the possibility of communal life, and the possibility of communal life was the basis for public commerce and domestic industry. Along with the myths and rituals of the cult of saints, to which men turned in the absence of an effective political authority, there was then a competing conception of a moral code, which was the potential basis for the pursuit of commerce and industry.

Among the Arabian Bedouins, the political community could be conceived in connection with a practical articulation of political strategies by which peace could be achieved. Among the Arabian settlers, the political community could be conceived in connection with a formal articulation of a moral code by which men in general would prosper. This was the setting in which a politico-religious movement could lead to the formation of a kind of state.[32] In the deserts and steppes, strategic political leadership could moderate the intertribal conflicts of the Bedouins. In this way, a political authority could realize those conditions in the deserts and steppes that were necessary for commerce and industry. In the settlements, there was the possibility of a religious movement that would condemn the myths and rituals of the cult of saints and invoke a code of personal and familial morality. In this way, a religious reformer could not only lay the basis in the settlements for commerce and industry, he could recommend such activities as an integral part of religious duties. An observation of Musil on the rhythms of Arabian political history suggests that the traditional Arabian state repeatedly took shape by the linkage of a political authority and a religious reformer:

> The sharp political and religious contrast between the settlers and the nomads, and the fact that the former are more or less dependent on the latter, have awakened among many settlers the idea that the one Allâh of the nomads is after all stronger than the numerous saints of the settlers and that therefore the religion of the former must be the truer. These ideas in the course of centuries

have given rise to various religious movements and have found their expression in the school of law of Ibn Ḥanbal, which has numerous adherents in eastern Arabia. From time to time these men attempt to reform the lives of their fellow citizens according to the teachings of Ibn Ḥanbal. For this purpose they generally make use of the power of a ruler and thereby strengthen his political influence. Such attempts have occurred and still occur almost every century.[33]

Musil suggests that the God of the Bedouins inspired these politico-religious movements. While this view grossly oversimplifies both the religious and political life of the settlers, it does nevertheless accurately state that without the Bedouins' moral pragmatism, the moral pragmatism of the settlers would have been little more than a sentiment.

The realization of such an Arabian state did not alter Bedouin conceptions of political experience in any extensive way. The head of state was more or less perceived as another tribal chief who had military and financial resources that an ordinary tribal chief did not have.[34] He had such resources, of course, precisely because his regime brought about a condition of general prosperity. In the settlements of Arabia, however, the realization of such a state confirmed religious conceptions that challenged the myths and rituals of the cult of saints in a fundamental way. For in the eyes of the settlers, a religious reform not only resolved the problem of a political threat from abroad, it turned men's attention to the pursuit of public commerce and domestic labor by which all men prospered. Nevertheless, the realization of such an Arabian state did not fundamentally resolve the problem of a popular investment in the organized use of weapons. It allayed this problem by enabling men to pursue their self-interests in a peaceful and constructive way. But if the prosperity upon which the state depended faltered, there was the threat of an explosion of anarchy. This means that the Arabian state always seemed to rest upon the "atmosphere" of a popular religious commitment. It seemed to the Arabians that if men just had the will to live in a moral way, the general welfare of humanity could be practically achieved.

In some ways, popular culture and society in Morocco was not very different from popular culture and society in Arabia. From very early times, the epoch of Near Eastern pastoral nomadism had played a decisive role in the formation of popular traditions in Morocco. From very early times, the cities and towns of Morocco were dependent upon long-distance trade and their role as local market centers. It was partly because of this similarity, no doubt, that Moroccan culture and society were so extensively Arabized during the early Islamic period. Nevertheless, the precise character of popular interests in Morocco and in Arabia was quite different. Outside the Moroccan cities, there was no great mass of mounted pastoral nomads. There was instead a rural population with the political culture of pastoralists and the productive interests of agriculturalists. The legitimate exercise of political authority was far more decisively compromised among these peoples than it was among the Arabian Bedouins. At the same time, these peoples were far more vulnerable to political disorder than were the Arabian Bedouins. Just because of this dilemma, Islam had a far more important role to play among the rural Moroccans than among the Arabian Bedouins. But just because of this same problem, the commitment of the rural Moroccans to the moral pragmatism of the sacred law of Islam was undermined at the same time as their commitment to the myths and rituals of the cult of saints was strengthened. On the political plane as well as on the religious plane, the architects of an Islamic state in Morocco had to proceed quite differently from the architects of an Islamic state in Arabia.

# Appendix I. Notes on some of the persons mentioned in more than one narrative or poem

1. Eben Sha'lân: the name of the family from which the Rwala traditionally drew their head chiefs.

2. Feyṣal: head chief of the Rwala around the middle of the nineteenth century. He died in 1864. See note 4 below.

3. Saṭṭâm: head chief of the Rwala in the latter part of the nineteenth century. He died in 1901. See note 4 below. Lady Anne Blunt met him in 1878 only a short time before his involvement in the death of Turki. She described him as follows: "Sotamm can boast that by right of birth he rules over a population of at least twenty thousand souls, and can bring five thousand men into the field . . . With all this, Sotamm himself does not appear to have much influence with his people (p. 345) . . . He was really pathetic in his lamentation about the manner in which he is obliged to sacrifice his own interests to the wishes of his people. *He* must become poor, that they may grow rich; *he* must find mares and camels, to satisfy the hunger of the Osmanlis, that the Roala may trade freely with the towns-people and fellahin, and soon he will be ruined. I have not much respect for Sotamm, but I cannot help liking and pitying him. He is only weak (Blunt, 1879, p. 349)."

4. Prince an-Nûri: head chief of the Rwala from 1905 through World War I. He was a personal friend of the ethnographer Alois Musil. Feyṣal, Saṭṭâm, and an-Nûri were the sons of three brothers. Their common paternal grandfather, Nâyef, was head chief of the Rwala during the first part of the nineteenth century.

5. Turki: head chief of the Fed'ân tribe during the latter part of the nineteenth century. He was killed by the Rwala who were at that time led by Saṭṭâm. Two stories of his death are presented in Chapter 4. Lady Anne Blunt, who met him in 1878 shortly before his death, described him as follows: "The half-witted Turki sat silent all the while I was drawing, but when I had finished and was going away he brought out three or four revolvers of English and American make to show me. He seemed to have a particular fancy for handling these fire-arms, pointing them recklessly all round, to the terror of men, women, and children in the tent, until the secretary took them away from him. He then made me a little set speech, from which it appeared that he was not such a fool, after all; for he had evidently shown me these revolvers only in order to lead up to the request that I would give him my own . . . [These men] have a bad reputation in the desert for everything except fighting (Blunt, 1879, p. 314)."

6. Khalaf: a lieutenant of Saṭṭâm during the campaign against Turki. One of the poems in Chapter 7 is attributed to him and another in Chapter 9 describes his heroism. He appears as a dark figure in the narratives which concern the Rwala chiefs. Musil's account of the later history of this man indicates that he was less than a faithful follower of Saṭṭâm and Prince an-Nûri: "The same Khalaf was the

most loyal follower of Fâres, son of Fahad eben Sha'lân, whom in 1910 the Government [Ottomans] nominated Prince of the Rwala. After an-Nûri's return from prison Khalaf fled to the Tûmân tribe and spurred them against his kinsmen. When in 1913 he had become reconciled with an-Nûri, he returned to his people, but in the winter of 1913–14 he was waylaid at 'Amûd by the Tûmân and slain (Musil, 1928a, pp. 109–10)." Fahad was one of two brothers of an-Nûri whom the latter had killed.

7. Muḥammad eben Smeyr: head chief of the Weld 'Ali during almost all of the last half of the nineteenth century. His tribe had special agreements with the pashas of Damascus with regard to providing protection for the pilgrims en route to Mecca. Sometimes he was at war with the Rwala, sometimes he had an alliance with them.

# Appendix II. Notes on some of the tribal groups mentioned in the narratives and poems

1. Rwala: a major ‘Aneze tribe of camel-herding nomads who summered near the Anti-Lebanon and wintered just north of the Nefûd desert.
2. Swâlme, Eshâje‘a, ‘Abdelle: primary allies of the Rwala in North Arabia.
3. Âl Jlâs: a name for the above three groups together with the Rwala.
4. Ḍana Muslim: a grouping of numerous tribes which divides into two main branches referred to as the Beni Wahab and the Âl Jlâs.
5. Weld ‘Ali: one of the most important tribes of the Beni Wahab grouping.
6. Fed‘ân, Sba‘a: two of the most important tribes of the Bishr grouping which parallels and opposes the Ḍana Muslim grouping. These two major groupings form the principal divisions of the ‘Aneze Bedouins of North Ababia.
7. Ḥwêṭât: a non-‘Aneze tribe of western North Arabia.
8. Sharârât: a non-‘Aneze tribe of western North Arabia.
9. Weld Sleymân: an ‘Aneze tribe of western central Arabia.
10. Shammar: a major non-‘Aneze tribe of Mesopotamia.

# Notes

## 1. The ethnography of Near Eastern tribal societies

1 Drápal (1972) has given an account of Musil's life. It includes a summary in German.

2 See, for example, Cole (1975), who provides an account of the Bedouin in modern Saudi Arabia.

3 See Lane (1908) and Musil (1928b). Musil's book *The Manners and Customs of the Rwala Bedouins* is hereafter abbreviated as *M & C* in the Notes.

4 Landberg (1919); Montagne in *Melanges Gaudefroy Demombynes* (1935–45); *idem* in *Melanges Maspero* (1934–53); *idem* (1935).

5 Landberg (1940), (1920–42).

6 Cantineau (1936), (1937). There is a criticism of Musil's work from the linguistic point of view in Cantineau (1936).

7 Doughty (1921); Montagne (1932), (1935), (1947). There are other ethnographic sources, such as Blunt (1879), Burckhardt (1831), Raswan (1935), and von Oppenheim (1939), but they do not add substantially to those mentioned in the text. Blunt encountered some of the people who are mentioned in the Rwala narratives and provides brief character sketches of these individuals. Raswan includes some pictures of these people as well as many pictures of Rwala camps, herds, and raiding parties. Von Oppenheim provides a brief history of the chiefs of the Rwala.

8 For example, the Yakut reindeer-herders, the Mongolian horse-herders, the Nuer cattle-herders, and the Tuareg camel-, sheep-, and goat-herders are all pastoral nomads, but they do not by any means share a common cultural tradition.

9 Zeuner (1963), Chaps. 6 and 7.

10 This atomism is reflected by the politically segmenting genealogies which are found among the pastoral nomads in the central Near East. Some features of these genealogies will be discussed in the next section of this chapter.

11 Kupper (1957).

12 Bulliet (1975). Also see the *Encyclopedia of Islam*, new ed., s.v. Badw.

13 Bulliet (1975), Chaps. 2, 3, and 4.

14 As mounted pastoral nomads, the North Arabian Bedouins represent one of the most extreme cases of Near Eastern pastoral nomadism. Among these people, the three crucial elements of this way of life – vulnerable domestic wealth, independent and scattered groups, and impressive personal instruments of aggression – all assumed an extreme form. Moreover, we have an exceptionally clear picture of how, over the course of many centuries, a

steady investment in personal instruments of aggression exacerbated the problem of political anarchy in North Arabia. The nomads in this part of the world acquired bows and arrows, and then metal weapons, such as knives and swords, at a very early date. This was followed by the refinement of the camel as a mount of war. Later, this beast was supplemented with the horse, a far more formidable military instrument and a far less practical possession in the desert and steppe than the camel. Nearer our own times, the Bedouins of North Arabia acquired various kinds of firearms, such as pistols and rifles, and on the eve of World War I, they were supplied with automatic weapons.

**15** See, for example, Caskel (1953), (1954), and Dostal (1967).

**16** Currently, Near Eastern scholars in the West are in the midst of revising their views about the character of the relationship between nomadic and sedentary peoples in the Near East. In general, they have qualified earlier ideas about the irredeemably destructive role of the nomads, the inevitability of a conflict of interest between sedentary and nomadic peoples, and the decisive role in Near Eastern history of dramatic and sudden movements of nomadic peoples outside their original homelands. See, for example, Lacoste (1966). The present study might be seen as taking part in such revisions. While it suggests, like earlier studies, that pastoral nomadism was the origin of a political problem, this problem is viewed as a feature of popular political experience in general. I have tried to conceive of the role of the pastoral nomads in Near Eastern history not by examining the occasions when they had a dramatic impact upon sedentary society, but by considering the possibility that their way of life had a routine and systematic influence upon social life.

**17** This aspect of popular Near Eastern traditions has often been somewhat apologetically underplayed by modern ethnographers. An article by Bourdieu in Peristiany (1965) and a book by Bujra (1971) are important exceptions to this rule.

**18** Elsewhere, Meeker (1975), I have shown how some of these cultural themes are differently expressed among Turkish-speaking and Arabic-speaking tribal and peasant peoples and how these differences can be traced to contrasts in the form of Central Asian and Arabian nomadism.

**19** Evans-Pritchard (1940).

**20** Evans-Pritchard (1949).

**21** For the Cyrenaican Bedouins, see Peters (1960); for the Somali nomads, see Lewis (1961); and for the Berbers of the Atlas, see Gellner (1969).

**22** See, for example, the various Cyrenaican interpretations in Peters (1967).

**23** See, for example, Peters (1967).

**24** The degree to which a tradition is oriented around political violence must always be distinguished from the question of the intensity of organized violence in a society at any given moment. In North Arabia, organized violence was a routine feature of political experience, but this does not mean that the Bedouins were necessarily more violent than other peoples over the long run. It does mean that the problem of organized violence was a serious and constant concern which shaped virtually every aspect of Bedouin social life.

**2. The personal voice and the uncertainty of relationships**

**1** Doughty (1921), Vol. I, p. 279.

**2** Ibid., p. 492.

**3** Ibid., p. 345-6.

**4** Ibid., p. 334.
**5** Ibid., p. 403.
**6** Ibid., p. 280–1.
**7** Ibid., p. 281.
**8** Ibid., p. 282.
**9** Musil *M & C*, p. 479.
**10** Musil *M & C*, pp. 417–18.
**11** Doughty (1921), Vol. I, pp. 322–3.
**12** Ibid., p. 259.
**13** Ibid., pp. 264–5.
**14** See, for example, "La Pharmacie de Platon" in Derrida (1967b) and De Man in Singleton (1969).
**15** See the article "Differance" in Derrida (1973).
**16** See Derrida (1967a) and the article "Differance" in Derrida (1973).
**17** Diringer (1968) hypothesizes that the first phonetic writing appeared in connection with a Semitic language at some time during the second quarter of the second millennium B.C., Vol. I, pp. 160–2. He locates this early alphabet in the eastern Mediterranean area and associates it with a political situation which "favoured the creation of a 'revolutionary' writing, a script which we can perhaps term 'democratic' (or rather a 'people's script'), as against the 'theocratic' scripts of Egypt, Mesopotamia, or China."

### 3. The composition of the voice and the popular investment in political adventures

**1** Here I have corrected what seems to be an obvious misprint in the original text. "Him who strengthens, who speaks the truth" has been corrected to read, "Him who strengthens him who speaks the truth."

### 4. Cautious and sensible chiefs and the strategic use of aggressive resources

**1** Musil (1908), pp. 232–3, and *M & C*, pp. 12–13, 291–2.
**2** Musil *M & C*, p. 471.
**3** See Musil's comment on the fate of Khalaf, Appendix I, n. 6.
**4** The actual characters of Saṭṭâm and Turki may not have corresponded altogether with the ideal figures which they represent in the tale. See Lady Anne Blunt's description of these two men whom she met shortly before the death of Turki, Appendix, n. 3 and n. 5.
**5** The tale reveals the implications of sovereignty in the desert and steppe. On the one hand, the mounted pastoralists, who had no need of a state, given their way of life, could only look upon a routinized form of political organization as an elaborate instrument of domination and oppression. On the other hand, a routinized form of political organization in the desert and steppe was always in part an elaborate instrument of domination and oppression, since it had no other function in an environment of mounted pastoralism. This is why Sa'dûn spends so much of his time in raids and wars. These features of sovereignty appear in more striking form in North Africa. They will be discussed briefly in Chapter 12.
**6** The incident of the fettering of the Rweyli tribesman receives, moreover, a considerable emphasis in terms of the amount of attention accorded to it. Al-

though it is a minor event, it reveals a crucial aspect of Sa'dûn's authority – the inhuman treatment of an ordinary human being. Note as well that this perception of a sovereign will, here represented by the acts of Sa'dûn, as unjust and cruel in its treatment of a simple humanity is a product of the inherent conflict among the mounted pastoralists between any form of state and the interests of the person, family, or communal group.

**5. Political authority, the metaphor of scriptural signification, and the metaphor of a domestic covering**

1 The concept of a sacred writing in a phonetic script has been of considerable importance since ancient times in the Near East. Such a concept is also generally connected with a notion of the structure of a politico-religious community. By discovering the hint of such a conception in a Bedouin tale, we can understand how this peculiar feature of Near Eastern religious traditions was rooted in popular experience in this part of the world.

2 Taken as a whole, the Bedouin materials recorded by Musil include an impressive variety of vocal metaphors. There is then every reason to believe that the Bedouins are extraordinarily sensitive to the implications of any minor detail that suggests a form of voice.

3 This recalls the pre-Islamic traditions in classical Arabic, "the days of the Arabs," which are derived directly or indirectly from accounts of intertribal conflicts in ancient Arabia. See *The Encyclopedia of Islam,* new ed., s.v. "*ayyâm al-'arab.*"

4 In this respect, the tale provides us with some understanding of how certain features of Islam resonated with Bedouin political experiences. Consider the first two verses of the Joseph Sura which have been translated as follows: "Alif lam ra (ا , ل , ر). These are the verses of the Glorious Book. We have revealed the Koran in the Arabic tongue so that you may understand it. In revealing this Koran We will recount to you the best of histories, though before We revealed it you were headless of Our signs," Dawood (1956), p. 38.

5 For example, the Kharijites of the early Islamic period stressed their involvement in continuous warfare with all unbelievers. The Bedouins are thought to have been an especially important element among the members of this particular Islamic sect.

6 See Antoun (1968) for a detailed discussion of the place of women in a traditional Near Eastern setting; and Granqvist (1931) and (1935) for a detailed ethnography of the life of women in a traditional Palestinian village.

7 For a glimpse of the degree to which the settlements could become embroiled in political anarchy, see Musil's accounts (1927) of his stay at al-Jowf, pp. 160–4, and his stay at Skâka, pp. 274–80. Also see Bujra (1971) and Boucheman (1935).

8 This also explains the intricacy of those Arabian conventions that dealt with personal behavior in the domain of domestic experience, such as hygienic practices and dietary regimes. Cf. Smith (1889).

9 See, for example, Granqvist (1931) and (1935), Cohen (1965), and Antoun (1972), who discuss the place of this custom in the course of the everyday life of Arabic-speaking villagers in recent times.

10 This pattern of marriage, shoring up a domestic interior against a political exterior, is especially characteristic of those peoples for whom the epoch of

Near Eastern pastoral nomadism emerged at a very early stage of their history and was carried to an especially extreme degree.

**11** As a contrast, consider the absence of any elaboration of wedding ceremonies among the Bedouins. Musil writes: "There are no special wedding ceremonies . . . Nobody is invited, nobody brings any wedding presents. There is no party, no dancing; neither the girls nor women sing or shout with joy. Often even the relatives of either the bridegroom or the bride do not know that there is going to be or has been a wedding. Neither does the slaughtering of a she-camel signify anything especially important, because an old or wounded animal is killed quite frequently. The tiny round tent, . . . alone shows that there has been a wedding. But if it was put up at sunset and the camp moves elsewhere next morning nobody takes notice of it, except the nearest neighbors" (*M & C,* p. 229).

**12** See Doughty (1921) for accounts of the moral fanaticism of the traditional Arabians.

**13** This problem will be discussed in more detail later in Part IV.

### 6. Rwala monotheism and the wish for authority

**1** The first version of the death of Turki touched upon this problem by suggesting that Saṭṭâm, a man of peace, could not avoid being drawn into the use of deadly instruments.

**2** In so far as an extreme example of Near Eastern pastoral nomadism (see the definition of this term in Chapter 1) provides an explanation of an extreme form of monotheism, so too the importance of Near Eastern pastoral nomadism in the arid zone explains the importance of monotheistic religions in this part of the world. The crucial features of Near Eastern monotheism in this regard are: a concept of God as a moral authority, a belief that such an authority presides over the design of the world at large, the association of such an authority with political conflict, the association of such an authority with the proper form of personal deeds and words, and finally the association of such an authority with a phonetic scripture.

**3** Musil *M & C,* p. 117.

**4** Ibid., pp. 674–5.

**5** Ibid., p. 675. Literally, *ash-sherq* refers to the east. Musil explains elsewhere in his ethnography that this same term should usually be translated as "the inner desert." Since the inner desert lies generally to the south on the Rwala migration route, Musil arrives at his translation of *ash-sherq* as "the southern mountain." Similarly, *yegharrebow* literally implies a movement toward the west, but should usually be translated as "moves toward the outer desert." Again such a movement would generally be toward the north, and so Musil arrives at the translation of *yegharrebow* as "moves to the northern mountain." In my opinion, the literal directional meaning of both these terms should have been retained in the translation of the myth.

### 7. Heroic skills and beastly energies

**1** Of the remaining seven poems, one was a written poem of fifty verses which had been presented to Prince an-Nûri, one was composed by a Ṣleyb, and five other poems of from two to five verses were composed and recited by an-Nûri or his slave, Selîm. In contrast, the other eight poems were oral poems composed by Bedouins and memorized by other Bedouins.

2 Musil (1908), pp. 233–4. My translation.
3 Ibid., pp. 235–6. My translation.
4 Musil *M & C,* p. 283.
5 This poem, Musil *M & C,* p. 579, was composed on an occasion when a report of an enemy attack omitted the fact that a Rwala party had already set out to take vengeance for the attack. The poet reverses the quality of the internal and terminal rhymes as he ridicules the precedence of speech over action.
6 Landberg (1919), p. 79. It is probable that the group from which Landberg collected this material was a marginal group of Rwala. The narratives and poems which he recorded are more like folk traditions than the narratives and poems which Musil collected. Also, Landberg interprets the "companions *eṣ-ṣaḥâba*" of verse 7 as a reference to the Companions of the Prophet. References to the Islamic tradition do not occur in the materials which Musil collected among the Rwala.
7 Landberg (1913), pp. 1660–1.
8 Ibid.
9 Landberg (1919).
10 Read *ekharaw* as *ek-haraw.*
11 The transcription, *w-'aḍm,* should no doubt be *w-'aẓm.*
12 Musil (1927), pp. 236–7.
13 The notation, h. 13a, should be read as "the first hemistich of verse 13." The notation, h. 13b, should be read as "the second hemistich of verse 13." This convention will be used throughout the remainder of the book.
14 Read *ḍaharha* as *ẓaharha.*
15 See previous note.
16 There is a possibility that the earliest meters in classical Arabic are associated in some similar way with the energy of mounts. See, e.g., Nicholson (1930), p. 74, n.1, who refers to a suggestion that the name of the most ancient metrical style, *rajaz,* is derived from a term which refers to a "tremor" in the muscles of a camel.
17 Read *wa-mqîḍahen* as *wa-mqîẓahen.*
18 The word *faḍaḥ* should perhaps be read as *faḍâ.*
19 In the original, *arkâbahom* reads *arqâbahom,* an obvious mistake in transcription.
20 Read *ḍhûr* as *ẓhûr.*
21 The transcription of *aḍ-ḍanâbîb* should probably be *aẓ-ẓanâbîb.*

**8. Poetic structure and the pressure of heroic interests**

1 Here I have in mind such societies as the American Indians of the Pacific Northwest, or the various peoples of the South Sea Islands. I have used the terms "tribal and archaic" to indicate a condition of statelessness and traditionalism.
2 I have noted that the ceremonial poem of raiding and warfare is composed according to strict canons of poetic form, while the composition of other kinds of poetry tends to relax these canons. Similarly, the less sophisticated settlers in North Arabia employ the opening image of riders on mounts and the two-part verse as purely formal devices, while the more sophisticated poets begin to borrow upon the poetic tradition in classical Arabic. If we examine the

poetic tradition in classical Arabic, we find that the most archaic poetic canons (riders and mounts, *rajaz* meters, internal and terminal rhymes) are very similar, although not quite identical, to the poetic conventions of the poem of raiding and warfare in North Arabia. That is to say, the closer one comes to the motivations and circumstances of camel-herding Bedouins, the more one finds that the strict canons of images of riders and mounts and two-part verses dominate the Arabian poetic tradition. And the further one moves from the motivations and circumstances of camel-herding Bedouins, the more one finds that the Arabian poets have freely varied or broken away from these strict canons.

3 While the exact translation of *qbaʿ neqḍaha* is in doubt, this conclusion is, I think, largely correct.

4 Among the settlers of North Arabia, one finds heroic romances, Musil *M & C*, pp. 12–13, 291–2, just as one finds such traditions among many peasant and tribal peoples throughout the arid zone. The absence of heroic romances among the North Arabian Bedouins indicates the extent to which personal and familial concerns had been thrown into question by a very extreme form of popular investment in aggressive resources (see Chapter 5, n. 11). The heroic romances among the settlers of North Arabia, it should also be noted, took the form of a narrative about one or a series of conflicts, together with several poems which were attributed to the individuals involved in the conflict. After the narrative was recited, the poems were recited in succession. See Landberg (1919) and Montagne (1935). This kind of heroic romance reflects once again the influence of the Bedouin way of life upon the traditions of the settlers. The very genre of the heroic romance among the settlers consists of a juxtaposition of two Bedouin genres: a narrative of a conflict and a poem composed by a participant in the conflict.

**9. Shadows and echoes of the priority of the concrete**

1 Read *tedhekeh* as *ted-hekeh.*

2 In classical Arabic, *ḍâmer* describes a camel or a horse which is lean and lank in the belly, a physical condition which suggests that the animal is a spirited mount. The term is also sometimes used to describe men. The classical gloss of the Rwala term *ḍamâyer,* "those who are lean and lank in the belly," seems to be more appropriate than Musil's "entrails," which is probably erroneous. The Rwala poet describes the nourishment of man's physique by news of war: "waters the lean and lank in the belly." In doing so, he employs a term which usually refers to the physique of spirited mounts, *ḍamâyer,* and thereby suggests that the physical energies of men, like the physical energies of beasts, have a crucial place in a struggle of riders on mounts.

3 It may seem odd to consider "news" as a form of expression. However, it must be recalled that political events among the Bedouins took a specific form just as the reports of these events took a specific form. All the ceremonial narratives are in this sense "news," even though they can also be described as traditional literary genres.

4 See Musil *M & C,* p. 387, v. 6: "A gold-colored bay, like a wolf broad in front, narrow in the back, *shaqra dhehûb w-kennaha-dh-dhîb maslûb.*" In the poem discussed in Chapter 7, section 4, we find the phrase "ostriches moving their upper parts, *heyqen yesîjen al-maṣâlîb.*" The word *maslûb* may therefore also be a pun on *al-maṣâlîb.*

5 The word *'arashet* has been mistranslated by Musil. According to Landberg (1920–42), this verb can be translated by the French term *broyer*. I have therefore translated *'arashet* as "did he grind."

## 10. The forms of segmentary politics and their relative absence among the North Arabian Bedouins

1 This point touches upon a problem which has been discussed at length in anthropology: the nature of kinship and marriage as a distinctive domain of human relationships. My point here is that the institutions of kinship and marriage, like any other institutions, take on a value which reflects the character of men's political experiences in the course of history. In this sense, kinship and marriage do not have a "nature."

2 In other words, an extreme differentiation of male and female roles took place under certain historical conditions. Circumstance placed a premium upon energy and action at the same time as childbearing represented a physical burden of considerable proportions. See the brief discussion of the patriarchal family and the seclusion of women in Chapter 5, section 7.

3 This explains why almost all the peoples of the arid zone have patrilineal traditions, as well as why there was a gradual shift in the arid zone from matrilineal to patrilineal traditions in ancient times. See, for example, the discussion of ancient Arabian matriliny in Smith (1885), Chap. 1. While this shift was sometimes interpreted as evidence that matriliny was a primordial institution which was followed by patriliny, it is more nearly the result of the increasing importance of a popular investment in aggressive resources, which tended to undermine matriliny and reinforce patriliny. The Tuareg, a camel-herding people of the Sahara with matrilineal institutions, simply prove that conditions favored but did not require patriliny.

4 This version of the structure of the tribal confederations in North Arabia is taken from von Oppenheim (1939), p. 113.

5 Musil *M & C*, p. 48.

6 Ibid., p. 51.

7 Ibid., p. 504.

8 In the poems in Chapter 7, sections 2 and 4, the Rwala and the Beni Wahab were at war with one another. In the poem in Chapter 8, section 3, the Rwala and the Beni Wahab were allied against the Fed'ân.

9 Montagne (1932), p. 65. My translation.

## 11. Political wildness and religious domesticity among the Cyrenaican Bedouins

1 Evans-Pritchard (1949), pp. 46–7.

2 Evans-Pritchard (1949) and Peters in Peristiany (1968).

3 And indeed, the problem even persists within the little group itself where obligations of political support strictly follow the lines of agnatic descent. This explains why patrilineal descent is traditionally such a crucial feature of communal political organization among the settlers of the central Near East. See, for example, Salîm (1962), Cohen (1965), Bujra (1971), and Antoun (1972).

4 Peters (1960).

5 Note that some names of political groupings represent a people as a collectivity, "the fleas," some as a group of descendants, "the sons of 'Ali," and some

as the inhabitants of a certain region, "the Westerners." Among the North Arabians, we find that the first kind of names predominate at the level of the tribe but the second kind of names predominate at the level of the little herding groups. As the Cyrenaicans have settled on their land, the first kind of names have been replaced with the second kind of names at the level of the tribe. At the same time they have also adopted a third type of name, the inhabitants of a certain region, which is very rare among the camel-herding Bedouins of North Arabia.

**6** Peters (1960) mentions that there were serious intertribal wars among the Cyrenaican Bedouins during the nineteenth century, but gives no details.

**7** Peters (1967), p. 278.

**8** Evans-Pritchard (1949), p. 54.

**9** Ibid., p. 59.

**10** The description which follows is drawn from Evans-Pritchard (1949). Map 2 is adapted from a similar map in his book.

**11** Map 3 has been reproduced from a map in Evans-Pritchard (1949).

**12** Montagne (1932).

**13** Evans-Pritchard (1949), p. 36.

**14** Peters (1967), p. 278.

**15** This description of the cult of saints in Cyrenaica is drawn from Evans-Pritchard (1949), Peters (1960), and idem in Peristiany (1968).

**16** Peters (1960), p. 46.

**17** Peters in Peristiany (1968), p. 168.

**18** Evans-Pritchard (1949), p. 79.

## 12. Narratives of the mystical power of saints in Morocco

**1** Dunn in Gellner and Micaud (1973), p. 85. The following two quotes from Dunn appear in the same place.

**2** Eickelman (1977), p. 41, states that in 1900 an estimated 93 percent of Morocco's population lived from a "combination of transhumant pastoralism of mixed herds of goats and sheep and the seasonal cultivation of wheat and barley."

**3** Montagne (1930) has discussed this problem at length. With regard to the independent Berber tribes of the Atlas, he observed: "To share in an equitable way the advantages of power among all the household heads and by doing so to maintain an anxious watchfulness over the ambitious men among them, these are the constant concerns of the internal political life of the little Berber republics," p. 269. My translation.

**4** See Montagne (1930).

**5** The work of Montagne has long been admired as an attempt to synthesize this complexity. See Seddon's introduction (1973) to his translation of Montagne.

**6** The diagram of the Beni Mtir tribe is adapted from Rassam (Vinogradov) in Gellner and Micaud (1973). It was recorded among a group of Berber-speaking Moroccans living in the region just between the plains and the foothills of the Middle Atlas.

**7** This paragraph and the two following are my reading of Montagne (1930), Spillman (1936), Berque (1955), Hart (1967), Gellner (1969), and Rassam (Vinogradov) in Gellner and Micaud (1973).

**8** Gellner (1969) insists so much upon the practicality and efficiency of segmentary institutions that he obscures the dimensions of the disaster to which these kinds of institutions were a response.

**9** The most important ethnographic studies of the traditional political role of saints in tribal Morocco are Gellner (1969) and Eickelman (1976). Also see Westermarck (1926).

**10** In this section, I have adopted the system of vowel transcription which is used by Eickelman (1976). The short vowels *a, i,* and *u* are replaced by the letters *ă, e,* and *o.* The long vowels *â, î, û* are replaced by the letters *a, i,* and *u.*

**11** For a brief discussion of the Maraboutic Crisis and its place in Moroccan historiography, see Eickelman (1976), Chap. 1.

**12** The description which follows is drawn from Eickelman (1976).

**13** Ibid., pp. 33–4.

**14** The story is given in the same form as it was published by Eickelman and Draioui (1973), except that the seven episodes have been numbered.

**15** This quotation is in verse (*saj*ʿ).

**16** Eickelman and Draioui (1973) note that this passage implies that it was spoken by the saint in the absence of his wife.

**17** According to Eickelman and Draioui (1973), the implication of this observation is that the saint was in a shrine.

**18** Eickelman and Draioui (1973) assume that this wife, the ʿUmariya, is the same woman as the wife in episodes 2, 3, and 4. According to my understanding of the tale, this is a different wife whom he has married in the new land.

**19** Eickelman and Draioui (1973) have pointed out the importance of this unorthodoxy.

**20** The story also insists upon this passage as an articulated *response* on the part of the saint by composing these lines in verse (*saj*ʿ).

**21** At this point the saint's ritual recognition of a religious authority is purely passive. It consists only of a vocal performance (*dker llah*). Later he will begin to employ a ritual instrument, just as the son employed such a ritual instrument (the camel) on his pilgrimages to Mecca.

**22** In this respect, we can see how the founding of the myths and rituals of the cult of saints went hand in hand with the establishment of cult centers as well as the proliferation of ritual specialists who were associated with these cult centers.

**23** Eickelman and Draioui (1973), n. 31.

**24** For a discussion of this model and its place in French colonial historiography, see Burke in Gellner and Micaud (1973).

**25** See, for example, Hart in Gellner and Micaud (1973).

**26** For a brief description of the character of these royal expeditions, see Geertz (1977).

**27** Geertz (1968), pp. 32–5.

**28** The title by which Lyusi addresses ben Nasir is probably "sheykh," which could be translated as well by "master" as by "teacher."

**29** Gellner (1969) has described how a popular interest in the existence of saints with *baraka* leads inevitably to a popular conviction that some particular man is indeed a saint with *baraka.*

**30** It is important to keep in mind that this story reflects the dilemma of an epoch of Moroccan political history rather than the actual character of any sultan or saint in Morocco. Almost all sultans attempted to legitimate their rule in terms of Islamic morality. They even claimed the status of a saint who was capable of exercising the power of *baraka.* See Geertz (1977). Likewise, almost all saints became implicated in the practical exercise of power. Some of them even became the virtual rulers of little principalities, which were more or less independent of the Sultan of Morocco. See Eickelman (1976). Nevertheless, any strategy of sultanship or sainthood, whatever shape it took, was always touched by the problems of the illegitimacy of political authority and the impracticality of religious authority.

**31** Cf. Burke (1969) and Lacoste (1974) who survey the various factors which determined the character of the state in North Africa. In this chapter, I have analyzed in detail only one of these factors which both the above authors refer to as a problem of "tribalism."

**32** These two dimensions can be clearly perceived in the early Islamic period. The Holy War of the Muslim warriors involved a practical articulation of political strategies that were aimed at the establishment of a religious community. After the success of the Holy War, the sacred Law of the Muslim scholars was derived as the basis for the practical articulation of this religious community.

**33** Musil (1928a), p. 257.

**34** See, for example, Musil's account (1927), p. 428, of the North Arabian Bedouins' view of the Ottoman Sultan as a tribal chief who simply had more power and wealth than most other chiefs.

# Bibliography


Antoun, Richard T. *Arab Village.* Bloomington: Indiana University Press, 1972.
"On the modesty of women in Arab Muslim villages." *American Anthropologist* 70 (1968), pp. 671-97.

Berque, Jacques. *Structures sociales du Haut-Atlas.* Paris: Presses Universitaires de France, 1955.

Blunt, Lady Anne. *Bedouin Tribes of the Euphrates.* New York: Harper and Brothers, 1879.

Boucheman, Albert de. *Une petite cité caravanière: Suḫné.* Documents d'Etudes Orientales 6. Paris: Institut Français de Damas, 1935.

Bourdieu, Pierre. "The sentiment of honor in Kabyle society," in J. G. Peristiany (ed.), *Honour and Shame.* London: Weidenfeld & Nicolson, 1965, pp. 191-241.

Bujra, A. S. *The Politics of Stratification: A Study of Political Change in a South Arabian Town.* London: Oxford University Press, 1971.

Bulliet, Richard W. *The Camel and the Wheel.* Cambridge, Mass.: Harvard University Press, 1975.

Burckhardt, J. L. *Notes on the Bedouins and the Wahabys.* London: Henry Coburn & Richard Bentley, 1831.

Burke, Edmund. "Morocco and the Near East: Reflections on some basic differences." *Archives Européenes de Sociologie* 10 (1969), pp. 70-94.
"The image of the Moroccan state in French ethnological literature: a new look at Lyautey's Berber policy," in Ernest Gellner and Charles Micaud (eds.), *Arabs and Berbers.* London: Duckworth, 1973, pp. 175-99.

Cantineau, J. "Etudes sur quelques parlers de nomades arabes d'Orient (premier article)." *Annales de l'Institut d'Etudes Orientales* 2 (1936), pp. 1-118.
"Etudes sur quelques parlers de nomades arabes d'Orient (second article)." *Annales de l'Institut d'Etudes Orientales* 3 (1937), pp. 119-237.

Caskel, W. *Die Bedeutung der Beduinen in der Geschichte der Araben.* Cologne: Oplander, 1953.
"The Bedouinisation of Arabia," in G. E. von Grunebaum (ed.), *Studies in Islamic Cultural History.* Menasha, Wis.: American Anthropological Association, 1954, pp. 36-46.

Cohen, Abner. *Arab Border-Villages in Israel.* Manchester: Manchester University Press, 1965.

Cole, Donald P. *Nomads of the Nomads.* Chicago: Aldine, 1975.

Dawood, N. J. *The Koran.* Harmondsworth: Penguin, 1956.

De Man, Paul. "The rhetoric of temporality," in C. Singleton (ed.), *Interpretation: Theory and Practice.* Baltimore: Johns Hopkins Press, 1969, pp. 173-209.

Derrida, Jacques. *De la grammatologie.* Paris: Les Editions de Minuit, 1967a.
*La dissemination.* Paris: Editions du Seuil, 1967b.
*Speech and Phenomena and Other Essays on Husserl's Theory of Signs.* Evanston: Northwestern University Press, 1973.
Diringer, David. *The Alphabet: A Key to the History of Mankind.* New York: Funk & Wagnalls, 1968.
Dostal, Walter. *Die Beduinen in Südarabien: Eine ethnologische Studie zur Entwicklung der Kamelwirtenkultur in Arabien.* Vienna: Berger, 1967.
Doughty, Charles M. *Travels in Arabia Deserta,* 2 vols. London: Jonathan Cape, 1921 (first published in 1888).
Drápal, Miloš. "Zivot a dílo Prof. Dr. Aloise Musila." *Folia: Facultatis Scientiarum Naturalium Universitatis Purkyniane Brunensis* 13 (1972), pp. 3-63.
Dunn, Ross E. "Berber imperialism: the Ait Atta expansion in southeast Morocco from 1870 to 1970," in Ernest Gellner and Charles Micaud (eds.), *Arabs and Berbers.* London: Duckworth, 1973, pp. 85-107.
Eickelman, Dale F. *Moroccan Islam.* Austin: University of Texas Press, 1976.
"Time in a complex society: A Moroccan example." *Ethnology* 16 (1977), pp. 39-55.
Eickelman, Dale F. and Bouzekri Draioui. "Islamic myths from western Morocco: Three texts." *Hespéris-Tamuda* 14 (1973), pp. 195-225.
*Encyclopedia of Islam.* Leiden: E. J. Brill, 1960.
Evans-Pritchard, E. E. *The Nuer: A Description of the Modes of Livelihood and Political Institutions of a Nilotic People.* Oxford: Clarendon Press, 1940.
*The Sanusi of Cyrenaica.* Oxford: Clarendon Press, 1949.
Geertz, Clifford. *Islam Observed.* New Haven: Yale University Press, 1968.
"Centers, kings, and charisma: Reflections on the symbolics of power," in J. Ben-David and T. Clark (eds.), *Culture and Its Creators.* Chicago: University of Chicago Press, 1977, pp. 150-71.
Gellner, Ernest. *The Saints of the Atlas.* London: Weidenfeld & Nicolson, 1969.
Granqvist, Hilma. *Marriage Conditions in a Palestinian Village Part I. Commentationes Humanarum Litterarum* 3, No. 8 (1931).
*Marriage Conditions in a Palestinian Village Part II. Commentationes Humanarum Litterarum* 6, No. 8 (1935).
Hart, David M. "Segmentary systems and the role of 'five fifths' in tribal Morocco." *Revue de l'Occident Musulman et de la Mediterranée* 3 (1967), pp. 35-65.
"The tribe in modern Morocco: two case studies," in Ernest Gellner and Charles Micaud (eds.), *Arabs and Berbers.* London: Duckworth, 1973, pp. 25-58.
Ibn Khaldûn. *The Muqaddimah.* Trans. by Franz Rosenthal. Princeton: Princeton University Press, 1967.
Kupper, Jean-Robert. *Les nomades en Mésopotamie au temps des rois de Mari.* Paris: Société d'Edition "Les Belles Lettres," 1957.
Lacoste, Yves. *Ibn Khaldoun.* Paris: François Maspero, 1966.
"General characteristics and fundamental structures of medieval North African society." *Economy and Society* 3 (1974), pp. 1-17.
Landberg, Carlo, Count. *La langue arabe et ses dialectes.* Leiden: E. J. Brill, 1905.
*Etudes sur les dialectes de l'Arabie méridionale: Daṯînah, Troisième Partie.* Leiden: E. J. Brill, 1913.
*Langue des bédouins 'anazeh.* Leiden: E. J. Brill, 1919.
*Glossaire datinois,* 3 vols. Leiden: E. J. Brill, 1920-42.

*Glossaire de la langue des bédouins 'anazeh.* Uppsala: Almqvist & Wiksells, 1940.

Lane, Edward W. *Manners and Customs of the Modern Egyptians.* London. J. M. Dent, 1908.

Lewis, I. M. *A Pastoral Democracy.* London: Oxford University Press, 1961.

Meeker, Michael. "Mounted pastoralism, the genres of heroism, and the Turkish and Arab ethnic presence in the Near East." Paper delivered at the conference on L'Acculturation turque dans l'Orient et la Mediterranée - emprunts et apports, November, 1975.

Montagne, Robert. *Les Berbères et le makhzen dans le sud du Maroc.* Paris: Librairie Félix Alcan, 1930.

"Notes sur la vie sociale et politique de l'Arabie du nord." *Revue des Études Islamique* 6 (1932), pp. 61-79.

"Salfet saye' alemsah, g'edd errmal," in *Mélanges Gaudefroy Demombynes.* Cairo: Imp. de l'Institut Français d'Archéologie Orientale, 1935-45, pp. 125-30.

"Le ghazou de saye' alemsah," in *Mélanges Maspero.* Cairo: Imp. de l'Institut Français d'Archéologie Orientale, 1934-53, pp. 411-16.

"Contes poétiques bédouins." *Bulletin d'Etudes Orientales* 5 (1935), pp. 33-121.

*La civilisation du desert.* Paris: Hachette, 1947.

Musil, Alois. *Arabia Petraea,* Vol. 3: *Ethnologischer Reisebericht.* Vienna: A. Holzhausen, 1908.

*Arabia Deserta.* American Geographical Society: Oriental Explorations and Studies, No. 2. New York: Crane, 1927.

*Northern Neǧd.* American Geographical Society, Oriental Explorations and Studies, No. 4. New York: Crane, 1928a.

*The Manners and Customs of the Rwala Bedouins.* American Geographical Society: Oriental Explorations and Studies, No. 6. New York: Crane, 1928b.

Nicholson, Reynold A. *A Literary History of the Arabs.* Cambridge, England: Cambridge University Press, 1930.

Oppenheim, Max Freiherr von. *Die Beduinen, Vol. I: Die Beduinenstämme in Mesopotamien und Syrien.* Leipzig: O. Harrassowitz, 1939.

Peters, Emrys. "The proliferation of segments in the lineage of the Bedouin of Cyrenaica." *Journal of the Royal Anthropological Institute* 90 (1960), pp. 29-51.

"Some structural aspects of the feud among the camel-herding Bedouin of Cyrenaica." *Africa: Journal of the International African Institute* 37 (1967), pp. 261-82.

"The tied and the free (Libya)," in J. G. Peristiany (ed.), *Contributions to Mediterranean Sociology.* Hague: Mouton, 1968, pp. 167-88.

Rassam (Vinogradov), Amal. "The socio-political organization of a Berber 'taraf' tribe: pre-protectorate Morocco," in Ernest Gellner and Charles Micaud (eds.), *Arabs and Berbers.* London: Duckworth, 1973, pp. 67-83.

Raswan, Carl R. "Tribal areas and migration lines of the North Arabian Bedouins." *Geographical Review* 20 (1930), pp. 494-502.

*Black Tents of Arabia.* Boston: Little, Brown, 1935.

Salim, S. M. *Marsh Dwellers of the Euphrates.* London: Athlone Press, 1962.

Seddon, J. David (trans.). "Introduction," in Robert Montagne, *The Berbers: Their Social and Political Organization.* London: Frank Cass, 1973.

Smith, W. Robertson. *Kinship and Marriage in Early Arabia.* London: Black, 1885.

*Lectures on the Religion of the Semites.* London: Black, 1889.

Spillman, Georges. *Les Ait Atta du Sahara et la pacification du Haut Dra.* Rabat: Editions Félix Moncho, 1936.
Westermarck, Edward. *Ritual and Belief in Morocco.* 2 vols. London: Macmillan, 1926.
Zeuner, Frederick E. *A History of Domesticated Animals.* New York: Harper and Row, 1963.

# Index

'Abdelle, 33-4, 36-40, 60, 189
Abu-d-Duhûr, 85, 190
Abu Zeyd, *see* 'Antar tales
affliction, *see* disease and affliction
Africa, 24
agnatic descent, *see* patrilineal descent
agriculture; and cult of saints, 211; and Cyrenaican Bedouins, 185-6, 193, 204-5; and North Arabian Bedouins, 16; and rural Moroccans, 243-4, 257 n2; in the Maghreb, 214-15; *see also* peasants; sedentary peoples; settlers, of Arabia
Âl Jlâs, 137, 189, 247
Allâh, *see* God
alphabet, 93; *see also* phonetic writing
'Alya herd, 54, 55, 190
American Indians, 254 n1
'Aneze, 3, 42, 188, 191, 247
'Antar tales, 52
anthropologists, 11-14, 95, 184, 196
anthropology, 11
Arabia, Western perception of, 24-5
Arabian Bedouins: and the Ṣleyb, 21-2; ceremonies and rituals, 28-9; esthetic and practical arts, 28; of today, 3; source materials, 5-6; *see also* Central Arabian Bedouins; North Arabian Bedouins
Arabic, classical, 114, 252 n3, 254 n2
arid zone: and centers of civilization, xi; and monotheism, 100; and Near Eastern pastoral nomadism, 8-10, 214; and North Arabian Bedouins, 183; and patrilineal and matrilineal descent, 256 n3; as an ethnographic region, 6-7
art, of verbal designs, 156
articulation: and strategies of theft, 41, 42-5; and the saint, 239; of political responses and political structures, 150; of space and time, 86-7; of verbal details, 166
artistic expression: and historical experience, 151-4; and poetry, 111-12
assemblies, 219, 220
awe, and the cult of saints, 211, 222-3, 233, 235, 238
*baraka,* 211, 213, 229, 231-2, 235, 258, n30; *see also* mystical power, and anarchy
behavior and experience, 91
Beni, *see* main part of proper name
Berbers, 12, 215, 224, 257 n3
biological drives, and political life, 23
Bishr, 188
Bleyhân eben Ḍeri, 32, 33-41, 41-5, 46-7, 106
blood money, 21, 206
blood price, 21, 122
body and mind, and a life of heroism, 160
Bulliet, Richard W., 8
Burke, Edmund, 259 n31
Caliph of Islam, 234-5
camel: conversion into a mount of war, 8; personal instrument of aggression, 9, 18-19; vulnerable domestic neccessity, 17-18
camel-herding nomadism: and long-distance trade, 8; and North Arabian camel saddle, 8; and poetic canons, 254 n2; as a crucial example, 100; as a way of life, 17-19, 25-6, 99; spread of, 8; *see also* mounted pastoral nomadism; Near Eastern pastoral nomadism; pastoral nomadism
camel-herding nomads; and cult of saints, 241; and shrines, 209-10; first appearance in North Arabia, 8; in Cyrenaica, 205; Rwala, 3; self-expression and beastly energies, 128
camel-theft, 19-20
Cantineau, J., xiv, 5
cattle-herding, 193, 203, 209
centers of civilization, xi, 7-8, 9, 214